P9-ELX-651

DEDICATION

I thank the many clients and customers who have trusted me and my teams to provide large-scale data processing solutions. I have learned as much from them as they have hopefully received from us, for it is they that own the fertile soil and the enriched backdrop for the experiences that make a book like this possible. With that, many thanks to the Remediator team, who have additional experience as knights-errant.

I also thank those who have encouraged me along the way, some of whom have already forgotten more than I'll ever know, and some who neither completely understand nor agree with all or part of the book's contents, and I'm okay with that. These include Kim Hall, Jody Mazolla, Dr. Craig Wood, Mark Kim, Ben Gonzales, Chris Day, Rampi Kandadai, Bryan Hunter, Marguerite Birmingham, Tony Cinello, Roy Sailor, Christopher Hyde, Darrell Lane, Hung-Chou Tai, Bill Herman, Bob Luke, Sandeep Sahai, Jim Thrasher, Mike Hirrlinger, Neal Birmingham, Dave Duncan, Cliff Lasser, Eric Overton, Lou Goldish, Jeff Endrulat, Arjun Malhotra, Dorothy Kuhn, Joe Vaughan, John Neese, Mike Adelman, Nick Galemmo, John Strong, Katie Madison, Daniel Wang, Marc Wrona, Colin May, Andy Pardoe, Barry Beville, Shashi Nittur, Chad Maggard.

I also acknowledge the many people at Netezza Corporation who have helped me (and many others) understand their technology and the vision behind it, in particular, Kim, Tim, Olga, Ray, Ralph, Martin, Mike S. Mike M., Mike T., Paul G., Paul J., Peter, Rick, Courtney, and Jerry, who all *make it happen*.

This book is dedicated to my sweet and beautiful wife, who has helped me without measure in the production of this work. Also to my three wonderful children, who make my own life "massively parallel" with no additional effort on their part.

And of course, to Enzees everywhere who have experienced the capabilities of the Netezza technology.

NETEZZA

The unauthorized tales of derring-do and high-adventures in resilient data processing solutions

DAVID BIRMINGHAM

Copyright © 2008 VMII - All rights reserved.

ISBN: 1-4392-0743-7
ISBN-13: 978-1-4392-0743-7

Visit www.booksurge.com to order additional copies.

Contents

WELCOME TO THE UNDERGROUND!

LADIES AND GENTS, step into the Netezza Underground where we'll examine most, or at least *many* - things Netezza, and how to get the most out of your big black box.

I call it this, *the big black box*, as a term of endearment, of course. It sits in the corner of our data center, rather casually and faithfully processing our enterprise data. It doesn't need care and feeding, a fleet of engineers or administrators. We don't need to show up each morning with table scraps, coo at the machine or find new ways to make it happy. It is as loyal as a puppy dog and as outright tail-kickin' performance as any five (or more) machines in our shop. I keep trying to think of a name for it that ends with "ator" (rhymes with Terminator). It's elusive.

Back to the subject - it's a black box. A rather packaged form of fire and (mostly) forget kind of data processing machine. As we take this journey, the upcoming sections will unfold a story. Tales of derring-do complete with ancient mystics, lost worlds, heroes and dragons. Perhaps that's a *little* dramatic, but we *shall* have fun, and we shall be entertained. It's written down somewhere, isn't it?

So when we consider Netezza's OnStream® architecture, its massively parallel data processing power, its ability to inhale and exhale data in BTUs, and its effortless upward scalability, we see that calling it a data processing platform somehow falls short. Some would call it an experience. Others would call it a happening. Call it whatever you want. It inhales, crunches and publishes Libraries-of-Congress-at-a-time – *and fast*. We're just here to offer some guidance, pointers, and show how to create a little wowey-zowey along the way.

Some readers may crack these pages wanting to know more about the machine before they get one. Still others may have one and want more out of their investment. Both groups (and anywhere in between) will find something in these pages. It's an interesting marketplace effect when a company like Netezza rises to so effectively assist us in our large-scale processing woes, when we want more info, we can't seem to find enough. Oh, it's out there, but often obfuscated by opinions of their competitors and the knowledge-darkness that accompanies *anything* new. In essence, people want to engage one of these, but want to lark around the marketplace first, and when they do, it seems like the lack of information is more prevalent than the availability of it. And in some case, clients have told me that the lack of definitive marketplace information makes it look like an underground, perhaps even a black market.

THE NETEZZA UNDERGROUND

Therefore, let it be known that while the title of the book implies dark alleys and subterranean knowledge shared in the catacombs, via flickering firelight, it is a function of literary irony and *purely* tongue-in-cheek. Many of you who already own the machine will readily understand that some degree of mystery exists for the uninitiated, and it is the intention of this discussion to bring the mysteries into the *light*, not take the discussion into the darkness. And while it's a black box on the outside, some (in the Underground) would want us to believe that it's a black box on the *inside*, and as strange and mysterious as the flickering firelight patterns on the Underground cavern walls. But it's not - so read on and find out why.

With that, many of Netezza's competitors run about in the Underground catacombs, offering one red herring or another to take our eyes off our goals, if only for a moment, to purchase *their* product. Part of their spiel might include offering the contents of this book as though it is definitive, meaning definitive in *their* favor. We need to keep in mind that Netezza faces the data warehousing and large-scale data processing problem domain, itself a highly challenging environment and filled with its own pitfalls and problems. The reader (and the competitor) should not ascribe the problems of the domain itself to the Netezza technology. The reader *can* assume, however, that the Netezza appliance will voraciously dispatch and consume these data processing problems, for breakfast.

We also see a pervasive effect among technologists. Invariably when we do whiteboard sessions and suggest best-practices with the machine, someone asks "Do we *have* to do this?" Which is sort of like asking a professor in a classroom, "Do we *have* to know this?" or perhaps "Is this going to be on the *test*?" The answers are obvious. "Proper" data warehouse implementation requires a wide range of capabilities that we'd rather not build ourselves, but instead focus on the more elusive aspects, *if only we could get past the basics!* Netezza has the basics covered, and a whole lot more. We won't find ourselves tuning for performance in the tactical weeds of ten layers of tightly woven software.

Finally, what consultant can *possibly* offer anything definitive about an *appliance*? It has 1001 uses and approaches. This book is a series of tales and commentaries, so don't take it as an owner's manual or "final word.". The only *reasonable* "final word", is in how the reader successfully deploys a solution with it! Keep in touch, and let us know how you're doing, and how many data warehousing dragons you've slain with it. This week, at least.

What's it good for? People ask us how we apply the machine, and the obvious answer is for data warehousing, but there's a *lot* more inside. Anyone facing large-scale processing, of any kind, will find enormous power in this technology. Not just financial and retail, but any form of operation that crunches large volumes *and/or* high complexities of data. This includes organizations dealing with scientific or analytic applications, oil-and-gas (mountains of geo-spatial information), transportation logistics (near-real-time operational capture and reporting), manufacturing and its attendant just-in-time requirements for high volumes of complex parts and materials. In fact, the applications are endless, because it's an *appliance*.

After all, if we have underpowered systems attacking a complex problem, once we harness the complexity, the data volumes radically increase. Likewise if we have a very large data volume, an underpowered system prohibits us from doing much more than basic stuff, meaning that the more complex stuff is out of reach. True to form, if we harness the sizes, we can express our complexities, and the volumes *likewise* radically escalate. Either way, we not only need a way to harness what we have right now, but brace ourselves for the escalating growth to follow.

But if we can't handle the information we have now, *what makes us think we can handle it later*? And if we install a system that only handles the here-and-now, what will we do when the immediate future arrives to crush us?

Netezza grows with our capacity. We can scramble on the existing business problems without ever having to worry about whether Netezza will break in midstream. We have the freedom to breathe, to grow and to *dream* about even more.

We'll review examples, and case studies. I thought the case studies at the end would provide larger context, but the water-cooler case studies are kind of fun too, so I'll provide the Case Study Short, just an in-context blurb to illustrate a point without the loss of momentum. Those who have a Netezza machine can appreciate momentum. Or rather, *acceleration*.

Disclaimer: Neither we, our progeny or forebears, are part of (nor beholden to) the Netezza sales cycle. Nor will we have one whit of awareness whether you purchase a Netezza appliance after reading this book. I'm a big fan of the Netezza product, and make no mystery of this, and sometimes marvel at why liking it seems to diminish my objectivity. If something works, and works well, I make no bones about it working well for anyone.

However, this book *is* for existing Netezza users so they can get a better bang for their Netezza buck. Others who read it might find it an interesting foray, but perhaps not as useful without the product in-hand. We'll also cover many aspects of data warehousing and bulk solutions harnessed by the Netezza technology, and thus where Netezza firmly fits in our various environments. So if you need some data warehouse stuff, it's in there.

This book is no substitute for vendor training. If you have a Netezza machine and haven't engaged the vendor's training program, some of the contents of this book might seem like a proto-language. Not to worry, just log onto their training site and get the boot-camp.

Also let it be known that this book is a completely *unauthorized* discussion, but in no way betrays the spirit or letter of non-disclosure concerning the technology. So says our attorney. The revelations herein deal with applications and implementations. If the reader wants engineering advice or information, get on the phone with the vendor. Their product support is top-notch, they love to talk about the nuts and bolts, and they actively disclaim any desire to enter a development lifecycle to deliver solutions or applications with you.

Which means of course, more for me (or people like me, if you will). If we want some implementation or application assistance after we've purchased the machine, this book will help. Knowledgeable professionals may help more (but again that's just the warehousing discipline, and true of *any* technology). The vendor's product engineers and support people are a lot like a sports coach in their approach. They'll show us the basic play, call it during the game, but we're the one carrying the ball on the field. And trust us on this: They've wrapped up all the hard stuff inside the box, so it's a lot easier on *all* of us. Our time-to-deployment is already compressed at the moment we break the plastic.

Some of the readers may find the Remediator team out on ITToolbox, shuffling about its hallways or, on occasion, dropping a post to Ab Initio Underground Blog. The entries therein clearly indicate that we have an affinity for parodies of movies, television, literature and the like. Expect to find parodies here as well, because the temptation is irresistible, and we are but mere mortals.

This book is by no means exhaustive or definitive. We suspect multiple editions might be in order as both the appliance industry and the products develop. We'll get around to those things too, if we find the time, and we don't forget.

Onward and upward.

Read the Product Label

Someone recently asked us, "Why does a Netezza project *fail*?" offered in the context of having "heard" that another Netezza project may have had a bumpy ride. This question is fair, because many data warehouse implementations have bumpy starts, so it's easy to blame the platform, or the lack of a proper one. Netezza projects "fail" for the same reasons that any *other* project can fail. It's an *appliance*. We would not blame our favorite, blessed and many-favored RDBMS for a failed data warehouse project. We would look elsewhere.

Wouldn't we?

By the time the reader browses the upcoming pages, the answer to this question will emerge, and perhaps the reader who needs the information now, before committing to an incorrect or marginal path, will find insights.

Pitfalls abound in bulk data processing, but are common to all data processing domains. Netezza is the kind of technology that can keep us out of the common pitfalls, for one simple reason: When a project goes into a steep dive, it needs power to climb out of it. Lots of power.

Netezza has it.

We would be significantly remiss in not warning you up front – to read the Netezza product label (or at least its data sheets). Some things it does well, some things it doesn't do at all. While we'll cover these issues in context, understand this:

Netezza is intended to circumscribe decades of core best practices in large-scale bulk processing and report delivery. You will see a flavor of mainframe-style operations and processing tricks that might be foreign to you. They are not foreign to the industry, and certainly not foreign to the domain of data warehousing, where bulk processing is the name of the game.

Netezza is an *Asymmetric Massively Parallel*® data warehouse and data processing appliance technology, combining the worlds of an SMP host and an MPP architecture. It works with data in *large* quantities at-a-time. Not *one* record-at-a-time. (In other words, it's not a transactional machine).

Decades ago on the original episodes of *Saturday Night Live*, one of the parody commercials was for a product that one of the characters squirted on his ice cream. It went off the side of the plate and onto the floor. The wife complained, *you got it all over the floor* to which the husband said, no problem, it's a floor wax, *and* a dessert topping. Meaning of course, that we can use the same substance for either purpose equally well.

By this analogy, Netezza is a floor wax, *not* a dessert topping. It's for heavy lifting and cleaning, not for the transactional, user-facing touch. Keep in mind that while it interoperates with our transactional machines, it is not *itself* a transactional machine. Netezza has extraordinary capabilities - for what Netezza is *intended* to do. But we've seen shops that will abuse the Netezza appliance no differently than abusing a regular household appliance. Don't toss Fluffy into the dryer and all that.

"No transactional for you!" - the Data Warehouse Nazi, *Seinfeld*.

Does this mean that we can use Netezza for "continuously streaming" data? Of course it does, and we'll get to that. We can process any kind of data, streaming intake included. But we need to understand that Netezza handles them in bulk. *Mind-morphing* bulk.

Also, we shouldn't short-change its effective impact by doing things in our *other* machines that are better suited in Netezza. Anything in our environment that deals with bulk, set-based processing should *find its way home* into our Netezza machine. That's where it belongs.

We now have a large-scale bulk-processor machine that can very nearly bend gravity in its power and throughput. Push the workload to it and don't hold back. Or, as the folks at the vendor headquarters are wont to say, get your data *Under Air.*

Of course, if we're not ready for the nosebleeds received from its stratospheric lift, perhaps we should look to the West, and not give it a second thought.

Advantages

The best part about working with Netezza is that we have the freedom to experiment with our ideas without taking a huge turnaround penalty. Imagine loading up thirty-million records into an SMP-based RDBMS to lark around with a few bulk-processing tests.

On second thought, don't imagine it. That's kind of scary. Sorry about that. Bad example.

On a gig fairly recent to one of my first introductions to Netezza, I worked with a client who had been painfully and laboriously stuffing their daily workload of fifteen million rows into a commodity RDBMS on a "standard" Wintel SMP platform - the load itself requiring two *hours* duration. We leveraged the Ab Initio product to push the information, so while Ab Initio's processing cycle finished in relative minutes of time, the remaining duration of the flow became two hours of pushing data into the database. This was akin to pushing half-dried concrete through a soda straw.

We contrast this to another gig where the customer required loading ten times this amount (both row count and size) of one-hundred-fifty-million rows into a data structure, to represent one day's worth of the customer's data. (This case study appears later).

Netezza loaded a million rows per *second*, a sustained intake of 50 megabytes per second. That's correct, 150 million rows in 150 seconds, or 2.5 minutes. We learned later that this was actually a *worst-case* loading scenario (owing to some undiscovered network issues). Even so, this initial performance number was a shocker. The vertigo-rush of this experience was mind-bending, and remains with us to this day. Give us a moment, we need to take a pause. Okay, we're back.

You get the picture. There is a *contrast*, but not a *comparison*. Fifteen million rows in two hours versus one-hundred-fifty million in less than three minutes.

THE NETEZZA UNDERGROUND

Once the data arrives inside, we can slice, dice and make Julie-Ann cry, but what we can't do - is take our fingers off the keyboard. It's a *drug* folks, like some funky kind of geekville crack that makes us crave another hit. The first time I saw it return a single, 1-terabyte query in just seconds, I was convinced. You think I'm kidding.

Okay, well, there's my *objective* assessment of Netezza for your enterprise data warehouse! Whooo-hooo!

Mythology: We find ourselves dispelling a lot of false product mythology. One of which goes like this: *The more data we load onto it, the slower it gets.* This is patent nonsense, and we'll examine why in these pages. While I don't have the cycles to chase down and dispel every Netezza myth and urban legend (largely fomented by disgruntled - er - *displaced* competitors) - hopefully this tour will give the reader enough information to separate fact from fiction.

I liken it to how the Secret Service is trained to deal with counterfeit cash. They're trained in counterfeit techniques, but can spot a counterfeit *bill* because they know the real thing so well. So the following pages follow this spirit, that the more you know about the real thing, the less impact the counterfeit mythology will have on you.

It is our intention, when approaching a technology of any kind, to make *informed* decisions about its capabilities and limitations. Heck, we do this when we buy lawn equipment too, don't we? So let's learn and assimilate, and have a little fun.

And no, the Netezza product was not sent to Earth by inhabitants of Rigel 12. This, too, is patent nonsense. The inhabitants of Rigel 12 know nothing of data warehousing. Ask anyone.

For Profiling: One of the major problems in data warehousing is in rarefying and distilling the most appropriate data structures for performance and longevity. We want to profile the data, knead it in our hands to squeeze out the fat, and find the best, right-sized internal structures to last us for awhile. With traditional technologies, this particular exercise is the most tedious, arduous and frankly error-prone, because every step is manual.

And there's *so much data!*

On a *traditional* platform, as we watch the seconds, then minutes and then hours of testing tick by, we might want to gnaw our arm off at the elbow to get out of this horrifyingly boring duty. We find ourselves staring at the machine, and the abyss of boredom beyond it, as though we can actually see it running. There is no relief. The gurus smile and say, "Pay your dues, dude, the rest of us had to."

In the old school, we profiled the data, put together a "viable" model, and might have *thought* we had it right, but we always needed more time to experiment. Just a little more time. In a traditional RDBMS, with gigantic, heavily-indexed data structures, we have as much trouble setting up a test as actually executing it. Without objective scalability, *today's* metrics on a traditional platform might be (and probably are) deceptive for processing *tomorrow's* data.

Practically speaking, we might actually be heading for a hardware upgrade even before our next annual salary review cycle kicks in. It's hard for the boss to remember that we saved the world nine months prior, when today we must request a hardware upgrade. We must time the request appropriately, and all that. Laugh now, but we know people who carefully manage capacity planning so the "bad news" never falls on a pay upgrade cycle. It's self-preservation, you see.

Oookay, now back to the issue at hand, and that is preliminary data profiling – crunchin' that data like there's no tomorrow. Strangely, we might actually be able to finish a lot of that crunching *today*, when on Netezza, our queries and data profiling activities are coming back in rapid-iteration cycles, in *seconds*. Not that we'll get it all done on the first day. (There's always tomorrow if we need extra time!) But in the end, we'll find ourselves with real daylight remaining at the end of the day, which may be kind of strange for some (getting to see the sunset on a regular basis and watch our kids grow up).

Case Study Short: One consultant noted that once upon a time he wanted to get data into a machine to test it. Once inside the Netezza machine, he just fired off the query and got the data back. Performing the same operation in an RDBMS, it never returned. Then someone told him of a "secret notation" he could place at the end of the query to give a special hint to the RDBMS. This worked, but still took over an hour to get the same data back that the Netezza machine had returned in mere seconds. We'll see this as a theme in our discussion: The SMP-based RDBMS engines often require secret hooks, special instructions and tuning practices that are only understood by the Shaolin priests. We'll call this discipline "engineering" so that its practitioners can save face, but suffice to say that the special-knowledge-thing keeps our business users nervous. They want something built, you know, like an *appliance*. They want it protected, you know, like an *asset*.

Ultimately we want a Netezza-facing set of data structures that harness the data and our creativity. But wait, there's even more. We don't *have* to do all the profiling in the beginning, just a first, best stab at it. What happens, for example, if we're halfway down the road and find an excellent opportunity to optimize even further? Should we shrug and say *alas, poor Yorick, I didn't know the data well enough?* Or should we just go for it and refactor? Netezza gives us the power to adapt along the way, if only we're willing to accept the responsibility such power gives us.

I'm fond of saying, at the end of the day, the technologist wants *the day to end*. Netezza buys back this time and actually makes the ride a little more fun. Those adrenalin junkies, accustomed to mainframe or Ab Initio-scaled power, will appreciate it too. No more slow data loads. No more slow extracts. The world is good, the birds are singing, the breeze is blowing and all the elected officials want to lower our taxes. Okay, that's a stretch, but the optimism *is* contagious.

Apart from the initial data profiling, we get a chance to see other kinds of structures in action. We'll see patterns emerge. What's that? Data patterns in billions of rows? Oh yes, it's in there! We'll consider some of those later, because they can directly assist in our data processing mission and keep things under control. After all, why put all of our ocean into a machine that can *actually* boil the ocean? Why not concentrate the heat, create some steam, and use it to run some information turbines for even *more* data power? Either way, we can focus our efforts on the business problems, not the technology problems. There is no "schema engineering".

And isn't all this - what we *want*?

This book will chop the problems and discussions into various categories, with "anonymized" case studies at the end. Overall we've geared it like a reference rather than a running editorial commentary. There's plenty of commentary smattered about, though. It's the way of things.

THE NETEZZA UNDERGROUND

The Netezza Developer Network (NDN)

Ahh, the "Enzee" community, of which the Remediator team are all members, is perhaps Netezza's greatest strength. If the reader is a member (and if not, *why* not?), the reader knows the power of bringing case-tested issues into the fold of the Netezza machine. In the NDN, the vendor and users alike encounter firsthand the problems and creative solutions that its own user base has implemented, and has the opportunity to see the patterns of reuse that it can boil directly into the architecture for increasing appliance value.

We'll discuss in the following chapters the various parts that make the Netezza appliance a machine that the developers love, because it does the things developers do, like the developers do them, and in a way that makes it fun. That the vendor actually *acts* on the user feedback, creates an environment that the open-software and open-system proponents have only written about but never actually realized.

In the NDN, it's for real.

And this is another aspect that raises the discussion from the shadows of the Underground, but in many ways creates a culture that itself seems Underground-ish (without all the shadows and flickering firelight). The main reason is, when you're part of the Enzee Universe, you're part of something different, and you know it. There's very little that's underground or hidden among us, and we welcome people into the fold the moment they embrace the technology. Its acquisition and deployment is a form of initiation, the crossing from one way of thinking into another, and a step into the light, not into the darkness of the Underground. Existing Enzee Universe members will cheer your entry, and lament your decision to go with another technology. Oddly, they know you'll be back, and the drinks and camaraderie will be waiting for you.

Whenever you're ready.

What's that? You're a business user and don't believe that your developers should have a little fun, perhaps even be re-introduced to what *sunlight* looks like? Unlike we might imagine, our technologists are not nocturnal creatures. They have families, children and other priorities that make life worth living. The Netezza machine is a platform they love to talk about, even when they're standing around the grill, roasting up a bunch of Johnsonville Brats.

Ahh, it's what life is made of.

In the NDN, users interact with the vendor and each other, and the ecosystem this has created, brings a problem-solving power and solution-centric strength to the domain that is nothing short of astounding. We're continually amazed at the responsiveness of the vendor to the repeating patterns their users encounter, and we're always pleasantly surprised when the vendor announces new support and features - *based on user feedback, no less!*

In fact, when the vendor says they're about to release thus-and-so, we often smile and think, "Of course you will. We knew you would." It's an odd form of symbiosis that is contagious among its user base and third-party ecosystem partners.

Innovation toward simplicity

Many years ago, someone introduced me to a processing paradigm described thus: We had a central MS-DOS-based disk drive on a high-bandwidth network. We had dozens of common desktop computers with access to these disk drives as a shared resource on a gigabit switch. Some of those computers operated as intake, sending data down to the drives, while others operated as batch processors. The data was physically stored on the drives in multiple parallel files, written in stripes on the drives to get the best power balance and reduce data skew at the hardware level. This sounds oddly like a Netezza setup, except all the machines were full-size desktop computers. Hundreds of them.

Now imagine that each of the desktop computers is running the same program, polling for data on the master disk drives. Now imagine that the common desktop program is not native C, Visual Basic or even .NET, but Microfocus *COBOL*. I could imagine a system-control language handling all the parallelism and orchestration, but COBOL? *Seriously?*

Now imagine that if we want to write an application for this, we're told that we have to write a common COBOL program, and carefully engineer its hooks into a substrate of deeper COBOL-based services that will interact with the common disk-drive system, all of which was a home-grown, hand-crafted control system.

In COBOL. Seriously.

Engineering minds (like me) accustomed to building very large scale parallel environments, understood the complexity and scale of the problem domain. The architects of this system did not. Apart from the abysmally poor choice of COBOL for a control language (my apologies, I still snicker at this), the rest of the architecture was an engineer's nightmare and an application developer's hell. When it was first described to me and several colleagues, I could make a case on half-a-whiteboard as to why this system had no viability whatsoever, and why embracing it was borderline insanity. After having constructed some of the most powerful expert systems and complex, real-time system control brains on the planet, I looked at this environment as nothing more than a toy. Imagine my surprise when the boss told us that we would embrace, assimilate and deploy this Medusa into our enterprise, forsaking all others!

I also noted, jokingly mind you, that whomever designed such an architecture must have really hated application developers. The environment sent developers through a crucible of testing and pernicious bug-fixing that looked as much like engineering as application development. But I was only joking about the architect's contempt for application developers. When I met the architect, I found out he really did hate application developers. Viscerally so. And this was not a joking matter.

The environment seemed to have come recommended, after all, a Texas-based telecommunications company had run with this product for many years, making its company very rich and its founders even richer. Our principals had the same delusions of grandeur (emphasis on the delusion part).

I noted at the time, and still feel the same way - embracing such a system for enterprise processing *is an act of desperation.*

It is also the Spirit of the *Underground.* Desperation leads people to do radical things, buy radical products and embrace radical assertions. It seems so *black market.* Someone is pulling the wool over our eyes, or over the eyes of our decision-makers. We make protective conclusions, that the product sales people are either deceived, or deceiv*ing*. Our natural instinct kicks in and we have to *save the day*. After all, no system is as powerful as the proponents claim, and nothing can possibly put numbers on the scoreboard as fast, well and accurately as its champions think, or seem to think. People who kick the Netezza tires hear these same radical things, hear these same astounding assertions and reach the same conclusions. Nothing is *that* good.

Or is it?

In some ways, the Netezza marketplace infusion fights against the muddy waters and underground assertions of those failures who have come before them. If we should go to the marketplace and attempt to discover products like Netezza, or those who have come before it, we might not find answers, or we might find answers in the wrong places, offered by the wrong people, with the wrong motive. An Underground motive. These are serious questions, requiring serious answers. The stakes are high.

The Spirit of the Underground has the look and appearance of a con-game. With a huge difference. My dad says that of all the criminals he's had to deal with (professionally as a prosecutor) that the con-artist is the most interesting. Because the con-artist preys on two very key things. First is the desperation of the "mark" to get what the mark wants, typically borne on greed. The second is the desire to do it secretly, because radical, stratospheric success is too good to be true, and if everyone knew about it, nothing would be left for our hapless mark. Keep it on the hush-hush, to make sure that nobody, not even those who might warn us off the bad decision, will know what we're about to do. And once it's done, we wish we'd told someone - *anyone* - besides the prosecutor we're now sharing the story with.

The spirit of *this* discussion is to share what we know of the product, so the con artists have no ground, no conversational traction and the schemes-manship is a non-issue. We can have objective, actionable information, and we know where we stand. More importantly, we're really trying to do it out in the open, not in the darkness of the underground. The stakes are high, we seek enlightenment, not shadowy patterns on the catacomb walls.

The marketplace is literally brimming with people whom I affectionately call "eccentric innovators". People with a "good" idea, the best of intentions, but who are in way, way, *way* over their heads. My standard response to the assertion of an eccentric innovator is actually found in a DMReview article called *Beware the Eccentric Innovator.* This was an essay on the *adverse* impact such an environment can have on a corporation, including the more significant impact it has on human resources and the many delicate questions of *Are you for real?* You see, technologists only want to embrace technologies and approaches that make them personally marketable, because they realize the blatant infidelity of IT organizations toward their own staffs. A layoff can and will occur at any time, and the technologist refuses to get locked into working with any technology that has no marketplace presence, or at least no *perceived* marketplace presence, which would limit the technologist's own career marketability in case of job loss.

Which is understood thus: Help me put my Medusa in place, and we'll engineer it to perfection. If a layoff comes, I'll give you a reference. To which the technologist mentally responds: A reference to whom? To the other companies who *aren't* using the Medusa? If there aren't any, will we be slinging burgers for awhile? Yes, the Medusa can turn careers to stone, too.

This DMReview article likens such innovators to the eccentricity of Caractacus Potts of *Chitty Chitty Bang Bang,* who thrilled us with his eccentric innovations, all very funny and humorous *because we're not actually administering them on our operations floor.* The article was prompted by my encounter with the aforementioned Medusa system (nicknamed Medusa, since it was highly tentacled and tended to turn application developers -and their managers - into stone). Until encountering the Medusa, I thought all such systems were obvious in their intentions and applications. Clearly the product of an opportunist, we should smile and wave, but not give it a second thought. Until Medusa, I had simply smiled, shrugged and passed it by as no consequence. Why would such an oddly designed (and poorly constructed) product have any marketplace viability at all? Who in their right mind would purchase such an obvious eccentricity?

A desperate person. A mark.

On the Medusa, its eccentric innovator/architect got frustrated with the inability of our company's principals and technologists to understand it, embrace it and run with it. What he hadn't considered, was that the technologists in our company weren't a bunch of runny-nosed kids. They *fully* understood his system, and had *rejected* it. For objective and reasonable causes. This realization stunned the innovator, so he packed his bags and hit the road.

Oddly, the technologists thought some of his ideas were good, so proceeded to build a variation of his architecture using commodity parts, with an RDBMS as the central hub. In other words, they thought that no difference existed between things that were parallel, and things that were *asynchronous*. This led to utter failure and multiple waves of layoffs for all involved. Including the desperate CIO who originally thought it was a good idea to embrace, and a better idea to extend. I suspect that none of those who attempted to extend the original Medusa, put it on their resumes as a marketable skill.

All that said, what has impressed me about the Netezza architecture is not its eccentricity, but its *simplicity*. It takes the obvious and makes it useful. It takes the realities of *scale* and puts them in a practical package. Its architecture is knowable, visible and easy to understand, no mysteries. Those who are in the pain of working with overwhelmed systems, will find its capabilities highly desirable.

What of those who are desperate? It is my policy, as it is those who work with me, that we never take advantage of a client's desperation. It goes back to a famous quote from W.C. Fields, who had been fired from one motion picture studio while on contract for $15 per day, which he requested as a starting salary at a new studio. His new boss objected, saying Fields should feel lucky to get $8 per day, reminding Fields that he'd been fired, and had no grounds for negotiation.

To which Fields simply said, "I see no reason for you to take advantage of my misfortune."

Indeed, the desperate among us are the most vulnerable. The Underground black market is in a word, predatory, gladly clearing a spot in front-row-center, near the campfire in Catacomb #3. The Enzee community, on the other hand, is one that protects it most vulnerable, not devours them. It is very interesting to see how Enzees greet a new member. Almost like a homecoming.

THE NETEZZA UNDERGROUND

What good are ya? Or, whaddya good at?

We get a lot of questions on the machine's practical uses, so let's look briefly at how some average customers might leverage the machine.

Query Acceleration: we load the machine with consumption-ready data, and the users pound the daylights out of it with complex queries. Quite frankly, lots of technologies can do this, even more if we swarm our engineers on them. Some technologists actually compare Netezza to other technologies on this basis alone. Missing the big picture entirely.

Master Data Repository: we load the machine with our master and reference data, hosting it inside for later utility

Parallel data processing engine: we load the data relatively raw into the machine, then perform transforms on it (using complex SQL statements) and pushing into another internal schema that faces the user. It arrives raw and ends up consumption-ready

Analytic calculations: in massively parallel form

Set-based, key-based and high-math: Problems that remain forever daunting, perhaps even elusive, in some cases impossible - within any other large-scale bulk processing domain.

Elusive relationships: such as topology maps, slowly-changing dimensions, error capture and reporting, etc. Once we cross over the high-scale walls in an RDBMs, these capabilities often evaporate.

"You don't have the big pic-*chah*!" Peter O'Toole as professor Wolper, *The Big Picture*.

The complete universe of Netezza applicability simply dwarfs our ability to define it. We can do inside the machine what has normally been the domain of ETL tools. We can process information in volumes and speeds that have normally been the domain of mainframes and massively parallel systems (Cray, Thinking Machines, Teradata, GAPP). We know users that leverage Netezza for *some* but rarely all of the above. If you're one of the types who pushes the envelope and uses it for everything, then excellent. If not, you're likely not getting the most value from the machine, but not to worry. The upcoming chapters will reveal how to get us there.

In style.

Roadmap to Scalability

People buy a Netezza machine with the expectation of scalability. This is not an implicit assumption, but an explicitly promised hope. It's on the product label and the tenor of every conversation associated with the machine. Of course, Netezza provides us with the *potential* for success, but cannot stop us from making other mistakes within our domain that hinder Netezza's effectiveness. To achieve scalability, we need to consider what makes it possible, and what we can do to achieve it, or for that matter, lose it after we have it.

- **Stability**- the first of three pillars of our environment. If we fail to achieve stability, or if our environment is already unstable, we can stop here. The more and disparate our storage mechanisms, the more the propensity for instability. We must stabilize in order to move forward. Netezza, as a self-contained appliance, offers a means to stabilize rapidly by reducing the overall system needs.

- **Adaptability**- the second of three pillars of our environment. While it stands that if an environment is not stable, neither is it adaptable. But without adaptability, we are doomed to endless cycles of rewrite and redeployment, sometimes for the tiniest incremental functionality. Netezza offers adaptability in the flexibility of its framework and the elimination of adaptation constraints. Not the least of which is the absence of index structures. The constant attention to index optimization in a traditional RDBMS is just one thorn in the side to administrators and operators, and only offers the constant appearance of instability. In addition, if we adapt once and are no longer adaptable thereafter, we are on a slippery slope toward instability.

- **Scalability**- the *third* of three pillars of our environment. This aspect is also dependent on the other two pillars. Without stability and adaptability, the whole notion of scalability is never within reach. Likewise if we can scale *only* once, we're not as adaptable as we thought. If we scale multiple times and lose our adaptability along the way, we have only scaled *into* instability. All three pillars must be kept in balance. Netezza allows us to scale in power simply by adding frames, and scale in storage with simple invoice events to unlock ever-present terabytes for our utilization. From there, the scalability is part of the appliance offering and requires far less customer-side direct engineering to achieve our scalability goals.

Scalability has dependencies and never arrives for free. It is likewise an asset that we should pursue, acquire, harness and *protect*. We can easily upgrade an unstable system and increase our capacity. We can then crank out more broken reports than ever before! We can likewise bolt-on clusters of application and third-party systems, rigging them together with plain vanilla connections, and our environment may have the *appearance* of interoperability. We'll see how adaptable it is when the business grows out of its capacity. Growth is the only true test of the strength of our systems.

Which is something of an irony, no? If our systems cannot scale, any new growth will crush them. But if we don't grow, how will we ever know?

Betty Crocker's Bake Sale

Any doubts about Netezza's performance? Think that the numbers you're hearing are just subject of urban legends? Nobody can query a terabyte in seconds, can they? An enterprise warehouse with no indexes? Pshaw!

Do a bake off.

Don't send Netezza Corp your data, have them come over to your place, and bring a machine. Load it up and watch it work. Touch it. Taste it. Handle it.

Believe it.

The only way to really appreciate what it can do - is to watch it happen, plain and simple. If we're someone who's never worked with the technology, this whole book will look like *words on a page*. The things we talk about – *like yesterday's news* – will be foreign and incomprehensible to someone who is ideologically committed to doing data warehousing *only* in a relational database, performing data integration *only* in an ETL tool, and using *only* indexes for query acceleration.

Not to say that we won't understand it, or can't understand it. The Netezza concepts are real, practical and easy to understand and implement. All the engineering is under-the-hood, so to speak, all we have to do is crank the ignition and go. However, just as owning a car has lots of responsibilities and assumes a general knowledge-base and proficiency in certain subject areas, likewise practically anyone with some data warehousing, data processing or software experience will pick it up in short order.

But someone without *any* knowledge of driving, shouldn't be behind the wheel anyhow. *Oui?*

This standardizing-on-simplicity (perhaps complexity-averse) approach is not necessarily the case with some of Netezza's competitors, who rather than reduce toward simplicity, have instead embraced much higher complexity. Not only do they embrace it, they invite us to join their "complexity party". Going with that, we have to embrace the same complexities that they tell us are *necessary* to process data in the required quantities. But we *don't* have to embrace them. There's a simpler way to do it.

And seeing is believing.

So snap to it, fire up the ovens and do a bake off.

What's in it for me?

One of our favorite anecdotes is the original Betty Crocker cake mix story. When the cake mixes first hit the shelves, they *stayed* on the shelves. In spite of rave reviews that the cakes were outstanding, they weren't moving. Nobody was buying.

Then Betty Crocker (not her real name) did some market surveys and learned that the people who normally made cakes from scratch, namely the housewives who were Betty's target market, had a beef with the cake, so to speak. *It didn't require any effort on their part*. Add water and make a cake. The hands actually doing it were superfluous. It seemed to *relegate* the importance of the *cook*. A cave man could do it. (Yikes, *now* we'll get mail!)

So Betty realized the error, and re-marketed the cakes to require two eggs. This simple change made the cooks feel as though they were part of the process, and the cake mixes *flew* off the shelves. Betty eventually retired a billionaire in Fiji. She doesn't accept visitors.

The point is, once we drop our black box on the floor and realize that it *really is* an appliance, this strange feeling suddenly arises. Almost like *what do they need me for*? Well, the Netezza machine isn't completely without administration, but it's part-time nevertheless. One of the primary reasons a hardcore engineer (i.e. *hero*) will eschew appliance technologies is the same reason the housewives did not buy the original cake mixes. The *perception* that it relegates them. But it's only *perception*.

Make no mistake, our (heroic) engineers will sometimes flock towards and fawn over the technologies that embrace higher complexity. It makes them starry-eyed, myopic and quite frankly dangerous to the business of processing data. They will invite more complexity to the table, like inviting a dragon inside the castle keep, all the while promising that dragon was, is and ever-shall-be under control. As keepers of the dragon, they are important. They are heroes. They are necessary. But the first time the dragon breathes fire, we will wonder - *what could we have possibly been thinking?*

With Netezza in the shop, another effect is afoot inside the mind of our boss and those around us. Creative juices are flowing. They're dreaming again. To think about what more they *could* do, including more business opportunities that were otherwise unavailable to them. Watch them burn out the Expo Dry-Erase markers as they brainstorm the future. The wave is rising.

Break out the board and ride it.

Even if the dream cycle hasn't started, we'll just bet our boss has a list of Very Important Initiatives that he's been wanting to get done for Quite Some Time. Now he has the power to Make Them Happen. Our suggestion, would be to embrace the future and master how the Netezza machine processes data. Start knocking off the items on that long-overdue wish list, and see if the boss isn't just happy as a peach.

Also – we shouldn't imagine that our boss *wants* us to firefight underpowered systems for the rest of our lives. Installing a Netezza machine might be the best way for her to reward us, and say she wants to keep us, and now she's pulled in some high-powered, really *fun* hardware and has just made our job tons easier than it used to be.

It's all good.

What's it gonna cost me?

We could give you the "underground" answer for this.

Imagine a Chazz Palminteri-styled accent: "Psst, hey kid, whatsit gonna cost ya to try it, and whatsit gonna cost ya *not* to? Say hello to my friend Guido, who will gladly cut you a contract without cutting your flesh. Thanks for stoppin' by."

Okay, so the underground is a rough place.

There's another way to ask this question, like our attorney would ask, "What do we *want* it to cost us?" It's a matter of expectations, no?

Yet another way to answer the question is: "If you have to ask, perhaps your problems really aren't big enough to worry about it. *Next*."

What you're probably *really* wanting is a set of real, dollar costs. The purchase. The upgrades. The scalability. The administration. The *muscle*. These are all excellent questions, and we're glad you asked them. We've already noted that we are in no wise part of the sales cycle of Netezza, and none of their principals, sales staff or others are even remotely aware that this book is underway and about to hit the shelves in time for – hmm – we'll have to pick a holiday. No matter – this book is for folks who already have one.

But for those who *don't* have one - we won't mince words with you (any more than we already have). But we will say:

We should *not* compare the Netezza technology to other products in the same way we would compare those other products *to each other*.

Why is that?

Netezza is self-contained CPU, disk storage and database engine, all rolled into a single appliance frame. A massively parallel (MPP) frame.

Contrast this to Oracle, Sybase IQ, GreenPlum, Ab Initio etc. all of which are *software products* that will require an additional purchase of *hardware and storage.* A commodity symmetric (SMP) frame.

Now don't get us wrong. We really like all these products. If you happen to have one or more, good for you. And you also know the truth of this statement, that the cost of the *software* product itself is only part of, perhaps a fraction of, the cost of the hardware to host it on, and likewise a fraction of the cost of disk storage. This is why people compare Ab Initio to Oracle – or GreenPlum to Sybase IQ, or Ab Initio to Informatica. All things being equal, the test or proof-of-concept will run *on the same hardware* for comparative purposes. So we compare one software product to another.

Not so with Netezza. We won't be putting Oracle on the same hardware as Netezza, nor will we test Greenplum or Ab Initio on it. So we need to keep this in mind – and we will repeat it for emphasis:

We should NOT compare Netezza to other products in the same manner as we compare those products *to each other.*

Batteries not included, among other things. Of course, just because we *should* not, doesn't mean people don't try (especially their competitors). Once upon a time, we attended a presentation with a competitor of Netezza's. They showed the "total cost" of the purchase of their *software product*, a similarly marketed data storage-and-query-acceleration solution, versus the total cost of the purchase of a Netezza *machine* – as if they were one and the same thing. This was a lopsided presentation, because they only showed the cost of their *software product,* not the cost of the hardware to put it on. Trust me, this "extra" hardware purchase can be a significant sticker-shock value. And once we've made the commitment to the software, the purchase-order train has left the station, so to speak, and the product vendor is *really* depending on this momentum to keep the deal "sealed".

Here's what we saw in the presentation, and we'll use percentages rather than real dollars. Partially because the costs of these machines will likely change over the shelf life of this book, and partially because consultants always speak in percentages. It's our native tongue.

Let's just say that the "software product" making its pitch, costs a relative $100. So we'll compare the initial $100 of software product compared to the relative outlay of cost for the Netezza product.

	Product for Sale	Netezza's Cost
Software Product	$100	$500
Required System	$100	$0 (in the box)
Required disk storage	$400	$0 (in the box)
Cost of Maintenance	$100	$25
Time to deploy	$200	$25

By the time we compare the *total works*, the "software product" not only has *four* times the ongoing maintenance cost (both labor and various vendor fees), it has a longer time/cost to deployment (and thus a more protracted cycle for enhancement). The overall cost of this particular core physical plant was more as well ($600 vs $500)– but the *software vendor* did not make it look that way.

So this is why I point it out: In the *underground*, people trade on secret and hidden knowledge. It's more like a full-disclosure problem than anything else. We can agree that the above comparison brings a major factor *to light*. Buying one of these *software* systems, with such significant *hidden* hardware sticker prices, is no different than having someone sell us a car and then claiming that the engine, transmission and tires are all separate purchases.

Consider the sales pitch of the "software product" versus its *actual cost to deploy*. It is (often) a factor of *five times* greater than what was actually presented in the sales pitch, which is at the very least a naïve approach to sales.

Or *is* it? (If the objective is to *make a sale*, after all)

For a contrast: An SMP platform is a general-purpose array of CPUs, not a purpose-built architecture. An MPP like Netezza is purpose-built, so we can demand and expect extraordinary performance within its designated solution domain. As such, the general-purpose nature of the SMP constrains it from rising above a maximum performance ceiling, that the MPP can effortlessly cross, *with the acceleration of a sonic boom*.

In a recent discussion, someone noted that a particular SMP-based RDBMS could out-perform a Netezza platform's speed, by writing data at the rate of 1.8 TB per hour. We asked for more specifics, and received an official TPC -H results spec, *and* discovered that this RDBMS was running on an eleven *million* dollar platform, containing *128* CPU cores! (In all fairness, they purchased it all-at-once and got a one-time discount of four million dollars, down to seven million dollars, so if we have this kind of cash lying around, *we could take advantage of the large-purchase discount too!*).

Hmm?

In anyone's imagination, is such a platform *remotely* viable, or even within monetary *reach*, of the average data processing environment? There's a difference between a functional home and a dream home, and we don't mind calling this 128-core platform what it is - a *dream* home - that people don't initially purchase, or even *grow* into. They would rather *jump* into from an existing environment that's rapidly losing power.

But do we *really need* to invest in such high-end hardware to get the physical performance we require? And once purchased, isn't Moore's law in effect from day *one?* (Marketplace technology moves on while our installation grows technology-stale over time). Will we *ever* get the chance to swap out those cores, the system storage or anything else, for faster, stronger marketplace upgrades - *as time wears on?* Overcoming Moore's law is automatically available with Netezza, along our continuum of ownership, through routine maintenance activity and not just upgrade-events.

In practically every performance-based discussion about a software product (in the above case, the RDBMS product), people don't even mention the *hardware* physics unless pressed for it. Almost as though they expect to hear "Well sure, on *that* platform." so it's as though they avoid mentioning the hardware, like this information might actually indict their favorite software product. It doesn't indict their software product at all, but simply shows that in apples-to-apples comparison, a competitor candidate platform emerges (Netezza), and the solution is never about *software alone.*

Performance is in the physics. Software can only use (or steal) the energy that's already there, and cannot manufacture more of it.

In the above case, the *storage alone* cost over four million dollars. So is this loading speed a reasonable metric for the software engine, or do we ignore the size, power and *cost* of the platform it's running on? Don't these play a part in the comparison too?

Of course they do.

As one of my colleagues likes to say "*Any* high-end hardware platform can make the *worst* software look like a champion. But I can't afford a *Cray!*"

For some comparative metrics, as of the inception of this book, a single Netezza frame could write its SPUs with data at speeds of over 700 gigabytes an hour. If we put 8 frames together (a 10800 Netezza machine) we have 896 SPUs with an aggregate write speed of over *6 terabytes an hour.* This utterly eclipses the aforementioned SMP / RDBMS performance (1.8 terabytes an hour).

However, if we're *only* after the equivalent 1.8 TB per hour, we could do this with *only 4* Netezza frames, or a 10400 machine, *half* the size of a maxed-out Netezza machine with power to spare - and - a **10400** won't cost even half this SMP's (discounted) seven *million* dollars!

So per our colleague's lament, we *can* have the power we need without investing in high-dollar, high-maintenance SMP platforms. And as noted, the SMP platform *requires* the additional power because its inefficient system architecture, and the inefficient RDBMS engine, both dissipate the precious processing energy rather than using it s*ynergistically for a focused purpose.*

So sales people – *chill* – and let us be clear: Each of these "other products" has a very strong set of core reasons to purchase them. Ab Initio, for example, does everything outside the database that we would normally do *inside* the database, and it serves the *critical* role of data transport to and from systems that are often unimaginably incompatible with each other. Ab Initio can source from practically any legacy system. It's a data processing *environment* that can handle movement and dispatch of large-scale information both in bulk *and* continuous operation, across our whole environment. And for the record, Ab Initio is the only known technology that can *load* Netezza at speeds approaching Netezza's ability to *intake* data.

Netezza doesn't do data transport. It's an appliance. It can consummately handle the bulk data processing on a mind-bending scale. It does on-demand query acceleration really well, but can do so much more without the data ever having to leave the machine. Data processing, but not the data *transport*.

But what of the other *appliances* that don't do data transport either? Aha! Now we can compare them more in how they will play in the environment.

So when we compare the products, we need to consider the *capabilities* we intend to leverage, the stated marketplace purpose / solution domain of the technology, the actual cost of deployment and the ongoing cost of maintenance. All of these matter, because once we've made the purchase, all of these questions will arise. If we don't have good answers for them *now*, what makes us think we'll have good answers for them *later*?

Our strongest suggestion, for the most objective comparison, is to:

- Get a complete list of all the hardware and software parts that will be necessary to make the solution "go"
- Get initial costs for all the parts.
- Get maintenance costs for all the parts, including licenses, service etc.
- Get costs for upgrading the parts, or adding to the parts
- Floor space, and yes, electricity, environment etc. Some appliances have a big footprint, Netezza does not.
- Cost of training, administrative support (anything "labor")
- When in doubt, perform a bake-off between them, just make sure the bake-off requires them to solve our *hardest* problem, not our weakest or marginal one. Don't make it easy for them, because what is easy for them might be very hard for us, and it might be hard on *day one* after the purchase.
- Now get the real growth numbers for the business, the data and expected capacity needs, and track a line from what it will cost now, versus what it will cost five years from now after the growth has been realized. The cost of the upgrades to keep up, licenses for more CPUs, all that stuff – will come into play.
- Now we must understand something else – what is the cost of doing *nothing*, and waiting for the growth to slowly eat the raised floor out from under our existing systems?

The above criteria are all reasonable to request and to review, and to use in selection and exclusion. While some nits might be missing, these criteria are the "big ticket" issues for cost and purchasing. Upon applying the criteria for total cost of ownership, we will see a *clear leader* emerge here, so we have objectivity in our selection.

A Clear Leader?

Some of you have already executed a proof-of-concept process and found it has taken "longer than expected." Your domain perhaps has ensconced technologies, for example, and Netezza is a

THE NETEZZA UNDERGROUND

threat to them. When a new kid moves into town, more talented at sports than all the others, reads poetry, listens to pop music and likes chick-flicks, the other boys on the sports teams glare at him. Suddenly the cheerleaders aren't cheering the team as much as they're cheering *him*. And now, he has dates with the prettiest girls in school!

No, we love to hate him, no matter how talented he is on the ball field, and no matter how many points he can put on the scoreboard, he is a threat in other ways. He makes the rest of us look bad, and he must be dealt with.

And you think I'm kidding?

We know of a number of Netezza install-bases that had protracted technology intake cycles because the existing ensconced technologies had vested interests in keeping Netezza *out*. Not because it couldn't out-perform them, but in side-by-side tests, it made the other systems *look bad*.

And we can't have *that*, now can we?

While a clear *technical* leader will emerge, the political machinery is always in play. This is where the Underground steps in, and it can get very interesting. Companies who finally purchase Netezza after a valiant competition with one of their competitors, sometimes lament that their internal infighting over the technologies was far more egregious than the proof-of-concept itself. These internal battles emerge with internal champions defending the existing technologies, and Netezza cast as an *uppity interloper* - probably one of those system-slam technologies that those dastardly consultants are always hawking to us!

In such skirmishes, the internal folks may win the day (temporarily), but they also have to put up or shut up. It's one thing to champion one's chosen technology simply because it's 'chosen', but it's plain embarrassing when we defend a player that cannot make it happen. These internal champions will spend a year or longer trying to get their favored son in shape for the company's future, only to realize that the favored son is a one-talent-wonder. It's not a multi-purpose data processing machine, but a technology with a rarefied skill set.

Sort of like hiring someone to plan a major city-wide convention because we've seen them so *skillfully* organize birthday parties.

When it comes to *scale*, the game is radically different. It's no longer about functionality alone, but performance. The competitor's internal champions are comfortable and perhaps addicted to their favorite son's special little features that make them giggle. But when push comes to shove, as it does when overworked systems are out of gas, the giggle isn't enough anymore. Not nearly enough.

Something we've noticed about the Enzees (those members of the Netezza Developers Network) and their supporters. There's a kind of unwritten "Enzee creed" that underpins conversations about the technology. Imagine a bunch of blackbelts standing around talking about their latest derring-do in the self-defense field. Confidence in their skills is unshakable, and they presently stand among their own in the conversation. They aren't chatting about common street-fighting, or pillow-fighting, but bouts with bloodthirsty, international champions who don't plan to exit the ring without drawing a pound of flesh. Uhh like our *end-users!* Others can enter the conversation, but only on the same level. This is one picture of the "spirit of Enzee", that the confidence in the technology is so deep and loyal, it brings these character elements to the fore.

One of which is, we don't have to "cheat" on a proof-of-concept. In fact, we can show Netezza in its "worst case" and still blow its competition into the weeds, so why would we need to fabricate any information? We don't - the technology really *can* deliver.

"The primary difference between a nobleman and a peasant, is that a peasant speaks his mind, and a nobleman minds his speech." - *written in glyphs on the Underground's stone walls, near the entrance to the Enzee community.*

We've noticed a certain "noble" behavior among Enzees. A sort of patient, loyal confidence, perhaps a *candid honesty* that is inexplicable and unattainable with other technologies. The Enzee "nobility" is more about attitude than position, and is revealed in how they speak about the technology and the problems it can solve. Sounds a little odd, we know, but if one attends a Netezza User's Conference, one gets a feel for this underpinning fabric.

More importantly, the Enzee community is loyal to a central, unstated mission, one that always takes the high road. Why is this important? Wouldn't it be easier to use underhanded techniques to close sales and capture revenue, or just to ensconce its community into a rarefied group of people? But that's just the polar opposite of the Enzee spirit. It's as though such a technique is a form of betrayal to the technology itself. The Enzees have too much respect for the technology to speak ill of it, or use underhanded techniques that would invite others to speak ill of it.

Everyone is *welcome*, all of us recognizing that the Data Wars have beaten us down, and we've come to the weapons depot to get reloaded, only to find a new kind of weapon. A multi-purpose weapon. More dangerous than *Blade's* sword, more elegant than a Light Saber, more effective than Silver Bullets and more versatile than Spiderman's webs. Enzees come to a place in-from-the-war-zone, still prepared to fight, but welcome by all who came before them.

Like warriors standing around a table, ale in hand with their new weapons at their sides, the recent arrivals only want to get outfitted. The veterans say, what size do you need, and how many?

No Really, What's it gonna cost me?

Build it or buy it. This is the ultimate choice each of us has in any given deployment. Not only for the initial power plant, but to actually roll out the application. O, that the *applications* would come pre-packaged, and all that. But they don't.

We'll have to build *something*, and it's important that this something isn't a laundry list of components that we have to build first, before ever even addressing the business functionality. We will *want* to build some components, it's just important not to re-invent the wheel in doing so.

What a *wrong* decision will cost us, is *time*.

For a data warehouse, it's important not to underestimate the cost of time to deploy, and the time to maintain. Labor costs something, and it's only measured in *time*. People often tell us how they cut corners on the cost of their hardware, only to throw a fleet of engineers at it to keep it going. The funny thing is, most enterprises have *zero* visibility to comparing these costs. Labor costs more, and if you have a gaggle of contractors on the job, believe that they make money from the labor, and have a vested interest in protecting the labor dollars, for themselves, and will never suggest the purchase of an appliance that reduces those dollars. What we can expect, and what we've seen firsthand, is a headlong run toward more complexity, because complexity means more labor dollars.

"You get what you pay for," written on the Underground walls as a reminder that if we buy *less power, we'll get less power. but if we're paying for contract labor dollars, we'll have people who want more of those labor dollars. We get more contractors, because we're paying for them. We get what we pay for.*

Some can readily see the problem for exactly what it is. Our staffs are usually applications people or operational users, not necessarily trained or experienced in high-end performance tuning. They do their best, call contractors or consultants to tune their environment, keep throwing money and time down the sinkhole when in reality, it's a bottomless pit.

Money and time later, they wish they had accepted the relatively lightweight "sting" of higher hardware costs, because *over time* it would have saved them so much more.

The question we must ask is – *How much is it gonna cost me – over time?*

In this context – it goes well beyond the pen-to-paper "total cost of ownership" in dollars alone. The inability to test is the inability to control quality and outcome. It's the cost of

- Reduced confidence in our user base
- Reduced job satisfaction among the IT staff
- Increased stress in all personnel - who make things happen by force-of-will
- Loss of key personnel by regular attrition, and time to train new ones in an artificially complex environment
- Inability of key business stakeholders to run the business with the firm's own information (keeping a pulse on their own business operation)
- Reduced confidence among external consumers (account holders, vendors, suppliers, etc)
- Reduced confidence in growing the business (unknown capacity)
- Inability to service business consumers/customers/accountholders due to firefighting or misfires in just a few business consumers' information
- General focus on business personnel in firefighting with their customers instead of traditional customer service activity
- Loss of confidence among business customers, loss of key (demanding) customers
- Acts of desperation (rather than business promotion) in giving away free business services to avoid losing a customer completely.
- Inability to objectively track new customer acquisition, customer service and customer loyalty, including the cost of defection of key customers to competitors
- **Inability to mitigate business risk**

- **Inability to capitalize on business opportunity**

The above represents the *short list.* Notice how – as the chosen technologies fail to support, or slowly degrade to the point they no longer support the business, the *people start to prop up the business with brute force and willpower.* Businesses based on electronic information – especially financial services businesses - cannot sustain this model. It will collapse of its own weight. It's just a matter of *time.*

I highlighted the last two, because these are core "unstated" purposes of *any* data warehouse from the outset. Chances are pretty high that our business users hold these two as a high priority, as things to actively pursue and apprehend. Without a strong, focused approach in harnessing the environment, they will remain as elusive as the wind itself.

Why are practically all our people running around on the floor, perhaps on roller skates, doing things with "legs, elbows and backs" that the machines *should* be doing for us?

The answer is simple: our personnel now work *for the machines,* not the machines for them. That's a scary thought, huh?

"Our data processing environment is a system of control," he said, producing a picture of a waiter - on roller skates. "to turn our staff into *this,*" - Lawrence Fishburn, *The Waitrix.*

DATA WAREHOUSE STUFF

FOR THOSE of us with some experience in bulk data processing (especially data warehousing), some of this chapter might read like a primer. That's okay, because once we read it, we might want to hand it off to one of our new-hires or someone that wants to know more (if we approve this message). So from the aspects of *general* data warehousing practices, we might find nothing new in this chapter.

But we're not dealing with general data warehousing. We're dealing with bulk data processing problems of extraordinary *scale*. Common data warehousing techniques and principles apply, but take on a larger, more daunting form. We'll address the common, leading to the scale, and in addressing both in context, we'll have hopefully done our job well, because data warehousing in general has gone *far* beyond innovation. It's as etched-in-stone via practice, theory and reality as any hard-wired motherboard of a desktop computer. Check out the TDWI website or any number of other sites on the subject. It's not light reading and very little (of the core) is *new*. However, what if someone noticed this, and wrapped an appliance around all this core knowledge? That's what we see with appliances in general, and Netezza in particular.

The *innovation*, we'll see, is in how Netezza has packaged all the hard-won data warehousing knowledge into a box. And a *very* powerful box at that. So if some of the aspects of this book appear remedial for the reader, it's not intended this way. Rather it's to provide *context* as to why Netezza does things in certain ways, and what underlying principle(s) might apply - to problems of *scale*. We point this out for a reason, because we see a number of books on the marketplace that some myopic reviewers and readers have disclaimed because they "talk down" to the reader. Trust us on this - the subject matter of data warehousing is a complex and daunting animal, and we have the highest respect for anyone who chooses to walk this path. It is for this reason we are imparting what we can to the reader, to help and assist.

For those readers who have applications in high-science or perhaps intensely algorithmic operations, this also applies, though it might not seem so at first. Any problem dealing with information of scale, requires the same core capabilities. So for those who do hard-core data warehousing, the terms in this section are second-nature. For those with no interest in data warehousing (the algorithm guys) - pay attention. You have a problem of scale, and need the same stuff the rest of us do. Netezza's got the stuff, so let's examine the capabilities in context.

That said, *context* is key, because if we don't understand the principles that Netezza has harnessed, how can we fully appreciate its purpose and destiny in our enterprise computing environment? In a case study, we'll see people misapply and abuse a Netezza machine, no differently than chaining a racehorse to a plow.

So I'm sitting in a conference room, surrounded by Really Smart People who are ready to Save The Company and run toward the Shining Future. The breeze is blowing and the surging crescendo of background music is playing, when suddenly the needle rips across the album as someone blurts from the back – they want to know "How does the mechanics of Netezza's *physical machinery* work?"

All of us slowly turn to the individual, wondering *why* he cares about this. The data is in the system, we can join and summarize whole terabytes in less than a minute, what does it matter how the "secret sauce" actually makes it *go?* More bizarre - the person asking the question used the actual vendor's terms for the various parts, literally wanting to know how the firmware and disk drives interact to conjure their sorcery.

Once upon a time, people desired a very consistent way to mow their lawns. One theme rang true – spinning metal blades. "We'll do it with spinning metal blades", said the engineers at Briggs and Stratton (or whomever originally invented it), so off they went to make a lawnmower. Honda, purveyors of automobiles, jumped into the fray with self-propelled versions, but *not innovating at all* on the theme of "spinning blades". The spinning blades seemed to be the best idea. John Deere purveyed large-scale tractors, and without innovating at all, and *lo* – there appeared spinning blades.

This is important to nail down one simple concept: spinning blades are how most people will mow their lawns. It's that simple.

So we visit our local lawn-and-power store and have a confab with a sales guy. He tells us all about the 22-inch mower he's just rolled to our feet. And then we ask him a question that he probably considers oblique and very strange:

"How does the Briggs-and-Stratton 2-cycle engine *actually* work?"

This person is a lawnmower sales guy, not a 2-cycle engineer. He gives us a card to call the engineers at Briggs-and-Stratton - but we don't rest until we know exactly, *precisely* how the 2-cycle engine operates.

We can see how ridiculous this is. What does it *matter* how the engine works, if the mower is still designed with *spinning blades* to efficiently cut the grass? What is our real, pressing need to know the internal workings, the firmware of the engine? On a hot day in the backyard, mowing and bagging the grass, will our minds feel anger, trepidation or anxiety with every step if we don't *absolutely* know how the 2-cycle engine operates? Or would most people just put their earbuds in place, punch the button on their *iPod* and walk mindlessly behind the mower, listening to their favorite tunes?

In fact, my only concern about how the 2-cycle engine works, is when it *doesn't*. Then I'll take it in for repair by professionals, because the lady-of-the-house doesn't pay me to know how a 2-cycle engine works, either. I get the day off.

Back to the story: We've met numerous people who get lost in the tactical weeds of the Netezza internal firmware and hardware engineering. What we need to know, to get the best out of the machine, is how it distributes and manages data so we can optimize our storage and application throughput. What we don't need to know, is how the 2-cycle engine works. I would have to ask, as someone mowing a lawn in the heat of the day, why do we *care*?

It's an *appliance*.

How do we extract innovation? By leveraging the stuff that's already inside. The NDN/Enzee community has a wide range of hardcore third-party product engineers that are actively integrating their products into Netezza, so that the whole is more valuable than the parts. This is the kind of innovation that accelerates the Enzee ecosystem, not perseverating on the internal hardware and machinery.

And to extend this – many of the people who ask these questions, consider themselves innovators. They want to take any technology they encounter and innovate on the internals, putting their mark on it, as it were. But – just as we cannot truly innovate on the theme of spinning metal blades, so we cannot innovate on the tried-and-true patterns of data warehousing. These patterns have always been with us, are not going away, and we need some serious, scalable power to deal with them.

And here's why: Once upon a time, data warehouse was born. Over the course of *decades*, the patterns of data warehouse operation and execution congealed into an identifiable, repeatable set of capabilities and patterns of operation. Just as most people mow their lawns with spinning blades, so do most people converge into a core set of data warehouse activities that are repeatable, immutable and highly desirable.

Netezza put pen to paper and built a machine to circumscribe the vast majority of these repeating patterns. The innovation *is in the box*. That's pretty much where our *warehouse* innovation stops. So it is incumbent upon us to innovate *while* using the machine's capabilities. And just as we would not lift the lawnmower (while spinning) to run it over the top of a hedge, so we will not use the Netezza machine for activities it wasn't designed for.

It's an *appliance*. It has a core focus. We should not innovate on its core engineering any more that we could innovate any other appliance's core engineering.

So, what *are* these magical, elusive capabilities that Netezza has put into the machine? I'm glad you asked, so I'll tell you, since we're in the Underground, and all of us are incognito. I'll jump on these a little deeper later – for now, step into our cavern:

- *Stability* – a stable, predictable and consistent foundation. Can't get anywhere without it.
- *Adaptability* – the need to move and shake quickly without destabilizing. Adaptation is key to embrace change. Not available on unstable platforms.
- *Scalability* – It's in the box, but because we get stability and adaptability too, scalability is more than just adding hardware. We can get really creative without high structural engineering.
- *Agile, rapid-iteration development* – the power in the machine allows us to freely experiment with whopping scales of data. It removes mysteries and distills our ideas to their core nuggets.
- *Everything inside* – all we need to process the information is inside the box (CPU, disk, memory). We don't need to leverage other horizontal technologies for the core bulk

processing mission.

- *Low cost* – for purchase, deployment, total cost of ownership, I've done surveys of other technologies, including Netezza's competitors. For many, we don't even have to put it to paper and measure it. The benefit is often obvious. We'll examine details later.
- *Small footprint* – the machine, it's cost and "bother" sometime scare managers because the machine just sits there and does its job without ever glowing, smoking, flashing, beeping or otherwise showing signs of apoplectic seizure on a regular basis. It has a small physical footprint, too. It's all good.
- *Low administration* – People ask "how many" administrators are necessary, but really it's just a part-time gig. Some of our own folks who do remote administration, cover multiple machines with a single person and multiple data centers with what anyone else would call a "skeleton" crew. The machine just runs itself. No kidding.
- *Visible operation* – All of the internal operations are visible on a panel, and there are no "black box" queries running on the black box. Setting up more visibility at the internal application or external access level is easy too.
- *Easy to understand* – The overall paradigm of Netezza is easy to understand and grasp for practically anyone who understands the data, regardless of whether they understand the technology. This is a core advantage of the appliance approach, that the user is relatively isolated from needing to know anything deeper, like how a 2-cycle engine works.
- *Sheer freakin' power, man!* – Okay, not our most professional assertion. But in the end, we will need power to get things done. Time-to-market is not a trifling matter. This isn't just extra power or an incremental boost. It is *hundreds* of times more power than we get in a traditional RDBMS, and can be *orders of magnitude* more powerful than a production-ready RDBMS environment. Developers close off functionality. Testers validate it. Production implementers certify it. The longest duration is now determined by our own administrative *lifecycle* overhead, not the actual delivery constraints.

And these are a *few* of my favorite things…

Extreme Physics

In science fiction and fantasy, we sometimes see forays into anomalous physics. One of the more popular forms is based on Black Holes. These were first predicted by math and later discovered in the cosmos. A black hole is basically a star that has collapsed onto itself, creating a gravity so dense that not even light can escape. It continually pulls more matter into itself, increasing its mass and density, and its gravitational strength.

An overwhelmed/overpowered RDBMS system can start taking on all the characteristics of a black hole. It becomes dense with function points and engineering, tightly woven algorithms and fine-tuned components. It then starts to pull more people into maintaining it, further increasing its functional density as they apply their brain power. It's a functional black hole, but when we speak of "lights out", we cannot apply it to our existing box because it requires lots of attention.

After a while, fewer people understand anything about its original functionality (what it was intended to do) and they are too afraid to touch anything inside it, for fear of breaking what it was *intended* to do in favor of what they *need* to do now. Paralysis sets in, people leave the company in frustration, some just find another job, and are replaced by others, and more knowledge leaves with them. It *functionally* becomes a black box, but it's really a black *hole*. And now, even the functionality that's inside it, the components we once used to shine light in the darkness, are now themselves black boxes. Likewise, no new functionality can be applied.

So we could say, it's so dense, no new *functionality* can escape!

We can no longer learn anything from it, because it's *schooling* us.

Quite unfortunately, in extreme physics if we cross the black hole's path, it's curtains *and* lights-out, quite literally. For a densely packed RDBMS system, we simply need to admit the fact that it's run its course and should be replaced with stronger technology. Is this *different* technology altogether? Dense means brittle. It has lost its stability, its adaptability, clearly is no longer scalable - and is no longer meeting our demands. We need to assess how we're *actually* using it. If it's not meeting our needs now, what would lead us to believe that a *bigger* version of the same thing is any better?

Recall that a black hole continues to gather density to itself, for no better reason than to get bigger. A bigger black hole is *still* a black hole.

Harnessing complexity

Many of you have seen the small *Towers of Hanoi* puzzle (depicted below) that has three posts and five or so disks of incrementally different sizes. The game is simple – the player stacks disks with the largest on bottom and smallest on top. We then move the disks one-at-a-time from one post to another, and at no time can a larger disk be placed on top of a smaller disk.

The objective is to get all disks from one post and onto another in the fewest possible moves. The third post provides a place for intermediate storage, you know, like a *temp* table.

Of course, we just gave you the rules for the game as *artificial* constraints. What if we could move them any way we wanted to and set aside the one-disk-at-a-time rule? Wouldn't we just pick up the whole stack and drop it on another post?

But wait - what if the disks were actually several hundred pounds each? We would have no choice but to move them one at a time. What if we had a crane or other power-lifting tool that could pick up all the disks at once, move them to another post and safely drop them? We get the same outcome, but without all the fuss. We just need a lot of power to make it happen.

Why is this applicable? This little puzzle looks a lot like many *underpowered* data processing environments. Or rather, it's the solution profile for many *overwhelmed* systems, moving things a piece at a time, carefully managing what-lands-where so we don't run-out-of-this-or that, attempting to harness the complexity of the problem based on entirely *artificial* constraints – because we are *powerless* to do otherwise. The data *and* processes have literally overpowered the systems to nearly cripple them.

Someone observing this end-state would see some highly repeatable patterns and symptoms. The running theme of it all, however, *looks a lot like this little game*. The following list is by no means exhaustive, and we'll examine these more in context later:

- *Protracted processing cycles* – when the systems start to run out of gas, an initial symptom is a missed bulk processing cycle window. If it repeats itself too many times without correction or a consistent solution, trouble's a-brewin'.
- *Poor or missing data management* – in order for information to acquire a state of reliability and consistency, we have to manage it. No differently than land, money in a bank account, or resource on a project. Data management is as much about automation as it is measuring the effectiveness of the automation, and everything else influencing the data's integrity.
- *Lots of dirty data* – usually the result of a lack of respect for how much real damage "just a little dirt" can cause, or how much the dirt in our data structures acts like sand in the gears of the machine. It steals energy, and *lots* of it.
- *Minimal to zero governance* – overall, governance is about boundaries, especially the boundaries we set for the people who interact with the information. Developers, operators, troubleshooters, administrators, end-users – the list is huge. If we fail to apply some minimal controls, we're already out of control. It's a lot easier to relax existing controls to accommodate exceptions than it is to apply controls after-the-fact.
- *Lots of spinning plates* – as the power runs down, our engineers are tempted to fix things with *rigging*. The more rigging, the more activities. The more activities, the less control. Plates will start to fall and shatter. It's just a matter of time.
- *Standardizing on the exceptions* – sometimes we start out in a happy state. Perhaps when Dick and Jane moved into their two-bedroom flat in Dover, Kent, they had all the room in the world. Five kids later, it's not enough room and they're not kidding anyone. For us, as the demand gets larger, the system holding it cannot remain the same. Likewise, we'll see our engineers start to use it in ways it was never intended (like having our children use sofas and rollaway beds). Soon the temporary structures become permanent ones. We have effectively standardized and institutionalized the *exceptions*, and now call them the *rule*. We've forgotten the "happy" state of the original environment, perhaps even lost focus on what it was ever intended to do.
- *Misapplication of the technology*- Some engineers "do what works" and cobble together extra parts or accessories in an effort to take pressure off the core. Still others will attempt to restructure or even re-characterize the solution using the same technology as before, when the technology itself is the culprit. Before engaging in a re-platform or even a re-structure, we must make sure we know what our end-state requirements are. Does our technology fit *what we're doing?* Or are we trying to fit *what we're doing* into the technology?
- *Eccentric innovation* – Using the systems and software in ways they were *never* intended. Often resulting in systems that few (to no) people can understand, maintain or enhance. More importantly, the presence of complexity invites *more* "innovation", or rather, more

eccentricity.

- *Forest for the trees* – the usual approach of tactical engineering is to solve spot-problems or gain back incremental wins. We often hear an engineer lament about needing orders-of-magnitude more processing power, not the incremental nibbles his staff currently offered up to him as "success".
- *Artificial complexity* – The last thing we want to do is institutionalize or standardize on complexity that only exists as an artifact. I'll repeat this effect several times in the book, because it's worth examining. It's a fairly repeatable pattern, in that our internal engineers might get exasperated dealing with all the complexity and come to their leadership with a recommendation for a high-powered system to deal with the *complexity*, rather than a high-powered system to deal with the *underpowered* environment. Many times, the apparent complexity is only artificial, a symptom of an overwhelmed system.

For all the above cases, the Netezza appliance has the ability to handily harness or eliminate the issues altogether. The right level of power and functionality sets aside all these concerns. We can now focus on the best approach for the business, and Netezza will close the distance.

Bulk Processing Practical Issues - aka Bulk-101

In our world, bulk-data processing and data warehousing are practically the same solution domain. While we might not be building a "data warehouse", every bulk-processing problem will always exhibit patterns found in very mature domain of data warehousing. So we don't have to construct an official data warehouse to benefit from its best practices.

Not very long ago my youngest son banged his head against the side of our pool. While there was no permanent damage, it did split open the skin and start bleeding. My son, ever the trooper, didn't pay it any mind until his mother offered a sincere (and animated) objection to the blood trickling down his neck. I put him in the car and spirited him to the emergency room. Here I was given two options: The doctor could stitch the cut back together, or he could apply surgical glue. (That's basically *super-glue*). I jumped on the *glue* option, and the doctor had me hold down my son while he applied the stuff.

Considering that the whole scenario was pretty scary for a two-year-old, my son did pretty well. He only screamed loud enough for the people in the *parking lot* to hear him. I didn't really care about the people at Starbucks on the other side. They have their own problems. My son kicked and bucked and generally let it be known that he'd rather keep the scar than have it glued shut. The doctor took one swipe with the glue, pinched the skin together for thirty seconds, and he was done. *Perhaps the longest thirty seconds of my life.* I could not imagine the doctor holding a needle and suture during this exercise.

The point being – super-glue has a lot of uses, but closing a suture might not occur to the average person. I'm glad it occurred to the doctor, but that's what he's paid for. In the end, I did not need for the doctor to apply all known surgical techniques or best practices in *surgery*. I needed for him to take a subset of his knowledge and apply it. If not for my sanity, for the sake of the poor people in the lobby awaiting *their turn*. They could hear the screams, too.

So to bulk processing. Examine and consider the various resources on data warehousing and leverage the practices, ideas and solutions discussed within this domain. It probably doesn't all apply even if we're building a HUMONGOUS data warehouse. But some of it *definitely* applies in bulk processing.

And one thing is crystal-clear. We won't find a bulk processing solution by trolling the resources centered on *transactional* processing. People who are only familiar with transactional processing generally cannot help us form an effective bulk-processing model. It is as foreign to them as the London Tube Trains are to a California beach surfer. *Trust me on this.*

We're occasionally asked (okay, we're asked a lot) about the things that make a data warehouse approach viable. We could look across the fruited plain at practically every kind of implementation in existence, and we would have a number of takeaways. These are practically impossible to prioritize, so I will list some of the "more" important ones at the top, with the remainder in an appendix for your reading pleasure.

The one I see violated or deviated from the most often is **Rule #10**. I speak on Rule #10 and find myself coaching people on Rule #10 just about everywhere I go. It's a very pervasive pitfall, in bulk data processing in general, and Data Warehousing in particular. Some of you have asked us to write whole dissertations on Rule #10, but I wonder if it will help? Rule #10 fights the tide of vendor marketing and hype. How can it be wrong, if it feels so right?

Right?

So let's just cut to the chase and get to Rule #10. It's the only one we really care about now, hmm? Well, if we *really* care about it, I guess we can just go there.

So here they are, in no particular order – but pay attention to Rule #10. You may well ask why it's #10 if its so all-fired important? That's an excellent question, so read on.

It's an Environment, not a Project

While this doesn't really count as a rule on its own, it is worth level-setting our expectations, and what you're about to bite off, or perhaps what's about to take a bite outta *you*.

So here we go.

Once we embark on the Data Warehouse path, it's like a journey with no true destination. While that sounds strange, what we're doing, is setting up an environment. As an example, when DisneyWorld first opened many, many moons ago, it had a very different look than it does now. The Magic Kingdom, while timeless, has been augmented by various other parks. MGM/Disney is the place for movie-nuts like me, where the Animal Kingdom, while not-a-zoo, is a wonderful place for kids that's just plain different from the Magic Kingdom. EPCOT (Experimental Prototype City Of Tomorrow) is the place for teenagers and adults, and has the most amazing thrill rides.

But when Disney Tokyo first opened, the Japanese people thought it would take six months to a year to "work out all the kinks". What they could not have known, is that the people who would be running the park, had been shuttled over to California and Florida and trained on the existing environments for *hundreds* of hours. The end result, when Disney Tokyo opened, it had flawless execution on *day one*.

This is the primary difference between delivering a project, and standing up a living environment.

The Netezza Underground

The data warehouse needs protocols, governance, operators, administrators, troubleshooters. We might have lots of folks in these various roles, or some folks wearing multiple hats. The point is - *take the problem seriously.*

Treating it as a *project* is a bad idea.

I was called into an environment as a "cleaner", for a series of "after-action" interviews. The CIO was chagrined that his recent data warehouse *project* was not only on the ropes, it was *in the tank*. Everyone knew, when I arrived, that one or more heads would roll, so every interview was a sober, in fact somber experience.

The outcome was not so grisly. My report to the CIO was that the project had not failed, it was just in an operational pause. You see, the project had simply reached a delivery point. If we see the data warehouse is a living environment, how can it *ever* be over? No, we just get to stopping points, the end of an *iteration*, and then we continue.

The only way we fail, is if we *quit*.

Imagine that our current, particular step in our environment is just step one. Or if we are reading this book trying to recover from what we think is egg on our face, the yolk's not really on us. It's just a pause in the activity. A way to catch our breath before the next phase of activity begins. More importantly, we need a way to set the expectations of those around us that the path to delivery is steady and incremental. Not once-for-all. If one group's requirements did not make it into this functional release, perhaps the next, perhaps spread out over a number of "nexts". Either way, we must pace ourselves. We are on a long-distance running tour. Fortunately, we can stop along the way, but we can't stop completely. A data warehouse is never done. Its problems never die. And hope springs eternal.

Remember this, if we remember nothing else about data warehouse delivery. Write it on the inside of our eyelids if we have to, but forget it at our peril.

*It is better to deliver the right answer **late**, than the wrong answer, or the broken answer, or the slow answer, **on schedule**.*

Many years ago, I worked with real-time systems. These were the *real*, real-time systems, not business-transactional. For those who understand real-time, it's like this: a robot balancing a broom on the palm of its hand. Now *that's* real-time.

In this realm, a universal maxim applies: the right answer late, is wrong. For military applications, if we can detect a Surface-to-Air-Missile (SAM) launch and notify the pilot in less than *five* seconds, it does the pilot no good if the SAM can reach his aircraft in *two* seconds. Likewise, if we have an innovation that fails to meet the time-to-market, our answer might be the next best thing to sliced bread, but if it's late, it's a copycat. The right answer. But it was late.

A data warehouse is not a real-time delivery problem. It is a more a function of user *confidence* than timing. Our time-to-market must be *completely* governed by the *quality* we deliver, not whether the solution is delivered *on time*. For example, one set of data warehouse users had to wait an entire month past the original project deadline to get access to their warehouse. If it had been delivered on time, it would have had "more crash than flash" and the warehouse implementers would never have recovered from it. User confidence isn't just an important aspect. It's the *only* aspect we care about.

The wrong answer on time, is still wrong. The wrong answer late, is still wrong.

They will remember.

Just like Disney Tokyo on Day One, the data warehouse we roll out first, will be the one they remember. No matter what we do to fix any issues with the first rollout, if it is perceived as falling short, the *perception is reality*. It is far better to never meet this perception, or embrace this reality, than it is to meet an artificial deadline. when we *know* that our work isn't ready.

This sounds a bit like expectation-management, and perhaps it partly is. Someone has to be the one to tell the users to wait, and someone has to take the heat when things aren't ready. But if we release things when they aren't ready, it can be disastrous.

Better to not release *at all* - trust me on this.

Case Study Short: One customer had a proprietary application with built-in invoicing, and they wanted the invoicing system linked to Oracle Financials. Okey-fine, we could export those invoices out of the system and into Oracle, but it would take some significant testing. This was the company's *money flow* after all.

The overall leader for all the projects said he wanted a deliverable from every team, every four weeks. Just schedule your workload on those boundaries, he adjured, and package up what you've done for the testers.

One month, our team did not meet the deadline. We had taken several of the major interfaces apart for functional rework, and were still in the process of testing them. Several days after we "missed" the deadline, the leader took our team into his office. The conversation shared here was quite a bit more animated, and I have changed the content to make the point.

"You know we had a release this past weekend."

"That's correct. First of the month, every month."

"But you didn't release anything."

"Nope"

(Icy stare) "You know the rule. Everyone releases, no matter what."

"No matter what?"

"No matter what."

"Okay, no problem, we can package up our stuff and deliver it today. We can have it on the testers' desks first thing in the morning."

"That's great, but why couldn't you do it on Friday, like everyone else?"

"It wasn't ready. It would have completely mangled the accounting system's entries and probably caused irreversible damage."

"Glad you got it fixed."

"It's not fixed yet, we're still testing it."

"But you said you could release it today."

"We sure can, we'll get right on it."

"But it's broken? Why would you – ohhhh, I get it. That's pretty funny, you're not taking me seriously, are you?"

"We gave you reasons last week why we would not release. Those reasons have not changed. We're taking this problem *very* seriously, and giving it the respect it deserves."

"And I'm not?"

"Not if you expect an arbitrary release on an artificial deadline, as you put it – *no matter what.* So if it doesn't matter to you that this thing will mangle the accounting system, we'll release it today."

(Icy stare) "Release it when it's ready."

"We fully intend to."

Crash not flash: One of our colleagues is fond of saying, "we can't release when it has more crash than flash." And this is exactly right. It doesn't have to be *perfect,* but over-the-top works just fine, and something that has the "wow" effect, works even better. But if it's full of noticeable and pernicious breakage, who are we kidding? It's *not* ready.

We are building an *environment*, where our data will live, breathe and all that stuff. Just as our own home is an environment where we might do all kinds of things from raising a family to inviting over the bridge club, people see our home as a living environment. The home itself never "fails", it just goes through cycles, new furniture, new carpet, etc. We swap out the old and swap in the new. We upgrade wherever we need to, just to improve the environment or keep it moving.

But get real. We don't invite guests over to a house-party without preparing for the party, and making the house ready for a party. Getting the house ready a week after the party does not serve the day of the party. And if we have broken windows, a missing door, who are we kidding? The house *isn't* ready.

If under construction, do we want to build an efficiency apartment that will not grow with us, or a functional multi-bedroom home that will serve our needs for the long term at a price we can afford, or a deluxe dream home on a high hill, that our boss will never pay for?

The efficiency apartment is right out, the dream home is just that, a dream for now, but the functional family-builder-kinda-home, that's doable and affordable. Funny thing is, Netezza lets us have *all three.* We can smoke-test our functionality on its smaller machines, we can deploy for performance on larger machines, and we can grow the machines at an acceptable and affordable rate. What's to complain about?

As for time-to-deploy a Netezza-centric solution, especially for a new data warehouse, very little is in our path to impede success. I can testify, as can many users, to practically loping into a full-scale rollout in a matter of months. How is this possible? The normally-protracted data testing cycle shrinks as we realize how fast we can turnaround our functional and integration tests, and get the users involved very early with working prototypes. If quality is key, then it's within our reach in short order and high confidence. The productivity lift for the initial rollout and the ongoing maintenance gives us lots more time to think about the problem-at-hand *and* a well-rounded solution, not just something for the fire-breathing users who want it delivered yesterday, or sooner.

"Can" versus "Should"

Okay, get ready for our rather preachy dissertation on the differences between liberty, license and responsibility. First, let it be known that I have no power of life or death, so whether you follow these musings or not, is of no consequence to me. It may, however, lead to consequences for you, good bad or indifferent. If we do things wrong, at the worst we'll probably waste some time. At best we'll learn a few things while we're wasting the time, so at least some of it was well-spent!

Getting off to a good start means some degree of balance between what we *can* do and what we *should* do. What makes a really solid data warehouse? Focusing on he the things we should. What makes a marginal data warehouse? Focusing on the things that don't matter, like those things we *can* do - today - that seem important but aren't.

In this respect, performance matters not.

What?

Looks, folks, we have a really powerful data processing machine. The worst thing we can possibly do now is to mess things up by myopically focusing on the one thing that should be the least of our concerns. Optimize here, tune there, do take some responsible steps in making things efficient. In short, the mind-bending power of the machine, out of the box, means we don't have to go through excruciatingly painful engineering and tuning exercises. We have power to adapt and refactor in shorter time frames, so our risk of error or misstep is lower.

Case Study Short: We had the opportunity to make a very elegant, easily-maintained environment. After the initial proof-of-concepts, we went through some profiling and tuning, settled on several core structures, and the project took off. We had already reduced their entire processing cycle from eighteen hours to forty minutes, *just by installing the machine.* After the first optimization exercise, we reduced this down to *twenty five minutes* without any significant effort.

We were about halfway through the effort when two of their folks called a meeting to discuss their "optimizations" to our original structures, that is, the ones they had *agreed* to use and, more importantly, that the client sponsor had *signed off* on.

They had come up with another set of processes and structures. It was more complex than the original, had some hardcore math scripts that ran in the background, included a set of cross-reference tables to assist in boosting performance. It was *hot!* Overall, it could reduce the entire processing time down to eighteen minutes, saving another *seven minutes* off the processing cycle! (And aren't *you excited* about this? It's a *twenty-percent* gain, at least!) Sometimes, just sometimes, those stones have a little more blood in them, don't they?

We can see the false economy here. It jumps off the page at the average analyst or architect – but the average tactical, *performance junkie* is staring at the page right now thinking "What's your point?"

The point is, if we have the choice to roll out an easily maintained model versus a more complex one, and the difference in performance is marginal, what's the real value in the boost?

Once we start talking about processing times that are measured in *minutes* rather than hours, and savings that reduce by *minutes* not hours, we can see that any additional talk of optimization is just noise on our eardrums.

So to clarify our original shock-value statement: Once we have things reasonably, tuned, performance matters not. What matters, is resilience, extensibility, adaptability and all the other capabilities we really, *really* want, but in the past were sacrificed on the altar of an underpowered system. We knew what we should do, but we *could* not. The power wasn't there.

In Netezza, another temptation arises. That what we *can* do is squeeze more blood from the stone. What we *should* do is leave the stone where it is. It's easy to maintain, and the overall cost-of ownership is low. Seven minutes faster is a *not* an even trade-off.

So don't focus on the things we get for free. Focus on *honoring* the things we get for free by working hard for the things we really would like to have, but have never been able to implement – *because the power wasn't there.*

I'll end it here "With great power comes great responsibility." And you know where that's from. Spiderman don't need no stinkin' workout program. Optimizing the Spidey is unnecessary.

So again, here are the rules in no particular order. I will offer the brief versions of #1 thru #9 here, racing to Rule #10, and expand on #1 thru #9 in a final chapter.

To once again, level-set the discussion. Think in terms of terabytes, not transactional systems or gigabyte-level warehouses. The following discussion is for *very-large-scale* data systems. The rules are different here, while oddly the same!

Rule #1 - Everything is requirements-driven.

Every environment finds itself replete with requirements, many of them deeply held but unspoken expectations. The business users don't really understand that when they left their former company, itself sporting a data warehouse that was designed and driven by a former industry guru, they were taking a step down in functionality when they joined our happy clan. Yes Virginia, there is real data warehouse functionality, somewhere over the rainbow. If you liked it so much, why did you leave?

Now we have a different requirement - punting terabytes not gigabytes, and housekeeping, maintenance and administration in a *mansion*, not a two-bedroom apartment. Or feeding hordes of people in a convention center, not a local corner deli. It is a problem of *scale*, where the same duties have completely different needs.

Many years ago, I was asked to help in a kitchen supporting a large youth gathering of over one-hundred teenagers. They would arrive for breakfast at 6am, and the chief cook had everything under control. She showed me four of the largest skillets I had ever seen, and produced five gallon-sized containers of liquid eggs. She took one of the containers and emptied half of it into one skillet and half in the other, commanding me to *scramble them up*. My only job that morning, was to keep those four skillets full and cooking until the containers were empty. The chief cook did the same with another of her assistants, but with bags of hash browns, and on down the line. By the time the teenagers arrived, we had a multi-course buffet laid out for them. When it was over, barely a morsel of food remained. Not only had the cook prepared enough, it was almost exactly enough. I was amazed and awed as to the chief cook's predictive ability's, but more importantly, the attention to *scale*.

Sort of like when we are told that we need to take a business trip to a foreign city. We're told we will have a car and a corporate apartment. We have an expectation for what "car" and "corporate apartment" actually mean. When we arrive, we find that we are actually sharing a car with dozens of other people, only one of which holds the keys and he's not parting with them for love or money. The corporate apartment is actually a three-bedroom villa with a common area, and we share a bedroom with eight other people. Not too bad once we get past sharing the bathroom and shower with strangers.

This is somehow – not what we *expected*. Someone provided the functionality, just not with any *scale*.

A whole mental list of unspoken expectations await us – from the operators, administrators, troubleshooters and maintenance developers. In terms of science, and the scientific method, we would call these folks *peer review*. They know better than anyone else the true quality of our work products. Does it *produce* what it's supposed to produce? Fine – but *how* does it produce those things? The process is directly tied to the quality of the outcome.

We must regard *all* requirements, not just the requirements reduced to a page by the business users. They think they are implicitly ordering all the stuff we are *supposed to do for free*.

And now, our primary requirement is the mastery of *scale*. The rest of the functionality won't matter if scale isn't under control. The rules are different now.

Rule #2 - Simplify and clarify

Rather than inject artificial complexity or more engineering. Bulk processing is simple. It it might not seem "cool" or "sexy" to build an input-process-output model. If we build it right, we don't get calls in the middle of the night. Underpowered or secondhand platforms make it harder. Build it right, do it right, get it done and go home happy – at 5pm – without expecting a midnight call.

We're talking about hundreds of millions, perhaps many billions of data rows. This is not a realm where high-complexity will serve our architecture. Examine any large-scale environment. While we may discern complexity, we should not directly interact with it or manage it. An appliance harnesses all the complexity out of sight and mind, so we can focus on the business problem. Don't embrace complexity, and throw away something that Netezza provides de-facto, a means to simplify and clarify, if for no better reason than we now have the power and muscle to do so.

With that, an enemy in moving from our old environment to our new Netezza home, is the assumption that the existing complexity is real, and not an artifact of performance engineering. Think carefully about the problem-at-hand, and don't let anyone fool you into thinking that the complexity is real. In any underpowered, over-engineered system, the complexity is artificial.

Case Study Short: The CIO had commissioned me to evaluate the operations center for opportunities to reduce staff. The center had too many people working in it, and he wanted to know why, After several days of operational review, including several evenings and early morning vigils in the operations center, we had a report, but he didn't want to hear it.

Each evening at midnight, the operations center turned into a beehive as the batch applications came online. Of some forty tape decks, the tape operators had already stacked dozens of empty tape cartridges on top of each one. When the batch systems took off, so did the tape drives. The tape operators popped the cartridges in and out of the drives like madmen, a frenzied activity that continued for hours.

Upon investigation, we learned that the batch applications used the tape drives for *intermediate storage* because the regular disk storage had run out of space. That's right - the tape drives were being used as application *workspace*. When we measured how much they used, we learned that they would have to nearly *triple* the existing disk drive space just to meet *fifty* percent capacity.

Look at all the artificial complexity. The tape drives burning into the ground. The extra people, the complexity of the applications to leverage the tape drives, and the list goes on. The environment had run out of power, so the people had found workarounds, the admins had applied engineering, all to artificially increase the environment's complexity.

Because it was running out of power. We will see this as a theme. When a system runs out of power, complexity increases as the engineers come to the rescue.

Case Study Short: The client had a variety of systems that coordinated data on and off their web site to support customer orders. When a customer completes an order, they said, it can sometimes take hours for the order to show up in the customer service zone. We want to reduce the latency so that if someone places an order and wants to call up and discuss it, we can pull it up with no issues.

"The Kid" in charge of putting together their initial architecture, had rendered a completely convoluted spaghetti flow drawing, with flow lines running all over the place. He then presented it to the principals with the offhand comment that he would need *$500k* in middleware to make it all work correctly. I redrafted the architecture with some very simple flow lines, like the boss had *expected* anyhow, and the meeting to discuss the two approaches was very interesting.

"Look, Boss, David is very experienced in data warehousing," said The Kid, "but I know my stuff, too. And we need all this technology. All of it."

The boss looked over at me, and something exchanged between us that I cannot completely explain. I simply said, "You don't need those products."

The boss looked directly at the kid and repeated, "I don't need those products."

The Kid was undaunted, and continued to make his case, all the while the boss was staring at me.

"These things are unnecessary," I simply said.

The boss looked up at The Kid and said, "These things are unnecessary."

Later in the day, one of my colleagues who had been present said, "That was like a Vulcan mind-meld, or that scene from Star Wars where Obi-Wan tells the soldiers to let them go about their business."

Yes, it was a little weird, but our minds were on the same page. The complexity was artificial. Say it any way you want.

"These aren't the 'droids you're looking for." Alec Guinness, *Star Wars.*

Rule #3 - Use correctly powered and scalable systems

Underpowered systems require our staff to use creative engineering tricks, generally to optimize hardware and schema definitions. Once-upon-a-time-powered systems that over time become over-powered (or over-taken) by volume and workload, often require rigorous review from top to bottom. Just to squeeze a little more blood from the stone.

We need to stop applying tactical extensions for performance-related fixes. This only invites creeping artificial complexity into the solution, where ultimately the artificial complexity becomes indistinguishable from the core.

And when I say that "underpowered systems require our staffs to..." - I'm not just talking about our IT staffs. Our business users will create an entire culture of workarounds so they can get their own work done. What is the real cost of doing business? And have we realistically measured this cost? Are we okay with our business users wasting time (and money in the form of labor hours) in manual workarounds rather than doing what we hired them to do - run our *business*?

Rule #4 - Governance

Our entire environment needs some rules that set expectations of the participants. Do whatever it takes to build the governance model into the architecture. This doesn't mean draconian steps, it simply sets the tone that rules exist, with an expectation of loyalty to them. Otherwise the developers will sense the freedom to mutate the architecture.

With no rules in place, are they really *violating* anything?

When developers are in the heat of battle, we need something in place that will encourage if not require them to comply, even if it is not convenient for them to do so. In many cases, the governance constraints are in place specifically to control runaway rogue activity, so that things *don't* end up in production within the same hour they were created, regardless of the level of testing applied.

It's ironic that the industry has run pell-mell toward rapid-application delivery, without realizing that something needs to be in place to slow the process down, at least a little bit, so we don't shoot ourselves in the foot to install something that really needs more testing.

But there's just *so much data!* our application developers will lament. Testing against this mountain of data is just so - so *boring.*

Netezza gives us the power to test it *all,* and provide higher quality in a shorter time frame anyhow. Why not leverage it for success, rather than forego it and accept the standard risks that the *standard* environments incur?

Rule #5 - Data management

If data management practices are missing, we'll see symptoms. We may not immediately recognize the symptoms. They may appear in various forms and mutations, but if we peel back the deceptive veneer, we'll recognize them.

- Manual workarounds for core data processing functions.
- Junk data, contamination, null, duplication, etc in the core data content
- Poorly formed or poorly functioning data model
- Systems and siloed applications that do not easily share information
- Data transport based on replication alone
- No challenge of data from external sources
- No reconciliation of regular external sources
- Information too difficult for average user to navigate

Rule #6 - Strong architectural approach

A classic maxim is simply that the surest sign of a good architecture is: good things automatically fall out of it. The surest sign of a marginal architecture is: the environment is constrained from providing much more than it already does (a black hole).

Sounds almost like we need a crystal ball, or a power-team of heavy-hitters down the hall that are the "go-to" people for architectural excellence. Perhaps we rent-an-architect to get us moving, but without some of his/her brains spilling into buckets for posterity, what is the real lifetime value of what we're doing? Those who come after us will not have taken ownership of the principles, will not appreciate the original sacrifices, etc. Woe is us.

Take a deep breath.

Architecture is *not* rocket science. Don't treat it like some kind of elusive pie-in-the sky goal. Go for *perfection*, but set your heart on *excellence*. Excellence is part of a malleable, adaptive approach, but perfection is brittle and largely unattainable. Adaptation is not only easier to achieve, it's usually not far away already. Perfection might be a noble goal, but excellence is a *journey*. The *road* to our goal is far more important than the goal itself.

No philosophy, that's just the way it is.

In a database environment, the architecture is largely expressed in the configuration of systems, storage and their interfaces. The connections between our systems, their bandwidth, the system components and the software environments on top of them. Netezza extends this further with its internal architecture, such that we have no additional interfaces apart from the lightweight objects we'll build inside, like tables, columns etc. These are all *structural* quantities.

So it's safe to say that our interfaces are all logical structures, such as database tables, views and the like. If we stabilize these as the outside world touches them, we have stabilized the architecture for the outside world. If these structures remain in flux, or can potentially change or break, we have an unstable architecture for the outside world. What does this mean? By publishing an interface, we declare victory to the end users - victory that we've harnessed their information-experience and that it shall remain stable forevermore.

But is this really true? How many warehouses directly expose their core tables to the users and their BI applications, only to discover later than a change, however minor, is necessary? Should we make the change and risk destabilization? If the tables aren't directly exposed, the architects have a buffer between the core and the user's interface. It is this interface - the published specification to the user, that we must protect for their sakes (and frankly, for our own). The best way to protect their experience and protect our freedom to support it, is to decouple them. Meaning: we don't give the users direct access to the core tables.

So, don't go all catatonic trying to get a perfect architecture. We should get our core requirements in order and quickly set up a framework architecture. Embrace adaptability rather than an etched-in-stone-we-need-to-know-everything-now approach. We'll want this framework / reference architecture as the springboard for our first iteration delivery, and then mature it to its functional and capability edges as we move along.

Netezza gives us the power to close this initial exercise very quickly because it has so many architectural principles inside the box already. We don't have to engineer our schemas or think up brilliant, far-reaching information plans. What we build now is functional now with minimal risk for later. We really can start small and move up. If we get into a bind, we can refactor (even the entire) data model in very short order. We have the power to move quickly, with lower risk of failure.

In other words, the adaptability is given to us in the form of raw power – we can leverage it to recover from a design mistake. Adaptability means more than just the ability to enhance an existing model, it means the ability to conform to new requirements without breaking anything, even if it means wholesale change of the data model. If we use strong architectural principles (decoupling, adaptive interfacing, etc) we have the power *and* the freedom to embrace change quickly.

Rule #7 - *Build the environment with the expectation of change.*

Separate the core architecture from the user-facing features. Put the architecture and the features on separate lifecycles. We should use our architecture as a set of building-block capabilities to support features. We add more building blocks if the features demand it.

This is the most resilient means to deal with user-facing change without destabilizing the core architecture. We should only modify the core architecture occasionally, not in rapid-fire form each time the user requests something.

Think of it like this: We buy a house and move right in. We can put our furniture (features) anywhere in the house we want. We can even have electricians and plumbers extend their respective systems. But we can't change load-bearing walls or foundational priorities. These are part of the architecture, the capabilities of the home, not its user-facing features and customizations.

We should build our applications and their attendant features as *consumers* of the core capabilities, while building the kinds of capabilities that all applications need.

Rule #8 – *Testability*

The sure sign of a flawed approach is the *inability* to test it. And this means rigorously test it. With a large-scale model, this is even more daunting, but even more critical. With more data, the more the potential for errors. It's just a matter of percent-error. Just keep in mind that a given percent-error in a small data warehouse might be acceptable, but on a larger scale, it's like poison.

We have to test functionality and performance separately and together. Yes, we really do need to test performance, because we really can design ourselves into a processing pitfall, even in

Netezza. But a performance test will allow us to correct it - and correct it *quickly*.

We have these overarching flow-facing *functional* requirements:

(1) every business rule in the flow is exercised and behaves as expected
(2) the flow doesn't break when introduced to production data
(3) it performs within the expected durations
(4) its duration does not grow as the data volume grows

Testing the above requires a fairly robust environment. We need functional (model) test data sets and baseline comparison protocols, and a production-quality test environment to check performance and data breakage.

The more complex we make the architecture, the harder it is to build-out a reliable test environment. We must simplify and clarify the delivery path for our work products

The testability of an environment has everything to do with its delivery highway. By this I mean the path from the developer's head, to the keyboard, and onward to production. This delivery highway has to be solid and robust, and any potholes in it are only there because we allow them to be, not because they belong. We'll get rid of those, too (or fill them in, whatever it takes). More on the highway later.

Rule #9 – Go Parallel

It's all in the hardware. As noted prior, bulk data processing is about *physics*. Any environment that accurately and efficiently leverages the physics is not very far off the mark.

"Go Parallel" does not mean "go asynchronous". That's transactional thinking, and will be summarily resolved in Rule #10. The spirit of "parallel" means leveraging our environment to *flow* data in *bulk*, not in units. Asynchronous equals units. Parallel equals bulk.

In *processing*, the physics is found in hardware bandwidth, and *lots* of it. Of course, just having the bandwidth languishing about does not constitute *parallel* processing. we need disk drives, CPUs and infrastructure to optimize their utilization. We can have a 32-way RDBMS machine, but to say that the RDBMS is processing in *parallel* is inaccurate, at least not "parallel processing" as we understand it.

Parallel processing differs from SMP multi-way processing in *so* many ways. Later, we'll examine the essence of a true parallel processing model and how Netezza embraces it at the architectural level.

And now, a drum roll please...

Rule #10 – Never do bulk inside a traditional RDBMS!

So let's make sure our terminology is correct. We have MPP and SMP, so I am specifically calling out Netezza as an Asymmetric Massively Parallel Processing® platform (MPP) and *not* a traditional RDBMS engine running on a multi-way Symmetric Multi-Processor (SMP). We can certainly interact with Netezza as an *RDBMS interface* for bulk-related extract/load/query activities, but not for transactional-style activities.

We *can* likewise implement a RDBMS for bulk processing, but the transactional nature of the traditional RDBMS is its Achilles heel, and will never scale for bulk. The Netezza platform has no transactional leanings, in fact no transactional capability *whatsoever*. It inhales data in quantity, and exhales it in quantity. Netezza breathes massive volumes of data like we breathe air. Likewise, it does not accept air *molecules*, only BTUs at-a-time.

With the traditional RDBMS, the engine *is in the way*, piles and piles of software between us and the physics – software that will ultimately serialize. It can never scale like a flow-based, bulk processing engine, because it is unable to by *design*. Using a traditional RDBMS, without a separately configured, high-powered data processing environment (like Ab Initio), we must invariably leverage stored procedures in our bulk processing, which likewise don't scale and further don't provide the necessary visibility for operators and administrators, troubleshooters or those who would monitor progress or recover from failure.

Stored procedures are like black boxes, and feel like ticking time bombs to more people than want to admit it. This is not about trusting the technology at all. Someone has to implement the technology. Often the process-visibility needs of the operators are dismissed or ignored. And if these fundamental needs are ignored, what else is being ignored? It's a nervous situation.

And with systems of *scale*, the nervousness only escalates.

Why is a stored procedure *bad*? Stored procedures are usually cursor-based execution of an *entity-at-a-time*. We will pull up an entity table and

(1) read each affected row

(2) apply a series of rules or operations to it, and

(3) take an action (such as an update or insert).

We think that because the stored procedure loads up local memory, lookup tables and the like, that we get some uptake that we wouldn't get if we performed the same operation asynchronously. This is an illusion. The real problem is that we are applying multiple rules to single entities (Multiple-Instruction-Single-Data). Even if we launch multiple-action SQL statements, like insert-into-select-from, the RDBMS will *still* treat it like serialized transactional processing. It cannot scale in parallel because its power-plant (server/disk) are not parallel. Clusters help a little, but still aren't massively parallel.

Apart from processing the data inside, we still have to load the data into the machine from outside. Relatively speaking, we won't see too many *initial* issues with plain-straight loading of an RDBMS. When we first roll it out, the RDBMS is to die for. It's when we want to *get data back out,* like ad-hoc queries, bulk processing and the like, that the malaise begins. We'll add an index here and there. Tune a table for this or that. Then we'll go back to the loading process that worked so well – the *first* time. After having applied all the index structures, it no longer loads as fast. Now we're broken on *both* ends. It's a predictable outcome. Our engineers will work on the tactical details to get more performance. More complexity ensues.

And because the *get-the-data-out* isn't supported without schema engineering, we can't test very well, either. Testing means we need to bulk-*compare* our results to a baseline, meaning we have to *get-the-data-out* of two data stores, not just one.

In fact, many users of Netezza know that to perform baseline testing, it's often easier and much faster to move data from the legacy system into Netezza to perform just such a raw baseline comparison. The penalty for the forklift from the legacy RDBMS is offset by the speed gained back in the high-intensity testing activity – that Netezza does *in parallel*.

Doing bulk processing inside the RDBMS is *such* a bad idea, in fact, and success for it *so* marginal, that it hardly bears a second look, yet so many environments make the mistake of not only using it, but embracing it and even standardizing on it. It's one thing to start out using it this way for convenience. We tend to forget that it just *won't* work out for us. We need to be on an active search for a *real* bulk processing solution.

And now: **Jurassic Park**. Many moons ago, Steven Spielberg's movie thrilled us – heck – it *still* thrills us. While most of the movie's dinosaurs are computer animated, many close-ups were of large robotic models. The T-Rex model (used extensively in the car-attack scene with the kids) had a pet name "Model-T". And now I shall ruin the ride for you. In the scene where the Raptors first enter the kitchen to come after the kids, when it kicks open the door, beyond this you can see the hands of a stagehand holding the robot upright, then they move away to the left.

The first introduction to the moviegoer of a giant resident of Jurassic Park, is the Brachiosaurus at the beginning of the movie, entirely computer animated. Why is this important? This fifteen seconds of movie magic was the result of *hundreds of hours* of computer crunching in their CGI animation studios, rarefying the image for the perfect "wow" effect.

RDBMS-based data warehouses are a lot like this. Some analytic and cube environments are like this. Why? Because they require us to take a huge data processing penalty in the *front* of the process, in order to gain the "agile consumer" benefit on the presentation. I spoke to an engineer from one of these analytics vendors once, specifically about this huge uptake penalty to get one of their agile datasets. He simply smiled and said, almost dismissively, "Well, that's the trade-off, isn't it?" *We* have to do the heavy lifting and high intensity restructure of the data, the loading, the cleansing and whatnot. The users get a crisp, elegant experience.

Just like in the movies.

Dare I say, that the technologists who deliver these things to our end users are tired. Just plain tired. It's *hard* work to get the data crunched and the machine running, and keep it running. It's horrifically tedious and time consuming to test and troubleshoot. O that we had some power to affect our fate!

O – *but we do*.

Netezza mitigates all this malaise of loading, crunching and data preparation. It handles the data intake at high speed. It handles the internal data processing at high speed. In fact, from the time of the data's arrival on Netezza's front door to its actually becoming consumption-ready – is a very short, breathless ride. And free of white-knuckles, at that! For many applications, we can leave the data's structure *totally* as-is. No star-schemas, no special indexing, no creative disk striping. It's all there, all the time, with no additional engineering or tuning on our part. In fact, any schema engineering we *actually* do will be to fulfill a *functional*, not *performance* requirement for the users.

How cool is that?

I always adjure the newborn Netezza users to shape their Netezza schema in a way they intend to *use* it. This usually means they should rethink and refactor their source schema, or the one they used for a proof-of concept. Because while it's great to compare apples-to-apples in a proofing exercise, this is *just* an exercise to get us out of the apple-orchard and across the street, to the *marketplace of ideas*.

I've sat across the table from dedicated database engineers, application developers and otherwise hard-working IT folk who squean down their eyes into slits and hiss "*What do you mean (my favorite database engine here) can't scale?*" It's as though I've shot their dog, spat on their child and told them their spouse was ugly, all in one small sentence. And even if I've *never* seen their dog - it's still personal. It's sometimes borderline religious. I was innocently *suggesting the right approach* when in their minds I've somehow declared *jihad*. Yes, well, it's not always about the technology, or the best choice. Sometimes what can and should be an objective discussion, affects people in very emotional ways.

I was working with a group on a competitive proof-of-concept with Netezza and several other products, and it was amazing how many engineering hoops the internal people were willing to jump through to make their pet technologies perform the same as Netezza. After several weeks of these hijinks, one of the leaders took them all aside and said this:

"You aren't doing (your pet technology) any favors by demonstrating to us that (your pet technology) requires all this engineering and brain power to achieve the same results that Netezza provides simply by turning on its power switch."

Well, there it is.

And that feedback still rings in my ears. Recall **Rule #2 - Simplify and Clarify.** These are large-scale problems. What this leader's technologists were demonstrating was simply this: We can *show* (our pet technology) in a good light, but we cannot *sustain* it over time. We'll work like dogs for the proof-of-concept, but at the end of the day, we won't stick around and work our tails off to keep (our pet technology) running at this bandwidth. The leaders can see it already.

In their *fatigue*.

Using (the pet technology) the *people* were doing the heavy lifting. In fact, they were temporarily signing up to do the work that the *machine* should be doing for them. And again, they'll sign up for this on a proof-of-concept because of the competitive nature of many technologists and their affinity for (their pet technology). But they won't sign up to maintain this level of intensity as an *operational* priority. It's just too steep.

So the above assertions are especially aligned toward those who feel that an RDBMS *really can* scale for bulk processing. Such a feeling is *just* that, an emotional attachment to the technology. People will expend a lot of physical and mental energy in loyalty to their favorite technology. Those same people, oddly enough, sometimes become Netezza's most vocal champions. We *must* objectively set aside feelings, be skeptical of vendor white-paper claims, and base our decisions on *empirical* observations. It's a science, after all.

THE NETEZZA UNDERGROUND

RDBMS engines do not scale for bulk processing.

Repeat it like a mantra if you have to, but drill it into you brain and down into your lumbar spine. Etch it on the inside of your eyelids. It won't betray you, mock you or otherwise sell you out. It is the safest bet, and many before you have made the bet, with big payoffs. Many before you have bet against it, and did not find success.

Never forget, the discussion is about more than just the technology. In many cases the *objective* choice is not what people *actually* make. Many times it's an emotional choice, or one borne on peer acceptance, or simply fear of failure. It's the way of things.

The primary reason that RDBMS bulk-scaling is not viable is due to the missing parts - core capability requirements that universally exist for all large-scale processing solutions. We cannot ignore these or treat them as secondary. They are the "day one" problems requiring our attention now, and we are expected to have under control already. If these capabilities are inherently missing from the RDBMS, how can we expect success? Certainly not as an objective conclusion.

The primary issues stand in our way of success when using a common RDBMS are in (bulk) Extraction, Transformation, Integration and Publication. These are core data warehouse / large-scale processing capabilities. The traditional, SMP-based RDBMS is *not* originally and deliberately configured to harness them. Rather, the traditional RDBMS is configured and designed to *include* them, but not make them bread-and-butter, baseline capabilities.

Not to belabor a point, but I'll periodically encounter someone who will argue that their technology does these things *very* well. Sometimes I engage the conversation, sometimes I don't. If I really want to hear someone tell me the same old story from another angle, I'll listen just for the sake of nuance. It doesn't change anything. Words don't solve bulk processing problems. Software doesn't either.

Only *physics* can make it happen. No physics, no solution.

Case Study Short: When comparing a common RDBMS technology to Netezza, the internal RDBMS proponents showed that they could make a very complex, all-in-one SQL statement to do exactly what the business wanted, where in Netezza we "had to" break it apart into several operations. This "several operations" approach, *they* used as a verbal battering ram to keep the Netezza proposal at bay. Never mind that their solution ran in fifty-nine minutes and Netezza's ran in ninety *seconds*. The confusion here is not whether their RDBMS *can* do these kinds of operations, but whether it *should*.

What our business users want to get away from, *really* want to get away from, are these multi-page, highly complex (and frankly scary) SQL operations that require high-end engineers to create and maintain. The Netezza solution (above) was simpler, easier to understand, more flexible, achieved exactly the same results in a fraction of the time. When defending a technology, we must be careful about what we're defending, and what spoken and unspoken message is delivered. The users *didn't want* the complex, all-in-one SQL statement, which was highly surprising to its proponents.

But think about what the users heard in context of a self-contained solution for anything else: We have two solutions for getting you to the store for grocery shopping. One is that you take that car over there on the driveway, hop in and make the trip. The other is that we call the neighbor and borrow their motorcycle, use it to drive down the street to someone who has a larger car, borrow the car (provided nobody else is using it) then make our trip, then when we come back, we have to use the motorcycle to carry one bag at a time back to our house. If we drive the motorcycle and second car very fast, we can likely match the speed of the first car as it goes to and from the store - only once.

Look how much additional complexity, additional work, extra *risk* and additional *human* participation it requires. People do not see (their technology) as adding this kind of complexity to a solution. More unfortunately, when *people* (not machines) do the heavy-lifting, whether they are technical or business employees, it's intangible and largely invisible.

Issue #1 – Extraction: When taking data from a database source, we're tempted to join multiple tables, perform a group-by or an order-by with the data on the way *out*. Keep in mind - all RDBMS engines ultimately serialize this operation. Even partitioned/parallel engines must ultimately serialize on the output. Even if we have the option to extract in parallel, such as with an Ab Initio Input Table component, we still miss that somewhere behind the output, the RDBMS serialized it first. What we want to avoid, is serialization on the inside, and this isn't always possible. Even partitioned databases have issues.

Extraction from a traditional RDBMS means avoiding any joining, filtering or sorting unless these operations *directly* serve a performance purpose to benefit the flow (rarely the case). Filtering is our first option. Joining is sometimes necessary if it enriches the flow with database-side reference data. Key-based operations of any kind will always bear a penalty. Rollup/group-by has marginal value to reduce the size of the outbound flow, but we sacrifice details on this altar when we can mitigate this with incremental extracts.

Some exceptions are available with partitioned databases, but we always invite the danger of database-side serialization unless we carefully engineer and tune the extract for our exact needs. We can *always* engineer it. And later when the engineering breaks, we'll *re-engineer* it. How many schemas can an engineer, engineer - if an engineer could engineer schemas? The answer is exactly zero. The *first* time we engineer the extraction, we are doomed to continuously engineering it thereafter – it will be a constant thorn in our side.

Engineered schemas are *unstable* schemas.

How to avoid this? We extract the individual raw table information and transport it to our processing engine. Whether this is Ab Initio or Netezza, we'd like to transport the information in its native table form. Trim columns and be wise about the size. The first extract is the hardest, incrementally thereafter.

Don't Join, Sort or Rollup on the source database, unless we can show it actually buys us something. Just rip the data out and go with it. We can do all the rest after it lands on the SPUs.

Issue #2 – Transformation: Applying a common set of business rules, calculations etc. to each row of a selected set. Think for a moment about the magnitude of this kind of operation, say, *millions* of rows, where we will apply some calculations, rules or other logic. Internal to the RDBMS, this is a cursor-based, record-at-a-time operation. We'll pull each record off the top of the set, examine it and re-insert/update it within the same cycle. Even for the engines that perform block-reads and block-writes of the information, it is horrendously slow. And I think I already said, *it will not scale.*

Our alternative is to write insert/select transform queries (the "T" in ELT) which are only marginally better and are still beholden to the weakness of the RDBMS engine. An insert/select transform in Netezza, however, leverages parallel tables for input and parallel tables for output. We won't see serialization unless we finally want to take the data out. Let the SPUs do the work. It's what they were born for.

We have another pervasive need in the transformation activity. The search for errors, anomalies, missing values and the like. We *could* do this at the row level, but in scales of information, row-level is no longer an option. We need to perform this activity in gross, sweeping movements.

I've heard people say that they would stop the intake of a billion records for the sake of just one erroneous record. This is transactional thinking. Our users will wonder why we didn't cordon off that "bad boy" into an administrative zone, forwarding the rest of the good data to its final resting place.

Errors are often needles-in-a-haystack. When dealing with scale, we need to peel the errors away in administrative form and allow someone to eyeball them, dealing with them offline without harming the records that really are good to go.

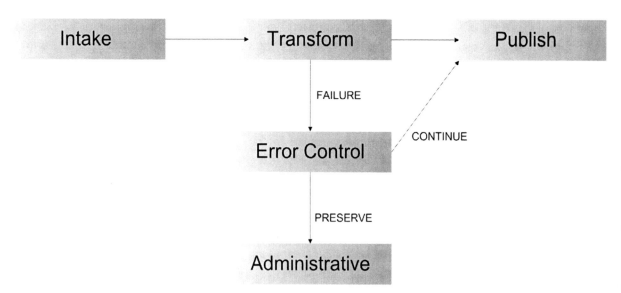

In the depiction (above) we see a standard model where the "happy path" transform/business rules follow the intake-transform-publish path. If an erroneous / anomalous record appears, it is peeled off for automated review in the Error Control zone, where we have collected all the user covenants for error correction. If the data can be automatically corrected according to a predefined covenant, we re-introduce it into the flow and continue. Otherwise we drop it to an administrative zone for user review. If after review, the noted error can be automatically fixed, this is added to the covenants in the Error Control. This keeps our true business rules separated from the exceptions, so that we can manage both in context.

Case Study Short: One group had a series of stored procedures that ran "bulk" operations against a major entity in their database. It pulled the entities one at a time, applied four business rules to each one, and then put the result in another table. Each operation took (more or less) 20 seconds. With 3500 entities, the total time for the operation to complete, on average, was multiple hours.

We broke this apart into four operations, one for each of the four business rules. Running one rule against 3500 entities-at-a-time, even joining three other tables and applying additional enrichments, required mere additional *seconds*. We finished all four rules, their attendant housekeeping and error control, in less than three (3) minutes. It's amazing what a little massively parallel can do.

Just to check our sanity, we went back to the RDBMS and applied this same approach, but the four queries in their best form still required many hours.

Case Study Short: One of our teams was asked to assess an environment sporting a 12-way Oracle platform where the Java-based "data cleansing" tapestry was rapidly pulling data out, cleansing it, and putting it back. Somehow they really believed that if they *simulated* a transactional environment with a grid-base computational model, they would get automatic and obvious lift from the database engine.

What nonsense.

Bulk processing is *bulk* processing, not performing a bunch of transactional operations-at-the-same-time. We pull the data *en masse*, process it in bulk, and put it back in *bulk*. We don't pull/push a record-at-a-time. That's not bulk processing. That's transactionally processing non-transactional data. Or more to the point: it's not parallel – it's *asynchronous*.

For a Netezza-based operation, the ability to perform SQL-based transforms is incredibly fast. The system has little to no row-level software overhead to get in our way (like the RDBMS engine does) and can pull data from one table and push it to another without degrading performance in the slightest. In fact, it's *engineered* to do it this way.

Issue #3 – Integration (Join/Sort/Rollup): Now we get to the gravitas of the operation. Do this activity in the ETL/Transport layer, or once we get it transported to Netezza, do it inside the box as part of an *ELT* protocol. *Don't* do it in the RDBMS source, and *don't do it in a RDBMS target*. Take care of it where we have the most power at our fingertips. Even on an RDBMS, the sort happens on the way out. The Join and Rollup, however, usually require some kind of Sort to support their work. We'll take the sorting penalty almost as a throwaway, won't we?

Ab Initio performs these operations in the flow, and can go parallel for as many CPUs as are available. It is arguably the most powerful product for its capability, but even running it 32-ways on a powerhouse Unix machine, we just might find more lift in some operations on the Netezza machine's 200+ CPU frame. The largest Netezza frame is over 800 CPUs, utterly eclipsing the power of any of our other environments. Enhancements (2009) to the machine will breach this limit into the many thousands of CPUs, supporting petabyte-scaled storage. In the meantime, we must simply balance the workload where it makes the most sense. Pay attention to the flow, not to the components in the flow - or the products configured in the flow.

We are optimizing *flows*.

Issue #4 – Publication: In an ETL context, this would be *loading*, or *pushing* data to its final resting place where the consumers have visibility to it. When we finish our processing cycle, we present the work to the users, in an easily accessible form (like a mart or cart, which is really nothing more than another engineered schema). For an RDBMS, we have to hit the target table directly, no staging tables allowed - we don't have the spare power for them, or the stored procedures to support them. Stored procedures or internal transforms would require the RDBMS to perform bulk processing work (see Rule #10). A star schema is not particularly hard to load We put the dimensions in first, then the facts, and off we go.

But there's more to it, isn't there? What if the data fails to load? We don't want the RDBMS involved in the recovery, either, since this, too is a bulk processing operation. We also don't want the rollback or logging turned on, nor the constraints or the index structures – because these cause row-level interactions with the bulk load, effectively involving the RDBMS in the bulk processing.

"Keep yer stinking paws off my data, you (expletive) dirty RDBMS!!"- the late Charlton Heston, *Planet of the RDBMSs*.

Fortunately in Netezza, these are *non-issues*. We can join and prep our data, using hundred(s)-way parallel tables for intermediate storage. No index structures in our way, and no relational constraints are enforced. What does this mean? We can intake dirty data, transform it and finalize it into consumption-ready form *inside* Netezza, without having to use an ETL environment to make it ready beforehand.

If the source data is already hosted in Netezza, we thankfully don't have to resort to schema engineering with marts, carts and star-schemas. We can optimize the data for the consumer, then push it to consumer-visible table, without ever leaving the confines of the machine. The consumer will always have a pleasant and consistent experience, no matter how much data shows up for the party. We'll abate our network overloading from large-scale data movement and alleviate heavy-lifting pressure from our ETL environment.

If we need physically outbound data, we can perform a high-speed internal extract and push the results to a Netezza external table. This is simply a way to package and reposit structured information for later quick-extraction, or downstream publication. The consumer can easily pick up the pre-fabricated table whenever it's convenient, and will not have to impose upon Netezza's CPUs or processing environment with joins/summaries etc to get the answer it wants. Netezza has already fabricated it, dropped it off to an internal depot, and the consumer just picks it up. More on this later.

The conclusion of this section is: RDBMS engines must simply take their place in the flow as a point of extract or a point of loading. In either of these activities, we should mitigate and eliminate the need for the RDBMS engine itself to get involved at the row-level *for any reason*.

Netezza on the other hand, is *in the zone* for this kind of work. We have CPU and disk power to punt around terabytes-at-a-time inside the machine. All we really need to worry about is getting the data *into* the machine.

Everything else happens inside.

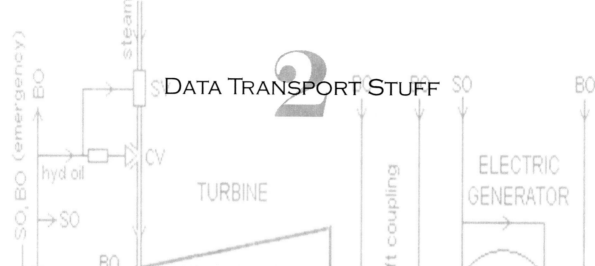

DATA TRANSPORT STUFF

WHILE OUR Netezza environment is a self-contained source of processing power, an important key is in feeding the animal, so to speak. We can have the most powerful lions on the planet, but if they're starving for food, they're probably not operating at peak, and so it goes with Netezza.

Netezza's intake capacity is largely "network speed" -driven. Whatever our network can support, Netezza will intake at that speed. With the new *StoragePad* capability (onboard EMC storage up to 10TB), we can pump data into the machine on the pad, and when we're ready to intake, we can do it at over a terabyte per hour *per frame* (on a 10800, that's 8TB per hour). Even though Netezza can inhale network-speed data, the network itself may not support its bandwidth (at the outset). We need to examine the feeding hardware configuration so that a slow network doesn't bottleneck the process or starve the machine. We'll provide some metrics later to show comparisons.

With an intake capacity like this, we now need to focus on getting the data *to* the machine. It is an appliance after all, and cannot operate without information. One of the most significant problems in bulk data processing and data warehousing in general, is in getting the data from its resident source and into the data processing target. As an example, one of the primary reasons why people use the Ab Initio product for data processing has as much to do with performance as its ability to adapt to legacy sources. No other product can perform extraction against so many disparate legacy sources so easily and effectively. A good thing, because we need a way to get the data *out*, and a place to put it once we're done with it.

Our objective with these technologies, is to keep the data *moving* until it reaches a final consumption state. We sometimes cannot afford to "hold" the data anywhere. The moment data lays down on a disk, it starts to become stale. We can collect it, tank it and move it in bursts or streams, but we'd better be moving it. Each time it lands on our enterprise SAN, we take a penalty to our flow of data, and we'd better get something back for it. Otherwise, why hold it at all? For any reason? Sometimes we'll use the intermediate storage as a collection point from which we'll initiate our batch window activities. For those businesses with an ever-growing business day, and an ever-shrinking batch window, at some point we'll need to embrace something continuous, where the system never sleeps. The popular storage vendors claim that their technology is the best place to *keep* the data. We don't want to keep the data. We want to *move* it.

"Harry never holds. Not for a minute, not for thirty seconds," the late James Coburn as Harry, a professional pickpocket, *Storage Vendors In Your Pocket.*

Data Transportation Issues

Of all the things we must embrace when processing information, it's operationally getting the data to a place (physically, logically, conceptually) where we can process it. We have options, like a scheduled, plain-straight copy, or an automated replication and the like. What we might miss in all this, that Netezza needs more than simple data intake, and doesn't want streaming data intake. It really wants data *block-pumped* into it, at network speed. Common replication mechanisms are often slow in bulk, often work like streaming feeds, and in single-record transactional form are highly inappropriate for Netezza's intake.

In addition, just because data leaves one place and lands on our Netezza machine, is no guarantee that it will arrive safely (the network could fail). In fact, we have lots of failure points between the external data sources and our machine. So many - that if one should actually rear its head, we might be hard pressed to recover from it, unless we have planned from the outset with a recovery framework. I discuss these later.

Some data transportation issues we need to harness include:

- Inventory of the data, whether by source, file, download, row-level etc.
- Source requirements, whether post-processing notifications or other
- Target requirements, a Netezza load-event prefers a functional minimum (discussed later) so we need to regard the target machine's constraints
- Target table requirements, whether non-nullable columns or relational constraints to resolve
- Failure points, whether the source system(s), the disk drives, connectivity and network, target capacity, etc during a data transfer event
- Incremental versus full data transfers
- Bundled / collected transfer assets (multiple files/feeds bundled as one)
- Record counts, for inbound, outbound, exceptions, etc. Some environments (like financial services) require us to harness every record and not lose even one.

We have a constellation of other issues that often arise, but the above are ever-present in an enterprise environment, and we do ourselves a disservice by neither regarding nor planning to deal with them. In most cases, a simple framework that fits our environment will do just fine. Other cases might require something more formal.

The point is, if we simply put these together to support a single application in the box, we have effectively stovepiped this as a feature rather than a reusable capability. We'll want to leverage this for the next application, so we should take steps now in formulating these things as an asset. We'll need it later, so the extra steps we'll take now will simply avoid stovepiping, in the spirit of adaptation.

Case Study Short: One environment pulled from a customer inventory system, summarized the data to the customer and fed it to several downstream systems. Each of those systems picked up their version of the information, processed it and passed it along. While none of the downstream systems were posting any losses or missing information, somewhere along the line, they had misplaced over fifty *million* dollars in customer transactions, lost in the flow. While this represented only one percent of the transactional flow, it was considerable enough to draw attention.

Oddly, when each flow handed off to its next downstream consumer, that consumer would only peel off what it needed and pass it along. When the final consumer used the data, it tossed the remainder. Somewhere along the flow, nobody picked up those additional fifty million dollars of transactions. Had they been invoiced? Was the company losing money or were these after-the-fact records?

In problems of *scale*, where this data was a fraction of billions of rows of data, how would we find such a needle-in-a-haystack? Large-scale bulk processors alone don't do it. We need to include some data transportation infrastructure to make sure we've leveraged the technology's power to harness the information. So we don't lose anything.

Like money.

The point is, data transportation is huge issue in most shops, and Netezza cannot process from nothing. Data *must* arrive on its front door, or at least within lasso distance of the machine.

I'll talk a bit later about the data loading scenarios we might encounter or embrace. Data publication is another story as well, because we want our consumers to receive clean, unadulterated information, not just the data that was sent to the machine sometime in the past. Using a Netezza machine for a simple consumption repository, or a store-and-forward resource, is nothing short of a lost opportunity. We have the extraordinary opportunity, and the amazing power of the machine to convert the *data* into actionable *information*.

Just like an ETL/data processing environment should scrub the data and present it, *load ready,* to the target, so our Netezza machine should, with *ELT*, scrub, prep and publish information *consumption ready* to our downstream. The difference is that it does so internally, to a *publication schema*.

Case Study Short: We reviewed a series of stored procedures that performed heavy aggregation in an RDBMS, solely to support performance and not any functional mandate. The procs congealed and converged data from the largest tables in the database, and reduced it to smaller, summarized form so the downstream extracts could have a one-stop-shop.

One problem, though, the data fields had not been completely scrubbed. So when the downstream consumer, in this case Business Objects, performed queries on the final tables, the BO developers had to wrap the query output's columns with is_valid(), is_null(), coalesce(), nvl() and all manner of data validation checks before presenting them to the user. Failure to perform these checks could cause presentation-level mayhem, because the data in the extraction table was so dirty.

So the folks making the extraction table missed an excellent opportunity. If they had only scrubbed the data while aggregating it, they could have reduced the need for Business Objects to do it on demand. In short, a problem that could have been fixed in the upstream, was punted to the downstream, *requiring overcoding in the downstream.* We must consider the downstream impact of our work, or lack thereof, because that BO environment could have been lightly coded, and thinner, more agile than its final, overcoded form. The problem of dirt must be resolved *somewhere*, and in this case, Business Objects was over-coded to harden itself from the dirt, and thus *artificially inflated* in its code size and complexity.

Simple failure to appropriately clean data can *cause* artificial complexity in downstream systems. Netezza has the power to overcome an issue like this in *minutes*, not hours. We should take advantage of its internal power to make the data 100% clean and consumption-ready. Make the data good for all the consumers. We have the power now.

"Use the power for good," Jonathan Kent to son Clark, *Superman, Data Warehouse Edition*

Information Theory and Chaos

One of the most pervasive problems in information management is in guaranteeing the integrity of the data itself. Data is different from information. Someone might want to argue this point, but suffice to say that information includes the raw data *and* its context. Without context, the data is just a bunch of characters in a file, or a table, or on a page.

So data management must preserve the context of the data and the data itself, and to faithfully store and retrieve both without losing the underpinning integrity of either. While all of that might sound remedial again, it's to make a point, so let's go there now.

Chaos never dies. It lies in wait for our data and is an ever-present enemy. It sits at each interface, waiting to kill and devour our information. Think of it in these terms. An animal to be hunted and placed in a cage to harm no more. Feed the animal. Put it on exhibit, but never forget that the animal will never die, it always wants out, and is always hungry. And it's an ever-present threat.

Whew!

Information theory provides a universal maxim, that data, left to itself, will lose its integrity in transition from one location to the next. Information theory also warns that the loss of integrity is cumulative, like the fax-of-a-fax. Once context is lost, the information is useless. Information theory goes a lot deeper than all this, so the takeaway we want to focus on is what applies to us – in the realm of information stewardship.

In stewardship space, the maxim applies: every time we touch the data, we should make it better for the next downstream consumer. Information theory requires us to embrace this philosophy as non-optional, and offers stern warnings to anyone who would ignore it, or for that matter, *delay* it (with the presumption that someone *else* downstream will deal with it).

When we move data from one place to the next, we should *never simply replicate.* I cannot list the total times I've been invited to a shop where the data movement was handled almost completely through replication. One might wonder – doesn't the replication process guarantee that the data we pick up is the same data we lay down?

And the answer is *no it doesn't*. But it *does* mean something else:

The same junk we start with, we carry with us.

The objective of stewardship is *not* to verify that the information and its context arrive as they started, but that they arrive *better* than they started. We should deliberately apply rules to the data so that every downstream consumer gets cleaner, sharper, more enriched information. If we merely copy the information, we miss an important opportunity that will never arise again, that the data was in our hands and we did nothing with it but pass it on. Ancient proverbs speak of this kind of "care" as poor stewardship, and a lack of loyalty and faithfulness, in this case, to the cause of the data's owners. In fact, they could have shipped the data out of the house to any number of vendors (for things like address scrubbing or data enrichment), and upon its return they would see the information in far better shape than when it left. Not just the new stuff, *all* the stuff.

When the data is in our hands, we need to do something with it, in flow-based form, before passing it on. For our purposes, a bulk flow is different than fielding tactical records. The ultimate goal in all this is to make sure the data arrives in better form, for whomever needs it. Especially if that whomever happens to be *us*.

"We can't make exceptions," Marlon Brando. *Warehouse Godfather.*

Case Study Short: Working with a group of engineers from a major consulting group, nameless for this example, they had built some fifteen or so core data processing components in Ab Initio to crunch and process information toward an expected end. Two of their team members were charged with constructing a utility loader to take the final work products to their respective target tables. One of these team members came to us and asked "You know, our utility graph is just supposed to pick up the file and shoot it to the database, but when the file arrives, it's full of junk. Now I need to know, how do I put a final transform in the loader to make sure it won't load junk?"

The answer to this question was simple: you *don't*. You need to get together with your team members and discover how, after *fifteen* flow-based applications touched the data, you *still* have junk in the flow. Well, we know Ab Initio wasn't the culprit, so perhaps the problem was between keyboard and chair? A quick review of those fifteen components revealed an interesting pattern.

Each of the components had scrubbed the data *for its own use* by using inline is_null() and is_valid() checks on the various columns, without ever applying a valid-value if the data was bogus. They were just doing the null-checks so the operation *at hand* would not fail. Ultimately the bad data remained bad, slipping through the cracks, and none of the components had taken responsibility for cleaning it.

Another pattern was quite obvious: that each subsequent application was *over-coded*, as much as thirty percent or more, with cascading null checks to make sure their own, localized operation did not fail. In short, every component had to harden itself from failure, when the upstream could have covered it and simplified things for every part of the downstream.

So we have several items of malaise:

- Starting point is dirty data
- Over-coded components to guard against local dirty data effects
- Dirty data scrubbed locally only
- Dirty data slipping through cracks
- Nobody claiming ownership of data to eliminate dirt
- End result is dirty data
- Dirt is a four-letter word

In a flow like the above, the pitfalls of information theory adjure that we challenge the data when it first arrives in our hands. *First and deliberately.* We don't wait for a downstream component to get lucky. We use this first gateway as a means to make the data better, and all downstream components benefit, and there's no dirt in the end because the dirt was purged in the beginning. From there, no component has permission to release dirt. Period.

- Starting point is dirty data
- We scrub the dirt and eliminate it
- Dirty data scrubbed once, first and deliberately
- Dirty data never gets past us
- Initial intake component claims ownership of data to eliminate dirt
- End result is clean data
- The downstream becomes lightly-coded applications with crisp and concise business rules
- Dirt remains a four-letter word – because dirt is *always a four letter word*

We should never become complacent about dirt. We must assume that the data we receive is dirty, and clean it, *then* release it. Then everyone consuming it downstream will benefit from it.

And of course, we will have embraced information theory head-on, knowing that dirt and chaos are waiting to make us look bad. Dirt and chaos never sleep, so we need deliberately constructed and regularly reviewed processes to make sure that dirt never seeps into the data warehouse.

In Netezza, we can transport dirty data into staging tables, then use the machine's internal parallel power to perform large-scale cleansing and integration before pushing it to its final target tables. It's okay to arrive dirty if we intend to give the data a bath.

But *do* give the data a bath!

Logistical Capacity Problems

What is *logistical* capacity?

We load up a train with a hundred boxcars and enough fuel to get us to the next station and beyond. We roll out of the station and within minutes are moving faster than most automobiles. In fact, we're on a bullet train. In the middle of the journey, we realize that some of the boxcars don't belong with us, but with another train. Likewise another train has our boxcars. How do we get those boxcars disconnected, sent back to our prior station so they can be on their way? Or retrieve our own boxcars? It's not a hard problem, but it has logistical issues. If this were a toy train, it's easy enough to pick up boxcars and move them because we have the power to do so. As the problem *scales* upward, with larger boxcars, we no longer have such options.

Let's say we have a database that we've rolled out into the production environment, and its data model originally had marginal to ugly performance. Now on a shining new platform, the hardware and technology mask the ugliness of the data model. *Any* high-powered hardware system can make a bad data model look good.

We now have a false sense of security, and proceed to point hundreds, then thousands of users and applications towards the marginal model. We find out later that we made some huge errors in the model, but now we can't go back. With all the thousands of consumers and potential breakage-points all over the enterprise, can we hope to reel the functionality back inside? This is like the locomotive leaving the station, now moving at 90 miles per hour, we might lose hope to change the track we're on. We need to find a way to get off the track, while the train is moving at full bore. The environment has now moved beyond our ability to reel it back in. It has breached our *logistical* capacity – the capacity we need to keep things under control. We will need extraordinary, perhaps painful measures to regain control.

And this just isn't the kind of thing you had planned for your shining new implementation.

"There's no time to change the road you're on," Robert Plant, *Warehouse to Heaven*

You'll hear a common tale from many purveyors of data warehouse appliances (note, I've never heard *this* from a Netezza rep): Take all your data and toss it, "as is" into the machine, and start using it in production without ever having to clean it up. All that dirt? No problem, our machine can make even the worst data model look like a million dollars.

And in the end, cost a million dollars, too.

To remediate.

In all fairness, Netezza product reps *will* tell you to throw your data into the machine "as is" for a *proof of concept*. After all, anyone can restructure a bad model to make their own hardware look good. It's when they take your model "as is" and show you multiple-X improvement, that you see the major advantages of *moving out* of your current home and into another one.

But just as we would not move our trash from our current home into our new one, nor should we take the trash from our old database environment. We especially should leave on the trash heap those vestigial summary tables that we had to artificially manufacture to squeeze power from every last ounce of strength the machine had, or once had, once upon a time.

Okay, that's a little extreme. We'll likely keep the tables and structures that face our downstream. We cannot afford to toss them out and destabilize our consumers. We really might need to keep those pesky summary tables, too. But largely for functional, *not* performance reasons.

I've already noted that we can use Netezza as a high-powered profiling machine. We should take the time to do this exercise, really get to know our data well, before blessing the new structures as the go-forward approach. It's an important exercise, not difficult and certainly not time consuming. We might end up with the original data structures we already had. Great, but now we *know*.

Why do this? After all, can't we just throw our bad data model into the new machine and hope for the best? Sure, we can *hope* for the best. Alice in Wonderland *hoped* for the best.

Why *hope* for the best when we now have the power to actually *deliver* the best? Why take a guess when we can know?

Case Study Short: I was called into an environment that had a lot of serious logistical issues. The people were running around in firefights, the DBAs pulling their hair out trying to defibrillate the servers during their peak usage. Every day brought a new management nightmare. More than once I heard a group of admins gather around a machine, one holding the paddles and shouting *"CLEAR!"*.

Placed before the assistant to the CIO, he told us a tale of woe. They had opted for a data warehouse appliance technology, one of Netezza's competitors, just two years prior. All was well. Everyone got bonuses. If the Sun was shining brighter anywhere else on the planet, nobody would have believed it.

Yet now the malaise was visible and the anxiety palpable. It had all started rearing its head some six months prior. In reality, they hadn't gotten more than a year or so of lift from their purchase and implementation. What had gone wrong?

Simply put – they had made the command decision to use their original transactional data structures "as is", forklifted their entire database into this next-generation technology, and pointed all their applications directly to it. This was the first, worst mistake. Everything else was just a symptom.

Here's why: If the data model was already that bad, then it's *already* stealing energy from its host. Moving it to a stronger host, this parasitic relationship will only escalate, draining the host of its lifeblood like some kind of macabre insect that lives in the host's stomach. It doesn't starve the host to death, it just never lets the host enjoy a healthy existence, ever again.

A friend of mine does missionary field work in Africa, and after working within a remote people-group culture for almost five years, a famine struck. He found himself among a starving people, and no villages around them had any food, either. Rather than abandon them, he decided he would stick it out.

After twenty days of no food, walking down a path one day, he started to choke. He felt something rising up inside his throat, and the more he coughed and gagged, the harder *it* tried to escape. *It* jumped out of his mouth, only partially, revealing the first foot of a thirty-foot tapeworm, living in his belly. He firmly pulled the worm out of his gullet, curling it into a pile on the ground. And left it there.

Crikeys!

The point is: If we deliberately starve the environment, the ugly worms will want to jump out of their own accord (we call them manual workarounds) They form the impetus to move to another, more powerful platform. But if we feed the same model with more power than it knows what to do with, the worms will grow. And grow hungrier. We *cannot* feed them enough.

Okay, so some of you are a little freaked-out by the analogy and application. *Good.* I wanted to focus attention to something that is very ugly about porting to a new environment. Leave the parasites in the old environment – and this could mean the original data model, too. Not to say that we can't take it with us, just that we should make no *de-facto* assumptions about its ongoing viability.

Use it for a proof-of-concept. Then emotionally disconnect from it. Using our new Netezza machine, we configure the tables and structures that will help us meet our critical *functional* mission. We might keep some of the old model, but should *not* be overly sentimental about it. We can put it on a powerpoint slide and revisit it on occasion. Talk fondly of it. But don't use it *de facto*. We'll use the parts that serve, but be prepared to leave the rest behind if we must.

It's equally important to keep a lid on the *configuration* of our environment as well. No differently than launching the aforementioned locomotive with no conductor at the helm, abdicating control at the outset, compared with losing control later in the game, still has the same outcome.

Chaos.

CONFIGURATION STUFF

THIS IS perhaps the most overlooked yet the most desired capability in the realm of any form of technology deliverable. What "configuration" means, is the ability to ***deliver***.

"Do it Right. Make it Faster. Don't Break Anything." - notation etched in the stone walls of the Underground catacombs. A rule of thumb to keep hapless wayfarers safely on their way.

I was in a crucible once where the entire team was just trying to get something out the door. One person was using version 4 of a widget even though the rest of us had upgraded to version 5. This merely scratched the surface. We had tools, directory structures, metadata, reference data – you name it. All in various states of delivery and none of them converging for us. Each time we scheduled a "delivery weekend", it was anyone's guess what would break next.

We weren't sure *what* would break, but we were sure of *breakage*. Just as sure as we could predict the sunrise the next morning (and our lack of sleep during the previous night). And this expectation of breakage is the surest sign we've lost control of the work products. We cannot deliver what is broken, and delivering a hairball isn't really delivery, it's just an exercise.

But what if the breakage isn't really the functionality? What if the breakage is due to something else? Something we didn't pay attention to, and now we must.

We simply must.

The Process-of-delivery, is key to quality

Something we take for granted practically every day, is that the *process* to make and deliver something determines the *quality* of the product. I know someone who has refused all his life to buy a car if it rolled off a Detroit assembly line on a Monday or a Friday, claiming that these are the worst two quality-assurance days for assembly plant workers. Perhaps this was accurate before robot assembly lines, but not as applicable these days.

Mrs. Fields Cookies has an interesting story. Mrs. Fields' husband created a computer program that could do things the way Mrs. Fields did things in the store. Mixing dough, baking cookies, basically telling the employees what to do, how and *when* to do it. As a matter of quality control, we always want people doing things the way we do them, or at least the way we'd like things done. When we get a model we like, we want to see more of it. It's hard to pull off without a quality control framework.

And that's all we're really talking about. How do we get things in their current state of readiness, assembled, packaged and delivered without the wheels falling off, the bytes biting back, and the chocolate chips bailing out of the dough - before we realize any dough for ourselves?

I have also been privy to more than one conversation among consultants or service-providers who consider all their hard-won efforts and claim, as though it was a revelation, that we could *package and sell it as a software product*. A casual word to the wise here - before making such a statement, one should visit a software product house and see what it *really* takes to make and market a software product. It's not something we casually decide to do over morning coffee. It requires some serious uptake and infrastructure.

Almost all of it focused on *quality* control. One bad delivery can spell curtains for the product. We don't experience this effect as dramatically within a captive audience (our company's user base), so we don't appreciate how merciless and fickle the open marketplace can be. Make no mistake, there might be people sitting in the same room as us, drawing a paycheck from the same company as us, and participating in the same 401k plan as us, but if they were given the option to use our work products or another, might pick the other.

If for no better reason than that *one bad delivery*.

Once upon a time.

They remember.

Delivery highway

A friend from Costa Rica declares that the main reason America has such great cars, is because America has such great highways, and how an American car on a Costa Rican road, wouldn't last a month. I knew he wasn't kidding. At the time, the roads there were *terrible*, a challenge for the sturdiest offroad vehicle.

The point is, our very best efforts in producing a quality product, are meaningless without a way to deliver it, and *repeatedly*. Even if we build the delivery highway, what's to stop someone from just *going offroad?* We know what an offroad vehicle looks like. Ruggedized, over-built to handle extra shock, muscled-up in infrastructure and hardware to go-the-distance. But we can't build all our applications with this level of hardening. It would cost us a fortune.

Clearly the better way is to put together a delivery highway that will support our applications automatically, with reusable, steady capabilities that are useful for all applications. Like a highway, every application enters by the on-ramp, has a smooth ride for the duration of the run, and exits at a known location in consistent manner.

Where is the offroad vehicle? Invisible and out of mind. It will show up sometime. Many applications, especially those built around stored procedures, present themselves as offroad vehicles - black boxes. They launch and "go dark" for extended periods, to the chagrin of our nervous operators. They will show up, we're sure of it.

Because Netezza *is* a black box (physically speaking), some may approach it with the fear that we can't know any more about what's going on inside it than we can know about our microwave ovens, or our Briggs-and-Stratton 2-cycle engine. But this is not the case. Netezza's admin panel and statusing/alerting ability give us all that (more on that later), and all we really need to do is focus on what *we need* to consistently deliver our application logic in the machine.

As fortune smiles upon us, Netezza's internal operating system is Linux, which itself is a strong foundation for all things operational and programmatic. All we really need to do (not to over-simplify) is to set up some consistent environments inside the machine that serve as our infrastructure for delivery.

Also what we want to get into, is the habit of *iterative* delivery. Early delivery, regular delivery, even if to our own testing staff or to a pre-production staging arena. We need to shake out all the bugs in the *delivery process itself*, and get rid of all the potholes and things that are in our way. One of our managers many years ago required us to produce a working logon screen and deliver it to the testing staff. While this seemed simplistic at the time, our packaging, delivery and implementation of this *one* screen shook out so many false assumptions that it paid for itself many times over. We could not imagine delivering hundreds of misconfigured screens to the testers, yet without this one exercise, we would have shot ourselves in the foot. Several times.

More importantly, we need a governance model to give our delivery priorities some teeth, and a governance-aligned infrastructure to give it *wings*. I am fond of saying that the developers should be in compliance *simply by participating in the infrastructure.*

So now, we have a mandate. Get the delivery highway in order. Make a "delivery #1". Then #2. By the time we roll into production, it's delivery #151. If that one has a bug, fix it and deliver #152. It should be that simple, smooth and easy, or all we've done is bitten off the same bitter herb for ourselves every time we deliver. Bite the herb once, and then install and shake out the things that will keep us from having to bite them off again.

Within Netezza, we have the general luxury of BASH shell, which is easy enough to understand and control (because it's just script after all). However, there's a temptation here, because script is not especially object-oriented or geared for reusability unless we actually use it that way. I know folks who have these x-levels-deep makefiles that can do practically anything short of reanimating the dead. But those did not come about for free. Neither will our delivery highway. (And you won't need anything *that* complex either). So if we don't like BASH, Perl is another lightweight option. Our group does things in BASH so we can all share stuff, because not all of us are fluent in Perl.

One of the best things we can do in Netezza is to decide how our schemas will be leveraged, and by what users, and for what purpose. If we have an intake protocol, do we need one schema, or more than one (to support multiple source I/O points and access credentials)? If we have a data processing thread, do we perform all of this inside one schema and publish to another, or keep it self-contained? Will we have multiple applications using these as resources, and if so, how are they managed?

What is the *master* configuration?

You see, in a "normal" database, we would assign one schema to an application. Now we have the freedom, perhaps the responsibility, to define internal appliance *capabilities*, and allow the various applications to leverage those capabilities in a configured environment. It's not that the Netezza machine itself requires us to do these things, but that they were never practical in other technologies, so why would we ever bother? Now we can have schemas for master data, reference data, staging data, published data – each one handling an architectural capability that we can leverage for multiple applications. Don't like the idea of multiple schemas? No worries, we *always* have the time to shake out the best fit. Kind of a weird feeling, all that extra time. All that extra power.

When we boil it down, applications have *function* points, but the architecture has *capabilities*. We need to leverage both inside the Netezza box, and balance their power for highest resilience. More on this in a later section.

What does an effective delivery highway look like? One of the questions it attempts to answer is – are we after Rapid Application Development, or Rapid Application *Delivery*? Rapid Application *Development* focuses only on the productivity of the *developer*, and not the overall *delivery cycle*. Rapid Application *Delivery* regards the needs of the end-user first, and wraps a framework around an architecture that *also* supports the developer. In this model, the developer is a component in the delivery cycle, not the center of the universe.

For example, when a developer receives a request for change, often the developer can turnaround the request rather quickly. In fact, some rapid-application-development environments allow a developer to turnaround a request in *minutes*. Some people hear this and say *you betcha!* Others ask *how do I get one of those?*

Not so fast. Or rather, perhaps this is not *as fast* as one might think. In many environments, a *methodology*-driven *monolithic-lifecycle* approach will steal the developer's thunder before the lightning has a chance to strike. The monolithic lifecycle will require an impact analysis, design, development, regression test and review, implementation and operational turnover. The regression test cycle alone can run the feature request into the weeds. I know of places that can't get a feature off the ground for months. Long after the developer has turned it around, the feature awaits the light of day, the user just awaits the *feature*. So much for rapid *anything*.

"I decided to send my help desk request a birthday card," actual quote from a business user, frustrated that his environment had such a long turnaround time, heralding the one-year anniversary of the request.

Case Study Short: Our clients assured us that they had only fifteen stored procedures to migrate from their old environment to the Netezza machine. They had already migrated one of them and it had only taken a few days. So they did the math and wanted to conscript us for only one month to do the remainder of the stored procedures. We told them that we would happily spend a month converting all their stored procedures over, with *simple* conversion. Our team proceeded in the task, accepted a check and left the building.

"How do we know the conversion is complete?" asked one of the principals.

I'd already had this conversation with him, but he was new at the game, so forgive me for toying with him a bit. "We converted the procedure, in the same manner that you converted the first one. How did you verify that the first one was complete?"

"When we finished translating the code," he said.

"So we finished translating the code. Per our agreement, you did not pay us to test the results, only convert the code. We do a lot of code conversions. It's pretty simple actually."

"But how do we know if you did it right?" he repeated.

"Well, you would have to test it, and if you find any issues, we'll be happy to come back and troubleshoot them for you."

"But - " he started to say, realizing that we'd already had this conversation. I had completely several white-board sessions with him on the necessity of conversion-and-test, not just conversion alone. He thought at the time that I was just trying to inflate the cost of the project. Now he was the proud owner of a lot of untested code. He'd paid for the conversion, and we'd offered him more. The longer this conversation wore on, the more it clarified - he had an expectation that conversion included *some* testing. He just wasn't willing to pay for it.

They looked at us with strange eyes at that point, because in their minds, the conversion really was only about the *development* effort, not the testing. After all, they had only converted (and not tested) the first stored procedure, and had not considered the additional time for testing, integration and production release.

Don't be naive, it's not *that* simple.

Case Study Short: We assured a group that we could get their entire environment converted from its old technology and into Netezza, even with hundreds of stored procedures to convert. At the eleventh hour, they let us know that they planned to use a Netezza competitor. We had specifically included in our contract that our schedule and deliverables assumed the presence of the Netezza 10100 as the development machine, because the whole schedule was pretty aggressive already. When we were told that the technology was about to change, we sent them a new contract. Nothing in particular had changed with the people or the money, but their choice of technologies had converted the project from a self-contained Netezza project and into a multi-platform data processing project, with an ETL product as the centerpiece. The competitor technology they had chosen was geared for query acceleration, not data processing. Where would we process the data now? In the ETL layer. A standard Jurassic Park model. It's interesting how the change in technology actually changes the focus and nature of the project and its deliverables.

What this also meant, was they would need to invest more money in their new reporting technology, and ramp up the ETL server as well. The principals were flummoxed. They had thought the purchase of this competitor technology would save them some money, but found out that the decision was about to cost them more. Why?

Because the data has to be processed. Somewhere. And the chosen reporting technology was five times slower for loading and writing data. Meaning it was also much slower for testing.

As a simple example: All of their existing stored procedures already performed multiple bulk select/from/insert operations. One in particular required around thirty minutes, but on the Netezza platform it ran "as is" in less than five minutes. On their "other platform", this same stored procedure ran in fifteen minutes. Still down from thirty, so it's not all bad. But consider the testing lifecycle. For each day of testing of the Netezza-based solution, it will take three days on the other platform. This literally inflates the project timeline from the *inside-out*.

This is no different than a person getting an estimate from a charter jet company for the duration of a flight, and finding out that even on their best corporate jets, they will get across country in less than an hour - and when they inquire as to how long it would take with a propeller plane, they learn it will take much longer and cost more, because they pay their pilots by the hour.

The point of all this is, the actual development cycle of these artifacts is usually a very short ride. The testing is the primary problem-at-hand, and this always requires an infrastructure and some *significant* power. If our environments are highly application-centric, we'll want to leverage the good ideas from other groups but cannot without building them from scratch ourselves. One delivery point will then experience one level of quality, while another delivery point will experience another.

They will then compare notes and weigh our teams in the balance.

Common weakness of "applications"

When we roll out our first application into production, everyone shouts for joy and the users sing our praises. They raise obelisks and etch our names on them, and generations tell of our derring-do. At least, it sounds good on paper.

Upon initial rollout. something interesting happens. The users tell us of all the *other* things they want the machine to do. We might not hear about them right away, but rest assured, they're thinking about it. All that humming power inside the machine, ready to churn ever more quantities of data, and ever more applications of the technology.

Oh, yes, they want more applications on it. So while our work is done and we ride into the sunset, another team follows. They build out a schema and their own directory structures, landing zones, etc. They might leverage part of what we did. Either way, it's another bouncing baby application.

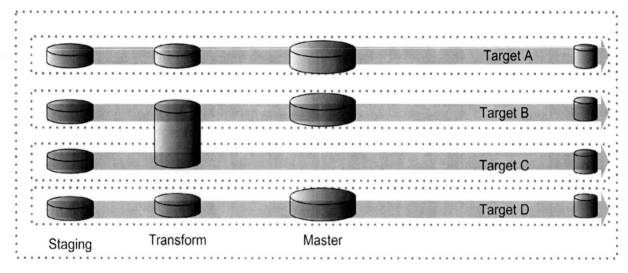

In the depiction (above) we now have our secondary app, and even a third and fourth application, all sharing the machine but little-else. We're using the machine's architecture, but not our own, and we're actually moving toward *stovepipes-in-a-box*. We *can* avoid this, and we *should* avoid this, if we decide to.

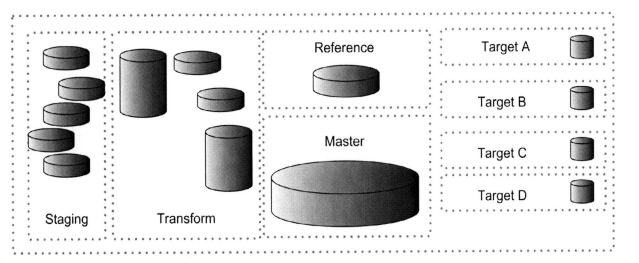

In the depiction (above) we've separated the capabilities into patterns, and have coalesced some functionality into capability. We have staging (intake), a transformation area (for administering our business rules, error records and reporting the health of our work), master and reference repositories, and finally the application views at the end of the chain. It is a better balance of functionality and capability. Or rather, we now have a capability-set that harness the machine's power, leading to the exposure of features to support the fire-breathing users.

What is all of this leading to?

Capability versus Feature

We must decide where our real architectural priorities are, and what roles the environment is intended to fulfill. In the *Delivery Highway* section above, I noted the separation of the architecture into multiple layers to achieved differently managed lifecycles. Here, we have a primary reason why the separation is so necessary. It has to do with stability, scalability and adaptability, all of which are found in leveraging the *systems* for highest throughput and the *feature-delivery* environment for highest user turnaround.

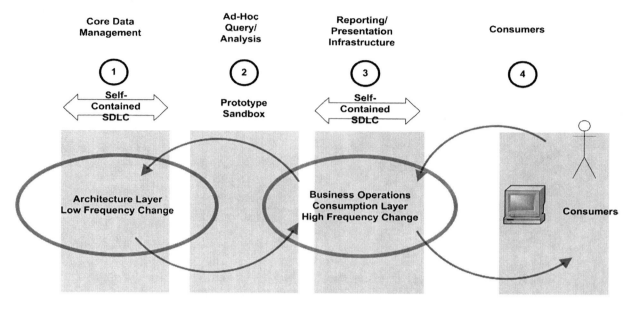

Architectural layer
- low-frequency change (self-contained lifecycle)
- capability-focused
- system-facing
- large-scale transform and integration
- deals directly with the "how" question
- managed by architects and IT staff

Consumption layer
- high-frequency change (self-contained lifecycle)
- feature-focused
- report development
- user-facing
- deals directly with the "what" question
- managed by business analysts, user-facing developers or ad-hoc users.

- The *core architecture* faces the systems and the hardware, and is comprised of capabilities. It is stable, with a slow lifecycle.
- The *user functionality* (reports, etc) and data work products, face the user, and are comprised of features. It is more volatile, with a fast lifecycle.
- A nether-world between the two that supports prototyping and ad-hoc reporting

Separating capability from feature, effectively componentizes and harnesses our risks, giving us the elusive stability, scalability, and ultimately the adaptability we need to keep our warehouse engine resilient and healthy.

An architecturally-driven approach will deliberately separate the environment into at least two (if not more) separately-styled lifecycles using the architecture itself. This breaks apart the monolithic application-centric lifecycle and allows the core to rapidly stabilize, while it s consumers leverage it for a higher-intensity lifecycle. It's a rapid-delivery model, because it embraces and harnesses change where the heat is highest, and stabilizes the architecture where the heat is lowest.

What this means, is that we must have a clean, healthy division between the layers of the overall environment, one that faces the systems/hardware and one that faces the users. The separated lifecycles yield a repeatable pattern. With this, we can deploy a consumption layer, allowing rapid, user-facing change in a harnessed environment. The users can run at much higher speed and temperature. The architectural layer stabilizes the system-facing functionality as reusable, building-block *capabilities*. It is important to keep these activities inside the same infrastructure to avoid out-of-control prototypes that muscle their way into the production zone.

How does this affect our *overall* delivery lifecycle?

For most user-facing change requests (in fact 90 percent or more) the report developers can rapidly deliver them without any affects on the architecture at all. We thus deliver features *and* a lifecycle (rapid delivery) closer to the users, even right into the user's control. This is key, because in order to support rapid delivery, we have to shorten the lifecycle between the user's request and the user's consumption. The best way to do is to *remove all forms of IT intervention* from the regular lifecycle. IT intervention is then reserved for implementing new capabilities, in the core.

For requests that need non-yet-existent capabilities (low frequency) these changes are sent back into the architecture for review and implementation. But they still have lower frequency and longer testing lifecycles. Either way, we get the best of both worlds.

And we give fire-breathing users rapid *delivery*. We're heroes. Vicariously, but heroes nonetheless.

What does this approach buy us? For one, we will start treating the core data warehouse architecture (tables, structures, etc) within context of their underpinning power-plant. Like an *asset*. The core data warehouse architecture then conforms to a *collection of capabilities*. We ask questions of "can we do this-or-that" in terms of what the *physics*-facing environment itself is *capable* of. We upgrade to support capabilities. We extend, cluster or enhance to provide lift to the capabilities. When something inside the core must change, it's a capability change, driven by things that face the systems and hardware, not the applications. It happens on a slower, more controlled cycle. While this describes its function, it does not dictate form. I see flavors of this scenario all across the fruited plain. Not because it's something I came up with, but because this approach has a natural gravitational attraction.

In the depiction (above) the architectural layer is separately configured from the business intelligence and reporting layer. Both operate and change in different lifecycles. The architecture faces the systems, forming capabilities. The BI environment faces the users, expressing features that are borne on capability. This effectively decouples the common dependencies we see when capability and feature are so intertwined and married that they are indistinguishable. We *must* distinguish them if we are to meet the performance, management, administrative, operational, scalable and adaptive goals, whilst continuing to satisfy the fire-breathing users who rapid-fire new requirements by the hour, if not by the minute. The feature-layer then, can move in high-speed iteration that is unavailable in a monolithic application. It doesn't take the regular intervention of IT staff to affect small user-facing changes. They control their own destiny.

Another danger, is that if the capability and feature are married, then changing a feature impacts a capability, and may destabilize a totally unrelated part of the environment. This will cause our architects to institutionalize full impact review for the tiniest of changes. Separating these two areas can mitigate this necessity.

And this is key, because the applications will require a *completely different, faster lifecycle* than the core architecture. The applications may change by the month, day, or even by hour in the case of ad-hoc environments. This level of dynamism in the *application* is ideal and healthy, but toxic for the architectural layer.

Here's a good example for those who use SQLServer, who might not believe. Or if you are a Netezza user and sit next to a Microsoft guru, here's some fuel for your discussion:

How often do you upgrade your SQLServer instance? How often do you apply patches? How often do you upgrade from one edition (say SQL2000 to SQL2005). How often do these things occur, and do they impact your applications? The answer *should* be "not very often". Do we expect such patches or upgrades to directly affect our applications, or to simply fix a bug (e.g security) or provide additional capability of a particular functional area? One thing is certain: *We expect it to be centric to the engine software, but we sometimes fear that it will impact our applications.*

And this is because an environment that is constructed with this technology is rarely built with the *expectation of change*. It lauds agile development, but only until it's actually deployed. That's when "agile" is at *risk* - when we actually need it *most*. Such applications actually enter their "half life" cycle and will eventually decay and devolve no matter what we pour into them, because they were not constructed to withstand ongoing, dynamic change. The database and the application are so inextricably linked, they are one and the same.

We cannot afford to make this mistake in a data warehouse. The warehouse core architecture must be *distinguishably* separate from the applications that consume it.

This means we need to characterize features as separate from capabilities. Since our warehouse is requirements-driven, features are always at the fore, but we need to boil them a bit to get the patterns - or capabilities - out of them. Some things in a data warehouse are non-optional, and the application-facing requirements will never mention them.

Things like operational control, logs of bulk job workload, capacity metrics, flow control, nightly batch / bulk SLA timelines and the like. Application users will only want to know that they have a hard deadline *in your face* for when the data – by hook or by crook – is ready for their consumption.

We thus defend the core architecture from the destabilizing effects of dynamic user requests. Each time a user wants something new, it needs a home. If the architecture is indistinguishable from the features, both are at risk for destabilization - with each and every request from the users.

Of course, we can load up all of our data in the Netezza machine and then drop a front-end like Microstrategy or Business Objects on it. Doesn't this embrace the principle of separation? No, it embraces the implementation of separation, but not the principle. We can only embrace the principle if we don't violate the implemented separation with leakage across the boundaries. I've seen people install this very configuration, then work diligently to commingle the two environments so that it looks like a monolithic application from the tables-and-columns, to the reports, to the disk drives. Just because it's implemented in its de-facto state, doesn't mean the implementers have embraced the principles for doing so.

So what is a feature? A feature itself is customized *consumer of capabilities*. Feature definitions are predominantly driven by user-facing requests. If a user isn't asking for it, then it's not requirements-driven (from the user side) and represents no threat to the stability of the data warehouse. The warehouse core is driven by other non-user-facing priorities, and should only require change in the case of a new or enhanced capability.

While we might implement some features on a user's desktop by a user-facing developer, at some point they will want to directly access the data warehouse to deliver information to the user. The data warehouse does not care how the feature-facing technologies present themselves, it only needs to know what the application will require. What data? What performance? What intersections, views or APIs? The core architecture only interfaces to the user-facing features via *interface* descriptions, so each one of these represents a collection of one or more architectural capabilities.

What happens if a capability does not exist, or requires enhancement to fulfill a feature? We simply characterize, construct and deploy the new capability. It might take more review, more impact-testing, but we should do it so infrequently that it won't have egregious workflow impact. What kind of lifecycle does this have? Somewhat volatile at inception, but rapidly stabilizing to the point that we might not see changes in the core data warehouse for months, even years. I know of one warehouse environment for a major retailer that has maintained the same architectural model for almost ten years, and has only been tweaked twice in that time to increase the width of some text columns. The environment was originally built with the separation of architecture and application in mind. Even when the application needed to upgrade across several *years* of server functionality (Windows NT 4.0 to Windows XP in one jump), the core information architecture did not even blink. Many of you have experienced the same thing, whether by good architectural design or accidental brilliance. (Take credit for the brilliance, life's too short...)

This kind of separation requires *a priori* commitment on the part of the architects, and the architects alone, to disallow applications to corrupt the core with spontaneous feature requests. This also requires us to think of our environment in terms of two (or more) distinct layers, rather than one end-to-end *monolithic* configuration.

As noted in *Delivery Highway* above, Netezza gives us the core capabilities right inside the box. What's left for us, is to instantiate a robust data model and management layer. We have to do this anyhow, so let's make sure that all our data priorities continue to face the system and do not inadvertently align with the user layer. If we allow the user layer, and its attendant rapid lifecycle, to bleed into the core information architecture, stability may erode, to the point where we lose the more desirable scalability and adaptability.

How does all this fit with a Netezza implementation? With Netezza, our architectural layer is largely already in place. Instantiating the data model and other infrastructure issues are likewise faster to implement. We can then put any reporting engine we want to – right on top of it. I say, right on top, but we'll want decoupled views in Netezza also, as I'm not a big fan of allowing external processes direct access to warehouse tables. In the end, we'll have a stable, resilient architecture and a high-speed report development environment. Many environments have a very long distance between where they currently are and the decoupled environments noted above. Many others aren't very far away at all.

Important note #1: Don't arbitrarily throw away what Netezza gives you for free. Don't make the mistake of driving a methodology-driven, monolithic-lifecycle approach into your Netezza-centric environment. Rather, let the arrival of Netezza provide the power and impetus to get *away* from the monolithic lifecycle.

Important note #2: Don't put "high walls" between the two lifecycles or people will find ways to use loopholes and exceptions to circumvent them. The lifecycles and functional separation serve a valuable purpose, but always keep an open mind to exceptions. Our simple advice is to harness the exceptions within a governance protocol (and not a steep one either) that invites people to have an open discussion about what they really need. Otherwise they will find workarounds, and we'll see secret hooks, hidden capabilities, you know, Underground stuff, creeping into the implementation.

Very often we can accommodate an "exception" within the existing framework. If it cannot, harness it like anything else, but don't let it exist outside the mainstream, or it will take a life of its own and become a tumor. You think I'm kidding about this, but if we give people an inch, they won't just take a mile, they'll take ten and put another ten in the bank. "Scope creep" is an inside joke. Scope is very rarely "creeping" – it's in full-bore freight-train runaway.

Guard your environment, and don't let exceptions rule it.

Expectation of change

The most significant error we can possibly make in constructing our data processing environment, is the assumption that when we are done, that we are *done*.

We are never done.

We must construct our environment, end-to-end, with the *expectation of change*, not the fear of it.

We are simply on a journey with operational and deliverable pauses. We can decide when and where (and why) these pauses occur, but we cannot assume that any given pause is a final stopping point, or that our decisions can ever reflect such a point of view.

It's a spirit of the environment that needs to jump off the pages of our project plans, become regular terminology in all of our conversations, and certainly become an institution in our interactions with end-users.

Now the good news, Netezza makes this part a lot easier to pull off. Here's one example why:

Anytime our end-users need more power in the machine, it's because they need to access the data in a different way, or need more (or different kinds) of data. Netezza lets us pull new data in and rapidly integrate it with practically zero impact. In fact, that's the *easy* part.

In any *other* environment, the users eventually start complaining about reduced performance in their queries. We attempt to fortify their experience by adding index structures or aggregations (engineering) but find that it affects our ability to load the tables (those pesky index structures are always in the way). So one way or another, the incremental changes coming down from the users, are affecting our architecture in major ways.

Rework and redesign are on the horizon. Perhaps closer than we think.

Again, Netezza's core architecture comes to the rescue. With the absence of index structures (Netezza has none), we never fear such a request from a user. We could even play a game with them. They make a request, we tell them it will take two weeks, they complain and negotiate, we deliver it in a few days, they think we are heroes. (What they never realize, is the we are doing nothing but watching a clock and setting a reminder in our Outlook Calendar as to when to notify them). Because the bottom line is, their request is *already* delivered. They don't need any additional help from us to slice-and-dice on any column they choose. In Netezza, *every* column is fair game for search and consumption, *all* the time. Of course, if they learn of the game, our goose is cooked. We need another way to set their expectations.

How about this? We tell them that a long time ago, we made the best decision we could have *ever* made, and rolled out a Netezza platform. And now, anyone can just trot on out there, and fearlessly create high-intensity applications. We'll help configure the *really* complicated stuff. If they run into any issues, they can give us a shout. Off they go.

Does this sound like a utopian, even *unbelievable* kind of conversation? Well, perhaps only *slightly* embellished for dramatic impact, but functionally not off the mark at all. Those who have a Netezza machine know what it can do.

The better part, is that we can blissfully go about the business of our regular jobs, without worrying that we'll have this conversation too many times before it goes away completely. The Netezza machine is an appliance, sitting in the corner doing its job without much regular intervention on our part.

Where we drop the ball, is in assuming that the Netezza machine will simply read our minds and we have no responsibility toward putting together reasonably efficient structures and internal processes. To emphasize, they only have to be *reasonably* efficient, not consummately engineered for the highest *possible* throughput. We can expect throughput galore just by dropping the machine on the raised floor. Now we actually have the luxury of focusing on the business application and operation, without assigning a fleet of engineers to keep it humming.

How do we brace for change? When interacting with the user's needs, or the processing needs of the subscribers, we have fewer priorities now – like developing appropriately sized and configured data structures, assimilating and managing the data, and integrating the structures to create useful information. We'll have other issues similar to this, but note that they are all functional and information-centric priorities, and have little to do with *performance*. We now have the odd pleasure of actually dealing with data, and not the extraordinary heroism of keeping our *systems* optimized.

Netezza gives us the power to *actively morph* our environment into the next-generation needs of our users - either a piece at a time or all-at-once. What we really want, is to get there a piece at a time, to avoid the logistical danger of a "forklift" event. Our problem, is that our current environments are loaded with massive amounts of data. Without Netezza-like power, we have no mastery of it. We are its slaves, and we can only hope for forklift *events*, which themselves require enough power to create a rift in the spacetime continuum.

Better to do it incrementally for the users. This way it's all *requirements-driven,* and every part has a purpose. Our largest danger in a forklift event is when other people get wind of it, and want to piggyback on it, radically inflating our scope, effort and risk. If we can assimilate their requirements incrementally, like inhaling, we minimize impact and everyone gets what they want.

Netezza gives us this flexibility and adaptability, but only if we deliberately embrace it as a priority, and the *expectation of change* is ever-present. It will cause our developers and testers to think in terms of "what if" a change should impose itself, rather than with the false hope that our *next* delivery, will be our *final* delivery.

I've seen this mentality play itself out in the construction of data models, pushing for non-adaptive decisions that later had to undergo painful remediation. The non-adaptive decisions were constrained by the technology.

Then we see people pushing for their favorite bulk processing mechanism. Whether stored procedures (which have marginal *everything)* or towards a more formal ETL environment. The same rules apply – if we build things as though it's a project, with no vision for the future, the non-adaptability will find permanent residence in the core of the architecture.

"How did you complete the project so rapidly?" asked Fluke LieStalker.

"We finally reached critical mass in our functionality, and it imploded," said Harsh Grader, from the dark side of the Red-Eye Nights.

"You mean? ---"

"Yes, the implosion created a rift in the spacetime continuum, and a wormhole, allowing us to go back in time."

"Back in time?"

"Yes, the project actually traded one day for one year. It took ten years to complete in our frame-of-reference, but only ten days in your time frame."

"That's incredible. I just have one question."

"Yes?"

"Did you meet Elvis?"

Case Study Short: We also see people pushing for non-adaptive system environments, including marginal purchases made with no inkling as to their impact. One CIO received a request for a high-powered storage system. The sticker-shock for the system nearly gave him a heart attack. After defibrillation and medication, he called some representatives that could give him Big Storage for a Cheap Price, cut a contract and had the stuff delivered at the end of the week. His chief systems guy met with him and asked why he'd made such a unilateral decision without discussion. The storage system the CIO had purchased was for Departmental File Storage, not for Data Processing. In fact, the vendor had a *specific* disclaimer in the front of their literature – *not for bulk data processing or data warehousing.*

It's bulk processing. *Always* read the product label

The CIO mandated the team to *make it work.* After much malaise, mayhem and wasted time, the CIO eventually had to make the larger purchase and redeploy the first underpowered system for – you guessed it – departmental file storage. One poor decision led them down a bad path entirely.

At least, some people know when to fold 'em. I know of several environments that have lumbered along with their slower I/O storage, continuing to avoid the pain of making the right purchase the *second* time.

Non-adaptive decisions appear in many forms. When we embrace and promote the spirit of the *expectation of change*, we realize that more thought is necessary for our decisions and directions. More up-front work, to receive the payoff later. What does this kind of approach look like? How do we guard against non-adaptive decisions? How to we keep our environment fueled with healthy decisions?

The most significant questions we can ask, at any point in the continuum of deployment, are "Will I have to revisit this later, and how can I fix it now so that I will never revisit it?" In other words, program it *once*, deliver it *forever*.

Configuration files and reference data

We have two broad categories of reference data. One is business-facing (discussed next) and one is administrative or application-facing. This second category is so aligned with metadata that it appears indistinguishable unless we wrap some context around it. In metadata space, configuration files provide initialization context so that an application can instantiate into a known state. Afterward, we have behavioral metadata that provides steering logic for application behaviors. This can be in the form of business rules (e.g. the Postgres SQL of Netezza or the DML business rules of Ab Initio) or can be simple instructional cues.

Business reference data can also serve to guide an application's execution thread, but is largely something used to enrich the primary business data with more context or value. The following anecdote gives us insight.

Case Study Short: One of our clients purchased another company and initiated the migration of the new company's data into its own databases, to assimilate its customers, instruments and business transactions.

A critical part of the application was the master cross-reference file mapping all of the second company's business, application and accounting codes into our client's. Our main concern was that they were managing this cross-reference file under a separate configuration management and versioning protocol than the master application. Whenever they promoted the master application to production, they would have to separately promote this highly critical file as well. We feared that this "human discipline" portion of the promotion (depending on humans instead of machines to automatically promote the assets) was an Achilles heel.

The issue at hand was not whether promoting them simultaneously made good sense, but whether the file *belonged* with the application. I know this sounds like a purist kind of argument, but the team felt that the file, being application-facing data, did not belong with the assets of the application itself. It integrated to the data that the application would process, and since none of that business data was part of the *application's* assets, they didn't think this file should be, either. It was categorized as *reference* data, not an application asset.

Our assertion was twofold - *one* that the file's data provided application steering logic and *two* that if someone forgot to promote the file along with the application, then the application would not run correctly and thus provide bad output. In short, a purist view of reference data is that it's not part of the application, but this was a *one-time*-execution. It required *special* handling.

In this case, both file and application had to be promoted *at the same time*. The rules of information theory apply here, which warn us that any transition of information from one environment to another has the potential for the loss of information. The application assets and this cross-reference file represented information. Dependence on humans, and not automated processes to abate the loss of information, is not a wise choice. Humans invariably inject procedural error. We are charged with setting up automated procedures so that the human cannot make a manual procedural error.

We are also charged with setting up a mission-critical, *automated* environment that in no way implicitly *trusts the discipline of a human*.

We were requested to a meeting held by the leaders overseeing this project, where we expressed our concern for this, and other aspects of their environment, that were not ready for prime time. They were willing to fix all the outstanding issues, which we frankly considered to be nits, but were almost adamant, based on *principle* mind you, that this cross-reference file was a non-issue and they had it under control. We tried to explain it one more time, with our concerns and potential outcome as the highlights. The project leader heard us out, then simply turned to our principal and said something like, *"Are we ever going to get past this?"*

At this point, it was clear that they had no intention of moving one inch on this issue, so we dropped it and we never discussed it again. The following weekend was their big-bang assimilation run. They kicked it off around six PM on Friday and it finally wrapped up all of its processing late Sunday evening. Everyone was happy, elated in fact, that the entire run had executed end-to-end with no stoppages or cancellations.

Monday morning, however, they learned the truth. The pesky cross-reference file had *not* been promoted into the production machine. The version they had run, while *mostly* correct, was not the correct version. They spent the next *two weeks* backing out the data that they had inserted to the master transactional systems. In the meantime, the project leader adjured the team to promote the cross-reference file into production, so that when they ran the transfer again, all would be well.

We maintained silence.

The next weekend, now three weeks having passed since the prior failed weekend. They were ready to roll. They kicked off the application at the same time and it finished at roughly the same time. When they arrived the next Monday, to their chagrin and horror, they found that the *wrong cross-reference file* had been promoted to the production environment. The developer who promoted it - thought they wanted it promoted from the *pre-production* machine, so he copied this one. What they really wanted was still on the *development* machine.

So now we have two lost weekends and by the time they performed the final run, were ten weeks behind.

All from a fixable configuration problem. One with an outcome *so* predictable, it made me look almost like a pre-cog.

The takeaway from all this, is to not get lost in nomenclature, the role or the spirit of what our application assets are "meant" to be, or are "supposed" to do. This is a science, we should treat it that way. "Purist" philosophies are sometimes impractical. Something that keeps coming up over and over again, is that anything we are doing manually to *configure* the environment, we should drive into configuration files that we can leverage *repeatedly*. Our "purist" discomfort with it now, will abate when we realize the benefit later. Taking this step allows us to build more and better applications that have a common foundation.

What the team above missed, is that they should have recognized weakness of the asset-promotion system and done something to *protect* themselves. But they didn't, and assumed that the human actors would make up for the weaknesses of technology using brute force-of-will or their own discipline. These are never reliable, so why would we *ever* depend on them? Or for that matter, disregard them as a critical failure point?

Reference data

Business Reference Data can also serve to guide an application's execution thread, but is largely used to enrich the primary business data with more context or value. We can also leverage other forms of reference data (to make our own lives easier.) Here's a quick taste:

- Business calendar – invaluable to determine what days actually count for business processing. For example, our business days might include all weekdays but not weekends. It might also include a weekly breakdown of five-week months or even thirteen-month years. We should never assume that our business calendar is the solar calendar. Nor should we assume that every day is a *processing* day.
- Time-zone windows - invaluable to determine when our zone-based windows appear, and when we can start processing one versus another. If we need to process Singapore's data now but not London's, we can start processing the Asian markets when they close, and prep for the close of the UK markets. The globalization of our business day may require us to bite off the work in different time-boxed chunks. One of our client does their end-of-day processing in a sweeping window of two-hour timeframes, one each for Asia, UK, American East coast and West coast. This allows them to deliver reports and end-of-day reconciliation to the Asian markets before the close-of-business on the West coast. Reference data gives us the rolling interval.
- Trade calendar – for trading environments, we know that the trading floors are only open on certain days and certain hours. If we trade internationally, we also have windows where some markets close while others are open.
- Stock ticker symbols – one of our clients receives stock trade requests for execution from a variety of members and individuals. The stock tickers have some odd characteristics. Some of them appear as four character, some as three, and some as either one with qualifiers such as OTC (Over-the-counter). Once inside the shop, the processing environment would scrub these incoming values to a common one they could use to interact with their vendors, using reference data. Then something new happened, the members and individuals wanted their data reported back *in the same form they had sent it.* And since every member used different qualifiers in different formats, the client had to make a decision – accommodate the request

or require all the members to otherwise comply. Wanting to be a good service provider, the client used member-facing cross-reference data, such that the ticker data coming to and from a given member was transparently interchanged with the correct information.

- Index symbols – the market indices have an equally dynamic flavor as the equities mentioned above. Cross-referencing is strong kung fu.
- Cross-referenced account codes – we often see cases where business-to-business interfaces have to interpolate, transpose or otherwise cross-reference external data with internal equivalents, coming and going.
- Cross-referenced industry codes – good examples include state codes, zip codes, IRS codes and various other published sources. We should pull what we need into our local environment and leverage it for consistency.
- Formula tables and cross-references - for scientific applications and those using pre-calculated tables, or for high-math applications (analytics, etc) requiring statistical reference or table information.
- Versioning - in all the above and more, we need a way to capture what the reference data was at a point-in-time. For regulatory compliance in financial systems, someone may ask to reproduce a report from two years back. Can we do this from the *valid* reference data for *that* time period? Versioning our reference data is a daunting task, indeed, but this is simply metadata of the reference data, and is itself reference data (does the rabbit-hole *have* a bottom?)

"Take the whole bottle of red pills, and I'll help you count the rabbit holes, and give them names," - Lawrence Fishburn, *Waitrix and Grommit, the Nurse of the Where-Rabbit.*

Netezza gives us organizational control over data through sheer muscle alone. Of course, in order to use reference data, we need to leverage it either as a *filter* or an *join-enrichment* to master data. Meaning that we apply the filter or join on-demand. These both align *perfectly* with Netezza's architecture and actually boost our performance *and* our control over the information.

An RDBMS will require us to import, index and publish the reference data, it won't let us do much more. One may ask, what else is there besides importing the data? How about reconciling it with its original source? Removing or housekeeping the information, scrubbing any creeping contamination or staleness? Some of these reference data stores can be enormous. How do we perform housekeeping and optimization on them without having to take the RDBMS offline for a maintenance cycle? Index maintenance alone will drag us into the weeds. Oh yeah, we can extract it into our ETL environment and then put it back. But people don't like doing that. They only like to use ETL when the data is going somewhere *else*.

It's *still* bulk processing, and people who embrace reference data as an invaluable resource sometimes find themselves in the malaise of bulk data processing *the reference data* in the RDBMS - where it's all stored (see Rule #10). We run out of gas, out of time and eventually out of patience and resolve. At some point we want to fix it, but don't have the power.

Alas.

In Netezza, we don't have these issues. We can do the housekeeping processes in the same relative minutes as we do normal data processing. We have additional options to physically partition the data (later) so we never experience a processing hiccup. Reference data then stays up to date, we never accumulate any source-driven contamination, and we have the ability to actually *version* the reference data in case we need to reproduce a result from the past. It's all good.

Operational resilience

One of the more interesting conversations we'll ever have is the breathless rant from the operators. The poor blokes and sheilas who received a brittle, poorly designed environment, administered with spit and bailing wire, and clearly the result of people who place no priority on the operators' personal time.

I've seen operators literally flash out, almost spinning into a cinder as they explain their environment. One of them even "fled the interview". What *the*? His peer told us that he'd been reprimanded by his boss for complaining all the time, and just one more complaint would get him fired. He thought the interview was a setup! Oh well, you never know what's in someone's head.

I had a conversation with the individual's boss and lightly skirted the issue. Seems that the operator had registered a series of very *valid* complaints, all of which were already on the top of our list, but the boss did not see these as priorities. Operators, in the boss' mind, were *supposed* to be the monkeys on the operations floor. It never occurred to him that the operations floor, if risk was reduced to zero, should be quiet as a tomb (cooling fans notwithstanding, of course).

From a bulk processing perspective, operational priorities include the ability for an operator to know, in no uncertain terms, that in the given batch cycle there is a finite set of work to do. How many tasks are complete? How many are remaining? Of those that are running, how far along are they? Are we on schedule? Are we ahead or behind? What percent-error exists? How can we do better?

If the architects and developers deliver an environment that cannot measure and publish the metrics, we've hamstrung our operators and created risks for ourselves. We have inconsistent implementations, application execution and design, and operational support in the form of logging, health reports and the like. We'll need more people, and the operational footprint will be more expensive.

In short, we can't measure *anything*. This is like driving in the dark without headlights. Or driving in the fog with the headlights on bright. At ninety miles an hour. The driver had better know the road. As for the passengers, you've never seen knuckles so white.

What do operators need most? Assurance and status. They need assurance that the processing cycle is on track, and if not, that they can get it back on track. They need status to know where they stand, in a form that's systematic and easy to understand. It should ideally deliver a message as to the health of what it just accomplished. Total records processed, total time, disk required, errors reported, percentage and counts that allow the operators to let the users know – *all is well* – and *what to do if it's not*. If it's not actionable, it's not practical.

In case we missed it, we just identified a *core capability* that we will need for all of our operations, not just one or a few. We need all the operations and applications playing inside the same visible, operational and manageable sandbox. Whenever a new bulk process enters the arena, it has to follow the same rules, start and finish the same way, and provide the same statistics while it's in the house. This is a very daunting thing for the programmers to tediously install for each application, so it's better if the developers can plug their stuff into a framework, like a capability, that already provides it. Of course, this will require the developer to align their work products with the framework. But this is exactly what we want, that they are in compliance *simply by participating*.

Views

I'm a fan of views if for only one reason – they *decouple* the external consumers from the core schema, in fact from the database itself, and give the implementers more control over supporting the consumer's experience. Of course, the better part of the view is that the business logic to produce the view's output is hosted and managed in one place - the view. Not across the vast expanse of the distributed application(s).

The Netezza view has a cool feature, in that an existing view can be replaced in one, non-interruptible operation, without having to drop it first and then replace it. This avoids the risk of disruption if anything should happen between these operations.

We have another benefit of Netezza views, that we can change the view without disrupting the currently active *read* operations. (Use the *create-or-replace-view* syntax).

Synonyms are the next section, which we could use to replace views, except that we cannot change a synonym with a create-or-replace. We have to drop-and-restore, potentially disrupting the user's experience. The danger is that if a user is currently reading the table underlying a view, the read will continue unabated. If a user comes to read the table through the synonym after we just dropped it (and before we restore it), we will risk the disruption of the user experience.

It is best to use these two capabilities in tandem. Recall that we can prep a table prior to turning the view loose on it. Likewise for a synonym. If we use a view to control the consumer's access to the synonym, we can configure another synonym to reference what we really want to see next, then simply reconfigure the view on top of the synonym . The new synonym will be assimilated with no issues. The old synonym is never dropped, because only the view has visibility to it.

The primary reason to use a Netezza view, then is to *steer* the entry points of users, primarily the *more automated* users. I say this because many architects and DBAs think that this decoupling is unnecessary for advanced tools like Business Objects, because these products have their own semantic layer. That's great, as long as we understand that those semantic layers belong to *them* not to *us*.

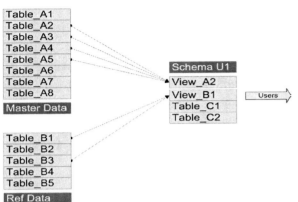

A view or synonym (left) keeps users from directly accessing the table structures, which is de-facto permission to raid all of our tables. This would be true of *any* RDBMS as well, especially where it concerns extraction-points from those databases. These systems provide a means to put an API *on top of* the tables, specifically to decouple the consumer's dependency on the underpinning structures.

Of course, if we let our BO group run around willy-nilly in the data warehouse, they will have permission to raid all of our tables, and when we need to restructure data for supporting additional applications, we risk disrupting our existing users *at the point of entry.*

Note in the graphic (above), how the view can use a complex SQL query to combine multiple tables into a single output. It is more powerful than a synonym, which is constrained to only and only one table.

Not wanting to go completely overboard with this, however, we might want to consider simply using synonyms for our ad-hoc users, considering that they need some general configurability but also some agility (meaning – less formality) in the interface. The objective is to use the best interface for the given constituency, and the closer we get to tools or automated access consumers, the more we need to decouple that consumer from the underlying data structures.

Synonyms for Configuration Control

Synonyms provide a means to alias our table structures and other entities. More importantly, we can synonym *across* schemas. For example, if we need to get read-access to a table in one schema while operating in the context of another, we would normally use the notation:

```
schema..table
```

Where the double-dot "`..`" notation gives us the cross-schema reference. However, Netezza will not allow us to *write* to a table in one schema while connected to another, we can only read from it.

I like that notation for batch style processing, because the people closest to the database are controlling it. But when it comes to a BI environment such as Business Objects, Cognos, etc, we might not want these products directly accessing the database schemas or tables anyhow, or have to worry about whether another external schema integrates with their own. It seems like too much structural dependency and tight coupling, *because it is*. So synonyms are a viable entry-point for our external users. I will deal with the cross-database scripting later, because for internal data processing, it can be a very powerful configuration tool.

A synonym *logically* resides as part of the *local* schema, and can point to data in other schemas, which means that we still can't write to it, but it certainly means that we can treat it like *local* inventory. This is a great configuration feature, but I still sometimes put the synonyms under a view, because I might not want to grant direct access to a core table, especially not its structure. A view keeps a consistent structure no matter what the underpinning structures might end up looking like over time. We can set up a view to consume any table or synonym, so the underpinning configuration remains decoupled from the user. We will always want to protect the freedom to restructure or refactor the underpinning data structures, but this is not always possible if they've been exposed to the outside world.

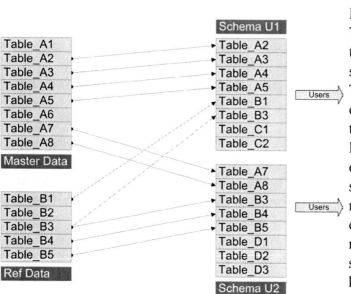

Note in the configuration (left), the Master Data and Ref Data are repositories. Their tables have synonyms attached to them in entirely different, user-facing schemas (Schema U1 and Schema U2). This allows a user base to log into their own schema and see their own *local* tables (Respectively C1/C2 and D1/D2/D3 above) commingled with read-only repository tables that are simply synonyms to their underlying physical repository table. Users have access to a discrete set of repository tables and no more. They all appear to be part of the same family, and the applications don't know the difference.

What if the underpinning table needs to change? Aren't we on the hook for having published this table's structure? Aren't we responsible for making sure that the consumers of the synonym are never disrupted?

Yes we *are*.

Keep in mind that the synonym is only viable to reference another single object, such as a table. The view (described prior) can reference multiple objects and can perform highly complex SQL queries as well. It is often a more viable, powerful and flexible decoupling option than a synonym alone.

Using synonyms (see depiction above), we can:
- Create a single schema containing bulk test data, and use synonyms to subscribe to it from other schemas
- Create a single schema containing reference data, likewise subscribing to it from other schemas

- Create a single schema containing shared repository data, exposing it via synonym to (one or more) schemas containing application-facing data
- Provide multiple schemas, each controlled by specific security options, for facing an external consumer or publisher, each containing the data necessary for that consumer, and containing (via synonym) shared data used by all consumers (or all schemas)
- Provide a metadata schema containing administrative, operational, configuration, statistical and other forms of common metadata, and expose the schema's tables, via synonym, to the remaining schemas
- Provide one or more schemas containing a repository of regression testing data, allowing the application (through synonyms) to transparently consume different schemas during testing.
- Provide a pre-production schema that we can "point" to in a production deployment, such that it behaves exactly the same as production for core reading tables, but has local pre-production tables for writing. Allows for a pre-production implementation with transparency in the configuration.
- Avoids the necessity to handle schema configuration in the application or with global configuration variables, reducing complexity and propensity for injection of human error
- Provide a "production backup" schema, so that if the production of the primary schema information should fail to meet an SLA, become corrupted or otherwise miss its readiness window, the users can be pointed (via synonyms) to the tables of a backup schema (usually containing the last-known-good results). It also allows production support people to scramble to fix the broken data, and later switch the users to the latest-and-greatest with a transparent synonym change.
- Relatively transparent configuration control

These are just a few examples of using synonyms to affect transparent configuration management. A configuration manager can then set up the synonyms as part of a central configuration model, under governance, and keep reasonable control without disrupting the individual application logic. It supports testing and pre-production deployment, lots of creative things.

Caveat: Unlike a view, a synonym has to be dropped, then reconfigured. The dropped synonym can create an issue with users that are already online. But a view/synonym combination can mitigate this, provided that only the view accesses the synonym.

Parameters for Configuration Control

While using schema-level synonyms provides us with a way to publish the data structures to external consumers, we also need to provide agility to the *internal* data consumers, that is, batch data processing and any bulk-related operations. Just as we would not require our core Java components to enter another component through the user's API, we should not require our bulk applications to jump through hoops either.

Of course, this requires some degree of discipline on the part of the architects, but no more than we would expect of the programmers who are actually laying down the scripts and SQL statements. Contrast these priorities with the following:

- **Product-centric** - A BI environment that manufactures SQL on-the-fly based upon a set of point-click semantic rules (features)
- **Internal / SQL-centric** - scripted environment with SQL statements that are hand-crafted and tuned for specific batch, bulk and flow effects (capabilities)

Between the two scenarios above, the synonyms are a great fit for products (scenario #1), but are simply in-the-way for canned internal work (scenario #2). We will have testers that want to have their own self-contained schema, perhaps several of them, and will not want to swap out whole banks of synonyms to perform their testing. It is far easier to provide some hooks to the various sources, and then environment variables to self-contain these hooks.

Ultimately we can always publish the schema for external users in any form that works best, but we should not push these configuration priorities too deeply into the testing and development environments because they will create artificial logistics. These serve to frustrate our delivery and raise more questions than answers in the environments that need to be answering all the questions!

In the end, we can override the environment variables with command-line parameters to point, pull, and manipulate our data experience with far greater agility. This takes a very simple form, keeping in mind that it is BASH-shell syntax.

```
export SOURCE_DB=mysource
export TARGET_DB=mytarget

$NZSQL  -d $TARGET_DB <<-!

Insert   into   myMainTable   select   *   from   ${SOURCE_DB}..
myMainTable;

!
```

Does this seem strangely verbose? Keep in mind that for system-level and lights-out component scripts, this form is the most agile and testable. We can derive sources instantaneously with a simple command-line override, without the invasive synonym changes we would otherwise require.

Here's a case where we combine the NZSQL statement into a Begin/End block as follows:

```
export SOURCE_DB=mysource
export TARGET_DB=mytarget

export NZSQL_START="$NZSQL -d $TARGET_DB <<!"
export NZSQL_END="!"
```

Now we would see the aforementioned construct as:

```
${NZSQL_START}

Insert    into    myMainTable    select    *    from    ${SOURCE_DB}..
myMainTable;

${NZSQL_END}
```

Here are two common scenarios:

Developer A makes some data processing scripts that transform several internal tables into several more consumption-ready tables for later publication. He wants to leverage the smaller testing tables in his local schema for his functional testing. After the tests are complete, he wants to point to some larger tables filled with model functional data as a source.

To do this with synonyms, he must drop his local tables (which he may desire to come back to shortly) and then add synonyms to his schema that point to the model data schema. Once he completes his tests, he must drop the synonyms and then re-establish his original testing tables.

Another option is to have yet another schema containing his test data, that he can synonym-swap back-and-forth with the model data synonyms. The problem here is that we have to maintain more scripts for this, effectively managing synonym-swap-scripts. It's just another system component. In the end, *some script* has to touch the base tables and organize them. All we're really discussing here is what level we want that to be.

I like helper-scripts, but *they* require configuration management, too.

The above is a very common testing scenario *for all technologies*. Much of our testing can be very tedious and mind-numbing, and we really need to remove the total number of steps it takes to perform setup. Someone with a tired, numbed mind, no matter how adept they are when initially slinging the business functionality, will find themselves fat-fingering things and wasting time - all very tedious and cumbersome. Especially when the final application logic runs in a lights-out component that will never see the light of day.

Developer B wants to drive the Netezza machine from an ETL environment, launching SQL statements remotely. He will send largely raw data into the machine, then launch a series of SQL statements that will command Netezza to transform the data from the raw form into consumption-ready form. Here we have a risk in the ETL environment's coupling to the Netezza internal environment - which we want to be as decoupled as possible. Rather than use parameters, we would use synonyms, and the ETL environment's references become transparent, but remains manageable by the Netezza administrators with little overhead. As this is a *formal* interface, we should have no issues in putting together formal scripts to deal with synonym-management issues.

The point of all this configuration-kung-fu, is to avoid standardizing on one-and-only-one scenario that will hamstring one or more of our technical staff. Netezza provides a lot of mix-and-match options, so our responsibility is simply to harness the ones that work best for the task at hand, for the given user base.

It's an *appliance*.

In all of the examples I'll provide in this book, I'll often include the parameter-driven form as the baseline, because the synonym-driven form is transparent to the examples.

Combining with a transactional database

Many transactional database environments will allow for views and stored procedures that can "reach across" or "drill through" to another machine to plumb its information. This is a great way to leverage Netezza, with one major point of interest:

Don't use Netezza for transactional I/O. It's a floor wax, not a dessert topping.

Many environments will put a front-end on top of their transactional environments and then allow the users to query-through to pull back history records from the Netezza repository. This is an *awesome* way to use the Netezza platform, because it's serving a reporting-styled purpose. It captures groups and lists of records rather than one-record-at-a-time pulls, and can also be optimized through read-only views or other structures.

But if we use it this way, we are committing to a read-only access in the spirit of user-side reporting queries. We *must* draw the line when it comes to writing *back* to Netezza in a transactional manner. We could *possibly* have the user interface launch a load procedure, or another internal SQL statement to produce a summary output, etc. But these are all still scanning queries that do not themselves receive data input from the user interface.

If we intend to take user interface transactional data to the Netezza machine, we will need to bundle it, "collector/ fan-in" style, into a large enough load to justify Netezza's intake. We have a number of ways to do this, discussed elsewhere in "Loading" and "Continuous Stuff".

Case Study Short: One environment had a gaggle of transactional servers that each opened a spontaneous Netezza ODBC interaction and dribbled over the handful of records they had just processed. With several dozen machines simultaneously performing this work, the user complained that Netezza did not seem to be performing as advertised.

We then restructured these operations to push their data to a collection repository, which Netezza would receive on regular intervals, effectively bundling the work (fanning-in) into larger data loads. Those who use Ab Initio's Continuous Flows product will recognize this as a "compute point". It is a *very* common EAI approach to "reservoir" data so that its delivery is more efficient.

Some will also recognize this as *serialization* even when we want to go parallel. If we have enough data to justify a parallel load, we should do it. But the above is in context of *not* having enough *at one time*, and the two are *not* the same. An example of this is also found in *MQSeries* and *MSMQ*, where we can program the queues to collect a certain quantity of information before initiating the downstream feeds. This maximizes the bandwidth of the network with right-sized feeds rather than swamping the network with the feed-related overhead. (every feed has some front/back overhead).

We'll discuss optimum loading sizes/intervals a little later.

Materialized views

The vendor is quick to suggest that we should keep "0 to 1" MVs per table, with the implicit assumption that MVs are an optimization, not a required feature. MVs can be very powerful tools to publish our data automatically through some discrete business rules. I would not advocate them for simple extraction. But MVs have a lot of power when it comes to supporting our run-of-the-mill query activities from a common BI platform.

In a common table, the zone map provides us with incredible filtration lift, but the MV takes it a step further, offering the ability to zone-map on any column data type, not just the de-facto integer-and-date in a common zone map.

Here's why: In a regular view, we'll be hitting the same tables as everyone else. That's fine, but the query efficiency will always move toward the "lowest SQL" denominator. As our tables increase in size, zone maps and other filtrations keep our tables running at top speed. We might find some order of higher efficiency by squeezing down the data size by columns and rows into a smaller subset. Typically the users don't really want to see *all* the data. Their queries usually fall within a discrete subset of activity, and the MV is just the ticket. As a configuration mechanism, it allows us to know exactly what parts of the given table are published to the users, the same effect we experience with a common view.

Think of an MV as a *kind* of cube, only with the parallel arrays powering it. Netezza throws us some caveats about their loading and maintenance. Pay attention to those, because they can create unnecessary angst if ignored. The MV is significant power-tool in the Netezza arsenal. It is a pre-fabricated form of oft-used information. The MV is also kind of like a query-extension for base tables. When the base gets too big and redundant, the MV is the happy, automatic medium between keeping the data in separate tables or doing schema engineering, which we definitely want to avoid.

The vendor has promised extensions to the MV with clustered bases, offering more multi-dimensional power in locating data. This is a lot like a MV on steroids, and if you can imagine a common RDBMS star-schema on a 32-shot Starbuck's latte, laced with crystal-meth - hey, you're in the ballpark. In the estimation of many, the technology we use is a lot like choosing the right drug. Some drugs are better than others, they claim, and it's the ones that offer the mellow after effect, with no paranoia, that we come back to, no?

This is your data on the RDBMS, and this is your data on Netezza, any questions?

As for configuration management, MVs are a step above the regular view interface and still provide the right level of decoupling, with the bonus of bringing the physical data closer to the user in more consumable form. Keep in mind what a configuration model intends to support –

A consistent user experience, using the most effective harness without tightly coupling anything together.

For common extracts, especially automated extracts or repetitive extracts, the MV is probably not the right choice. We can serve plain-straight extracts with external tables, and when the user comes to get the data, they don't hit the SPUs at all, but get the same extract performance as if they had. I dive a little deeper into external tables elsewhere.

Summary Table Kung Fu

Invariably on a migration project, we hear the technologist blurt that the summary tables are all going away. The users freak-out of course, because the summary tables are their window to the universe of data, and they need them badly. Announcing their demise is often a very painful event for some.

In fact, it might turn into a painful event for *us* as well, because these technology decisions have political ramifications. Sometimes the users put up a hard wall and say they must have their existing summaries restored and supported. They have a real concern that we must take seriously, and is a breach of configuration control if we do not. Their existing consuming interfaces access our published interfaces, the summary tables, and as publishers we have an unconditional covenant to support what we've published. So let's just do that. Give them the summary table and be done with it. Considering that it only takes minutes to manufacture one, this might not be something worth fighting over.

What we *can* do, is give them the summary table and put a view on top of it. The users enter the data through the view, consume the summary table and all is right with the world. Our political woes have abated - with an added benefit. We can now revisit the summary table anytime we like and use the view interface to perform the summary operation on-demand.

"I'm uncomfortable that we have an unlicensed, untested warehouse solution on our backs," said Aykroyd.

"I blame myself," said Ramis.

"So do I," said Murray.

- DataWarehouseBusters

Boot Camp Stuff

HERE WE launch into several chapters on essential performance stuff. We have some groundwork to cover first, since the Netezza platform harnesses so many things for free, it's important to use the machine in the spirit of its original construction. At least, to get the best user experience.

All apologies if some of it sounds remedial. We're just being a little more thorough than necessary for some readers, perhaps not as thorough as others would like. But these are *Essential* Netezza, not *Compleat* Netezza.

Strategy vs Tactical

A sage said once that some people plan the work, and some people work the plan. The former is strategy and the latter is tactical. Strategy vs Tactical has many shapes and sizes, but for most development projects we will always have some degree of chaotic activity, especially if we want to embrace an agile model. Some overseers regard this madness with a skeptical eye, so we need a way to explain the madness - it boils down to whether there is method in the madness, rather than madness in the method.

Case Study Short: The following is an anecdote from a California-based colleague and a client on the West Coast, used by permission.

"Our team plus the client's team were all in a room trying to decide the best approach to prove out a Netezza platform, and the best method to determine if we had in fact proven it. One of the leaders said that each of us should take his own track, and by doing so (and keeping up with our own activities) we can each assault the mountain from a different angle, and compare notes when we got to the top. An objection to this was that if each person took a different path, some might take shortcuts, some might not make it to the top at all.

Another leader objected for a different reason, saying that we already knew what we wanted to do and how to go about it, let's just take a general path up the mountain, with the whole team in one "assault" crew so to speak. This way we could all leverage each other's strengths and learn together along the way. The first leader disagreed with this, but nobody else did. It seemed like the right thing to do, so we took this path.

And what do you know - it really was the right thing to do.

When we wrapped up the first assault on the mountaintop, we had gained immeasurable understanding (separately and as a team) in a very short period of time. The first aforementioned leader continued to claim that our approach had been too *limiting*. That we did not give ourselves the freedom to find the best way up the mountain, only the most expedient, given the size of the team. *So many* combinations still existed, he asserted, and we should examine all of them.

Upon decompressing with several after-action meetings, we discussed what we had done with each turn of the path up the mountain. We looked at this and tweaked that. We added this and tuned that. This same leader offered a number of different "additional" solutions (discussed next) that he felt a broader approach would have honored. When we asked him what those things might be, he started describing additional tactics that we had not only considered, *they were actually a part* of the go-to-production solution now underway in testing.

When this leader learned that we had actually applied what he felt like were *his* innovative ideas, he looked like he'd somehow been betrayed. He said that if we really had deviated from our stated path in such a manner, this would have been "cheating".

Now, when you're in the zone of solving someone's business-critical and time-sensitive processing problem, it's not exactly cheating to find the best path and apply it. None of us had a clue what he was talking about. Cheating? Was this some kind of test? A contest? We were confused.

So at this point we learned something important. Either this particular leader did not know how to articulate his own strategies, or we did not know how to articulate ours. As with most things, the truth is always in the middle. What he said that he *wanted* to do, was have everyone go their separate way up the mountain. What we collectively *decided* to do, was to go up the mountain as a team, dynamically investigating the path and conforming our assault to the shape of the mountain, in whatever upward-meandering form this might take.

What the leader actually *heard*, was that we intended to take a *razor's edge* path up the mountain, with no deviations whatsoever. "

People hear different things. So we'll be as clear as possible - *solving problems with Netezza requires us to think about problems differently than we have in the past.*

Do not be afraid to experiment with good ideas. More importantly, *do not* be afraid to experiment with ideas that would be *insane* in a more constraining RDBMS context!

But *do not* innovate on what we think might be a good data warehousing solution if it does not leverage the full strength of the box, and more importantly, if it is actually counter to the full strength of the box.

Netezza applications can appear counter-intuitive in many ways. One of the things we really need to form a healthy mistrust for, is our understanding of how RDBMS engines solve bulk processing problems. We have a Netezza machine now. We must leave our transactional processing skills at the door, take deep breath and *jump*.

Once upon a time, we floated along on a gondola in Venice (if you've never been to Venice, neither have I, just work with me here). We close our eyes just for a moment, and suddenly assaulting our ears are the sounds of hammers and tools. Looking up, we don't see Venice anymore. We see a long beach filled with a primitive people, in primitive dress, building a large structure of unknown purpose. We have somehow been catapulted through space and time, to another place where people think about problems-of-scale in a different way.

They don't talk about table spaces, but about data sets, channel-connects, virtual machines and Direct-Access-Storage-Device (DASD) but they call it DazzDee. Sometimes they call it Great-and-Powerful-Dazz-Dee, or shout "DazzDee Be Praised". We see tape drives and tape silos, hear the large scale wind-tunnel of air-cooling blowing through the raised-floor enclosure. People speak quietly about jobs, but not jobs where we work, rather jobs that work for us. They are on a schedule, but not a schedule for the people to follow, a schedule that is *following* the people.

They speak of side-by-side jobs and inline jobs. Pending jobs, completed jobs and job logs. We look around and don't see any logs, stumps or trees of any kind, and marvel at their language. They speak of flat-files, rollback segments, parallel threads and ancient, magical acronyms and glyphs blasted on the walls, obelisks and megaliths, such as EBCDIC, IMS and VSAM.

We wonder that we have stepped back in time, to a place where "big blue" dinosaurs ruled the earth, and people had to solve large-scale problems in a different way. If we need to take down a mammoth, one might say, we need to use the god of COBOL. COBOL is the lord of big data. It will slay big data and devour it in the eventide with herbs and savors, the minstrels will sing a madrigal and all the peasants shall rejoice.

We have entered the Lost World. The place where big-data problems were solved one and only one way. Batch data processing. Bulk equals batch. Batch equals bulk. And transactional stuff is handled by the cousin of the witch Circe, an all-seeing, all knowing witch with one big green eye. Her name is Cee-Ess, with the all-seeing eye. We call her See-Eye-Cee-Ess (CICS).

The *horror.*

We really want this dream to end. *It is a dream, isn't it?*

We tap our heels together and chant repeatedly. Some of us will chant "There's no place like Redmond". Others will want to climb the mountain, penetrate the fog and consult the oracle, a mystic who seems to be everywhere at once. We want our feet back on the ground. Some say terra-firma, others say terra-data. What will we do? There must be a way to get back to whence we came.

After all, we have transactions to close, procedures to store, and servers to cluster.

Do not fear. Our mind has not been temporarily taken over by aliens, there is no chip in our head. Everything that is around us has an explanation. We just need to understand something. The world of bulk processing is not the transactional world. It is a bulk processing world, the world that computer science was born in and ruled computing thought for decades before client-server was ever born, and certainly before Al Gore didn't invent the Internet.

And while we can have all the doubts and concerns about global warming that we see fit, understand that Grace Hopper didn't worry about the ice caps or perma-frost, she worried about whether or not her machine would cap its capacity before completing its *bulk* data processing mission on time and in budget without *frosting* over. All this at a time in history when completing by the end of *month* was considered a feat of derring-do, and its knights-errant the equivalent of dragon-slayers.

Certainly computing has come a long way, but the tried-and-true methods and practices of bulk data processing are a lost art form, perhaps even a lost world.

We should not be surprised if we find ourselves wanting to use the Netezza platform like a transactional machine. Just don't succumb to the temptation. Netezza is not a transactional machine. Period. We'll examine more reasons why in the upcoming sections.

Also, don't be surprised if we find ourselves "coming up with" some interesting ways to solve problems that are counter-intuitive to transactional thinking. These are likely not new ideas, but primordial, original thoughts, bubbling up through our instincts, and we could probably make a movie out of it if we could only get together with the Netezza machine into a sensory-deprivation tank...

We now force ourselves, perhaps *will* ourselves, to think about the problems differently than we would in a transactional environment. Even if we have to think in terms of "if we had to process this as a flat file..." or "if this were a memory-based data problem..." Trust me, once the creative juices start to flow, we won't want to quit.

While the other monkeys are throwing bones at the black Netezza monolith in the middle of the raised floor, our applications will generate dreams inside it.

"Open the iPod, Dave," HAL the computer, *2001 a Y2K Oddysey*.

Physics

"You can't get past the physics," said an old professor of mine, "When things will only move so fast, you have to give 'em more power, or create less drain. Performance is always about the juice in the *hardware* and how efficiently you use it. Software is a cost center. You can't create power with it."

We had a very interesting, and animated, conversation with someone who believed that their (favorite software product here) could beat a Netezza machine without any additional effort. I said that I would put their software product on my laptop, and take it through its paces. He had a strange expression while he realized the irony. His (favorite software product here) needed powerful *hardware*, or there would *be* no contest.

With Netezza, the power is in the hardware already. It's a self-contained appliance. More importantly, the power is in the *architecture* of the appliance. Hardware alone still does not equate to performance, any more than unharnessed lightning represents a useful power source.

Some of you know of my sideline passion for pine-car derby. In a race, all of the contestants receive a block of wood and a bag of parts (axles and wheels) and have to go away for a few weeks to convert these basic parts into a race car. Upon return, each car has to meet certain size and weight limitations, to make things fair. The cars are placed at the top of a 40-foot track and released simultaneously. The first one to the finish line wins. In newfangled races, each lane is clocked, so the real measurement is in the total seconds from start-to-finish. Our fastest-car-ever practically flew down the track, covering the distance in 2.63 seconds. The next competitor finished in less than a car length (about seven inches behind) at 2.70 seconds. But we've seen closer races, winning within 1/1000th of a second.

And no, I'm not one of those testosterone-based life forms bobbing my eyebrows about secret designs while the other cars smoke mine into the weeds. Rather than operate on hit-or-miss, we took the bull by the horns and optimized the car based on *physics*. Since it's free-wheeling, gravity is the only power source. Everybody's car starts at the top of the track, with the same amount of gravity and potential energy. That's why there's a five-ounce limit on the car's weight.

One might think that a ten-ounce car would beat the others, but this is a false assumption. If such a car did not efficiently use its resources, found only in the car's balance and in its axles, that car would lose too. Why the car's balance? If it's too heavy on front or back, it will create drag on its axles, so when it's at the bottom of the track on the straightaway, it will look like it's just put on brakes. Why the attention to the axles? This is where the most friction is focused, and where we lose all our energy to heat.

Of course, my oldest son and I had a wonderful time racing these cars together, capturing a few blue ribbons along the way, but my daughter and youngest son do not share the passion. *Yet.*

There's always a "yet" isn't there?

Stealing energy: This is the most important takeaway: All the pine-cars have the same potential energy, just as all our programs, flows and such have the same number of resources (CPUs, gigs of RAM, disk drives). We cannot manufacture more CPUs any more than we can manufacture more gravity for our little pine car. How well it performs is a function of how well we leverage the resource and how efficiently we burn it. *We cannot allow inefficient design to steal our energy.*

So the real question has nothing to do with the software. If the hardware itself has no ability to meet our processing deadlines, why do we imagine that software will somehow rise up and overcome the problem? I spoke to an eccentric innovator once who honestly believed that his (favorite technology here) could do the same work of the mainframes. When we took it through a smoke test and it was found lacking (processing less than one percent of the required workload), he was flummoxed. He claimed (or rather disclaimed) our test. Clearly we had programmed the software wrong, used (his favorite technology) wrong, or some such.

No. The *hardware* was *physically* unable to keep up. Why is this so difficult to understand? We even took him to a white-board, showing that on a good day with the sun shining, no part of his hardware even possessed the bandwidth to move a fourth of the mainframe's data. "Get over it," we heard him say, "You keep talking as though the hardware has something to do with it!"

Keep an eye on that guy. Seriously.

Tug of war: In friendly team tug-of-war championships, one team piles its people on its side of the rope, likewise the opposing team on the other side. They pull until one side wins, usually because one side has more people.

But in a *real* competition, it's done by member count. In professional competition, it's done by *weight*. Such that the two teams have to be equally matched in aggregate weight. This is because many teams will get a pig farmer named Cletus as their anchor, himself weighing 400 pounds or more, such that there's no way the opposing team will get him to budge. But if the weight limits are used, the opposing team will get another player, perhaps two more players. More players is *one* key to winning, the weight constraint is just to make it fair.

So our little band of brothers was pitted against another group that had several of the university football players on it. We were sunk, we knew. No way could we beat them. While we got some concessions on weight (we added two more people to our side), they mixed-and-matched likewise. Why all the passion about a tug-of-war match? Our team had risen to the top of a campus-wide competition, and this contest would decide the best team on campus. No pressure there.

One of our team members, also one of the strongest people I've ever met, got an injury the day before the big match, precluding his participation. Could anything get worse? He told me "You can still win this. It's not really about the count or strength of people, it's how you act as a team that counts most."

Pulling together: He went on to tell me that most tug-of-war teams will start pulling the moment the referee says "go". He said the way to win, is if everyone immediately pulls just enough to keep the rope from moving away, then on a single command, *we all pull at once*. This leverages our collective power into the pull, rather than all of us pulling arbitrarily and dissipating our strength. Someone needs to call a cadence. Everyone pulls on the rhythm of the cadence. You'd think with competitive rowing teams having done this for centuries, the technique would be obvious, right?

At the competition, the injured team member called the cadence, and we pulled the other team over the line - like they were a gaggle of schoolchildren. I was stunned by how quickly and almost effortlessly we'd won the competition.

The takeaway on all this: *Power is found in numbers, but only if the numbers move in synergy, not in arbitrary motion, and not competing with one another.*

Translate this to our own processing models. What if one of our tug-of-war team members was asked to join another team – in the *middle* of the contest? What if our team member was asked to switch sides of the rope, playing for the *other* team for a moment, then coming back?

But this is exactly how we experience our SMP computing resources. We launch programs that compete with each other for RAM, CPU, disk drive and network bandwidth, wondering why a program that runs by itself in ten minutes, somehow takes an hour to run when we put it into production, and on a much more powerful machine.

The answer is not in the amount of power, but in the efficiency of its utilization. Stolen energy is lost energy, and the energy is a finite pool.

RDBMS "Physics"

In a traditional RDBMS, we access machine physics using software-described index structures. This isn't *true* physics, but how the *software* leverages physics, and with it we must embrace index maintenance and management. For very large databases, this is an Achilles' Heel. We sometimes find that it takes longer to rebuild index structures than it does to actually process the data.

Index structures don't exist in Netezza. This is one of those counter-intuitive things about the machine. This shouldn't scare us, but liberate us. It's the best of all worlds to have a higher-performing machine *without indexing* and thus without index maintenance, than it is to have one that uses index structures, if only for our intellectual comfort.

In the traditional RDBMS, the index structures assist with locating the individual rows of data.

They don't help (much at all) when we want to process a large portion of the table. They may assist us in filtering for the sake of a read-only query, but they are obstacles when we want to load the data. *Loading* of the data into the RDBMS tables is a key capability that even the best databases struggle with. Index maintenance and construction often happens after the load, and is often a huge performance hit.

Netezza gets us out of this miry clay. We have to think about the problems a little differently, and it's anything but painfully different. It's actually a source of liberation, as we will later see.

Flow is hydraulic: "All flow equations," an astrophysicist told me once, "boil down to the same several core *hydraulic* equations. Whether it's electricity, water, data, it doesn't matter, they will rigorously obey *hydraulics*."

While at the time, I understood this statement in terms of optics, how cameras capture analog and deliver to digital media and vice-versa, the statement has universally applied in every instance where I've needed to apply *flow*. While I studied the same physics as this astrophysicist, I did not see such an application or pattern jump out at me. Partly because while one is in college, there's no practical reason to derive this level of understanding, and partly because academics who teach it, don't see it either. High-speed, very-large-scale data processing was *all* R&D when I graduated, so what would they know of it? In that time frame, large-scale bulk data processing was still the domain of the mainframe. Break out the COBOL, fire up the green screen. Turn off the irritating keyclick *beep* of the TTY terminal and *start coding*.

Pipelining of data is an important means to leverage hydraulics. For example, if we take data from one place, process it and put it back, is this more or less efficient than taking data, processing it, then handing it off to *another* downstream component to process, while we process the next element of data? As long as our pipelined components are not competing with each other for resources, this is a very efficient way to get data moving and keep it moving. It's a kind of virtual bucket-brigade, or a relay-race.

While we may functionally pipeline inside Netezza using certain styles of operation, pipelining will really come into play when we get to the aspects of large-scale enterprise computing, where the Netezza machine itself is one of these components. If we implement a flow where we efficiently use Netezza's intake-processing-output power, we have a means to manage capacity for the entire flow of data in a very visible manner.

For now, let's jump into another subject, a key factor in bulk-processing success.

The Interface

Once the machine is ensconced and nestled onto our network, all we really need is a connection session (I personally prefer Putty) to interact with its Linux host, or an ODBC/JDBC connection to interact with its database structures, and we're all set.

Netezza uses a *Postgres* facade, so anything we send to it must comply to the Postgres protocol, apart from plain-straight ANSI-99 Structured Query Language. Netezza has some additional commands for maintenance and housekeeping, and slightly extended syntax to assist in table creation. But we'll find that talking to the machine is simple with no special handling.

Way back when, Netezza purchased the rights to the Postgres engine, kept the interactive facade and tossed the rest. It is essentially a facade to the underpinning Netezza magic, no differently than a steering wheel and stick shift are the human adaptive interfaces to the power of the Maserati, or the Ferrari. Just go out in the garage and check (ha, kidding). In any case, we don't expect to interact with any other kind of high-powered engine on the surface of the engine's metal, so Netezza won't make us do so, either. We want a pretty interface, and a pretty functional one too. Netezza has one, and it's well-documented on the internet in various places, for free. Ask for Postgres by name at your local web browser.

What's more, we can automate its interface anywhere Linux or ODBC/JDBC is understood, and the support for both protocols is ubiquitous and pervasive. We can hop onto practically any web site explaining BASH shell, Bourne Shell or the other shells that Linux supports. Pick one and run with it.

In fact, the interfacing to the machine and its database is so canned and consistent, it hardly bears any mention. We feel somewhat guilty for adding a few paragraphs for it, but when proofreading someone said "Hey, you didn't mention Postgres."

Now we have, and here we are!

The Parts

First, we must understand that the *architecture*, not really the component parts, is the strength of the Netezza system. The parts are largely plug-and-play. It's what they are plugging-and-playing *into*, that counts the most.

If we examine Netezza's *general* architecture, superficially it's actually pretty simple stuff. The magic is in the synergy of the physics. But we do need to understand the parts in order to understand the whole, so to get a *general* idea of how it operates, form a mental picture of the following description:

The Netezza platform is a massively parallel array of CPU processors. Each one has a dedicated disk drive. There's some hardware magic in how the CPU and drive talk to each other, and if you need the details, you can speak to a Netezza engineer all about it. This CPU/Disk/Magic component is called a "SPU", for "Snippet Processing Unit."

Now let's say we have 100 of these SPUs in a frame. When we create a database table, it will logically appear as a single table, but will *physically* exist across all the SPUs. If we then load the table with a "random distribution" from a source of say 100,000 records, each SPU will receive 1000 records.

Now if we perform a query against this logical table, the SQL statement will apply to *all SPUs at the same time*. Each will operate on its own physical part of the table. It does not need visibility to the data in the other SPUs. Each SPU will return a result based upon what the query has asked for, and the data it can locally see. The next level of processing will assemble the results per the query.

Important to note – the SPUs talk to each other on Netezza's high-bandwidth internal network, (its *fabric*) so perform cross-talk of workload and information in dynamic and creative ways to drive the machine's overall activity for a given query. If the SPUs need to join multiple tables together, for example, the keys for the given join might not be co-located on the SPU, so the SPUs will cross-talk to affect the appropriate join. Once again, the synergy of the SPUs is the primary magic.

And like the tug-of-war, if we are truly trying to master the *data*, the SPUs working in lockstep cadence will pull the data over the line. Effortlessly.

A Field Programmable Gate Array (FPGA) coordinates all local SPU activity. It contains all of Netezza's control software and firmware. The FPGA applies the primary filtration logic of any given SQL statement so that the data physically leaving the disk is *only* the data that will meet the SQL's selection criteria. This is very powerful in that it essentially tells the SPU where *not to look* for data on the physical drive. For any given query, the 'where not to look" is a larger and more important piece of information than the data itself.

A latest feature of the SPU is the ability to put custom C-language programs on the SPU itself. This allows us to perform custom, User-Defined-Functions (UDFs) on the data down inside the power of the SPU (without having to know a lot of details about the SPU magic). The SPU then becomes the massively parallel platform for our *custom* algorithms. UDFs are worthy of a deep dive in an entirely separate volume, but I'll talk about them a bit more later.

Power Consumption

"It's because I'm *green,* isn't it?" – Jim Carrey as *The Grinch*, after being ignored by a cab in downtown Whoville.

Since a given Netezza frame has upwards of 112 of these self-contained SPU assemblies, and 108 of them in active service, it's a lot like having 112 miniature desktop computers all in one place. The engineers had to pay careful attention to how much heat this assembly would produce. Not just to be viable, but to be practical.

I recall one day at home my desktop felt like it was "running slow". None of the programs were as agile as normal, almost like the CPU power had been cut in half. I popped open the machine and took a look inside. The five-dollar fan that sat on top of the CPU had not only gone out, it had *melted* into the motherboard. I replaced it and *voila!* The machine was back to normal.

Heat affects machine performance. We inherently understand this, so to get the best performance, Netezza engineers would need to find the best parts that worked together in the best synergy, to remove all inter-component contentions or incompatibilities that might create heat. So Netezza did this, for the hardware components on the SPU itself. It was a practical thing to do, because otherwise the entire frame could radiate like an oven.

A star is born - an entire Netezza frame produces less than 5kw of heat, requiring only 12k BTU of cooling. Contrast this to 90+ kw for the average-to-large SMP server frame with a comparable data processing role. Switching to Netezza can dramatically change the electrical and cooling footprint of our raised floor environment. In essence, they "went green" because it was practical.

What we'll discuss in following chapters, is how to best leverage Netezza's array of SPUs and how they manage the tables for application and processing effects. We won't take a deep dive into the SPU's internal magic, mostly because it's not necessary.

Missing Parts – No Index Structures

The absence of index structures is the most-often-asked-question we receive about the machine's internal workings. We engaged the Netezza '07 Users Conference and it was *very* well attended, with a number of curious would-be owners coming to kick-the-tires and all that.

Standing near our firm's exhibition booth, one of these curious onlookers started asking general questions about the machine. In case you haven't noticed, we generally hold back our excitement about the box. *Not.*

And at one point he asked, "I heard there were no indexes in the database."

"That's right," we said simply.

He squeezed his eyes together, as if we had just told him that the sky was green, "How can that *possibly* work?"

What he was experiencing, and what you might ask in your mind right now – was an effect of the counter-intuitive vertigo we get when trying to map what we think we know into a platform that defies it. The absence of index structures is actually a non-issue when we consider the *anti-indexing* strategy of the machine. Rather than take instructions on *what to find*, it formulates instructions on *what to ignore*. So, not only does the *absence* of index structures turn computing on its head, Netezza takes it to the next level, too.

In a massively parallel system like Netezza, every query is potentially a full-table-scan. Before you get concerned about whether or not this affects performance, *don't.* Its built-in filtration what-to-ignore mechanisms remind us to use and leverage filters in creative ways. If we currently eschew the notion of correlated queries because of performance hits, we must understand and embrace this as a kind of filtration. In addition, the *row*-level, *attribute*-level filtration, gives Netezza the instructions it needs to *dance around on the disk* rather than *slogging through* a sea of data.

What this capability *will* affect is how we solve a data processing problem. But trust me, performance is not an issue. Those of you with a Netezza machine, know of whence I speak. In some cases, since the disks are always spinning, the FPGA is always reading, and now we just need to tell it what we want to peel off for us. We don't care about the rest, it just stays on the disk for later, or whenever. It's like the rest of the data isn't even there.

As we noted earlier on mythology, we have lots of options here to avoid scanning the entire table, no differently than we would want to avoid scanning an entire table in an RDBMS. In Netezza's case, most of this avoidance is right ar our fingertips rather than something we have to engineer.

Missing Parts - Stored procedures

But are they "missing", *really?*

People ask quite a bit about stored procedures in Netezza. All the major database systems have them, they say, so why not Netezza, hmm? What's that? You didn't *know* that Netezza has no stored procedures? What if we told you that stored procedure *functionality* is actually supported *even better* in the onboard Linux environment, an option you might not have available (or have considered) in your RDBMS technology? How on earth does Linux support a stored procedure *better* than the proprietary technology of our RDBMS? Before we get into this subject, allow us to vent a wee bit on the stored procedure. Or to repackage a quote from Disney's *Mary Poppins*:

"What do you get when you feed the clients? Fat clients!" Dick Van Dyke as Dawes Senior, *Servers Poppin'.*

Once upon a time there was an application. It had lots of client-side functionality and over time, became too unwieldy to manage. Fat clients, we called them. Each time we deployed one fat client, we had to deploy them *all*. If one fat client issued a SQL statement a certain way, all of them had to, so up with the version numbers and onward with deploying those big fat clients.

Then along came thin clients and web apps, and lo, there were portals. Behind the portals (or APIs) we had systematic access to the database. Simple views were not enough, cried the app-dev team. We need to centralize the *interactions* so that we can have several database operations going on at once, in the same session, to maintain integrity. And lo, there were stored procedures assisting those applications in fulfilling their *transactional* processing mission. The more logic we could put into the database, the less logic we had in the client. We thinned out those clients, didn't we? All the way down to where it had the same "thin-ness" of a "TTY green screen".

You know, like the mainframe.

Then something else happened. People wanted reports. Not just a report off the data itself, but some summaries, algorithms and statistics applied, you know, business rules. They tried a reporting server, but it was too slow, so the de-facto way to get the data into reportable shape was to actually shape it. They didn't want to pull the data into a middle tier unless it was ready to exit, for the report. So they baked up some stored procedures to do the work internally, and this seemed like a good idea at the time.

It still *seems* like a good idea.

But in the context of an RDBMS, someone might say "Yeah, verily – forsooth we shall use cursor-based, looping-constructed, stored procedures for bulk processing." And thus proceeded to knit *multiple-instruction-multiple-data* bulk processes together using stored procedures. They had no choice - because the RDBMS did not support single-instruction-multiple-data (MPP / flow based) operation. So now, rather than run in the single-instruction direction, our engineers have run the *opposite* direction toward more multiple-instruction mayhem.

After much wailing and malaise, a single voice cried "Turn back! It's not safe here!" But the vendors said "Nay! The stored procedures are good for thee! Yeah, verily see how they sparkle with the morning dew, and dost align thy data processing architecture *forever* bound with our proprietary products - and cost the prettiest of thy pennies. And what stored procedures have joined (customer and vendor), let no consultant put asunder!"

Even though we *think* ourselves hopelessly dependent on stored procedures for bulk data processing, we still might want out. We might see the danger coming and want to warn our CIO, the CEO and the Justice League, but alas, nobody will hear. We become that single voice saying "Turn back".

The stored procedures were originally for *transactional support*. They do *multiple-instruction-single-data* operations. Here, we make a looping construct with if-then-else operations inside it, and browse-the-cursor to operate on *one-unit-at-a-time.*

We were told once that the lack of SQL if-then-else looping was a drawback for Netezza, *but is this really true?* No, because we *won't* be using cursor-based, unit-at-a-time processing. We'll be using flow-based, massively parallel, *bulk-at-a-time* processing. Within this paradigm, we can leverage User-Defined-Functions and case-when-else constructs down at the column level while we are punting *terabytes*-at-a-time.

But we won't process a unit-at-a-time. That's *transactional* thinking.

And no, we don't feel any need to offer up a primer on BASH Shell. For those who are unfamiliar with shell programming and control, suffice to say that this is one of several ideal homes for flow control logic. Many people using other, non-Netezza environments ask for more power in fully parameterizing and componentizing their SQL statement logic. BASH shell gives us these options almost transparently, where the typical RDBMS stored procedure is far less malleable.

When we've implemented a bulk-processing solution in the RDBMS stored procedures, and they seem to be running just fine, only one thing can change this equation – and the minds of the dedicated. It will be time and growth. If our environment grows over time, it will rapidly approach the capacity limit of our multiple-instruction, stored-procedure paradigm. Once this happens, a single three-letter acronym will shake the foundation stones of our CIO's office building. Those three letters are S-L-A. Service Level Agreement. Meaning that our warehouse has to be up and available by a certain time, and has to be available for certain hours. Miss these windows repeatedly, and we'll have some 'splainin' to do.

Stored procedures are highly functional, but they don't scale. See Rule #10. They don't scale. (they *really* don't!)

In small-or-large *bulk* processing terms, the stored procedure has only one role - to help the vendor keep his machine ensconced for as long as possible at our site. Unhooking from this level of functional dependency is difficult, sometimes very difficult, but not impossible. The vendor depends on this high wall to keep those license fees comin'. Don't expect them to say "hey, you really can do it all *without* stored procedures".

Please.

When it comes to bulk data processing, not only *can* we do it without stored procedures, we *should* do it without stored procedures. Stored procedures are by definition *enslaved* to the database engine (and Rule #10 says this is a poor way to do data processing). We need a way to face the physics, and leverage the hardware. An RDBMS won't get it done, and a stored procedure only *institutionalizes* "not getting it done".

All that said, without Netezza, the only option we have is a middle tier. Those of you who hate the middle tier won't find any comfort there either. Apart from Ab Initio, few products will scale into the millions and billions of records you need to process. We'll need hardware for Ab Initio, too, because it is also a software product. One way or another, if we intend to scale, we won't be able to do it in the bowels of the RDBMS. Accept this reality now.

Netezza has no *proprietary* stored procedures. Through Linux, however, we get the benefit of multi-stage SQL execution, including the ability to pass environment and configuration variables (exported $ vars) to dynamically shape a SQL statement, so we get even more flexibility. We can also bundle up repeating patterns of SQL and control in shell script, invoking them as objects. So rather than regard "no proprietary stored procs" as a bad thing or as a feature deficit, we can count our blessings that our dependency on the machine will never grow out of control. On the flip side, we might need multi-stage operations in the Netezza machine, so how do we pull this off?

We have two ways, discussed elsewhere in multi-stage processing, but I'll summarize here - we invoke an *nzsql* session using:

- Our external ETL / Data processing environment.
- BASH shell in Netezza's Linux environment
- Promise from the vendor to support SQL-side looping soon

The ETL environment, if we have one, is the very best way to control the Netezza machine (simply launching SQL statements through *nzsql* from a flow-based environment) with the ETL as the control harness). The second option is good for places with no ETL environment. Most BASH shell is simple, manageable, straightforward and easy to understand. By placing a Netezza query in the BASH shell script and wrapping it with simple notations, we can execute the script and it will execute the query. The third option, promised by the vendor in upcoming releases, will allow us to loop inside the SQL statement context. But not to process one-entity-at-a-time. Looping in an RDBMS is for entity-at-a-time processing, but in Netezza is not.

The primary benefit here is the visibility of the SQL statement(s), coupled with the ability to leverage $ parameters and export variables, each containing either a parameter we use in the SQL statement, or even a snippet of a SQL statement that we concatenate into a skeleton to make a completed statement.

Here's a simple example:

```
nzsql -d mydatabase <<-!

Sql statement number one here;
Sql statement number two here;
Create temp table mytemp as select * from mytable;
Insert into mytemp select * from mytable where active_day =
now();
Sql statement number three here;
Sql statement number etc here;


!
```

By placing the above in a shell script file, we only need to make the file executable in Unix (chmod) and then invoke it from the command line. When the above statement executes, it will pipe the SQL statements one at a time into the *nzsql* instance, treating the entire list of SQL statement as a self-contained transactional session. Note the creation and filling of a temporary table. This table will be dropped at the close of the *nzsql* instance.

We can then launch the scripts remotely, usually with a job-control or scheduling mechanism. In BASH Shell, we can still do all the looping, variable manipulation etc that comes with a more advanced product. Just keep in mind this universal principle of the Netezza machine:

We only send SQL statements. Netezza only operates in terms of firing off a SQL statement to it, so why does it matter (to Netezza) where the statement comes from?

When we think about it, most bulk-processing stored procedures are just a pile of SQL statements that run one after another. The problem is that they run inside a black-box process with no operational visibility as to it status.

And so inefficiently.

A primary reason why we say *leverage your ETL environment* to harness and manage these SQL statements, is because most ETL environment have additional ways to harness the metadata and *lineage* of the SQL statements into a more visualized flow form for review by data analysts and the like. We'd rather have them walking through a *graphical* flow description than just reviewing a pile of SQL statements, wouldn't we? If our ETL environment has the visibility and metadata functionality to do this, we should leverage it as a matter of good stewardship.

Case Study Short: One client asked us to port one of their RDBMS stored procedures into Netezza. We decided to use the aforementioned simplified shell script notation. It contained over twenty individual SQL statements and numerous temporary tables. The version on the RDBMS ran in twenty-eight minutes. We ported it "as is" with no tuning, optimization or other work to a 10100 machine. It ran, first time, in less than *90 seconds*. Suddenly we had a new problem, that the SQL statements were zipping in and out of eyesight so quickly, we barely had time to blink.

With Netezza, we can actually *see* each query the script launches (through the passive Admin window) and can also analyze them, and the processes launching them, for later tuning. Once completed, we can review the actual execution because the query remains in the admin log for this purpose. This gives us high visibility and operational control without any additional effort. If we're launching these in BASH shell, it's easy enough to keep job logs. It's also easy to create reusable script components that have specific tasks or categories of tasks. This accelerates testing and generally makes the environment a bit healthier and more flexible.

Our practice group has a jump-start framework that we bring with us to a client site to get a project moving rapidly. It's just a collection of script-based patterns that seem to repeat themselves everywhere we go. BASH shell is so easy to work with, you, too can make your own version of this, in fairly short order, and start reaping the benefits (and no, you can't have *ours*!). Another option is Perl, which some find to be much more readable and manageable, without the constraints of simple script. All these things are true – you need to do what works – for *you*.

So whether we use a more formal, flow-based (and visual) control mechanism like an ETL environment, or we just use the utilities available in Linux BASH shell – the functionality is there to get the job done. Neither path is especially hard, nor will paint us into a corner. We just need to pick one (for now!) and run with it. Whether ETL or BASH, we are not bound to either one. The Netezza machine only wants SQL statements.

When migrating from a heavily stored-procedure environment like the typical RDBMS, our advice is to take the existing stored procedures and replicate their *functionality* - in *another* way (we'll describe some here). Use the above aforementioned nzsql notation to convert the stored procedures and capture the original functionality. We can then baseline the existing data and processes, and use them later for regression testing when an error rears its head. It is likely, even healthy, that our stored procedures can migrate "as is" to the Netezza machine. Once we get them in place, we have the power and turnaround time to whip them into better, more integrated shape. We'll want to perform some basic due diligence, and of course, test the daylights out of the new solution.

What is important, however is that in thinking about solving the problem a new way, it won't surprise us how creative and generally productive we'll become in rather short order. RDBMS stored procedures cannot offer such a boost. As black-box procedures, we would still have to build the functionality (through human discipline) that we get for free with Netezza. Why build it? Life's too short.

Implied Parts – Filter tables

Important to note – we will talk about "filter tables" throughout this book, so let's define what one is, and is not. First, there is no special table type of "filter" in Netezza. A filter table is an application *role*, and is just a means to use a regular SPU-based table in the catalog, but we can apply it to have a special *duty* of filtration on a larger, master table.

As we look under Netezza's covers, we find the repeating theme of "I can find anything you want, just tell me where *not* to look". The Netezza architecture aligns itself to searching-by-filtration, so what better means to assist its architecture than with a table dedicated to the role of filtration?

How does a filter table work?

Any way we want it to. It's our table, not Netezza's.

Normally, we join our master table with our filter table, using either a "where not exists" or a "where exists" syntax in correlated-query form. The result will be based on the join/anti-join on our filter table. This seems simple and plain-vanilla, until we realize that without index structures, we can leverage filter tables literally for free, and it actually buys us more power and simplicity, not less. For example, let's say we're tracking duplicate records in a master table. The master table contains some twenty-billion records, so we might not want to "just delete" the duplicates if there is an alternative. By placing record identifiers into a filter table, we can join the filter table to the master with a "where not exists", and the duplicate records will be scrubbed in the join's *output*.

And with no index structures, it has extraordinary value and power. We would not dream of using such a structure in an RDBMS. The indexes alone would border on insanity.

Now, before imagining that we'll have to put infrastructure around the filtration, keep in mind that in data processing space, we'll only have to do leverage the filter once as we move toward the downstream. We can do this same trick with error/reject records, audit records versioning for slowly-changing dimensions, topology mapping, creative data intersections, and any number of other ways to tag records as "special" without actually *modifying* the master record. If the objective is to create a final workstream product, we would not include the filtered records in the product, but use the filter table to make the clean, consumption-ready version of the output. *The external consumers never know the filter tables exist.*

This also plays well into extensibility, because if we physically tag the master records with a status, and another status type should come along, we might need to add another status flag to the table. In the filter-table paradigm, we would not modify the master table. We likely will not have to modify the filter table, either, if it's a table that can accept a notation-column as to what its given entry represents. I've seen a single filter table used for tracking duplicates, anomalies, error-rejects and administrative rejects, all tagged with the status of what got rejected and why. It's a one-stop-shop.

Our primary data structures remain stable. We are then able to develop capabilities around the filter tables to serve a wide variety of uses, rather than application-specific implementations. We will find a recurring theme – a pattern – in how we use many of the filter tables, so it's important to package it as a reusable capability.

Hidden Parts – System Catalog

I like to leverage the system catalog whenever I'm building pattern-based scenarios. For example, if we want to copy one table to another, we might want to execute some overhead operations if this copy is more of a transform, or transition for operational reasons. we'd rather be able to define common protocols for all repetitive activities. We see this in design-pattern space, where we find ourselves coding and re-coding what looks like slightly different operations, but most of the activities are the same, and patterns emerge.

A common system-catalog scenario is the desire to create a table that is identical or similar to an original. We can directly manufacture one table from another with the Create-Table-As-Select - CTAS (affectionately pronounced See-Tazz) as in the following notation:

```
Create table new_customers as select * from
    customers limit 0;
```

The "limit 0" notation tells the statement to return 0 records in the query, but the *select* statement has delivered up the complete table definition.

Hasn't it?

Well, it hasn't given us the distribution key, which *could* be a very important part, indeed. We could always trail the statement with "distribute on random" and be done with it. For many temporary tables, this is often the best bet anyhow. But what if we want more? What if we want to organize the table's distribution by the original key, or by a different key? Is there a way to do this without hard-wiring the *create* statement?

We do have some options, one of which is the catalog. Many of you already know what to do with this, so I'll give you the tidbits that can get you jump-started, and you can do the rest.

```
${NZSQL} -d ${TARGET_DB} -A -t <<EOF > ${DDL_WORKFILE} 2>&1
select attname, format_type, coldefault, attnotnull, atttypid
from
_v_relation_column where name='${TARGET_TABLE}'
order by attnum  ;
EOF
```

The above BASH Shell notation will send the output of the query to the file contained in DLL_WORKFILE. I've provided some $ parameters to show where they would fit, but let's say that we have a TARGET_DB that has the value of **myDB**, and TARGET_TABLE of **myTable**, sending output to **myFILE**. It would interpolate to this:

```
nzsql -d myDB -A -t <<EOF > myFILE 2>&1
select attname, format_type, coldefault,
   attnotnull, atttypid from
   _v_relation_column where name='myTable'
   order by attnum  ;
EOF
```

Examine the _v_relation_column table for more insights on other elements you might need.

For a distribution key, we just access a different catalog table:

```
select attname from _v_table_dist_map where
   tablename='${TARGET_TABLE}';
```

Keep in mind that if this query returns a null data set, it doesn't mean that there's no distribution, only that there aren't any keys, meaning that the distribution is *random*. So now we can shape our create statement, but there is a subtle difference between the DDL for creating on random, and on distribution keys. It is the presence of parenthesis, so take care when shaping a create statement like this.

```
Distribute on (key1, key2, key3, etc);
Distribute on random;
```

This is important, so don't miss it: We can quickly and easily manufacture fully functional tables for intermediate (or persistent) use, with the confidence that the minimal DDL is *all that is required* to define the table.

Unlike more complex RDBMS systems **requiring dozens if not hundreds of object**s to accurately define (or redefine) a table, we can do it with simple, visible metadata.

This minimalist-DDL aspect actually unlocks enormous freedom and configuration power to leverage the catalog for all kinds of metadata-driven activities.

SIMD - Single instruction multiple data

This particular aspect of Netezza is what first drew me into its engineering model. The first part of my career (mid-late '80s), I worked with massively parallel arrays used in processing infrared video for military attack aircraft. For that system, almost all of the magic was in the hardware. It would stage a frame of video into the parallel array, blast a series of instructions into it, then move the results to the next stage of the pipeline.

This "series of instructions" was blasted, one instruction at a time, to all processors in the array, all at once. Each processor would behave somewhat differently based on the image data in its own memory and the cross-talk it shared with neighbor processors.

This model is highly effective in spreading out workload, but still keeping all workers "tugging" together. In the early '90s, I worked with a group that needed to store satellite imagery at high speed and high resolution. The solution, all in the hardware, was to break the streaming image apart by its individual pixels, then break apart the pixel itself into bits, then stream the pixel-bits to different disk drives (disk drives were *very* slow back then). This would allow the system to break apart the data into manageable chunks and not saturate (choke) the pipeline while trying to intake such large quantities of data. Short version – spread the workload out among the workers, and pipeline it to parallel streams.

The Netezza platform does this on several levels. Firstly, the CPUs themselves are called "Snippet Processing Units" for a reason. Whenever we issue a SQL statement to the box, the Netezza host immediately breaks the statement apart into "snippets" of work. Any given SQL statement, you see, is really only a pattern of known activities. Filter, Join, Summary, Sort, Transform, and the like. These activities are presented to the level in Netezza where they are the most effective, for the context of the given SQL statement.

For example, if we have a Select statement that needs to pull back all rows from last month's transactions for a given region and district of geography, the query might look like this:

```
Select column1, column2 from Transactions where
    region=1, district=27 and tran_date
    between '01/01/2008' and '01/31/2008'
```

Netezza will see that the filters (after the "where" clause) can be pushed directly to the SPU, so that everything in the "where" clause is sent to all SPUs for resolution. Some SPUs may have no data whatsoever that fits inside the criteria. Others may have only a few rows. Either way, the SPUs have their orders, will search their local *physical* portion of the *logical* table, and return an answer. They don't care one whit what happens after this.

The SIMD model is characterized by a single, focused operation, distributed to multiple actors, affecting millions of rows at a time. The multiple parts of the SQL statement are then pipelined to take the data to its natural conclusion. Where we might enter the noted SQL statement above, we understand it as:

Fetch->Columns with Formatting->Table->Using Filter

Where Netezza will essentially execute it as:

SQL->Decompose->SPU->Scan w/ Filter->Assemble->Publish

Note how the SQL statement's activities are essentially *pipelined* into a flow of activity, not a single SQL statement's worth of work? We can see how single-instruction, multiple data applies in this case, but how does it compare to the other types of instruction models? These other models are all *Multiple*-Instruction, not just a variation, but the polar opposite of a Single-Instruction model. one is the Multiple-Instruction, Single-Data model (MISD, depicted below).

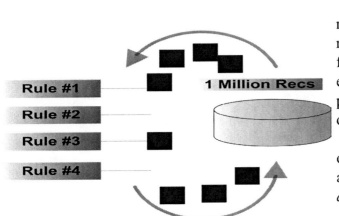

In the depiction (left) we have our millions of records passing through all the rules - such that if we have four and only four business rule actions, we'll pull out every record, touch it, taste it, handle it and put it back. It feels like we're in control, doesn't it?

MISD models attempt to perform lots of work inside a parenthetic boundary, such as a transactional boundary, *on one piece of data at a time.*

We can have multiple-instruction-single-data (MISD), or multiple-instruction-multiple-data (MIMD), but either way, we execute *multiple* instructions against a single unit of work at a time.

We might see data enter the MISD lair, and while it is in the clutches of the API, multiple disparate stored procedures pick it apart like carrion and whisk it off to its final resting place. The picture here, is that the single specific point of data is the center of attention, being pounded upon like a gauntlet, by multiple disparate processes before its release. It is the polar opposite of the SIMD model, where a single process operates on millions of data points at a time.

The MIMD (multiple-instruction-multiple-data) model is the typical model of RISC-based systems and RDBMS engines. They will accept multiple disparate instructions and apply them to multiple disparate data stores, all multi-tasking to get the work done. MIMD/MISD models are ideal for transactional systems - but SIMD models are not. Just as SIMD models are ideal for bulk processing - but MIMD models are not.

Data processing environments such as Ab Initio use a flavor of SIMD that coalesces certain patterns of operation into component form. The components comprise the flow, and each component operates on the complete flow, pipelined as one-component-at-a-time. The primary difference here is the pipelining effect (next) such that when one component is done with a given record, it may pass it on to the next downstream component. Each component will operate on all records, but the workload is again spread out. This model could be called a Single-Component-Multiple-Data model, but this only describes how it applies a given operation, not how it manages the entire flow.

Ab Initio allows us to keep the data in memory-based flows for as long as we possibly can. Still, the only other SMP alternative to this is to leapfrog the data on and off the disk rather than keeping it in memory for as long as possible. Some people abuse the Ab Initio model using this method, simply by creating what are called "toy graphs" that read a file, perform some relatively isolated operation, and then put the data back into a file, only to repeat the same scenario with the next isolated operation. In actuality, these isolated operations should be strung together with flows inside a single, more complex application, and keep the data off the disk completely. Stringing toy-graphs together is a worst-practice and borderline product abuse, because it's an SMP-based disk drive system, so will not behave the same way as the Netezza parallel storage.

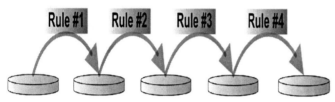

In the depiction left, we have our million records pulled from the drives, passed through a single rule and dropped back onto the drives. An SMP has little choice here except for some engineered disk striping and volume management.

However, Netezza does not lift the whole of the data from the drives and plop it back down again like its SMP-based competitors.

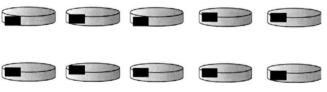

In the depiction left, we have a subset of 10 Netezza SPUs each depicting the location of a single table stored there. I have depicted it as occupying the same physical location on each drive, but try to think of it as a logical part of the drive. The physical drive actually owns its portion of the file.

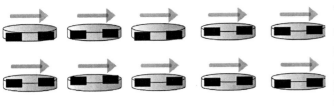

In the depiction left, we see Netezza "moving" the data, but it doesn't lift the entire table into memory only to plop it down again. Rather each SPU simply moves its portion of the data to another location, but the tables's contents never leave the SPU's control. This is massively parallel transformation, and the reason why it beats the SMP equivalent.

MIMD and SIMD contrast: To best highlight the differences between the Multiple-Instruction model and the Single-Instruction model, here are some examples of flow-based throughput we might experience in practical terms.

SIMD-Military outfitters: Soldiers are queued and then streamed into multiple barracks. Each barrack has a line of tables. The soldier checks in at each table, procures his gear from that table (based on the soldier's role, destination and the like), and moves on. If the given table does not have what he needs, he is provided a fulfillment card, but they don't waste time with him at the table itself. By the time he gets past all tables, he is either fully outfitted, or has one or more exception fulfillments to present to a waiting administrator, also found at a row of tables. The administrator deals with exceptions, so the flow continues to move. It's all about flow. Single instruction, multiple soldier. When the solder gets into the field, the military operations will run this way also. A general will give an order, and it will affect large-scale movements. He does not give his orders to each soldier personally.

SIMD-Road Rally/Derby: In this example, the participants are given a destination and a time frame. They must arrive at the destination by the given time frame, or they're out of the race. When they arrive at the destination, they are given a new destination and new time frame. In each case, the exception is the "tardiness" and the flow continues unabated. The participants receive their new instructions on-the-fly – upon arrival. Single instruction multiple contestant. A "scavenger hunt" is a similar model, where the participants get their new instructions or clues upon arrival.

SIMD-College Registration. When entering the registration room at a college or university (typically a gymnasium) we see rows and rows of tables from each school and each department in those schools. We run about to each school, finding a class that fits our schedule and meets our requirements. The representatives from each school sit at their tables, ready to assist. But we are the actors in the flow. We can flit about like butterflies, ignoring the tables we don't care about and queuing up at the tables that matter. In essence, we know what to ignore, because it's not on our sheet of stuff. When we're done, we see the registrar, pay the money and then go buy our books.

Netezza sees a SQL statement the same way we see the sheet of stuff. We know what we're looking for, and go directly to it, knowing what to ignore.

SIMD-Automotive factory: Take a visit to one of these to discover how they can roll cars off the line in under a minute-at-a-time. Parts are pre-assembled into sub-assemblies, one part at a time as they convey down the line. Each person (or machine) adds parts along the way, and we would watch the automobile take shape. As we get into the customization/options set of the journey, the auto frame is conveyed past various stations. Each station identifies the assembly as either something to ignore or something to regard. The appropriate customization is applied, or not, and it continues its conveyance, one customization at a time. When it's time to get painted down, the assembly will be channeled to a painting station that is already outfitted with the given spray-heads and color pumps. It is very time-consuming to trade these colors out for each car, and more efficient to roll the car into a painting bay that is already configured with the necessary colors.

The assembly-line format has the appearance of the Multiple-Instruction-Single-Data model, but it's not. The entities are flowing through stations, where singular actions are applied, the same singular actions to each entity that flows through. The action-station has no context of continuity, and only knows that when an entity is before it, there is one and only one thing to do.

If we invoke such assembly-lines with common objects and components, we'd better have a way to guarantee an unstoppable flow. In the plant, the conveyor guarantees that the entities will continue forward movement at a certain pace. A common object model does not. It allows the objects to capture-and-hold instead of guaranteeing momentum. Substrates like Ab Initio keep the flow moving, where each component attacks the data upon arrival with a rarefied instruction set. This is a flow-based assembly line, not a common object-modeled string-of-rules.

Ever wonder why the Dodge Caravan / Chrysler Voyager, or the Dodge Durango / Dakota, have identical construction but superficial differences? Once upon a time, the only differences between the two vans, was the front grill. This process of applying a single-instruction as the assemblies flow by, is the only way to achieve economies of *scale*.

And scaling is what we're talking about, not just operational functionality. What if they put each car assembly on a big platform and brought all the parts *to it*, assembling it completely before rolling it out of the factory? This would be a MISD model, and highly inefficient for *scale*. If they tried to make multiple platforms for multiple cars, this would be a MIMD model, likewise inefficient for *scale*.

MIMD-Pizza Delivery: Our pizza delivery guy will receive an order, then they might *make* the pizza in assembly-line fashion. Then the delivery guy takes the pizza out to the car, runs it over to our house and comes back. He does not have the option of going to the next house because he's got no pizza with him. If he's going to the same neighborhood for several orders, he'll take multiple pizzas with him and deliver them all. In our neighborhood, the Domino's delivery guy will bring just one pizza if there's no others in the queue. Their competitors will actually wait a little longer for some more to enter the queue before delivering the pizza. After a few soggy pizzas from these folks, we see the wisdom in delivery right-away, even though it is the most inefficient if they want to move the product with higher volume and less effort. While this *looks* like a distributed delivery model, it's really not. The delivery guy *must* come back to the shop for a round-trip, effectively wasting the gas and time on the *return leg*.

This is also a consumption-point scenario. The delivery guy is like our transactional applications, sending an instruction to fetch data from the user (the pizza order) and receiving one-way consumption-point delivery to the end consumers. Transactional models are round-trips initiated from the consumer, not the purveyor.

SIMD-Rail cars / Shipping: The flip side of the pizza delivery model, is the *flow* delivery model. In shipping, we would never allow the container to move without loading it first, so ideally, there are no "wasted legs". Our trucks would travel to one place, unload their stuff, immediately re-load and come back. Airlines do round-trips with passengers and cargo, but work hard to fill *each* leg with both, so that no trip is wasted. The Pizza Delivery guy above would only have this option if each of the delivery points was making pizza, rather than being the consumption-point.

The flight attendants (or the pre-recorded message) will give the usual fasten-your-belt safety spiel at the beginning of the flight, offering the same (multiple) instructions to each person at the same time, but it's still MIMD, because SIMD would be inefficient, we're not *flowing* anywhere.

MIMD-Cookie Delivery; We really like Girl-Scout cookies. My niece is a girl scout and each year we're good for a blockbuster order of Thin Mints. We put them in the freezer in the garage. Never had a frozen thin-mint? You're missing out on life, in my humble opinion. We noted, however that even though we only buy those cookies, others in our neighborhood will buy more kinds of cookies. Upon the delivery time, some bright spark in the central office tells everyone to deliver the thin-mints first, then the others last. Partly because the thin mints are so popular, the boxes really fill up their local storage space quickly. So even if a person's *completed* order is all in-house and they could take everything with them, they focus on the thin-mints first.

This is no different that the Pizza-delivery scenario above, in that it takes the cookies to the consumption point, wasting the return leg. It is even more inefficient when it arbitrarily invites two wasted return legs and bewildered customers, who don't understand why they get part of the order in the morning, and part in the evening. Whether this is policy for such organizations, it must change! We want *all* our cookies on the first trip!

Capacity, we need it

Switching gears. Capacity planning, in a nutshell, is an 80/20 rule. While the actual mileage may vary, for initial and ongoing aspects of planning, an 80/20 rule will keep us safe. What does this mean?

On any given day, 80 percent of our systems are available for useful work, the remaining 20 percent is implicitly reserved for system activity, recovery and the like – a "red zone" safety net. We cannot build systems with the assumption that our "safety net" is part of our regular resource pool. Otherwise when our system activities spike into the "red zone", they risk a hard crash, or at least debilitate our systems and user base. We inherently understand this.

What is not obvious to some, is that if only 80 percent of our environment is available for useful work, we cannot sit idly by while our business grows and we start to approach the limits of he 80 percent boundary. The 80 percent boundary is best regarded as a hard wall. It is better to plan for more capacity, moving the hard wall away from us, than it is to approach the hard wall, see it looming, and start looking for ways to slow down the hard-wall's approach (usually through creative capacity engineering).

With an SMP-based environment, we usually get "one free upgrade", that is, we can push the hard wall away from us by upgrading our hardware, perhaps even our software, but we usually only get one of those (unless we fix other things along the way). In a typical SMP scenario, simply adding more / better / stronger hardware, is a tactical fix.

Unless we are in a Netezza machine. Then a hardware upgrade not only pushes the wall away, it practically sends it over the horizon and out of sight.

On a traditional SMP system, the hardware upgrade event *should* serve as a shot across our bow, so to speak, prompting our engineers to find a better and simpler way to do things, not more complex ways to do things. But over time, that's not usually how it turns out. The purchase of hardware is seen by engineers as a last-time-one-time purchase, mainly because the people purchasing it do not make the process easy or fast. Rather than engage this purchasing uptake again, engineers will set about doing what they do best, *engineer*, and slowly the systems will devolve into artificial complexity. Once this happens, the system becomes its own parasite, stealing its own energy to perform its own work.

Many "organically grown" environments look like this, where parts are added and functionalities bolted-on along-the-way, eventually leading to a functional-but-not-scalable outcome. The black hole we wanted to avoid, is now with us.

Planning ahead: We must start capacity planning when even while approaching the "80 percent" mark of our "80 percent" resource pool. Now, that's kind of scary, considering that this may launch a capacity planning exercise when the environment reaches about 60 percent of its *total* capacity. Think about it, if we have a 1000 gigabyte environment, and we know that 200 gigabytes is off-limits for recovery and the like, this leaves only 800 gigabytes for actual use. 80 percent of this is 640 gigabytes, the point at which we need to start capacity planning. Can you imagine walking up to our boss and saying, "It's capacity planning time." When our boss looks at utilization, he will see that only *64 percent* of the *total* resources are used.

"Wait a little longer," will be the invariable response.

Now let's go back in time, and discover how we got to this 640 gigabyte number. Was the space filled up at 500 gigabytes when we installed the system? I hope not, because we would have filled up that 140 gigabytes rather rapidly. So where was the water-mark when we installed the system? I can tell you where it *should* have been – at 20 percent of the 80 percent – that's *160 gigabytes* – which is very close to *15 percent of overall capacity*. We have yet to see a system installed where the admins and overseers told their bosses, "We have one and a half terabytes of active storage, and since this constitutes a fifteen-percent water-mark of the overall environment, we estimate we will need ten terabytes to start out. Rather, they might ask for around five terabytes, if that, and wonder why the capacity evaporates only a few months into its implementation.

Two rules apply here: **Workspace** rule, and the **Costner** rule.

Workspace rule: For any given bulk processing environment, we will need workspace. For the past two decades, a very consistent number has arisen for the workspace needs in a data warehouse or a bulk processing model.

It's 6-x.

We've seen hapless admins trying to squeeze a few more gigabytes here and there out of their bulk processing environment, where it never occurred to them that a healthy storage availability should be in the terabytes. "It's wasteful", one admin told us directly. "If we provide that much storage capacity, they'll use it up. But if we don't provide it, they can't use it, now *can* they?"

What?

We have a tough time not biting our tongue on these kinds of conversations. It tends to mean that while a real problem exists, someone isn't taking it seriously, and is telling others to "live with it" when what they really mean is "survive without it". I've seen lots of information systems "surviving" on breadcrumbs. Some were not *ever* healthy data processing environments, and the information systems suffered. If the information systems suffer, their users suffer, and the business suffers with them.

What does "6-x" actually mean? If our final data warehouse consumption-ready storage is a terabyte in size, we will need *six* terabytes of workspace to get the data into shape for this outcome. Examining the above estimate – when we told the bosses that we needed ten terabytes for the capacity plan, we did not include this "6-x" multiplier. The ten terabytes was only to support the growth of the *final* product. What we really meant to say, was that we need that much for the consumption-ready production portion, and another *eight* terabytes for workspace.

Not to worry, our boss won't buy us eighteen terabytes either. But for now, if we really tell the boss we only need five terabytes, can we now see how far off the mark this is, and why the capacity evaporates within months of implementation?

Costner rule: (okay, I made this up). This is from Kevin Costner's movie, *Field of Dreams*, where the catch phrase was, "If you build it, they will come". And we have to give fair warning, if we build this environment correctly, it will draw *more* users like bees to honey, and we will have more work on our plate than we ever dreamed of, with or without the *Field*. If this happens, our capacity plan might be *kaput* as well, because it might now grow in leaps and bounds beyond what we could ever have expected.

Contrast this to the **Homer Simpson** rule (yes, I made this up, too) – that if we really screw things up, we'll be back at our desk fixing things - which brings us back to *doh*!

Or rather, back to *dough*. It costs a lot of dough to fix things, and I'm not making this part up.

So it seems we cannot win the day. If we do a good job or a bad one, we're back at our desk blasting away on the keyboard. The good news is, that if we did a good job, we can conscript others and delegate the work against a robust framework. If we did a lousy job, we'll be working alone, eating alone, all that stuff.

"Things have turned out exactly as they should be," said Meta-Morpheus.
"Oh, how do you know?" asked Neon, punching the elevator button.
"Because we all still have jobs."

-- *The Waitrix, Re-Moded*

Capacity is more than the production system: And consider this, if we have an environment that is tens of terabytes in potential size, what does that say of our pre-production testing environment, our functional testing environment and our development environment(s)?

We all know from prior experience that these supporting environments can sometimes dwarf the production environment in size and capacity needs, collectively by a factor of four or more.

So what was it we said? Five terabytes? Is that really going to be enough? If the above metrics are true, it means we need 20-x or more, and we know that our bosses won't sign off on 100 terabytes to support a target database of a couple of terabytes.

Now can we see, in no uncertain terms, how the capacity we planned for, even the larger and over-the-top numbers we suggested, somehow evaporated within months of implementation?

Case study short: At a major retailer, we knew that the target data mart would be roughly 20 gigabytes in size. We specified a storage array size of 300 gigabytes. Our boss came to us, stunned that we would suggest such an incredibly steep number. We reminded him of the 6-x rule, and also that we would need a pre-production environment and a development environment, all sharing the same array. While this worked out (on paper) to 360 gigabytes, We thought we could get by with 300 gig if everyone managed their resources. Our boss walked away dazed and confused. He really thought we were nuts.

Halfway into the project, we had to bolt-on an additional 150 gigabytes to the environment, 450 gigabytes total, so even our initial estimate fell short. Oddly, by this time our boss was already running another project, encountering the same problem, and was already imploring that project's architect to dial back the space requirements. A short conference call on the issue brought it to resolution, but our boss remained unhappy. At the time, we had full corporate memberships to The Data Warehouse Institute (TDWI) and got some of their consultants on the phone. Their number was even higher (8-x), but our boss remained unconvinced.

Your current leaders may likewise remain unconvinced. Don't confuse him/her with the facts. Fair warning.

How Does Netezza Solve This? We're glad you asked that question, considering that, if the problem is real, and Netezza can't solve it, can't we just move on to the next subject?

We first buy a Netezza machine, let's say a 10100 with 12.5 terabytes on it, or perhaps a 10200 with 25 terabytes on it. Our boss may well ask, *do you need 25 terabytes?* And the answer might be no, at least *not now*. Not to worry, all we have to do is license the storage *we want*, and leave the rest. It's called Capacity-on-Demand and it works really well.

Note that all 25 terabytes are *physically* present on the machine, but if we don't pay for them, they are hidden behind a license key. We only pay for what we license. This means we can buy a 10200 with 216 SPUs of pure processing juice, but only license, say 6 terabytes. If we need more, we shoot an invoice to the vendor, unlock more storage and off we go. No hardware changes, swaps or configuration changes. We keep the CPU power and get more storage. The best part, we pay as we go, rather than pay a lot for a lot of what we're not using *yet*, perhaps even for a *while* yet. If we need more CPU power, we add another frame (another 108 CPUs and another 12.5 terabytes). It's transparent and painless.

How cool is that?

And as we noted with the mythology of Netezza, the Capacity-on-Demand is said by competitors to be a false economy. They claim that Netezza gets slower as we add more data. This is nonsense, and easily proven with the physics. Nothing is hidden inside the box. We can always test it. Like we said, the Underground is a function of literary irony. We can find everything we need to know inside the black box, because it's only a black box on the outside.

How ironic is that?

Our Operations center has several major priorities for capacity. One is the sheer *storage* capacity, which is often eaten up by redundancy. If we can consolidate our storage into fewer locations, such as with Netezza, we reduce our redundancy and gain greater control over capacity. Another issue is *data transportation*, but again if we reduce our complexity and consolidate functionality into the Netezza machine, many transportation needs are covered with in-machine data copies, not touching the network at all. Another hot-button for capacity is found in our most voracious applications, our *reporting* environment. Netezza provides extraordinary power for scaling our reporting capacity. We will find that it consummately harnesses our capacity issues so well, that we'll spend the majority of our time dealing with business application needs, not capacity tuning.

And isn't that what we *want*?

Compression

In 2007 we saw an additional incoming arrow in the Netezza quiver that is bound to raise the eyebrows of some - and the hackles of others. This is data compression, and it's *really* cool.

Now what would we *normally* expect from a data compression? If we can load our data in 30 minutes now, surely compression will take longer for intake no? And if we query compressed data, surely the engine has to unwrap the compressed stuff before examining it, affecting outbound performance, no?

No.

True to form, Netezza's architecture is antithetical to this kind of thinking. For Netezza, compressing the data simply means less to store and less to write, reducing overall write cycles and loading times. One might well ask, where do they put the data they compressed out? They handle it the same way *functionally* that any good compression algorithm does, except they do it before actually writing the data.

Likewise when reading the data, recall that Netezza's read cycle is based on knowing *what to ignore*. Since parts of this compressed data is, by definition, something to ignore, Netezza passes right over the "fluff" and pulls the real data. Either way, the architecture allows the SPUs to only write to the disk what must be, and only read from the disk what counts, excluding all others.

We can see that in a traditional technology, the compression can add an unhealthy percentage to the write and read times. It's a necessary penalty, we are told, to get the space back from the disk drives. A tradeoff, a necessary evil.

Tradeoff. I hate that word.

Not with Netezza. Some users in beta have seen as high as 3 to 1 compression, with a boost in performance besides. Some users have seen no higher than fifty percent compression, but everyone's actual mileage will vary. Try the compression to get some capacity back. It costs nothing to give it a test drive, and we'll get something back for it no matter what.

People are often stunned at the whole idea of gaining space *and* performance when using compression. Yes, it surprises everyone, just like scanning a terabyte in seconds. Seeing is believing, so flip the switch and believe it.

Flow-based operations

You'll see me regularly use the terminology of "upstream" and "downstream". A data warehouse has an upstream (data sources) and a downstream (target marts and others). The flow is what happens in the middle, but we have to carefully identify what this means, because it's a frame-of-reference.

For example, if I am receiving data from your upstream system, I may process it and send it downstream. If I join your team for a week, I will see your environment as my primary flow, and will see my original environment as the downstream. This might sound a little "remedial" but I'm making a point. Most shops see sources and targets but don't consider things in terms of upstream and downstream. This is potentially hazardous, because if we exist in an upstream position, we must harness our flows so that we don't create artificial work for our downstream.

As a simple example, let's say we let dirty data into the downstream, and those processes in turn crunch the data and prep it for their own downstream, say a Business Objects instance. The dirt arrives on the BO front door, and now a BO developer will have to deal with it. We could have dealt with it when it was in our hands, but we did not.

Someone will have to deal with it, or it will arrive dirty to the user, and they will require someone to deal with it. Where do we deal with it? In the upstream. First and deliberately. We never wait, watch or wonder, we just clean it the first time we encounter it.

Bulk data processing is like moving water through pipes. Any choke-point in the pipe will starve the downstream resources. It won't matter how powerful a machine we have as a final receptacle, if the pathway to it is filled with pot-holes, thin pipes and other issues.

In a plumbing system, we see several themes. To get large amounts out of one area and into another, such as storm drainage, smaller pipes (1' to 3') move to larger pipes (3' to 6'). Larger pipes stay larger, offloading their flows to smaller pipes along the way, eventually emptying their contents. The objective is to maintain momentum of water with no backups.

In traffic flow scenarios, we see a balance of the two models, realizing that humans are dynamic thinkers and may exit a thoroughfare to avoid heavy traffic. Small inlets feed larger ones, the backups occur at the flow exchanges, the outlets or in sheer volume of flow. Humans are not like water, however. Someone arbitrarily putting on their brakes far ahead of traffic, can cause hundreds of cars behind it to likewise brake. Unlike water, the cars are not pushed from behind. Nor are they moving at a road-harnessed speed like a network packet or a train on a track. Why do they follow common hydraulic rules? It's a flow, and they all *still* act the same way.

Case Study Short: Visiting a colleague in another large city, we hopped in his car to go see a client. Once on the tollway, the large signs overhead invited us to use the fast lanes to the left, but only if we had a tolltag. My colleague moved toward the right lanes.

"Need some change?" I asked.

"No, I have a tolltag."

"But we're not in a fast lane," I observed.

"It's only fast at certain times of the day," he noted, "All the other lanes take a tolltag, too."

When we crested the next rise, we surveyed a monstrous line of cars backed up in the "fast" lanes, yet all the other lanes were empty. My friend whipped past this line in the outside lane, bypassing over a thousand cars moving like snails in the fast lane, shot through the toll booth and rejoined the relatively thin traffic on the other side.

The takeaway here - my colleague understood traffic flow, while the other drivers melded into the "herd". Doing things like other people do them, just because the various latent signs "say so" is an artifact of the "herd mentality", mindless obedience to doing things the way we've always done them, like a Jurassic Park processing model and the RDBMS load-and-query model.

Break free, ignore the "herd management" signs and optimize the *flow*.

How does this apply to technology? Operators and developers will dynamically kick off multiple application programs, all running on the same road, all using system resources. The systems *arbitrarily* throttle their workload to keep from stomping on each other. Like the cars, the programs compete for resources, and each would run faster if nothing else were in its way.

Why all the examples? Most developers do not see their environment as a flow. They see the environment as a collection of components. Years and years of object-modeling and object design, componentizing, compartmentalizing and isolation have led to a kind of inbred thinking that starts with components-first. If the components run on a common flow-based substrate (like Ab Initio or other component-based flow product) then we have some additional power. However, *we typically understand* components as standalone instances of work, procedures etc Shared-nothing resources and want to operate in physical and functional isolation.

For transactional scenarios, years and years of Enterprise Java Beans and all the other componentized operation have grown a wide array of highly functional capabilities, all of which are largely useless for bulk processing and in many ways are not optimal for EAI-based processing either. Customers are finding that fork-lifting their Java-based Medusa with thousands of venomous heads into a common controlled harness like Ab Initio's Continuous Flows environment, provides enormous lift and radically reduces complexity in one fell swoop.

Netezza fits very nicely into this model, because when all is said and done, environments like Ab Initio already produce and process libraries-of-Congress-at-a-time and need a place to land it. Likewise, many of the processes and procedures that Ab Initio "could" execute are often better suited for execution in Netezza, *after* the data arrives. While a 32-processor Ab Initio server may sound like mind-bending power, it won't always compete well, in some operations, against Netezza's baseline 216-processor platform. The bottom line: balance the power in both environments and don't treat either one like a component.

It's a flow.

What does a flow look like? At the point the data arrives in our enterprise, until the time it finds a final resting place in our environment, constitutes a flow. For reporting systems, this may look like pulling data from one or more transactional environments, enriching it with reference data, and formatting into a consumption-ready form. All of this takes power and space – lots of it. We should never underestimate how much capacity we'll need to develop it, much less put it into production and operate it.

While this might not be a comprehensive boot camp, it sets the stage for what we need to look for, and what we want to purchase, or not, to get economies of scale in data processing. If we already have a Netezza machine, some of this already rings true. If we don't have one, and are trying to solve the problem through components and jumping-java-beans, maybe we need to take a deep breath.

Stop kicking the tires, call the vendor, and see what it can really do.

"I'm in the market, as it were," Johnny Adept as Captain Jack Sparrow, *Gyrates of the Javabbean.*

5 DISTRIBUTION STUFF

ONE OF THE MOST significant ways that we mate our information problem to the Netezza architecture is in how we actually lay the data down on the disk drives. As noted in the prior chapter (Boot Camp) we now have all these parallel-processing SPUs and we need to get data onto them in the most optimum form. When we distribute the data, we physically send information to each of the SPUs, represented in the catalog as a single logical table. Anytime we perform a query or activity on the table, it affects all the SPUs, because that's where it physically exists.

People then start to ask a lot of questions about how to distribute the data and what the implications are for doing so. We have a lot of options, but only a few are troublesome. So let's just examine some guidelines. If we stay within these as a rule of thumb, leaving the others open for free experimentation, we'll have a good experience and we'll learn more about the machine.

Once we're ready to work with the real data, we'll want to instantiate some tables. This process is simple and very-low-overhead. In fact, the DDL required to make the tables of our current RDBMS data warehouse, versus those required to make the same tables in Netezza, the total number of instructions is reduced by ninety percent or more. If you have an RDBMS admin screen handy, pop it open and examine the entire DDL instruction set for making a single table, and the thousands of objects created when we need to make a new table.

When we do this in Netezza, it's radically reduced because the appliance architecture has already canned and predefined all of the decisions and objects we would normally manage ourselves in the RDBMS . Netezza takes care of all the tablespace and storage, we have no indexes, and so the final product is a thin layer of DDL compared to its RDBMS counterpart.

A primary difference in the Netezza table definition, is the *distribution key*.

For the record, the standard RDBMS partition is *not* the same as a distribution. The RDBMS partition is an attempt to second-guess the user's desires by putting physical data into a logical boundary of some kind, like a day's worth of data. If our query cannot find the data there, the RDBMS might just dim the lights trying to find the information. Those who use Ab Initio have a different definition for partitions also, which itself is a key-based means to manage the same flow of information, scaled in a different manner.

What is distribution? It is method that we use to spread the data out on the disk drives. It's closer to *striping* than partitioning. There's a logical element to it, but it doesn't require us to put a lot of data in *one* place. We put all the data *all over* the place.

When we create a table, we can define the distribution as keyless, or "random", or we can define it as one-to-four columns (as keys) on the table itself. Whenever we load data into the table, the host will dispatch each record to a SPU based on the given distribution. The evenness of the distribution is called skew. High skew in the SPUs is very bad. Low to zero skew is what we're after. Distributions always have skew.

If random, it will land the records evenly in a round-robin form across the SPUs (depicted below). Random distribution mean *even* distribution, and practically guarantees zero skew, or as close to zero as is physically possible It also means that when we join the data in one table to another, the optimizer will have to ship the data from the SPUs containing one table into the SPUs containing the data for the other table. It knows enough to push the smaller table to the larger table, but either way it will ship some data. If we're only dealing with the key columns (as in a filtration scenario) this can be *very* powerful.

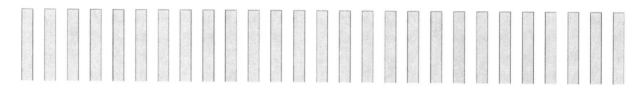

If distributing on a key (data column), upon insertion, Netezza will hash the given column and dispatch the record to the appropriate SPU based on the hash result. The benefit here is that all same-keys will land on the same SPU. So if we have more than one table distributed on the same keys, their respective records will be co-located on the same SPU. Netezza will recognize this automatically, and if these tables are later joined on those keys, Netezza is aware of the co-location and leverages it. Typically when we distribute on a key, we won't get a completely even distribution (depicted below), but a "ragged edge". This is fine, as long as the skew is within acceptable limits.

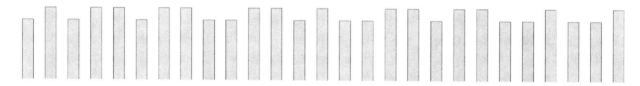

The primary logistical quantity to consider in all this, is that the Netezza machine doesn't regard the column *names* to determine how to hash or what to hash. It does NOT attempt to understand that the customer_id key on one table *means the same* as the cust_id key on another.

What it will hash on, and distribute on - is the column's *data type* and its *value*.

And this makes sense, doesn't it? If we have a customer_id on one table with the value of 21987 and a cust_id on another table with the same value, and we distribute both tables on these respective columns, they *will* hash to the same SPU. Later, when we join on customer_id and cust_id, it so happens that both tables are distributed on this same data type and value, and thus *will* reside on the same SPU. A query joining them, will *automatically* initiate a co-located join, because they are the same data type. It does not assume that the columns have any relationship at all. They have a common *data type*. This is all that counts.

The SPU doesn't care what the data in the column *means*. It only cares that they are the same data type. If they are the same data type, are both distribution keys, and appear in a join, the SPU will see that the tables are distributed on a column of the same data type. It will also correctly surmise that *because* the tables are distributed on columns of the same *data type*, their values are co-located and don't need to leave the SPUs to get an accurate join.

Can we see now how the data *meaning* and column *name* just don't matter? I've had white-board sessions with old and new users alike trying to help them understand this simplest of concepts. If you're not grasping it now, think on it for a bit, perform some simple operations on your own Netezza machine, and you'll see how it works.

Here's a simple example: Let's take an inventory table, distributed on inventory_id, which is a four-bit integer. The 450th inventory ID (out of 5000 items) is for large chocolate bars and has a value of *458998*. This inventory ID will hash to SPU 55 of our 108 SPUs when it loads to the inventory table.

Let's take a customer table, distributed on a key of customer_id which is also four-bit integer. We'll load up 55,000 customers nationwide, distributed on the customer_id, the 35,578th of which happens to have a customer_id of *458998*. When we load the customer table, this value will get hashed and sent to SPU 55 of our 108 SPUs.

Can we see a pattern here? The customer_id and inventory_id are of the same data type and value, so even if the values themselves are identical **but unrelated**, they will hash to the same SPU. The Netezza machine isn't trying to guess how we will use them. We know from the business model that the inventory_id and the customer_id are unrelated, so we would never join on them. If we did, these two records would get a hit (and might be the *only* two records that get a hit!).

But, what will happen when we join these tables, is that the SPU will recognize that both their distribution keys are of the same data type, and will therefore perform co-located joins on all SPUs. As noted, only one of the SPUs will get a hit, SPU number 55, because by serendipity the unrelated values happen to be the same, for one "match".

If, however, we have a customer_address table that we've also distributed on cust_id, which just happens to be the same data type and value of the customer table, and is *related* to the customer table, we can then join the customer and the customer_address and expect it to get lots of hits (they are related) and for every hit to happen on the same SPU.

However, if the cust_id on the customer_address table contains the same value as its related parent, but is instead a data type of varchar(10), it will not *hash* to the same SPU as its integer counterpart. Because they are different data types, they really do contain different values, because their binary form of data is represented and stored differently. These records will not exist as co-located on the same SPU as their integer counterparts might in the other table.

One user asked, "How does the engine know that the customer_id of one table is the same thing as the customer_id of another table?"

The answer is that it *doesn't*, and more importantly, doesn't *need* to. If upon loading, it examines the data type and value, it will push the same value to the same SPU every time. When we join, the engine knows that the tables are distributed on the same data type, so will co-locate a join on their distribution keys. It will always work, because the distribution keys are the same type. It is not Netezza's concern as to whether the columns have the same *meaning*, or if the data in the columns is even *related*.

One user complained that this was a drawback, in that relational databases inherently have this knowledge but Netezza does not.

Is this *really* true?

When we define a model in a relational database, such as the aforementioned customer and customer_address tables, what *about* the table definition tells us that the customer_id and the cust_id on the respective tables have any relationship at all? It is something we *apply* to the table that gives it this meaning, because it is *not* something the RDBMS inherently knows. Likewise we can still attempt to join the customer table to the inventory table on bogus identifiers. Nothing stops us from using the data wrong.

So back to the Netezza scenario. Why would we distribute the tables on one key-column and then attempt to join them on another? Don't we know enough about how to join our own data? Of course we do. And we can apply metadata hints to the tables so that our BI and more intelligent metadata-driven environments can connect the dots - that the customer_id and cust_id have the same *applied* meaning on their respective tables.

But this has nothing to do with *distribution*. When we select a column for key-based distribution, it is with the full intent that we will use it against another, likewise distributed table. There's not a lot of reason to distribute on a key-value otherwise.

If we simply want to forego all this and distribute on random, that's perfectly fine. We'll find that the Netezza optimizer still has our back, and won't penalize us for using and sticking with the random distribution. We often tell people to start out random, so we get a baseline for the worst-case in performance (which is still mind-bending), then move toward key-based as the use-cases clarify things for us.

However, when randomly distributed and we need to join two tables, it's guaranteed that the join-keys are not co-located on the same SPU, so the engine will either redistribute or broadcast the keys from one table to get them closer to the other. Netezza will be smart about it, moving the keys for the smaller table to the larger, among other things. But it still has to ship data around. If the smaller table is really small, this is a non-issue and not worthy of further consideration. If the tables are of considerable size, it behooves us to examine a key-based distribution because we can get more boost out of it. How much boost? Usually around 2x, but if we're doing a lot of work in one operation, that 2x can rapidly multiply to 10x or *much* higher depending on the nature of the query. The point is - seriously examine key-based distribution for optimizations, but don't be disappointed if random is the only option. The data and its use-cases are the rule here.

A caveat about distribution, is that some key combinations will hash alike, inadvertently dogpiling records onto one or more SPUs, significantly *skewing* the distribution of the physical data. If we need to use a key, we *should* pick the key that gives us the best distribution on the SPUs. However, until we can profile the data and get a handle on its layout, we should use the *random* distribution and it will guarantee a clean spread. What of those bad-boy values? Make them randomly-negative or remove them completely from the table. Keep in mind that the key-based distribution has to serve us, and if the data won't do it, use something that will. We've seen people apply incremental surrogates to the records as they arrive, then distribute on the surrogates, and then later join on the surrogates. It's guaranteed to be a random distribution, and a manageable co-located join.

Once loaded, we can bring up the *nzadmin* utility window to examine the graphical display of the table's distribution. This graphical display is a bar-chart with a vertical bar showing each SPU's relative load compared to the others. Ideally we want to see a smooth "flat-top" across this chart (guaranteed with random distribution).

When we use a key-based distribution, we should expect to see this chart have a "ragged edge", but not dramatically so. A very ragged edge means there's too much skew and we need more granularity.

Why the bother? Why not just load the data and hope for the best?

Skew University, or Skew-U

Case Study Short: The customer loaded the data according to a key that they thought was reasonably random. When they examined the *nzadmin* graph, everything seemed fine, with the data evenly distributed among the SPUs. With performance unacceptably slow whenever they queried this table, they wanted to understand why.

We examined the distribution (depicted above) and noted that the first SPU in the display was "spiked" with a bar many times taller than the remaining 215 SPUs, which were all a smooth flat-top. We asked the developer what the "spike" was all about, and he dismissed it, continuing with the conversation as though it was a non-issue.

Oh, it's an issue, In fact, the *only* issue there is. A spike of data on a single SPU will cause all the SPUs to appear slow, but they're really not. The overloaded SPU is doing the lion's share of the work, and the customer's not getting any real benefit of parallelism.

Keep in mind *why* we distribute data. So we can spread the workload out and get more CPUs/Disk-Drives attacking the problem. If even one of our SPUs is "slow" compared to the others, rest assured that all the others will return their answers rather quickly. *Then the query will wait on the slowest SPUs*. Even with a ragged-edge chart, the *tallest* bars represent the SPUs that will take the longest time to return. The entire query is only as fast as the slowest SPU's turnaround time.

The outcome of the above situation was an interesting discovery. The keys for that first SPU were all "0", an invalid value anyhow. We asked the developer how "zero-value keys" had made it into the database when such a condition should never happen, and he was stunned. As it turned out, a pernicious bug existed in one of the upstream feeds, inadvertently zapping the key. More unfortunately, this was a billing system and the zero-key meant that the downstream billing system would never connect the key with its attendant account! Bottom line – the invoices were financially short. They were foregoing revenue because it wasn't generating an invoice.

And Netezza helped them find it.

This is why profiling is such a big deal. It gets us in touch with the data on a scale that is otherwise elusive, or impossible to understand, because of its *sheer volume alone.*

Case Study Short: The customer had their original RDBMS tables partitioned on *date*, so felt that if it worked in one place, why not another? So the DBAs proceeded to distribute the data on the SPUS by the same value, the transaction-date, and it looked evenly distributed. Fact, the SPUS had practically no data-skew at all.

So why were their queries so *slow*? Several minutes for the simplest query?

In actuality, if the user launched a query within a given date-range, the query would only include one or two of the SPUS, making these few do all the work while the others remained idle. Once these were redistributed to *random*, the queries consistently returned in seconds. This wasn't a form of data skew, but *process* skew.

Yes, skew comes in many forms. We need to know our data, so we don't accidently skew ourselves.

Case Study Short: The customer loaded data to randomly distributed tables. Three of the tables were dimension tables, sporting over 100,000 rows each. The fact table contained over one billion rows. Upon joining the fact table to one of the dimensions, the query returned in less than ten seconds. When including a second dimension, the query returned in just over fifteen seconds. The customer then distributed the data with the fact table and the first dimension on a common key, causing them to join in co-location on the SPUs. The return time for the first query was now eight seconds. But when adding the second table, was *less than five seconds*.

Seems that under the covers, the first situation required the host to send the dimensional information from both tables to the fact data, distributing the data toward the fact table, and competing with each other on the internal network. With the co-located situation, the first dimension joined with the fact on the SPU and their preliminary result was very small, shipping its result toward the second dimension, instead of the fact table, for an even shorter turnaround time.

Whew! Got all that? The optimizer makes all these decisions, and countless others, on-the-fly. Aren't you glad we can just call it at five seconds and not care what happens under the covers? It's an appliance, so what's under the covers is, well, you know, *covered*.

Why do we care?

Case Study Short: The customer, an international shipper, loaded their customer transactional data onto the machine, distributing the information on the customer_id. The information both loaded slowly and their queries ran with unacceptable performance. Upon reviewing the SPU distribution, the graphic looked like a mountain range with tall peaks and deep valleys.

Seems that some of their customers (large companies) had a lot of shipping activity while others (their mom-and-pop outlets) didn't have much at all. The large-scale customer_ids dogpiled themselves heavily onto a relatively few SPUS. The customer then opted for random distribution because most of their queries would use the customer_id, and none of the other keys had any value in the distribution. Later in the deployment, they learned that one of the fact tables could benefit from co-located joins on transaction_id, and a distribution on this value was nearly random anyhow. By distributing on transaction_id, they did not harm the majority of queries, but instead boosted the queries that benefitted from co-location of the transaction_id.

The point is, distribution keys provide optimization from the random baseline. We'll get awesome performance from the baseline alone. In some cases, distribution keys provide significant lift while in others, only extra gravy.

But gravy isn't bad, either.

Case Study Short: One environment had billions of records in one table and we needed to self-join the table on other keys, multiple times. Rather than perform the self-join, we carved out two temporary tables, one representing the columns-of-interest for the parent in the join, and one representing the children-of-interest. We then cross-joined these two tables for the many slice-and-dice operations required to get the answers. The overall time to carve out the smaller tables and then join, took far less time than multiple-self-joining the master table. We additionally distributed the carved-out tables on keys that co-located their joins, boosting the power further. The overall reduction in time for this operation more than paid for the effort, by a factor of fifty-to-one.

While co-located joins sound cool and sexy, they're not always the best fit. We should fit the distribution for the task-at-hand and not make arbitrary all-or-nothing declarations about what kind to use. One of our colleagues said that his environment required (by governance policy) key-based distribution for *all* tables, and mandated that if someone needed random distribution, they should manufacture a random sequence, apply it to the table and use the sequence as the distribution key. Do what works, but keep it simple.

Can't I just join without co-location?

Sure, just distribute on random. It's what most people do anyhow when they get their first machine on the floor. Keep in mind that co-located joins are an application *optimization* that gives us additional boost over the regular on-demand hash-join that is normally in play when the distribution is random. Also – when the distribution is random, the SPUs cross-talk during the query operation, effectively shipping *keys* around so that all joins are essentially co-located anyhow. So we don't really lose anything with the random distribution. Netezza has our back.

The Netezza machine performs very sophisticated data filtration. In one example, we joined several tables, then added another, and another. Each time we added another table to the join, the machine's speed *got faster*. How is this possible? The magic of filtration.

In our particular case, the smaller tables' keys were being pulled and shipped to the other SPUs where the larger tables existed. This allowed the SPUs to leverage these keys in-memory to filter the larger tables before the data exited the hardware. This is only one scenario of many that the SPUs will use to intelligently optimize a given query.

However (don't you hate that word?) there is a pitfall here. While it looks like we might be able to dogpile as many tables into a join as we like, this is rarely the best approach. We should break apart such a massive operation, into its constituent sub-operations and perform several SQL statements using intermediate tables. This is more maintainable and loses nothing.

Intermediate tables? We still *need* those? Yes and no. We can sometimes find optimization in intermediate tables by pre-filtering larger quantities of data into smaller quantities *before* performing a more complex operation on it. This is especially true if we plan to execute several similar operations against the same tables. We can squeeze down the data to its necessary parts, churn it within this context, and then toss the workspace with zero penalties and all the benefits of a shorter operation.

Benchmark several options and run with the best one. *Don't* be afraid to experiment and do things we would never do in an RDBMS. Netezza is highly flexible and gives us the power to play around with terabytes at a time. We will always need to take a few stabs at those long-running operations (multiple queries that might collectively take ten minutes or longer) to see if we can *easily* shave a few minutes off, maybe *lots* of minutes off. Remember that the minutes we save now in these basic exercises will translate to many hours of savings over the lifetime of our solution.

I'm also not suggesting that we *engineer* a solution to squeeze blood from the machine. Over-engineering will only shorten the lifecycle of our solution, because new requirements will require re-engineering. This is simply an *optimization* exercise to get the most comfortable fit between performance and long-term manageability. Now we have a machine that lets us freely and confidently do both.

How much optimization can we really expect? After all, it would seem that if our anticipated lift isn't very high, the discussion seems like more engineering and thought-labor for very little return. The typical random distribution runs at about eighty percent (or more) of what the machine could do to assist in boosting a single join. Distribution keys, especially for queries that run more frequently, can rapidly move us into the 99+ percentile.

But we have another consideration - what if we need to execute a series of operations on the same tables, such as in boiling various quantities from the base tables? We see this in scientific computing, linear analysis, time-series crunching and the like. In many cases, the actual data in the larger table is a small subset we can drag into a smaller subset, then beat the daylights out of it. We can take this opportunity to redistribute the data into the key we intend to use. We have lots of options. It's an appliance, so experiment and tune, but do keep it simple.

If we find ourselves engineering things, we're doing something wrong, or we're addicted to the adrenalin. A true sign of addiction is that the technologists claim that they can stop anytime they want to. Once upon a time, we wondered if the vendor would offer addiction-counseling, or perhaps detox programs for the adrenalin junkies craving another acceleration hit. But that's not how a Netezza-dealer works. They *want* to keep us hooked, so we keep coming back for more.

It's insidious, no?

6 LOADING UP WITH STUFF

IN JUST about every environment I've worked in or around, the "long pole in the tent" so to speak, invariably boiled down to load-time. Whether it's actually moving data into the machine, or performing write-centric ELT inside the machine. Writing data to disk. That's what it's all about. And it's where Netezza's competitors often choke.

"It's the Jurassic Park model,", the major vendors will explain to us. We have to pay a lot in the front (loading and transformation) in order to achieve the nimble query results on the front end. Oh sure, they'll say, loading is an issue. Get the data to us and we'll turn off indexing during the load, turn it back on after the load, not to worry, we'll spread that work out so you don't know the difference. But either way, ya gatta pay.

But we *do* know the difference. In the Jurassic Park model, the heavy-lifting is done in the flow - crunching and shaping the data on the way to its end-point. When data arrives from our ETL flow, it's not only *load ready*, it's *consumption-ready* too. So the database is largely off the hook for anything more than getting the data inside. If it takes an hour, or two, that's okay. If it takes twenty minutes for a small load, an hour for a large one, that's okay, too. If we've leveraged a utility loader for the RDBMS, we've obeyed Rule #10 and kept the database out of the row-level data processing loop.

Haven't we?

"Ya gatta pay the dues, tah get da benefits. Tanks for stoppin' by," overheard in the Underground catacombs, to several hapless travelers who wanted data warehousing for free.

What if we could obviate all these considerations, getting the data into the machine so that it's actually available sooner? Available for what? Who cares? It's *available*. Keep in mind that from the time the data processing flow begins until the data is *actually* available – is the time we're trying to shorten. It's *flow* optimization. Players that don't play well in the flow optimizations are the players that like to touch, taste, handle and share vacation pictures with each and every row as it arrives into the system.

Enough!

What if we could just open a pipeline and pour the data inside like liquid? What if we could just press a button and have the data inhaled, like it was oxygen? Do we really *need* to touch every water molecule to get it inside? Of course not! This is the weakness of the RDBMS that we have deftly sidestepped with our purchase of the Big Black Box.

Data intake is perhaps where Netezza shines brightest among the constellation of enterprise products. No known technology (that's right, not even Ab Initio) can keep up with the ability of Netezza to inhale data. That's no slight on Ab Initio itself, because it can only go so fast as its own physical plant will allow. The point is, Ab Initio is a lean, mean environment, conscripting every last ounce of performance from its power-plant *by design*, and Netezza will *still* be waiting on it, checking its wristwatch for the data to show up. That's because Ab Initio is a software product, beholden to the physical plant it's sitting on, and Netezza is a hardware product, waiting on the other hardware products to catch up.

This section deals with plain-vanilla loading and some of the continuous flow issues that are one level higher. We'll deal with these in more context in *Continuous Stuff*.

Under the covers, the Netezza 10200 machine has bound dual gigabit network cards, each answering on a different IP. We can load to both simultaneously *at network speed*. This means *double* our actual network speed. Do we fully understand the implications of this capability? We're talking about pushing data at over *150* megabytes per second, upwards of *600* gigabytes per hour as it lands on the disk, and even more with compression.

"There's certainly more than one way to skin a cat," he said. "But we should not stop at cats alone. Our clients have animals in all shapes and sizes. We like to think of ourselves as animal-neutral when it comes to skinning them. In fact, one could say we're in the *pelt*-making business," - John Cleese, *Fawlty Data*

Case Study Short: In a proof-of-concept, the client charged us with examining their existing technology for how it would pass certain capability tests, then compare it to Netezza and one of its competitors. The client's existing technology loaded the 15 GB test file in several hours. All of the IT staff thought that a load time of anything less than an hour would be impossible.

While setting things up, the competitor's technology came online first, and its internal proponents could not wait to execute the loading test for it. The performance number they received back was *37 minutes*. The technologists were *stunned*. We saw emails flying all over the place, singing the praises of this competitor technology. They performed jumping-high-fives, asked each other out to lunch, patted themselves on the back, shared all budgets in common and had a luv-fest. Woodstock, anyone? They'd found their white knight! Let's just stop now and pause for a moment of silent reverence for this earth-shaking event, marking a moment in history, and *we were there*.

After rolling our eyes for the fifth time, I asked one of the senior technologists if they had experienced any network issues. He didn't understand why I had asked the question, until I raised the concern "It seems a little slow."

All the noise in the room stopped, with all eyes on me. They could not believe what they'd just heard. So flippantly had I maligned their newfound favorite son, you'd think I'd had said "Suzuki" at a Harley Davidson rally.

The lead DBA sputtered, "No, no, this is fast, very fast. We've never seen anything so fast."

We left the room, feeling their eyes on us, but smilin'-on-the-inside.

The Netezza machine arrived the next day and we executed the same load test on it. All the technologists watched as we kicked off the load. They waited for a few minutes at the flashing prompt, then dispersed to go about their business. No sooner had they found their way back to their desks than we quipped, "It's done."

The lead DBA looked up at us, staring as though we were joking. Then he saw that the prompt had indeed returned. We performed a simple "select count(*)" on the table, and it showed that all the records had indeed arrived, safe and sound.

In five minutes.

"You originally said that any time under an hour would be acceptable, *right?*" We tried to confirm without gloating. Honestly, we had bitten our lip the day before, but *Spartacus* had just entered the arena, so it was hard not to cheer. "And you said that thirty minutes was just over-the-top more than you ever expected, right?"

We wondered that we would not need smelling salts or *something* to break him out of his trance as he stared, mesmerized at the Putty session with the raw timing on it.

This ladies and gentlemen, was a *Kodak* moment.

Flat Files

We'll put this notation up front so there's no mistake or confusion. In bulk data processing, we need to nestle ourselves as close to the hardware physics as possible, minimizing the total times our software touches it, and maximizing its hardware-based control.

The closest thing we can get to, under our immediate control, is the flat file. We've seen one developer after another "try to do it" with a flat-file *aversion*. We hear excuses with everything from "flat files look too much like mainframe work" to "I thought we were past all this" - as though flat files have no more a place in computing than does Fortran.

I've frightened you now, because you might be thinking the next section is on Fortran, but it's not. Flat files are easily configurable, manageable and maintainable. Some people will deny the usefulness of flat files with their dying breath. Others understand them only as a "necessary evil" so treat them like noise. We then avoid wrapping them with strong data management because we expect them to go away, and don't want to waste any effort on institutionalizing them. But flat files aren't going away. We need to take the plunge, circumscribe them with protocols and support so they don't bite us, and treat them as necessary, not a necessary evil.

One of the worst things we can do, is disregard the role of the flat file as though we don't need it. The next worst thing we can do, is embrace it and abuse it. Flat files have a place in the loading stream, but not in the regular flow. If we use flat-files as simple intermediate storage for a component-based flow (e.g. Ab Initio) we will see a "leapfrog" effect as our data comes on and off the disk drives. In hardware terms, our data will literally meet itself coming and going on the SAN connection, causing our entire flow to devolve into an I/O-bound state. No, flat files are for dropping off the work products of one flow, in one zone of processing, to publish the content into another zone of processing. Keep this zone-of-processing mindset, we would see Ab Initio only save data to disk when it needed to checkpoint the data, or when it needed to drop off the content in preparation for sending it on to the database.

The most appropriate use of flat files around the Netezza machine, is when we need to intake or publish. Netezza external tables can help with both. But we also need to regard the infrastructure associated with flat-file handling. It's simple, but not optional.

When it comes to loading, or any kind of intake protocol, think carefully about how flat files may (or should) play a role, embrace it and run with it. If we treat them like noise, we will miss an important opportunity. We'll address this again for outtake and publication. Just keep in mind that flat files are a mainstay of large-scale bulk processing. Put some protocol, infrastructure and governance around managing them, and keep the performance fires burning.

Intake Protocol Example

I'll talk about some intake ideas in a bit, but for now let's examine some of the things we'll need in the way of intake rules or protocols. We're running a warehouse. We have inventory (records) kept in bins or carrels (tables) likewise kept in areas (schemas) in our overall warehouse building, (our operational environment). We need to initiate traceability as far *up* the intake chain as we can possibly go without actually leaving the building. In some cases, we might do just that, leave the building, to use traceability markers even from our external providers.

What's that? Your tech staff just wants to load some data? *Sigh.* Move on to the **Loading** section (next). But for those who want to solve enterprise problems, stay put. We'll get to loading momentarily.

Some "high audit" financial environments often require us to maintain very strict control over their client and peer intake. In many cases, client intake comes through a localized system that we will extract on a periodic basis. The external provider (or business-to-business) intake usually arrives in the form of a transmission, flat file or other medium. So in a high-audit environment, we have to track the following (minimum) information, often used to steer the intake protocol, like an *intake_audit* table, or an intake audit log file.

- Intake ID – unique identifier we can use for referencing this particular intake event.
- Source – where did it come from, a special client, a new client, a client with special handling requirements, etc.
- Media – file, table, source system, queue, automatic extract, download, etc
- Media Name / Instance Name – like a file name, queue name, source system extract name, etc
- Size – how big is the file, extract, etc
- Date time – always need a point-in-time reference. Bigger customers will send several a day throughout the day.
- Row count – how many actual rows in the transmission
- Notification / contact – who and how to contact individuals who are tracking status
- A reference as to when to expect the transmission, if the publisher is under an SLA

Something that we'll encounter on a regular basis: our upstream publishers will want to know that their data arrived correctly, on time and was processed, and the outcome status of that process. Many of them will not acknowledge that they need or want something like this. But the first time a file is lost in the transmission, they'll wonder why we don't have this capability. They will ask for it, as though it should have been there all along. And will wonder why we cannot answer for it.

Firstly, to handle the noted tracking functionality above, a simple (transactional) table structure will do the trick. A running log file will work just as well. If we use a database table, we don't want it to be inside Netezza, since appending to this table would be a transactional-style hit on the machine. We *can* however, install a Netezza external table, itself with an underpinning flat file as its source. We can then append (in Unix) to this flat file any data we wish. If we want to examine it, we can pull it into a regular Netezza table and toss it when we're done. It's easy to do, and handy for later traceability.

For automated upstream extracts, the world is our oyster. It's fairly easy to set up a scenario where we extract the data and then send a notification to an operator as to the status. All of our internal system-to-system operations can enjoy this kind of care and feeding.

But what about external sources, the ones we don't control? These normally appear in the form of a downloaded network/internet feed (reference data) or an inbound FTP file. Either way, a file will land in a file repository somewhere and we'll have to deal with it. Who do we notify that the intake is complete? An operator for starters. *Someone* wants to know. These processes are neither created nor operated in a vacuum.

Of course, if a publisher is passive, like reference data, it does not actually "send" us anything. We fetch it in our own good time, but we still need to notify someone that the process was initiated and its outcome.

Then we have people who owe us a feed, one that they will initiate. We likely have a hard deadline on when it's supposed to show up. One of our clients is a nationwide retail chain. All of its stores transmit their transactional files to a central repository every fifteen minutes. Over five thousand stores, that means twenty thousand files arriving every hour. Some don't make it and have to be re-transmitted. Some of the store owners doubt a transmission and re-transmit, creating a duplicate to deal with. All of the files and their contents require inventory control. It's not trivial or simple to deal with, but it's not particularly complex if we deal with it systematically and deliberately.

Case Study Short: One data feed supplier had a heated conversation with the data management company's CIO. He'd sent all of his feeds over in the prior evening but they had not been processed. One of the help desk people said that they had never received the files. The supplier took this conversation very personally, and asked directly if the help desk person was calling him a liar. Such awkward conversations are not only unexpected, but unnecessary. The CIO said that he wanted to fix this problem by proactively sending acknowledgements to the data suppliers, notifying them of the safe arrival and disposition of their inputs (or the lack of same).

What if the file is supposed to show up but never does? What if the intake data fails to load? We might need to account for these and other exception scenarios, and the intake audit can help.

For example, if the final file is supposed to show up by 6pm and normally shows up before 5pm, wouldn't it be courteous, even proactive, to send the supplier a friendly email to this effect *in time for them to do something about it?* If they miss the deadline for no better reason than an internal hiccup, we can help them avoid missing the deadline with a simple messaging protocol.

What if the files are really big, and the intake processing attempts to read them before they are completely written down on disk? (happens a lot with big FTP files).

Our best bet is to require the supplier to send a *trailer* file along with the data file, as long as the trailer file is sent directly after the data file. Some people reading this will say, of course you would send a trailer file, and it doesn't matter how big the file is! And this is exactly right. Why would we use a trailer file for the large files only, rather than using one for all files? If we set up this protocol now, it will never outgrow us. If we have a different protocol for files based on size alone, what happens when a smaller file becomes a larger file? Do we renegotiate the intake process?

Case Study Short: One environment had ensconced a popular EAI orchestration product for all their EAI and B2B needs. In the analysis, one of their intake protocols opened an inbound flat file and compared its contents with that of the trailer file, matching the noted size, row count, etc. before proceeding. Once validated, it forwarded the file into a common pool of files, later ingested by Ab Initio for larger-scale intake. Since this orchestration mechanism handled all files big and small, an internal debate ensued as to whether the larger files should be processed by Ab Initio, with the smaller files processed by the orchestration. This initiated another discussion around what would happen if a smaller file "became" a larger file? Do we redeploy the file's intake from the orchestrator to Ab Initio when the time is right? What happens when a larger file shrinks? Do we redeploy it under the orchestration's umbrella?

You can see how strange this conversation sounds. What does it matter as to the size of the file? It is more important to have a *consistent intake mechanism.* For the time being, all of the files would start out under the orchestration umbrella. The developers on the team then cut deals with the purveyors of the larger files to have them transmitted in parts over the course of the day, reducing their size and increasing their frequency. This leveled out all the file sizes and let the orchestration environment, you know, orchestrate.

As noted prior, don't get lost in purist arguments. Fix the *problem.*

The trailer file should carry exactly the same name as the data file, but with a different extension. It will be very small, holding only the metadata for the data file:

- Data file name
- Data file size
- Data row count
- Some of the source info noted above
- Other metadata (you pick)

This allows a canned intake process to pull the trailer file, match it to a target table, then perform the actual load intake in a more reusable componentized form. The intake process will:

- Send an acknowledgement to the sender when the trailer file arrives.
- Process the file and cross-check against the trailer for row counts and/or bytes counts
- Send another acknowledgement to the sender when processed successfully (or otherwise)
- If your sender has a service-level-agreement that the file should arrive within a certain window – if the file does not arrive within one-third of the window's expiration, transmit a warning message to the file's sender.
- Continue sending periodic warning messages until the file arrives.
- Negotiate with the sender as to the content, timing and frequency of these and any other messages.

As we can see, there's more to *some* intake protocols than might meet the eye. What we'll examine in the next pages are ways to leverage these things to lock down our intake into the same rock-solid machine-form as the box it's sitting on.

And seriously, we don't have to put the above functionality into the Netezza machine itself. If we've already done it, fine, it won't hurt anything at all. Lots of folks have other options in an ETL environment or commodity tools.

The point is, we need these things and we should build them into the intake. Netezza provides the power to manage the additional throughput that these operations require, or the power to seamlessly dovetail into what we already have.

Loading

We have several simple ways to push data into the machine. What we have here is a need to get data into the box, in *quantity*.

One of our colleagues does amateur car racing. Each year he goes out to Texas Motor Speedway near Dallas and they do an open-house, so to speak. Another friend noted that when they do this on his own local track, he has to use a car that can *easily* top 160 miles per hour. When you get to the first curve, he explained, it is so steep that if you're moving at less than this speed, the car will just slide down the track. The speed is what keeps the car on the curve, and it's got a "necessary minimum."

Netezza has a "necessary minimum" for a loading event. It works out to be about one gigabyte. Anything less than this in inefficient for Netezza. If this is all we have, then load away. But if we have a lot of little files, we should fan-in to a single load stream to meet the necessary minimum. The fan-in collector paradigm is one I'll repeat in other places, because it seems to rear its head quite a bit. Mainly because some folks (transactional thinkers) want to treat Netezza like a dessert topping, that is, a transactional system, and believe trickle-feeding it is okay stuff.

If we're going Unix-To-Unix, we can do this very easily with a common *cat* utility. Before rolling your eyes, think about what *cat* will do for us. It will pick up the data off the disk and shoot it into a memory-based pipeline. It will not write back to the disk, and won't be keeping anything in memory. Functionally speaking, *cat* gets it done.

Here's another take: Whenever we hear about people using *cat* in data processing, it's usually to pick up a pack of serial files and make another big-fat serial file, a total waste of time. Here, though, we're pushing the results into *memory*. Off-the-disk-and-into-ether as far as the *cat* is concerned. What *other* function would we use to pick up files and put them one-at-a-time into a pipe, carefully stripping off the end-of-file markers until the last one? We don't want to go parallel here, because the objective is to act as a *collector* for fan-in. Even if we wrote a C-language program to do the same thing as *cat*, it would still be *doing the same thing*, in the same way. So why not just use *cat*? Reinventing the wheel doesn't buy us anything. *It's just a file copy.*

So where do we send the data?

The Netezza platform has an onboard and client form of its utility loader, called *nzload*. The nzload utility does all the magic of connecting to the Netezza machine and delivering the data to a target table. If we need to *cat* the data together, we simply instantiate a named pipe (Linux FIFO), launch the nzload to read the named pipe, then cat the files into the named pipe. This effectively performs the functional fan-in using common, documented (and memory-based) Unix utilities, and will never run out of gas.

Of course, if we only have one file to load, we just invoke nzload and shoot it. No mess, no fuss. If we find ourselves invoking nzload a lot, that is frequently for each table whether the files are large enough or not, it is still *logistically* better to fan-in the large files, even if there's only one on occasion, to support a single, infrequent loading event. In this regard, *nzload* will always see one large stream, whether it originates as a large file, multiple small files or whatever, *nzload* won't care. It will read the FIFO/pipe, and it will be the responsibility of a fan-in collector to fill it.

The conclusion of this, is that if using a *fan-in* to a pipe is the most flexible form of loading in all cases, why not just build our whole intake infrastructure for a fan-in? In some of the installations we've done, we just standardize on the pipes and fanning-in, and whether we have one big file or hundreds of little ones, small files or large, or anything in between - it always works.

One of the most important things about standing up an infrastructure of capabilities, is to make it the *most* resilient so we never have to go *back*, for any reason. Here, by standardizing on nzload, cat and fan-in to a FIFO, we effectively embrace a model that will never run out of gas and we'll never have to refactor no matter how many or few, big or small files we have.

In a white-board session, some Netezza users had a special problem in getting data *out* of an underpowered RDBMS into Netezza. They likewise had some issues getting data *in* to the same underpowered RDBMS using Netezza. Another consultant in the room was tempted to offer up mocking questions as to why they would ever tie Netezza to a slower technology, but we knew where they were coming from. Bulk extract from their RDBMS was always problematic. Likewise in the other direction for loading. Such a product seems to be its own worst enemy in data warehousing. Not to worry - see the loading tips in *Continuous Stuff* for some pointers on this. We'll need to trickle the data over rather than bulk-load, and most RDBMS technologies won't mind this kind of operation all that much, it's a transactional system after all.

Programmatic Loading via "pull"

Yet another means to get data into the machine, is to point the *intake* functions to the network, while they actually execute under Linux on the Netezza machine. This simply means that the loading infrastructure for data intake is centered in the Netezza box, increasing its value as an enterprise bulk processing asset. In this configuration, we don't create significant infrastructure *around* the machine. Externally, we only need to get data onto a mounted volume where Netezza can see it, and Linux can do the rest.

Some external dangers exist here. The place we will read data from has to itself receive the data from somewhere. Why is this an issue? The typical SAN device that Netezza would reach out and read from, has *excellent* read speeds, often network-speeds. However, those devices sometimes have abysmal *write* speeds. I've seen SANs that will deliver data in relative seconds on a *read* compared to the equivalent *minutes* another process requires to write the data to the SAN. This means the SAN is sometimes a poor choice for store-and-forward to support Netezza's intake flow.

In one case, the SAN had one-sixth the write speed as read speed (according to its vendor sheet!). In another case, the SAN had one *thirtieth* the write speed versus read speed. In yet another, we found that the write-speed was *4 megabytes a second*. Considering that most gigabit networks can transmit data at *80 megabytes a second,* we've sort of hamstrung ourselves, haven't we? Before using the SAN as part of the enterprise store-and-forward, find out what the true throughput really is.

Pay attention to the write speed.

If we go this route, we should measure the *actual* write-speed of the device and plan on this being our maximum throughput rate. With Netezza's dual network cards, it can intake data at double this network speed, or *160 megabytes a second.* We can see how a common SAN can slow us down.

Can we also see how a traditional SMP-based RDBMS, using a similar SAN for storage, cannot compete with the intake capacity of the Netezza machine?

Another solution is just as viable, without the same flow drag. If we have an intermediate server, sometimes the server's *local* storage is faster on the write speed than an enterprise SAN. We can examine just about any enterprise server, most especially the more popular Solaris, AIX and HP servers, and their I/O for writing data is far faster than some enterprise SANs. Your actual mileage may vary, but don't allow strange numbers to fool you when trying to get data written to the SAN. Most people don't realize how slow their SANs are until they *measure* them when attempting bulk-processing store-and-forward. Some SANs and network appliance storage systems (e.g. NFS-mounted systems) even have disclaimers in their product literature that they are *not* applicable for data warehousing.

Take them seriously on this claim. Uh, *read the product label*?

If latency is not an issue (we have a midnight batch window we're waiting on anyhow) then just drop and collect the files on the SAN and don't give them a second thought. The files don't need to be anywhere else right away, and the Netezza machine will not pick them up until midnight or later, so no worries. As noted prior, the new *StoragePad* capability will provide 10 TB of onboard EMC-class write-speed for files destined for the Netezza domain. This option is stellar for applications that have lots of inbound files to write, store and manage.

Now we get to the actual pull of the data, and this simply requires a mount-point for the Netezza machine. Considering that we can configure much of Unix, we can envision easily supporting multiple mount-points as a simple metadata-described capability. Past this, we just need the 'root' path for the *source* of the data. We also need a way to designate the load's *target* table. Both of these are easily programmable, so not really much of an issue either. We can still use the 'cat' into named-pipe (FIFO) scenario mentioned earlier, where the pipes are owned by the Netezza machine. We invoke a local nzload, reading from the pipe, then 'cat' the remote files into the local pipe. What could be simpler?

Not so fast - we have something else to consider. What if this process *fails*? If the remote disk should fail, the network disconnects, the 'cat' hiccups from error, or nzload fails from bad data - we didn't *actually* succeed, and these are only the *obvious* points of failure. Our method should cover the failure points, *and* other intake considerations all in one place.

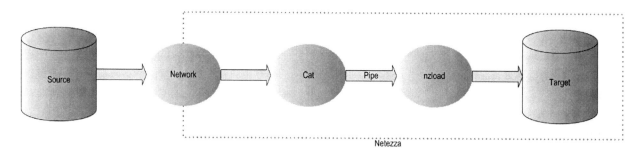

In the depiction (above) we can see the potential *external* points of failure already. We need a way to mitigate the external points of failure prior to the data's actual arrival on the target table.

I've mentioned in the prior section how we can intake tens of gigabytes in minutes. This gives us the luxury of time for some additional transform cycles. An inconvenient truth is that intake flat files often hold bad data, networks hiccup, disk drives interrupt their output, and sometimes they happen all at once. We cannot afford simple system or bad-data issues stopping us from completing the mission, and we don't have to.

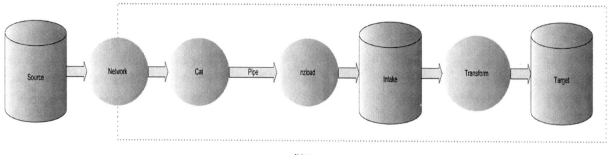

In the depiction (above) the *temporary intake table* creates a clean break between the risks of intake and the final landing of the target table, *plus* the ability to perform a scrubbing / enrichment cycle before landing in the target table.

To mitigate intake failure points, we set up a temporary intake table (using normal SPU-based parallel, not an external table) that is identical to the target table with one important difference – the columns are all nullable or flattened data types, and the table is randomly distributed. By performing the intake into this intermediate intake table, we achieve the intake decoupling we desire.

Now if anything happens with the network, the files, the data – anything at all – the load to the intake table will have failed. We can correct the issues as necessary, and try it again. But here's the takeaway: if the process fails, we can functionally and logically treat it *just as if it never happened*.

Note also how this aligns to the **Rule #5**, Data Management, where we challenge the data first, and deliberately, to mitigate the infusion of trash into the downstream.

"It never happened," President of the United States Jack Ryan, Tom Clancy's *Debt of Honor,* when announcing how he would fix the irreversible effects of a runaway terrorist-induced stock-market virus, by resetting all trading systems to the original state as of one hour before the virus struck.

Moving on, with the data in the intake table, we can now execute a transform-style query (*insert-into-target-select-from-intake*) that takes the data from the intake to the target table. In this query, we will transform all nulls, correct all inline information, perhaps even enrich the target table with metadata or reference data. Once complete, we drop the intake table and we're done.

Keep in mind, the *nzload* is a wrapper to the Netezza external table, so in many ways is handling the data intake of conforming the file content into the internal table. This is good, because it's adapting all the parsing and other activities we might have to do otherwise.

This two-phase intake is really not affected by how many / how large the intake files are. Because it faces the SPUs, it has fast intake and transform. For the above noted POC intake, we can pull the data into the machine and perform the transform *in less than eight minutes* total. In fact, we could perform the load (five minutes) and multiple full-table transforms (15 of them) before we ever exceed the *load* time of Netezza's nearest competitor. *Behold* the data processing power we have, and the nearly *luxurious* data processing time to get things done right, assimilating the flow rather than accepting risk.

Once again, the primary benefit of the Netezza-centric *pull* of the data, is that the satellite systems don't have to know anything about, or actually interact with, the Netezza machine's load cycle, Automated processes simply drop off the intake files to a common staging depot with the expectation that Netezza (or a supporting process) will perform the intake at some later time. It decouples the upstream from the downstream, and generally reduces overall failure points in the delivery cycle. It also aligns with (centralized) data management practices and publish-subscribe protocols.

As an additional benefit, we can manage metadata reports. For example, which files were part of the intake, how big they were and how long they took to load. All of this is visible to the Netezza processing and can be deposited in report logs for health checks and operational integrity.

It is a false assumption that the intake transfer will always finish happily. We might get 99.99% happiness over time, but the 0.01% sadness is often *much* sadness, if we don't have a plan to recover ourselves into happiness again. Does this sound like a self-help mantra? It might, only because we are adjuring you to help yourself, and do yourself a favor. Build some data transfer infrastructure into your environment!

What does the intake table look like? It looks exactly like our target table, or rather, like our target table *minus* the additional columns we've added for overhead. What's that, your target table looks identical to the source feed? You don't have any surrogates, audit identifiers or other enrichments applied during intake? And why not? Oookay, read the prior section, and come back.

Now we need to map the incoming feed to the target table via an intermediate table. This means we need a table definition that bridges the file structure into the target table.

May we suggest the use of catalog metadata to this effect? After all, we have a catalog definition of the target table don't we? We know what columns we added to enrich it from the original file load, don't we? Why can't we just map these extra columns and populate them as part of the intake? We'll load the intake information into the temporary intake table, then copy it to the target, enriching it along the way. If we treat every inbound data source this way, we have the beginnings of an intake cycle *component*.

Externally-initiated loading. If an external system pushes data towards the Netezza machine, it should likewise push it into a staging table or landing zone. From here, the external system will remotely invoke the next stage of Netezza processing, or the Netezza machine can just pick up the work on an internally scheduled boundary. Either way, some "next stage" of activity will perform the secondary intake into our master repository from our dirty landing zone. In a continuous environment, this process-handoff is especially important because we don't want external systems arbitrarily imposing high-intensity processing activities on a machine that has time-critical SLAs.

If we set up a landing zone correctly, we don't really need "formal" landing zones (although setting aside an internal schema for this purpose is good for configuration). Let's examine the mechanics and the pattern, and we'll see some highly reusable logic here, that applies to all of our inbound feeds.

- Data arrives, targeting a specific table
- We take the DDL of the specific table and re-manufacture the table structure as an intake table, nullable columns and the works (very simple operation, we can use the existing table's DDL definition right off the catalog)
- We intake the data into the intake table
- We transform the data from the intake table to the target, using an insert/select construct
- When we insert/select, we perform the columnwise cleansing necessary for the intake, primarily setting all a default value for all inbound columns that show up containing NULL. We can also perform other common transformations here, but only those that are for general intake protocol, not necessarily those for the target table itself.
- Drop the intake table
- Send success/failure report to any external component that is waiting for the notification.
- Start the next downstream process

Of the above operations, the creation of the temporary intake table seems the most tedious. The Netezza catalog provides a simple means to capture and understand the table's DDL. All we need to add is the nullable notations and other housekeeping.

The copying of the temporary intake table into the target seems likewise daunting, but it is also straightforward. Both the creation and the copy can be driven with simple scripts and metadata from the system catalog, so are reusable components for any table we choose.

What does this buy us, exactly? We have yet to see an environment where the data intake protocol did not need fortification. Here are some reasons why:

- The sender can go offline in the middle of the process
- The network can fail
- The overall hardware on either end can fail
- The operator can interrupt the operation
- Another process can kill the operation
- A troubleshooter can kill the operation
- A bad data element can bomb off the load

What we're really dealing with, is the subtle nuances between two systems and the potential for failure at the system level. Here are the firewalls that the above process provides:

- We get an automatic *structural* adaptation between the inbound data and the target table. Inter-system adaptation is always a necessary evil, and in this case, it's in there.
- We know that the intake won't fail because of dirty data alone, because we're *allowing* dirty data into the temporary table.
- Inter-system data intake does not face the target table, so we avoid the corruption of the target if the intake fails
- If the operation fails in the middle of transfer, we can still drop the intake table
- If the operation fails, we can repeat from the start, not in the middle, avoiding midstream corruption or duplicated data.
- Only when the data has fully arrived, do we close the inter-system connection and send the data downstream.
- If the process fails *anywhere* in the inter-system interaction, we can throw away all of our work and start over, without regard to downstream corruption
- We can include an Audit infrastructure for free, since a data load is always a traceable operation. (discussed later)
- We can treat the entire operation as *throwaway*, for any inter-system error, even one that does not stop the transfer.

Often when we explain the use of these temporary intake tables, people balk, and glare at us askance. Their objection is simply this: The above described protocol means we will have to land the data into the Netezza database *twice*, not just once. This means once for the intake table and once for the final copy. They scratch their heads, wondering what we must be thinking, because, they surmise, *this would be inefficient in any other database engine.* And they would be right.

However, in the smallest Netezza production machine, we'll receive data into a 216-way parallel table, and likewise copy it into a 216-way parallel table. Dividing the work 216 ways is *far* different than what *any other database engine* can do. So not to belabor a point, *we must think about the problems and their solutions differently than we are accustomed to.*

The above described operation is something that is sorely needed in data warehouse intake protocols. Would we arbitrarily avoid using it because it seems – *counter-intuitive?* No, Netezza gives us the power plant to do things the right way. We should embrace this power and leverage it for the good of all mankind (okay, that's a little dramatic), but at least for the integrity of our warehouse, the protection of the inter-system flow, and the protection of our target tables from corruption due to failure.

And uh, protect our *personal* time from late-night operator calls when an application fails?

And here's another consideration: We can load data into Netezza and transform it for validation in a fraction of the time Netezza's competitors do a simple load. We have the luxury of doing it right, so let's do it.

Zone Mapping – Make the Most

I'll note periodically (like now) that one reason Netezza can forego index structures is in how it leverages mass filtration to *avoid touching* the data, rather than index-searching to *go find* the data, or gross scanning to slog *through* the data. This avoidance-filtration theme is something Netezza has down to a hardcore science, one that we can leverage in many creative ways to get higher degrees of lift without much additional effort.

One of Netezza's coolest capabilities is the *automatic* ability to leverage zone maps. What a zone-map does is allow us to lay down data in a specific ordering, with a given column as the logical key-marker for the *zones* of data. For example, if data is arriving by the day, being laid down in date order, we can mark each record with the date just by setting the date's value in a given column, and Netezza will automatically track the data as it arrives, marking the daily transitions. If we then query the table using the date column as a filter, Netezza will *automatically* ignore the zones that don't contain the given filter value, and focus *physically and logically* on the specific zone containing the data we want. This allows us to get a massive performance boost from nothing more than the sheer organized arrival of the data itself.

The zone map is a lot like Oracle's partitions, but it is massively parallel. Because it tracks the zone values of all date and integer values, we don't have to guess which one it might be tracking. It tracks the zones for the columns and values using these data types.

Of course, if any data arrives out of order, it breaks the zone map. We'll still get the right answer, but it won't come back quite as quickly. The zone map is *automatically applied* as data arrives, to anything that is an integer or date format. So if we have zone-map quantities that are in character form, we need to provide an integer equivalent and we get the same benefit - we can now use this integer equivalent as a zone map. Also keep in mind that just because the data doesn't arrive in the given order, doesn't mean we can't use it as a zone map *later*. We can always restructure data, and with Netezza's power, it's just not painful at all.

Case Study Short: We used some data enrichment processes early in the data processing cycle. When the time arrived to do some additional processing on the given very large tables, we carved *subset* tables out of the original (pulling on the columns we cared about) filtered and *sorted* them based on the already-present zone-mappable values. This action not only reduced the overall data size of the primary tables, it organized the data into their zone maps *automatically* as we wrote the table. Then our next processing actions, some high-intensity operations, leveraged this smaller table rather than the original, then *tossed it* when we were done.

The result of this was to reduce the overall data processing time *by over ninety-five-percent* over the equivalent operations in the original tables. The zone maps caused our rapid-fire integration operations to target very specific portions of the tables, ignoring the remaining content. This kind of boost appears automatically with zone maps. And note how we simply and casually tossed away the work products when we were done. The objective is to *reduce* the flow time, not preserve intermediate work products.

We might find an even more creative use for zone maps, but don't imagine that we *have* to initially intake the data in zone-map form. We have lots of time to transform the data into a more consumable form. Take the opportunity as it arises, which might be at the beginning of the cycle, perhaps later.

And this is a primary takeaway of Netezza-centric transformation – we can very often pull all the data from a table, filter what we don't care about, transform it and lay it down in zone-map order – and then do the query rather than access the original tables. If it's a single, fire-and-forget query, just do it. But if we really need to churn the data, we can pull the data into a more process-friendly form, then beat the daylights out of it. All the activities will take a shorter cycle than if we didn't take the extra transform step.

In the next and later sections, we'll look at more variations on intake in other contexts, especially a *continuous* context.

"The purpose of the web site is to drive the customers to the store," said the principal.

"But we're spending millions of dollars to achieve this," lamented the CFO.

"Hey, doesn't this retail chain also own a national car-rental chain?" asked the troubleshooter.

"Yes, what of it?"

"For this kind of cash, we could rent cars, drive around neighborhoods and take them to the stores."

"What?"

"If the objective is to drive them to the stores, and all."

7 BULK DATA PROCESSING STUFF

IN THE realm of bulk data processing, when we talk to some who currently use the machine, it's sometimes in their original "Jurassic Park" model. They perform all the integration, transformation and other activities before data arrives on the machine, then appears "consumption-ready". The users get a wildly nimble, agile and responsive experience. It's all good.

If our flow-based data processing environment is especially robust (say, Ab Initio), we probably won't have anything to worry about for awhile. Still, the internals of Netezza have *all those CPUs,* and it's practically guaranteed that we can leverage at least *some* of its internal power, right away. As noted in a prior section, it is invariable that we will need to process the data after it arrives. Rather than pull it out just to put it back, Netezza's internal power can help us transform the information without ever leaving the box.

Another inline objective is to reduce the *overall* clock-time (flow time) of the flow as it arrives to its destination tables, *even if those destination tables are post-arrival processing in Netezza.* This balances the power where it fits best. Netezza has a sweet-spot in set-based, bulk, key-based integration and transformation. Let's not treat Netezza as a common read-only query accelerator, when we can do so much more with it. If we target an intake/staging table as the first ingress of data, whomp the daylights out of it, then push to its internal destination table, we've used Netezza in a more expanded role.

For those without a formal ETL environment or who intend to jump right in with a bulk processing solution *inside-the-box* we're about to dive deep.

What is a Netezza transaction?

You will see this word *transaction* in two forms in this book.

Transactional *processing* - dispatching one (or few) rows-at-a-time in a Multiple-Instruction model. Entity-facing stored procedures follow this model, and is native to the RDBMS. Netezza does *not* do transactional processing. Period.

Transactional *session* - performing one or more SQL statements in a session where they can share immediate context, such as temporary tables and variables, and inserted rows stamped with the same transactional session ID (createxid). When the session closes, all temporary assets evaporate. The transactional session is what we might functionally call a stored procedure or an instance of SQLPlus in Oracle terms. Netezza provides for transactional sessions so we can execute multiple SQL statements in functional context. All of the application functionality of a common stored procedure is present. Clearly it is not compiled and *stored* in the database, but it does the same stuff.

By this measure, we *never* perform transactional processing in Netezza, but we may *extensively* leverage transactional sessions for bulk processing.

Row Identification – We need it

Let's say we're working in a physical warehouse, with inventory stored in its various sections. We'll find the inventory in their own bins, likely tagged with something to track them. A SKU, or some other unique means to know when they arrive, where they are located, and when they leave, should someone order them out.

In fact, for practically every example we could provide for resource or asset management, from processes, to people, to systems and their results, *identification* is critical. We want to know *where* something came from, *where* it went to and *what* happened to it in between. We don't want to know what happened to a group or set of like-kinds, but specific, distinguishable uniqueness. We want a consistent way to handle it. We know we need something akin to registering a manufacturer's identifier (bar code / UPC) because this is a common standard. For our purposes, we don't want to use the *actual* manufacturer's identification approach (the source system), because each manufacturer can do it differently.

Mapping this to our data warehouse, we have a need to track the inventory that enters our environment. If we are the final target after a another high-intensity data processing environment, we'll apply the identification there. But if we are the first-on-deck, about to intake and crunch the data through a series of transforms, enrichments and integration processes, we need to keep track of what we're doing, and what's happening to the inventory as it passes through.

The simplest and most effective way to cover this is to give each row it's own "SKU" so to speak, a unique identifier. We can tie this to the natural-key identification of the inventory through surrogate keys. But even if we don't do this, we still need a way to identify the inventory. We know of some shops that mark records with unique IDs without regard to its natural keys. Before we get wrapped around the axle on whether or not to use cross-referenced surrogates, we *still* need unique identification. This part is non-optional. Whatever additional value we can derive from it, great. I'll speak of them in terms of surrogate keys, because we get additional value in using them this way.

Note - I'm not a big fan of surrogate/natural-key cross-reference tables in Netezza, even for slowly-changing dimensions. We'll talk about those, but assigning surrogates-on-the-fly without cross reference is perfectly viable for transactions or places were we don't care about slowly-changing dimensions, because transactions themselves don't change. Transactions *are* the change. What we really care about, is not losing track of all this fast-moving stuff. And if it's fast-moving stuff, chances are even higher that we need to do something fast with it, and losing track of it doesn't serve this goal. In the end, surrogates are the most nimble and objective means to track our fast-moving inventory, and since the changes are associated with transactions, we should embrace them and run with them.

However, some caveats are in order. When we add a row to a Netezza table, the machine will assign a row-id to this new row "for free". Just keep something in mind: the Netezza row-id is not persistent in the way we might think. For example, if we pick these rows up and insert them into another table, or even into the same table – they all get brand new Netezza row-ids, free of charge. Another caveat exists here, in that incremental backups rely on these rowids as well, so re-churning them throws away our incremental backup references. Take care when making *new* table copies.

However, we can leverage these embedded row-ids rather easily as long as we don't get carried away. As noted in a prior section, we need to perform preliminary data cleansing when data first arrives. We also need to perform some data preparation and pre-housekeeping. Any of these processes could use the Netezza row-ids as a temporary identifier, for intermediate steps, inside a transactional session, like for a temporary table (but not as a persistent reference).

A best practice is to assign unique, persistent integer identifiers to each inbound row. We know people who eschew such identifiers, favoring instead natural keys for their data modeling needs. We can see value in using natural keys. And if we need to cross-reference them with surrogates, We also understand how it complicates surrogate key management and the potential disconnections if we lose the cross-reference. We're sure we could list several more superficial reasons for not using surrogates and centering firmly on natural keys. You probably know what they are as well.

For this discussion, I'll offer a few *performance* reasons for leveraging surrogate keys. If we want performance, we don't want natural varchar keys. Some may object to this, and frankly it doesn't matter who you're talking to, or what technology they're talking about, *make them perform a proof-of-concept*. No matter how many times they try, their natural varchar keys will never beat an integer surrogate. Integers can beat natural keys, in some cases, by 100 to 1. Don't be fooled. This is science. Do a proof-of-concept.

Many years ago I worked with a hardware engineer who needed to assemble some analog circuitry. The overall voltage that would pass through the hardware was simply mind-bending, likewise with the overall amperage. He had a set of lockstep procedures he followed, and did not like anyone's casual dismissal of even the simplest part of the protocol. The more we interacted with him, the more we realized the wisdom of each step, and why he eschewed nay-sayers so harshly. No, we did not need such protocols when changing a light bulb or installing a ceiling fan. However, with the level of voltage and amperage he worked with, one simple misstep meant instant, inglorious *death*. While a misstep in our warehouse doesn't have the same stakes, we're still dealing with a problem of *scale*. We'll take steps that don't make any sense for smaller systems.

The primary reasons to use a surrogate (with details to follow afterward).
- Identification – row gets stamped once, we can always find it
- Performance – can't beat it
- Configuration – assists with troubleshooting

- Traceability – provides objective means to track the record through the flows
- Isolation – disconnects us from source and target, we have complete control
- Integration – clean, crisp and elegant data model, clarifying our relationships
- Intersection – we can leverage the surrogate for flexible, creative data intersections

When we want to form intersections between the dimensions and transactions, we'll want clean/crisp and fast connections. Only integers can do this *in bulk*, and rarely does an upstream source consistently apply these. However, here's an interesting rule to follow: if the dimensions and subjects already have integer identifiers, use them. It is highly unlikely (especially in mature ERP/EAI systems like Peoplesoft, etc) that an integer identifier is not already a strong surrogate identifier. This will eliminate the need to capture surrogate/natural key cross-references. Upstream systems rarely stamp their transactional data with a unique integer. If they are, well and good, because today's mature systems likewise implement strong surrogates. But if they don't, we can stamp the incoming transactions with incremental surrogates on arrival (Netezza *sequence*), and since they are non-repeating and not slowly-changing-dimension problems, we *still* don't have to track them in a surrogate cross-reference!

The point is, don't assume that just because we're embracing surrogates that it is necessary to embrace an elaborate means to cross-reference source keys to our surrogates. I'm not a fan of arbitrary over-complication, but in a troubleshooting crunch, we know what's valuable, too. Surrogates give us traceability.

Identification – Whenever data first arrives into our warehouse environment, we need an objective and proactive means to *permanently* identify it. Not only must we identify its source, but maintain track of it through the flows so we don't lose control of it. Controlling and harnessing the inventory is critical. Our users expect this capability at the very least.

What if we were to depend on the upstream source/extract system's identification method and incorporate it as our own? What if the upstream system did not have good control? What if the expectation of our data warehouse users is just that – we will *finally* get control of the data? Abdicating this control to the upstream system is *what we are trying to get away from.*

Harnessing the data, controlling it inside a data management protocol, is the goal. When the data enters our inventory, we stamp it, record its presence and otherwise assimilate it into the warehouse *as our own*. Once inside, *we own it* and we are responsible for it.

It is not a best practice to simply inhale data into our environment with no controls over the what, how, when and why of the inhalation. We can only record these aspects on the data itself. We'll need all that, because we have to scrub the data, synchronize it with other sources, and otherwise make it consumption-ready for a completely different user constituency in the downstream.

One thing is for certain, they will want to know that we have gained control of the information, have never lost control and never will. We cannot do this without proactive and objective means to own and inventory the data.

Does all this control sound draconian? What happens when we need to troubleshoot some erroneous data? Where do we start? In one or several records among *billions*, can we back-trace the rules that touched it, reproduce its path and find the bug? Or for that matter, verify that it's a real bug? An error in the data?

We're talking about problems of *scale*, and troubleshooting in *scale*.

Performance – Here's a simple test: Take a Netezza table with a varchar(10) unique key and replicate the same table with the same key. Now add ten million records to each table. Now join on the tables, using the given key, to get a simple answer like a "count". Pay attention to the duration of the join.

Now let's convert the keys to an integer and perform the same test. We will find that the difference in performance can be as much a 100 to 1. This is not unique to Netezza. Try the same test with SQLServer, Oracle or Sybase. In every case we'll find that the boost is in orders of magnitude, certainly no less than ten times the performance with the integer.

I once worked with an inexperienced lad who knew we had a 13-digit all-numeric key that was sourced as a character field We suggested to convert it to big-integer to get better performance. His quip was that it would "only save us five bytes" (converting 13 characters to 8 bytes). This of course, is a statement borne on the myopic trust of a database engine's software, not the physics that is actually doing the work. *Integer* kicks *character's* tail, every time it's tried.

Here's the mechanics of a how a CPU works when it wants to perform a key-based operation. If the variable is a varchar, the operation will (under the covers) compare the keys one-character-at-a-time until it reaches a conclusion. Some machines will compare several characters at a time, but either way it will compare, in software or firmware, the *contents* of the two keys, usually with some kind of looping operation. (Of course, we won't know the difference in the SQL statement, all of this happens under-the-covers).

Conversely with an integer key, the comparison happens on the hardware of the CPU, usually in a *register right on the silicon*, with a plain-straight *integer subtraction*. Can we now see how using a varchar key is actually a detriment to performance? The integer gives us the boost by aligning with the *physics* of the machine, rather than the varchar that aligns with software running on it,, perhaps firmware running inside it, but not directly on the hardware.

Of course, if we intend to convert the alphanumeric varchars to integer, we *might* need a cross-reference strategy to assign and re-assign the same surrogate for a given natural key.

Configuration: One of the most ignored but perhaps the most valuable aspects of data processing, is how we deal with the configuration of the data itself. After all, the keys in one table will join to the keys in another. If we have multiple versions of the data, for regression, development, performance and the like, they'd better all integrate correctly. But what if they don't?

What if they don't *need* to? For example, in volume performance testing, we can objectively test only the join-duration on the surrogates, not the natural keys. This means we can artificially replicate the data to 5x or 10x its original size, incrementing the surrogate keys with it, to get a valid performance test. But only good row identification, *outside* the natural keys, give us this capability.

And what of the migration and promotion of various work products such as reference data, configuration and initialization data, or just slowly-moving cross-reference information? Without surrogate key identifiers, we have more difficulty tracking what intersects to where, and it won't matter how fast we can integrate bad data. The wrong answer, late or on time, is still wrong.

Data management is as much about the configuration of the data as it is the contents. Do we need synonym links to our regression base? What happens when we integrate disparate keys to our on-the-fly test? In every aspect of development and production implementation, the configuration of the information can and will be a final arbiter of the system's performance and processing integrity.

Surrogates make it easy, in fact, almost transparent.

And then, with slowly changing dimensions we need identification anyhow don't we? We'll need the original identifier appearing multiple times, along with its version number. We also need a way to perform this as a consistent, table-independent capability rather than a solution that faces a single table only. Versioning of live data like this is often critical in financial services environments, where the version is actually tracking changes-of-state in an instrument's maturity or availability.

Traceability – As data moves through our pipelines, we might have very good identification of its original form, its current configuration and state, but what of the processes used to arrive at these end-states? At any point in time, the data is only as good as the processes cranking it out.

What process ran? When? On what source and target? Did we encounter problems? Where were they reported? *Were* they reported? Is the data ready? If not now, when?

Without traceability, we're in the dark before the processes begin, while they're running and after they've completed. We have no true way of knowing where we stand. Or for that matter, if where we stand is bad, how do we make it good? And if where we stand is good, how do we make it better?

Questions, questions.

Here is a typical traceability scenario. We load 100 million rows to an internal staging table from four disparate sources. We cleanse the records and reposit them to tables that an external set of users will consume and report on. We likewise perform several operations that produce records that contain erroneous or junk contents, duplicate records, or records that don't connect to the internal model. Of this processing, we spend an undefined amount of time in each of five workload stages include Assimilation, Cleanse/Deduplication, Integration, Transformation/Summary and Publication.

In the middle of the processing, something fails, bombs off and the processes stop completely. A troubleshooter shows up and sees that the last executing query happened to be inside the Transformation/Rollup processing, on the third step of seven. Our driving process, an external scheduler, likewise confirms that the third step died.

Armed with this information, what is the troubleshooter to do? Restart the process from the beginning, where it left off, or some prior point? Will he have to clean up any intermediate work, and if so where, and are there more than one target for cleanup? And how will we surgically identify the specific records to pull out? What is the protocol?

Now let's fast forward to the end of the process, and let's say it ran just fine. In our logic above, we discover several thousand junk records, a hundred non-integrating records, a number of duplicate records. We have either marked the records as such, or we have removed them to a holding area. Now the troubleshooter asks: Of these records, what job produced them and when? What source did they come from? Who should we report these errors to? Are these errors correctable at all? Will they be recurring, and is there a way to correct them in-line with business rules rather than have them error-off all the time? Which processing run produced them, and which step of that processing run? Was it a recovered process or did it run to completion?

Questions, questions.

Providing traceability to the environment is one part programming, one part planning and one part having the foresight to stamp our data inventory with unique identification, so that we can lay down an audit-trail of what is happening when, and which records participated, and why. Sounds daunting? It's not. But it's virtually impossible - at *scale* - without surrogate keys.

Isolation – If the incoming keys from the source system are already in integer form, it's tempting to use them for our data warehouse surrogates. If we can know that they will remain stable in the source, it's even more tempting. Just keep in mind that we need surrogates for *relational isolation*, meaning that even if the natural key were to change, we could still maintain the relational integrity of the warehouse entities. Otherwise we allow the changes in the source systems to directly impact and destabilize our warehouse model.

We must strategically and deliberately avoid this possibility. Our warehouse model should be impervious to the changes in upstream or downstream systems. If we fail to logically isolate it, we could see problems with integrity slowly start to creep in. Over time, the contamination can become irreversible and even institutionalized. I've noted that some ERP environments already rigorously enforce this isolation, for *themselves*. We could leverage it, but must understand the risk. Nothing is for free.

Applying surrogates makes our relational model crisp and elegant, connected only by surrogates and not the double/triple natural keys we find in many sources. Armed with this level of elegance, we now have the freedom to take the data to another level of integration.

In addition, when using surrogates, the natural keys reduce to attributes, not anchors for integration. If they should change, we have a problem only at the data level, not the data *model* level. And which is better, to handle the change of a key in a slowly changing dimension, or to lose the relationship forever because the key itself is disconnected?

Case Study Short: One retailer wanted a system to track the sales activity of their employees for purposes of training, rewards and the like. When we asked what they were using for unique identification, they said they had applied a surrogate key. One of our developers innocently asked why they weren't using Social Security Number, which seemed like a perfect natural-slash-integer-surrogate combination for employee tracking. The answer was at first surprising. The analyst quipped, "Because the social security number can change."

This was a new realization to our development staff, because none of us had ever heard of a social security number changing. It is perhaps the most persistent and unique form of identification in the United States. This being a era prior to identification theft, one of us asked the most obvious question:

How?

"When the Human Resource personnel first enters the employee's information," said the analyst, "When the employee is first hired. They can fat-finger the information, which could remain in the system for quite some time before it's discovered. By that time, the employee's internal information would be hopelessly tied to a key that will have to change, to what it was supposed to be in the first place."

So, a Social Security Number really *can* change! The point being, we should not arbitrarily use them (natural keys) as relational keys in our data warehouse no matter how good they look. This doesn't mean we should never use them. The key word is arbitrarily, you know, like a knee-jerk decision without giving it more thought.

Thankfully, Netezza has no relational constraints. We can join on any column, and all columns behave as keys. We have no indexes, so all columns are fair game. We can then join on whatever suits us, search on any column or value we choose, and we take no penalty for such approaches. We can always optimize things, but we don't have penalties for issuing strange or unexpected operations.

Also thankfully, Netezza has the power to allow us to morph the data into any form we choose. In other words, take a library-of-congress worth of data and shape it like so much play-doh. If we don't have an adaptive approach, we might miss some things. But we'll never be completely painted into a corner, or driven into a ditch.

I recall many years ago getting my car stuck in a patch of mud. I walked down the highway to the nearest house, where lived the owner of a monster-truck sporting super-wide gumbo mudders as the tires of choice. The owner drove me back to my car, attached a winch line and delivered the car from its trap like pulling a toy wagon.

Power and capability. Netezza has it.

With the surrogate we also get a measure of *structural isolation* - if we've added the surrogate to the original structure, and re-characterized the structure itself into a Netezza form, it places all participants on notice that the structure is owned and operated by the warehouse environment, not simply assimilated, unchallenged, from the original source systems. Isolation means functional, structural *and* relational, so we can take it to the next level – *behavioral* isolation inside the machine. Once we own the structures, they must cross an adaptation boundary in order to be fully assimilated. This boundary will protect all the hard-won behaviors and processes internal to our warehouse.

It all starts with the surrogate.

Integration – In the scope of connecting our data together, let's say we have tables that use several columns as a composite primary key. If we migrate this connection into our data model, we will have multiple columns connecting our keys down there, too. Why would we do this? Is there value in fork-lifting the source relational model into the warehouse?

What if we have multiple sources? This is very common, and we will find that the source-side integration keys for one source don't track in type or content to the others. More importantly, they are usually not synchronized either.

Let's say we have three columns in one primary table that correspond to three columns in several relational tables. The columns are invariably necessary in the transactional system to enforce transactional integrity constraints, enabling the model to push back on programs that might violate them, in turn pushing back on users who needed to correct their data entry. The multiple keys serve purposes of transparently controlling workflow on screens, to assist users. They have no purpose in a data warehouse, where users will only *search* on the key values, not enter new ones.

And since we are in the context of Netezza, which uses no index structures, it won't matter what we search on, will it? So we don't have to deal with indexing of columns or other artificial performance scenarios. Using Netezza means we dispense with those traditional "obstacle" constructs and make everything elegant, simple and useful.

So our best bet is to convert that natural key (especially those multiple columns) into its own unique identifier, and likewise apply that identifier to the relational tables, such that they are now connected by the single, isolated, high-performance integer surrogate, and not the multiple, tightly-coupled, low-performance natural keys.

Intersection – Here's where the power of surrogates pays off big-time. While integration activities link together the known business relationships of the data. Intersection structures integrate the subtle, sometimes barely-discoverable patterns in the information.

Think about this: We have a choice of two modeling techniques. One is that a sub-table carries the key of a primary table on its record definition. Another is that an intersection table carries the key of the sub-table and the key of the primary table. Or we have an intersection that carries both these keys and the key of a seemingly unrelated table, that would otherwise not cleanly integrate. Yet now they have a context - the intersection table.

The intersection structure is more flexible and adaptable. If we want to form wild and strange relationships between otherwise disparate tables, we can do so quite easily with intersections. Problem is, these are daunting and impractical in an RDBMS, but in Netezza, to our advantage, just another filter mechanism.

The best example of this is a common star-schema. This structure is nothing more than a multidimensional intersection of our business entities and their related activities. It is a formal relational model, and for performance is best represented and supported with integer surrogate keys. The star-schema has a limitation, however, in that the fact table usually centers on, you know, facts. The fact-less fact table typically forms intersections with no additional information.

In this context, the intersection contains the disparate keys and the *metadata* to describe the relationship. This metadata can be dynamic and malleable. We'll examine this deeper in GROKs.

Our ad-hoc report users may plumb the data and find even more information. Retailers may want to connect same-store sales business units. Financial systems may want to connect a customer's financial instruments and activity (loans, accounts, trading, mutual funds, etc) that are often held in siloed, dedicated systems for their respective purposes, with no direct ability to integrate them completely, and certainly no "normal" relational hooks.

What of trading systems that simply report their date-and-time trade stamp, when we might want to see them at the trading-day level? Invariably such systems have a trade-day business calendar, implicit or otherwise, but it might not be visible in the warehouse. Retailers likewise use business-day calendars in their regular work, yet most of their systems do not directly integrate a "master". In the warehouse, we can use surrogates to intersect the information to trade-day/business day structures for even more query power and visibility to the business operation.

The business-day calendar construct allows us to use simple intersection for purposes of *synchronization.* Most warehouses that extract from multiple sources are constantly fighting synchronization issues across the sources. Calendars and implicitly enforced intersections are clean, visible ways to connect the data in time-sensitive context.

We will find that ad-hoc querying and profiling produce a wide range of repeatable and exploitable patterns that allow us to link the data together in creative ways. The surrogate key makes intersections easy to manufacture, maintain and understand.

Assignment and Re-Assignment – Whenever we first apply a surrogate key to a given data point, we have some considerations. If we just want it for row identification, such as non-repeatable incoming transactions, we don't have to deal with anything else. Sometimes just assigning the new integer row-id is good enough. Other times we'll want to re-use this initial assignment. Some reasons why include:

- The target database failed and we need to reconstruct the key-value pairs
- One target table went corrupt and we need to reconstruct it as it was
- A natural key appears as a primary key on one table and a foreign key on another. We want to assign the surrogate as a primary here and the same surrogate as a foreign there.
- We want all our downstream data marts and targets to carry the same row identifier for the same data, no matter which downstream it ends up in.
- We want to incrementally apply the same row identifier to an updated/changed record so that it matches up with its original version later (i.e. slowly changing dimension).

The most direct way to handle this is to maintain cross-reference *files*. Not tables, but files that contain all the cross-reference information. At the beginning of the processing cycle, load up some working tables with the cross-reference data (it's only key-value information, and can usually load up in seconds). Why use files and not persistent tables? The main reason is for quick backup, another is for versioning. It is practically impossible to properly version a *table* for this purpose. When we're all done, we'll take any changes we made to the table and append it to the file, then truncate the table. Regular backups will keep us from losing the cross-reference.

For every natural key arriving – we simply compare it to the cross-reference table value(s). We might have more than one key in the table, after all, for multi-part keys. If the key exists, re-assign the existing surrogate. If not, assign a new one and make an entry into the table. For all primary-key intakes, do them first, so the foreign-key intakes will already have matches waiting for them. This scenario provides a centralized clearinghouse for all the keys and makes their cross-referencing completely transparent. For example, if we have three separate sources tables, each of them carrying a subtly different value for a stock ticker symbol, we can easily set up a way for them to share the same surrogate yet maintain their original values. This is true for any set of sources, that the common keys get cross-referenced to another number.

Why do this? In one action we have
- *isolated* our data structures both functionally and relationally from their sources, decoupling us from any dependency.
- *integrated* all the sources to a common center with one practically effortless sweep
- *simplified* and *standardized* on the highest-performing (and most elegant) keys and relational

structure to perform high-intensity data processing

- boosted our performance practically for free, in a way that anyone can understand and consistently apply

User-Defined Functions

This capability is new on the scene as of 2007 and is already blowing the socks off every other streaming analytics platform on the planet. There is no close second.

Fair warning - this book will not deal with UDFs in detail. We're working on this in another form. For now, we'll just examine what they do and how they apply, with more in a later section.

A UDF is a custom program that we write ourselves and install on the massively parallel hardware, itself appearing as any of the other Netezza built-in functions. We invoke it by including it in the SQL statement, and once invoked, executes on the SPUs in massively parallel.

With a user-defined function, we write a simple C++ program that is compiled and placed directly into the library of SPU software components. Whenever the SPU activates, under certain conditions, it will load and execute this component just like any of its other built-in functions. We can write *any custom operation we want* and it will run as-many-ways parallel as SPUs on the machine. Got a 10100? Our custom UDF will run 108-ways parallel, inline with the query.

I've seen demonstrations of this capability and our own group is working on several applications as packaged offerings. The speed and power only adds to the gravity-bending nature of Netezza's data processing engine.

This takes the realm of *stored procedure* out of the zone of a canned, single-threaded process, and into a massively parallel, heavy lifting performance engine that invites custom designs and business rules directly from the users, in their mission-critical applications. Software houses like SAS, Actuate and others are burning their analytics algorithms into place, increasing the value of their products.

What if we have a common algorithm that all of the online users leverage when they query data? What if the algorithm is used by some and not others? What if we simply provide a function call in the query stream, appearing like any other function call, that provides the business calculation automatically? Isn't this what we *want?* No distributed algorithms or special data handling in the BI tool. Sure, the user *can* do it that way, but now they no longer *have* to. And the sheer power of invoking the algorithm multi-ways parallel as we gather the data, versus applying it serially, on a desktop device, after the data arrives – well – the difference should be obvious. And in practical performance space, the difference *is* obvious.

Some of you may have no desire whatsoever to pursue this kind of advanced capability (but you should!). Still, this feature is new enough at the moment that we've not yet wrapped any best or favorite practices around it, but it's coming.

In-Box Processing (ELT)

For those of us immersed in data warehouse technologies, the acronym ETL (Extract/Transform/Load) is ubiquitous. Variations on this have included adding a "v" – EvTL, where the "v" stands for "validation". Adding the "v" to the acronym is indicative of the pervasive need to remind people about the lack of integrity in external data. The first thing we will always want to do when the data arrives from its original home is to challenge its integrity. No data should enter unchallenged.

No free ride.

ETL gave birth to many technologies and challenged the capabilities of many more, like those that originally did plain straight ETL, including Informatica and Datastage. Along came Ab Initio as more of a data processing environment that *also* performed ETL, and did all of it better, stronger and faster than their preceding competitors. So the others have tried to catch up, offering what could be considered "more" than ETL, but it's hard to fight one's own branding.

And along came the platform environments, first Teradata, which has a lot of stuff in the box that other database systems do. For the longest time, Teradata was the only machine environment dedicated to large-scale data processing – er – *bulk* processing lest any of you transactional gurus are confused. Teradata rightly identified that the performance solution resides squarely in the *physics*, not in the software of the engine.

Along then, come a bunch of folks at Netezza who likewise saw the solution in the physics, but decided that rather than focus on a set of proprietary hardware, they would leverage 100% commodity parts like hard drives and CPUs anyone could get at factory cost, and then wrap this into their own architecture. This embraces Moore's law, gaining the natural lift of commodity improvement with each new machine's construction, rather than being enslaved to a particular point-in-time power profile. It's all good.

But in the appliance genre for data warehousing, these are the only two players of any significance (as of this writing). Several other hot competitors are nipping at their heels, but we have yet to see if their radar signature is real or bogus, so we'll have to wait on the verdict of the marketplace. Other appliances do query acceleration, Sybase IQ, Vertica, Greenplum and Dautaupia come to mind, but all align with an SMP hardware platform, not an MPP platform. If all we need is query acceleration, these products can help. But if that's all we need, we could program/engineer our RDBMS environment to give us query acceleration.

The "ELT" paradigm, that is, Extract/Load/Transform, is different, in that it only requires us to transport the data into the box and get it loaded. (Extract/ Load). Past this, all the heavy-lifting transformations happen inside the machine (Transform) in the way of a data processing engine.

So the marketplace has come full circle, in that we continue to recognize the power of the "iron" to perform bulk processing. The primary difference in the mainframe machines is in the highly proprietary vertical of all the hardware and its wiring. Inside Netezza, every part is off-the-shelf and the "magic" is in their configuration, and the firmware binding the configuration together. It's a beautiful thing.

"The firmware is in all SPUS, it surrounds them, penetrates them and binds the SPUs together," - Sir Alec Guinness as JustWan CanShoMe, *Data Wars - The Revenge of the Red-Eye.*

So back to ELT and what it buys us. We can now perform all of our bulk data processing inside the machine, meaning that we can join, sort, rollup, integrate, cleanse and perform all the row-level or set-level processing we could ever want to do, in massively parallel.

As a bonus, Netezza's UDFs allow us to program our own proprietary optimizations directly onto the core hardware and run them in massively parallel mode. What does this mean to us? Every complex calculation we once had to perform by pulling the raw columns out, executing the work and putting it back, we can now do using the UDFs, and in many cases without the data ever having to travel all that far from its home.

Many environments will use their ETL layer to cleanse, transform and load their flows into a final target. At some point they use Netezza for that final target, but continue to use it as a repository, like a drop-off zone. They load the data, the users consume the data, the formula works, all is well.

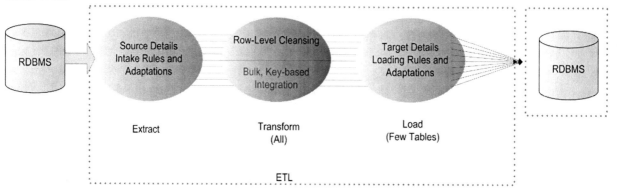

In the "ETL" depiction above, we see a typical Jurassic Park model. We extract from the sources, perform all of our row-level cleansing, then bulk integration and consolidation. Starting with many tables we would squeeze it down to few. We would trim columns, enrich others, and otherwise make the data 100% consumption-ready at the point of flow-exit in the database *load*.

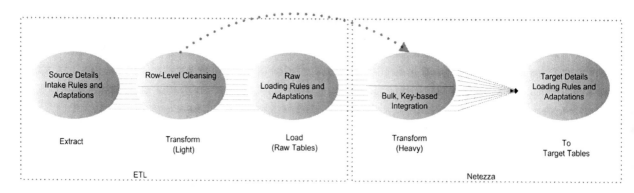

For "ELT", as noted in the depiction above, we break apart the heavy-lifting section of the transform and get it into the Netezza machine. Then in our source-to-load path, we do detailed row-level cleansing and validation, but leave set-based heavy lifting for later.

The question for resolution, is how much more power *could* we derive from the machine? After all, if our ETL environment has only eight processors, perhaps twelve, perhaps a whopping thirty-two processor machine, even if we use a parallel engine like Ab Initio – we will *still* have 216 processors in a Netezza production machine - *216 processors* to perform real data processing work. Did we simply load it and consume it, and miss the opportunity to offload more of our bulk data processing *into* it? We need to examine our opportunities and balance the power.

And in context, our set-based operations are a primary target, but our statistical, analytic and scientific algorithms are prime candidates, too. If we can move these high-order calculations into Netezza's parallel environment, we will experience immediate lift and stronger scalability. In row-level cleansing prior to entry into Netezza, we need to "skinny down" this part of the operation so that it doesn't do anything more than row-level pass-through checks. We don't want to do any lookups, joins, calculations or other heavy operations that Netezza can handle better in parallel. Review them all, assume nothing is off-limits.

It means we might load (somewhat) more tables and transfer (somewhat) more non-integrated data, but we'll be getting it into a machine that can not only intake the additional quantity, but once inside can consolidate, mold and integrate it with more power and speed than the ETL scenario can.

Of note in the above depiction is that it is likely that we will have more non-integrated feeds rather than a few integrated feeds. That's okay, because we want to integrate once we get *inside*. A note of caution, however. Don't normalize the information unless you have a lot of it, such as a feed that is very large, and normalizing it actually keeps it large, this is better than breaking apart a large flow into two or more much smaller flows. We should always benchmark such things to make sure we get the best bandwidth on the intake. As an example, if we have one flow that is about two gigabytes in size, and normalize it to several flows that are half a gigabyte in size, we need to remember that Netezza does best with a gigabyte or above on the intake. Will this change the point at which we might want to break the data apart? It might, so we need to benchmark it for best fit. If we already have a flow (such as an ETL flow) that is doing all this work on-the-fly, that's great. Don't arbitrarily re-consolidate it without testing the benefit. However, if developing a new flow, it might not behoove us to break apart and normalize the information prior to intake, especially if it will adversely affect the intake performance. In any suggestion I offer like this, always assume that I expect people to benchmark it for best fit.

Flow Control and Multi-Stage Processes

In a prior section we noted the inherently sticky logistics of flow-based processing inside machine. The data isn't flowing to or from the machine in this case, it's just flowing *inside* it. It's undergoing transformation and integration, but it's all in the box. Without some visibility, how can we know where we stand? More importantly, how can we preserve the lineage of what happened-to-what-data-when?

If we use an ETL environment to load/drive Netezza, we have no hands-on control over the physical data once it has left our hands. The transition between one processing environment to the next (e.g. the "load" cycle") actually transitions physical *ownership* between our ETL-based data processing domain and the external environment (whether this external environment is a database, a web site, an external FTP site, etc. doesn't matter). The same problem remains, we no longer have ownership of the data in the ETL flow. It's been handed off.

Examine how an ETL environment handles a multi-stage load process, such as loading the tables of a star schema. It will first load all of the dimensions, then finally load the fact table(s), Then manufacture any necessary summaries from these assets. If all goes well, we can push data to each table and sit back while the systems do their work. ELT environments do this operation as a shared-nothing scenario, so error/rollback across these shared-nothings that have no context with each other, requires forethought.

The sticky issues arise when this process fails in the middle. Recovery, checkpoint, restart – are all part of the flow-based control scenario. Anyone can bolt one process on top of another. The real trick is in how we quickly and accurately restart in case of failure. Some things to consider include:

- Which part of the process were we on?
- Were we loading an actual target or a temporary table?
- Were we preparing a workspace in anticipation of the final load?
- Do we need to back out some of the already-loaded data so as not to duplicate?
- If we back out some data, is it only for the last table that was (partially) loaded, or do we have to go back further in the process?
- Do we need to restart completely, and if so, how do we back out the data already loaded?
- For that matter, what if the final result completed fine, but we later find that we loaded corrupted data and now need to back it *all* out. How to support this?
- Is some of the load-ready data still resident in ETL load-ready files? Can we start with this asset, or do we have to regress further back?

For any of the above, we can see how a common ETL tool is on the "outside looking in" and cannot automatically affect any of it. We can deal with checkpointing inside the ETL environment itself, but now we're talking about multiple coordinated transfers against multiple tables *outside* of the ETL's control. The rollback strategy has to be *constructed*, because neither the database nor the ETL environment will do this automatically for us.

This is not specific to Netezza, as we would have to do the same thing on any database platform. This is an "ELT" related issue, applicable to any environment trying to coordinate across system boundaries.

One of the most effective ways to accomplish this is to keep an AUDIT table with some simple job control mechanics inside its structure. This is a transactional-style structure, so we should not store it in the Netezza machine. We could, however, form its functionality in the Netezza machine using flat files, like simple log files. Either way, we must deliberately harness the flow control. Netezza itself is an appliance. It can launch a flow of work and assist with execution, but if we want to recover or restart, we have to build some infrastructure around it.

Many Netezza shops can now process their data in a fraction of the time it used to take on their RDBMS machines. What was once 20+ hours is down to 20+ minutes, so there's no real impetus to formalize a checkpoint/restart scenario. If the load fails, they will back out everything, not just a partial rollback and restart-instream. After all, if our cycle window is four hours and we can execute everything in twenty minutes, our restart and recovery risk is very low, almost nonexistent. For those with tighter windows, however, the following discussion is applicable.

The legends are a little spotty, but way back when, in the days when big-blue dinosaurs ruled the earth, we would find these strange hieroglyphic notations and cuneiform images, commonly called Job Control Language (JCL) . With JCL we would submit our program to the gods of the underworld, and the underworld would then spirit the soul of our program to the appropriate muse, interact with this muse and then spirit an answer back to us. Many times the program made a simple request for the muse to perform one or more duties.

The JCL instructions used steps. Each step was a required configuration parameter, instruction, invocation or other directive to the underworld. We could track the status of the underworld's progress through the interactive crystal ball, or Job Status Panel, itself rising from the mystic green soup of TTY.

The salient takeaway here, is that these systems depended on *stepwise instructions for each transition of control*. We don't have to dive into the soup to affect this in Netezza, but we still have need of the steps. If we are to manufacture such a flow-based recovery scenario, we will need to account for the following concepts:

- Job or Flow – an identifiable application of logic. Generally synonymous with "Job"
- Job or Flow Name – a unique (textual) identifier which denotes the Flow by name rather than number.
- Job ID or Batch ID. a unique (integer) identifier that is assigned to an instance of the Job/ Flow when it first instantiates. This will allow the operator to restart the Job by ID, not by name. This is *not* the Unix PID. It is generated and assigned by whatever is controlling the application, like a scheduler. We can also capture it from a database sequence generator.
- Step – an indivisible, auditable portion of work inside the Job. (multiple Steps comprise a Job).
- Step Name – the unique (textual) identifier which denotes the Step's activity against the database or the system
- Step Source and Target – the unique (textual) identifier(s) which denotes the Step's source and target activity against the database or the system
- Checkpoint – a logical marker that allows the Job to close off a Step as "completed". This allows a recovery mechanism to start at the last checkpoint rather than the beginning of the flow. It is ideal to make each Step a de-facto checkpoint, but we may find that this is too granular.
- *Audit ID* – a unique integer identifier that is assigned to a Step prior to invoking it. The Audit ID will be "stamped" on each record in the target tables affected by the given Step. This ID has other names and contexts, such as Rule ID or Control ID. The objective is to identify what part of the flow created or affected a given row or table.

Note that *none* of the above constructs exist inherently in any "ELT" context for *any* platform, and likewise not the Netezza platform. Also, *none* of them exist as a cohesive set of coordinated quantities inside our ETL, batch control or other flow-control mechanisms. We again emphasize that these controls don't exist in any other database environment either, so it's not a knock on Netezza to point out their absence. What we're pointing out is that we need these things, and we will have to build some or all of them, because they don't show up for free.

Note that I highlighted the Audit ID. This value is dynamically formed (e.g. a sequence generator) and is stamped on each and every record created by its instructions. This allows us to rollback this auditable step simply by purging everything in its target table(s) that use the given Audit ID.

Also, depending on the level of control we want over the data, we might want to apply one or more of these quantities as physical columns in our target data tables. We can use an AUDIT table, mentioned earlier, that maintains records of the Flow, Job and Step. We then pass the Audit ID to each individual target-table row. If we need to trace the row back to a Job, we can do it through the Audit ID. One way or another, we have to stamp our work products with something that tells us how they arrived and what produced them. It is more traceable to make this more granular, depicting a step, rather than more general, such as an overall batch job.

If our only need is to completely rollback the work products of a given batch job, then the batch job identifier will do just fine. But some folks pass this through as the Audit ID or Step ID, in the anticipation that it might become more granular in the future. The point being, if we standardize on the Job ID now we cannot easily make it more granular later. We can always provide for the granularity now without actually applying it. This is the more adaptive approach.

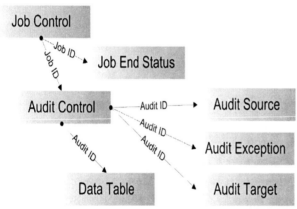

In the depiction (left) the job control instance gets a unique ID, start time and launches multiple, auditable steps. Each step gets an Audit ID which tracks the instance of the step, its source and targets and any exceptions, but also gets persisted with each row of our target data. This provides process-level lineage and traceability.

When each step closes, and when the job itself closes, we collect total rows, job end time and duration, any status, etc.

So now each of our target tables will carry an additional "big integer" Audit_ID field. This will tell us which Step of a given Job created the given record. We can then look back to our Audit Table to find which Job owns the given Audit_ID. This is all handy since we'll only need to add this once, and it's only one binary column. Once installed, each record added to the warehouse will now contain an identifier for the Batch Step that created it, tied back to a Batch Job that drove its creation.

In our new Audit table, we will track flow and step progress, maintaining the ability, all in one place, to control the fate of our data and the progress of the flow itself. Whichever method we choose to implement the minimum parts, we can be certain that the effort is necessary and will serve us in the long term. How we choose to implement it, will simply require the noted features. We need to track some other stuff, too, like the start and stop times of the job and its steps, total-count of records affected and exceptions produced, if any.

This scenario is provided as a framework, and rather than using it to "scare" you away from using Netezza, it is intended to highlight some issues associated with any type of multi-stage "ELT" scenario, no matter what the technology.

We can choose to embrace the minimum of this that we desire. Just keep in mind that when we start troubleshooting errors in tables that each can contain billions of records, it is important to have traceability to the Jobs and Steps that created the data (the business logic), not just the given Job that produced the output. So even if we don't use it for checkpointing, it's great for traceability.

It is also by no means exhaustive. I've taken the above framework to a variety of clients and installed customized tweaked-and-tuned derivations of it. But the framework itself is essentially the same and holds to the same control, traceability and recovery priorities. If you've already implemented something similar, leverage it. We were in one shop where several DBAs thought that these Audit IDs took up too much space and should be ripped out. Resist such nonsense. DBAs won't find themselves troubleshooting billions of records at a time. Perhaps in that shop, nobody else does either, because they *can't*. Of course, just installing the capability increases our accountability, something that not everyone might happily embrace.

Some final thoughts on multi-stage processing.

If we already have an external ETL / data processing solution in place, or we are putting one together, we should leverage it to manage the above recovery scenario, or one similar to it. Internal BASH-shell scripts and control language are just fine, too - but if we have something more advanced, consider using it as the first option.

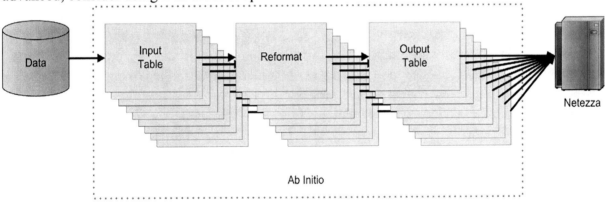

In the depiction (above) Ab Initio is shown launched in multiple instances of a utility loader, effectively moving the data from source to Netezza, structuring and cleansing the data without performing any bulk integration.

Ab Initio is actually better at bulk integration than any of its competitors, so don't take this simplistic depiction as a definitive use for the Ab Initio product.

Note that the source tables above are just moved from source to target with row-level cleansing but no integration or consolidation.

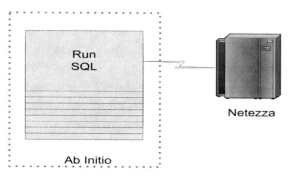

Now examine the depiction (left) where a series of Run-SQL components, each executing in a separate phase, simply fire off their SQL statements to the Netezza platform. These SQL statements can be either single-statement operation or multi-statement sessions. Netezza won't care either way. When we understand that all the Netezza platform wants is a SQL statement, and no more, it radically simplifies our configuration.

If we have already deployed a full-scale data processing solution like Ab Initio, or just an ETL solution, we should also leverage it for the actual job execution and flow control for *Netezza*. You might find that your ETL environment is ultimately "just throwing SQL statements over the wall." This is ideal, considering that the overall flow will become highly visible and out-in-the-open, rather than buried under-the-covers in scripts or other forms of control language. Mature ETL environments can also automatically wrap "lineage metadata" around such SQL statements, further providing visual lineage to the activities.

Now, don't get me wrong, scripts and control language are just as viable if you have not yet instantiated an ETL environment. But if you have, We suggest using it, simply because it will assist in managing a wider range of flow-based issues, including job logs and other forms of data control, as well as connectivity and data transport to and from the Netezza platform.

One of our customers used an ETL solution to perform the data transport into, the job control against, and the data export out of Netezza, all *controlled* from the framework of the ETL environment. The Netezza machine was just another component in the flow. And this is a great way to handle Netezza. It's an appliance - and we should be able to add it as a component, albeit a powerful one, to an existing arsenal of data processing systems.

That said, even the vendor sees the power in scaling the machines to higher levels. For example, what if we take two 10800 machines, each sporting over 200 terabytes of storage and 896 SPUs, and use them side-by-side as components of a larger environment? Now what if we added eight more of these, or ten more, fifty more? Does it really matter (apart from sheer real-estate) what the environment's functional mission is? Adding another machine, like adding a frame, should be as simple as that, just like a component in a larger flow.

As we would expect from an appliance.

Pipelining

Pipelining, in a nutshell, is the capability to have more than one operation in a flow driving work, usually through active upstream and downstream components. It's the ability to keep a lot of balls in the air without ever touching the ground (or running *aground* on the disk drives). If we consider how an environment like Ab Initio deals with pipelining in an application, think of a Visio data flow diagram with components on it and flows in between (this is similar to what an Ab Initio application looks like, except the rendering *is* the application).

Let's say a Reformat component will receive a flow, start working on records, and then pass each processed record to its next downstream neighbor. Let's say that neighbor is a Filter component, followed by a Sort component. What we'll see, is that Record-1 will arrive at the Sort while Record-2 is inside the Filter, while Record-3 is being worked on by the Reformat, etc. Each component is busy with *its part of the flow*. What this means, is that we don't wait on the Reformat operation to complete before beginning the Filter operation. Data is ready when the prior component is done with it.

So for flow optimization, an important factor is keeping a lot of balls in the air, so to speak, avoid serializing to the disk unless its necessary. We don't want to leap-frog on and off the disk between operations, because this will absolutely kill our performance.

What of how Netezza does internal processing? As noted in an earlier section, the Netezza SQL statement is broken into snippets, and their activities pipelined from the lowest to the highest level of the SQL Statement's activity. But wait - Isn't it true that when we *Select* from a table only to *Insert* to another one, that we're incurring this "leap-frog" penalty by design? How can we avoid the "leap-frog" effect - if this is the essence of a query's activity?

Not to worry, the primary difference is that we'll won't really be leapfrogging in the traditional sense. In true leapfrogging, the CPUs fight each other for disk and system resources. In Netezza, we'll be moving data in 200+ ways parallel. On a 10200, it's like 216 lily-pads to land the data on, so the overall *logical* footprint looks large, but practically speaking, it's really not. So we'll *not only* have 216 lily-pads, but 216 frogs on those lily-pads. When we want to move-the-frog, so to speak, the frog will just shift its position on its own lily-pad, not jump to another one.

Pipelining with Netezza comes in two forms. One is the use of Netezza as a sort of "chugging engine", which we'll examine with a case study later. In this scenario, Netezza is a processing component of a continuously moving data flow. In the second form, Netezza's internal computing power can be made to pipeline without any additional creativity on our part, it's just how the hardware works and how its features play out in our favor. Both are likewise useful for batch operations, your actual mileage may vary, so always benchmark an approach, or call a professional. We are always happy to help.

The reason to call this out: We can inadvertently negate the built-in pipelining by dog-piling a lot of instructions into one SQL statement. I've seen this done in traditional RDBMS engines, where one SQL statement can span ten pages or more. In the RDBMS MIMD model, this is one way to optimize a query operation. We won't do this in Netezza because we don't have to. SIMD *rules* the day, and it's already working for us.

When Netezza chops the SQL statement into snippets, each one representing a component of work. The snippets are then circumscribed with operational directives, and the directives are carried out starting with the SPU, then rising out of the SPU as the data results are assembled and finally delivered. Each component of work represents a bulk *subset* of an overall bulk result set. We see a pipeline then, for bulk operations rather than simply pipelining at the record level. This is especially ideal for large-scale set-based integration, joining very large tables in massively parallel form.

When loading smaller, more frequent intakes with *nzload*, we can designate that the intake be to an external table, which is essentially a flat file with a Netezza table definition on top of it. When we write to this animal, it is writing the data to local host disk, not actually into the SPUs. If the SPUs are busy doing something else, we won't be imposing on them. Once the nzload completes, the Netezza machine can then assimilate the data internally at its own pace and schedule, so we don't disrupt anything critical with our intake activity (again, for smaller, more frequent intakes).

Don't use *nzload* this way for larger intakes – take it straight to the SPUs. If using an external table, we can manage the files it creates on each intake operation, bundle these files into an intake directory and then load them all-at-once when a threshold or interval presents itself.

These are simple examples of functional pipelining. If we have complex internal transforms, breaking them into smaller units of work (on the same bulk content) not only increases their overall performance, but also their visibility and maintainability, If we have disparate external processes loading data to Netezza, their activities can easily swamp the machine with onesy-twosy bits of work. (*caning* the machine, as one of our British colleagues puts it) If we accumulate this workload in another way, we have the ability to perform a more efficient intake to the SPUs, activating them when there is sufficient threshold of work to justify it.

Why do this? As mentioned in another section, Netezza can intake a million records per second, or it can intake one record per second. If we send over a million records at once, we get the lift. If we send over one record-at-a-time a million times, it takes a million seconds. Likewise if we perform an insert/select transform one-record-at-a-time, it will display the same profile - single-records have poor performance where millions/billions of records make the machine shine.

We don't want slowdown on the intake, or on the internal ELT.

I've noted that it takes about a gigabyte's worth of data to justify the nzload's startup and shutdown overhead, and to justify the SPU intake activities. In the above noted case, we manufactured twenty million rows to create a gigabyte of data. We then did an nzload intake of this file, and it took about 20 seconds, or one million rows per second. Considering that Netezza can intake over five hundred gigabytes an hour, we felt that we really weren't pushing the box all that much. We doubled and tripled the data size, but it still hovered around a million rows per second for the intake. When we started reducing the total size, to half a gigabyte or less, *it took roughly the same amount of duration, but clearly loaded fewer rows per second.*

If we want to use Netezza in a continuously-styled pipeline, we cannot treat it like the aforementioned stored procedure processing, where one record arrives at a time, and is dispatched one at a time. This is the most inefficient means to use a Netezza platform.

What do we really need? We must consider Netezza's workload as a form of *capacitance*, perhaps like a tank with a high-water mark. We push data to Netezza to fill a tank to a high-water mark, and when the threshold triggers, we command Netezza to intake the information. This threshold can watch record count, time-between-intakes, or both. For example, load the data when it hits three million records, or when the duration reaches five minutes, whichever comes first. This allows us to address peak inputs and low-tide inputs, with no more than five minutes latency. If we see that five minutes is much too long, we reel it into something more useful and realistic (likewise if too short).

Note – the above triggers on row count and time are not inherent to Netezza. However, both are simple to implement if we have a cohesive intake protocol.

The external tables help us on output as well, because once we are done with our internal Netezza processing, we have two options. We can (a) allow external users to hit the SPU-based tables containing the final work products or (b) pre-select the data from SPU-based tables and publish it to an external table. When the consumer comes to get the data, it receives it from the external table without activating the SPUs at all. This is enormously helpful if the SPUs happen to be actively working on a processing problem when the consumer arrives to get the information.

Another Ab Initio example: If we were to look under the covers of Ab Initio, we would see that each component has an input buffer and an output buffer. This allows each component to read or write its work product with independent timing from its upstream or downstream neighbors. The output buffer of one component interacts with the input buffer of the next, etc.

What we see with Netezza, is that (for continuous operations) the external tables can receive the data in input buffer form. For outtake, the external tables can effectively publish the work products in output buffer form, and the Netezza SPUs sit between these operational bookends, doing all the necessary work.

But this only converts Netezza itself into component for a larger flow, as a part of a larger pipeline. It doesn't really express pipelining internally to the Netezza machine. To say "it's in there" is probably trite, but I'd have to commit to explaining how a 2-cycle engine works, and this isn't necessary.

Handling Landing Zones

In the Netezza context, I'll characterize data warehouse flows into two very broad categories. The first has a mature data flow environment (ETL, Ab Initio, etc.) before Netezza lands on the floor. The second does not, and consequently must stand up the Netezza machine by itself, perhaps leveraging a less formal commodity or utility data flow environment just to feed it.

In the first category, data will ideally arrive on the Netezza machine in good condition, perhaps as "load ready" as its predecessor required. If its predecessor was an underpowered RDBMS, then the data might be *very* clean, if for no better reason than to avoid an RDBMS's tendency to bomb off as bad data arrives. On the other hand, if its predecessor was Teradata, we might find that our ETL data will arrive in less-than-pristine form, because someone was leveraging Teradata's in-box processing for this task.

The reason to note the above, is that our data flow engineers may swear to us that the data is *as clean as it needs to be*. They also might swear to us that the functions (inside Teradata for example) to clean the information will require extraordinary uptake and functional transfer over to Netezza.

Ignore both of these claims.

The data is *never* as clean as it "needs to be", no matter how long we've been working with it. Our former environment is always hiding and masking bugs. Who's to say that the masks aren't really a detriment to performance, and when we move over to Netezza those masks will evaporate? Not to worry, there's enough power under our fingertips now to square this issue away quite handily.

In addition, functionally porting from one technology to another, especially a mature functioning environment, and *most especially* a data warehouse flow, is simple and straightforward, with very few mysteries or pitfalls. It's more of a testing exercise than a development or technical exercise. The sky isn't falling. It's clearing. This is a good thing.

But what if we've never set this up before? We have no formal data transportation mechanism and all the data is essentially dirty? Once again, this is the assumption we *should* make at the outset, regardless of the claims of our engineers to the contrary.

Dirty Landing Zone: When dirty data first arrives on the Netezza machine, we need to drop it into a dirty landing zone. Call it an intake table, or a group of tables in an intake schema designed for this purpose, but it's a place where data *first* lands, where we will deliberately challenge it, before introducing it to the master repository.

If we have access to Ab Initio, we can forego the staging tables, primarily because it's within our reach to cleanse the data before it arrives, and Ab Initio does it better. Other data processing/ETL environments are robust for row/column cleansing, but either way, we won't assume that just because one of them is available, that we can receive the data into our master repository without challenging it. Lots of environments that have Netezza *don't* have an ETL scenario, so this discussion makes no assumptions.

A landing zone is simply a table to receive the original data in its dirtiest (or most questionable) form. The columns are nullable and the table(s) all use random distribution. The priority here is in getting the data through the intake cycle, which itself can be very intense and error prone. Not error-prone because of Netezza, but because we are transmitting and receiving data *across two or more system boundaries*. Logistically, landing zones and staging areas provide a lot of value if leveraged for a functional purpose. However, one of these is *not* the Operational Data Store.

Operational Data Stores (ODS)

A starry-eyed designer hands us an Expo Dry Erase marker, points to a white board and asks us to lay out a design for an Operational Data Store. The first thing we do is draw a big question mark on the board and hold our breath. Yes, he's read all the white papers and especially the age-worn web sites on how to do it right, so he wants to test our acumen. We're ready to go there, but this is a lot like asking us how we would design a way to get drinking water into our house. We do it by calling a plumber. The process and procedure for installing and operating one is canned and predictable, and people may install one and euphorically declare victory, not realizing that we really don't need one.

Operational Data Stores have a use, but lately these are a rare and dying breed because their original purpose was twofold - to take pressure off the flow of data and to synchronize it. Once the technologies caught up with the flow, the ODS waned in its usefulness and value. The following discussion is on some ODS pitfalls we will commonly encounter, and hopefully will underscore what we're really signing up for when we use these three little letters.

They seem important, but are they?

The wrong way to build an ODS is to make it our staging area or inline system of record for the downstream warehouse. If we've done this, we are probably already experiencing its destabilizing effects, and are wondering why.

Here's why:

An RDBMS-hosted operational data store faces operational and ad-hoc users, and we must tailor it to fit their needs. As operational users, they see the data in third-normal-form, as we would expect a clean staging area to appear. It seems like the obvious store-and-forward location for the downstream EDW too, but it's not. The ODS must be geared and fitted for the utility of its users, not be a system of record for the warehouse. The ODS therefore, is itself a dedicated environment with a volatile and demanding user base, like a user-facing *mart*. They will want us to add information here, an index there, a new table over there, etc. In essence, the ODS is actually a *target* work-product of a dedicated flow with its own user base, not appropriate as the intermediate landing zone of another one.

And consequently as a functional asset, is also a *moving* target.

The Warehouse, on the other hand, needs the data for other reasons. It will perform interesting intersections, optimizations, summaries and data restructuring that the ODS doesn't need or care about. It seems that the Warehouse and the ODS are operating at cross-purposes for user-bases with highly disparate roles and requirements.

Here are some symptoms of this problematic configuration:

- Changes to the ODS are frequent, its users are demanding and transactional-facing
- Changes to the Data Warehouse "should" only occur when the data itself changes. But we find ourselves tweaking it often, usually whenever a change in the ODS occurs.
- We find high-walls of adaptation built between the ODS and the Data Warehouse, treating the ODS like another transactional source
- We cannot easily make independent changes to the Warehouse without affecting the ODS, because the Warehouse is dependent on the ODS for a feed.
- Likewise we cannot easily make independent changes to ODS without impact analysis, because we cannot afford to destabilize our primary consumer, the Warehouse.

To solve these problems, it is far easier to treat the ODS as standalone target *endpoint*, where the warehouse is not dependent on the ODS contents (or even for the ODS to be running). Likewise the data warehouse is a standalone target. Both the warehouse and ODS then consume independently configured flows. They may share staging zone and upstream sources, but they are not directly coupled or dependent on each other. This configuration provides the right level of isolation / decoupling and immediately stabilizes both.

Now if we consider the symptoms, we've mitigated all of them, and then some.

- Changes to the ODS are frequent, its users are demanding and transactional-facing – *non-issue, as now we can support them as often as we like*
- Changes to the Data Warehouse "should" only occur when the data changes. But we find ourselves tweaking it whenever a change in the ODS occurs – *no longer an issue, because the Warehouse will no longer be coupled to the ODS*
- We have high-walls of adaptation built between the ODS and the Data Warehouse, treating the ODS like another transactional source – *no longer necessary, since the ODS is no*

longer a system of record
- We cannot easily make independent changes to the Warehouse without affecting the ODS, because the Warehouse is dependent on the ODS for a feed – *no longer an issue, since the Warehouse and ODS are decoupled*
- We cannot easily make independent changes to ODS without impact analysis, because we cannot afford to destabilize our primary consumer, the Warehouse – *no longer an issue, the ODS is no longer an intermediate system of record*

We'll see a lot of information on the web about the good, bad and ugly of Operational Data Stores. The best value in an operational data store, is to serve its users. The only way to most effectively do this, is to make it a standalone target.

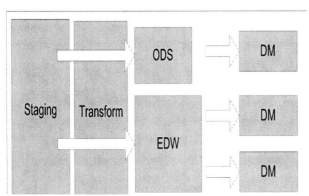

In the depiction (left) we see staging tables that receive the inbound data from its various sources. We can use a separate schema for these, bearing in mind that intake is a *capability*, not necessarily an application-centric need.

We can then use a transformation schema, a place where we can make and toss all the intermediate storage we want.

External applications then consume the DM schemas.

Housekeeping functions can keep it clean and tidy without having to deal with capability-centric issues smattered all over the place. We then drop the finished products into their respective Reference and Master schemas, and use these as anchors to downstream targets. The targets themselves are standalone schemas using local tables, synonyms and views to the Reference and Master stores. These represent finished/published applications. Some of the DMs may have very specific tables for their own consumption, while leveraging the common EDW and even the ODS tables for other needs (as conformed dimensions and the like).

When our users ask for an ODS, they want the daily snapshot of the data for operational reasons. What they *don't* want is the raw information. They want it *unfiltered*, but not completely *raw*. This implicit requirement changes the nature of the data, in that we will send it through the same crucible as the EDW information, performing the row-level cleansing and bulk-integration with the environment, but we won't carve off any of the errors or anomalies, largely because this is something the operational users are actually looking for. What they finally want, is clean, integrated, but *unfiltered* information.

So how do we provide an integrated-but-unfiltered view of the data as an ODS, and also provide an integrated-but-filtered view of the data as the EDW?

The answer is obvious - filter tables provide all we need here. I'm not suggesting that we have to use the same tables for the ODS as the EDW, but filter tables provide enough functionality to keep us from having to make separately configured structures for the sake of filtration only. The structures may look identical though physically separate. The filter table is what makes them behave differently. What does this mean? We can deploy a day's snapshot to an operational view using the identical table structure as the EDW equivalent, without any filter structures to control it. Over in the EDW, we use the same master structure but use a companion filter table on it. This keeps the two synchronized for the sake of filtration. Any differences in the two will be a function of user-requested features, not filtration capability. (Our master structures remain uncluttered).

The objective is to avoid creating various, standalone, application-centric streams of activities and structures, and do our best to capture architecture-centric capabilities as reusable assets for all applications. The applications then become consumers of the capabilities. It is a more resilient model than standalone, stovepiped applications, even when inside the same machine.

How do we accomplish this? We need to examine our existing flows, and even if it means replicating or restructuring existing logic to support both ODS and EDW areas (which is rarely the case) we need to take this important step to stabilize the ODS and the Warehouse. If we have access to Ab Initio, we can leverage this environment as a "bus" to simply peel off the data from the flow on the way to the Warehouse. This allows the ODS to be dependent only on the flows that lead up to it, likewise the Warehouse, but also allows them to experience reuse in the components that precede both of them in the flow.

All that said, the ODS is something of a non-sequitur in Netezza (it is often noticeably missing). We can still make one as an independent target, but it doesn't matter if we maintain a highly normalized view of the data *unless the consuming users want it that way*. The warehouse doesn't need it in this form, the ODS users do. This is what we meant by, build it to suit your users, on *their* requirements. The warehouse has no requirement for data in this form, but the ODS users do. Fit it to *them*, not for the warehouse.

This means that in the above data intake protocol (prior chapter), we can use the data intake to land the inbound table in clean form, and leverage this as an ODS-style source since it always contains the most-recent data. We can then copy / transform from this source into the final-consumption form of the ODS.

But think about this - if we call it an ODS, people will align their *thinking* and their *expectations* towards it. If we redefine it as more of an operational mart, perhaps even an integrated-but-unfiltered mart, we have a means to control its destiny without *white-paper purists* trying to redeploy or reconfigure it.

Watch out for those white-paper-purists. They're everywhere.

Lastly, it only *seems* counter-intuitive to target the ODS as a destination and not as an intermediate system of record. It only *seems* counter-intuitive to eliminate the ODS as an institutional storage point. Ignore these feelings and forge ahead, and you will not encounter the aforementioned destabilizing symptoms, or the attendant workload to prop them up.

Truncate vs Delete

In the Netezza machine, we have a couple of ways of dispatching records out of our view. One is the Truncate and one is Delete. Now, keep in mind that the Truncate completely and irreversibly clears a tables contents. The Delete, not so.

Whenever we *delete* records in Netezza, it's more like a "soft delete". The records are removed from view of the normal query processes, but they're not completely gone. Nor will they be recycled (their space won't be used on the next insert). Some competitors have claimed that by leaving the record "hole" in place, this means we'll have to slog through it on our next query. Again this is nonsense mythology. Netezza deals with data bases on where *not to look*, a deleted record is by definition in a place we will *never look* during a query. Myth. Busted.

The side benefit is that if should accidentally delete records during development, we can *get the records back*. We would not desire to make this aspect a part of regular operational activity, nor should you. Tinkering with the machine at this level is best left to a product engineer. While the restoration operation is reasonably straightforward and will give us back what is lost, doing this on a regular - especially operational - basis is a clear sign that something is wrong or lacking discipline in our procedures and practices. I dare say that institutionalizing a restore-from-delete may likely institutionalize a problem we'd rather control another way.

So while I'll say that it's possible to do, get one of your product support folks on the phone, tell them what you need and let them restore it for you. I'm not sidestepping here. I know how to make it happen. I also know how dangerous it can be in the wrong hands, an that I shouldn't offer it up *in print.* In the end, the fewer that know this, the better, so assures the vendor, and so I agree.

The most significant issue, however, is that the delete does not really remove the records from the table's reserved storage space. If we delete again and again over time with no housekeeping, we will see our machine's available SPU storage space start to diminish and we might wonder why. A simple excursion into the Netezza admin panel will reveal all, that the table is taking up a lot of space for the deleted records it is holding, but that we cannot see. This tells us we need cleanup if we are to recover the space for useful work.

Likewise for updating (since an update is a whole-row delete/insert combination). We will find that repeated update without cleanup will leave us with a lot of unusable space.

If we want to leave the data in place and simply recover the unused space, we would use the *nzreclaim* utility. The best way to describe this operation is functionally like a disk-defrag, but not quite so egregious, because we are compressing out the space in 200+ ways parallel. I've seen this operation take no longer than a few minutes for very large tables when we're using block-reclaim. However, it can take as long as twenty minutes, which for a continuous environment is unacceptable, but for standard data warehousing is perfectly acceptable.

As for frequency, in a typical data warehouse scenarios, we won't find ourselves needing to cleanup even our most active tables more than once a week, perhaps even once a month. Again if this is the case, just use *nzreclaim* and reclaim the lost space. It's not expensive when we do it as part of a night-time or off-peak housekeeping function. If we have a continuous model, the insert/truncate model is perhaps more appropriate, because in continuous operations we won't get a regular housekeeping cycle to reclaim the data, and the data is moving pretty fast already.

We can put some lightweight housekeeping around it and keep everyone safe from harm. The vendor is always improving these aspects of the machine, so I expect its performance to only increase. At some point the *nzreclaim* latency will evaporate altogether.

Insert-Only vs Delete or Update

Running in a continuous environment, an engineer called us to his desk and showed us that his Netezza machine was losing table space. "It's disappearing on me", he said, "and I don't know how to get it back. Is the machine corrupted?"

When we shared with him the administrative requirement of the delete and update operations, he was at first disturbed, then suddenly ecstatic. Like the pieces of a puzzle had snapped together in his head, he closed his eyes and said, "*That's* why we should use insert-only!"

Okay, so what's an "insert-only"??

Firstly, let's do a little background. In most database environments, deleting and updating are as natural as breathing. Netezza provides for both, but we need to understand the mechanics of each. The short version is this:

- Insert – appends a record to the target table. Netezza does this best with millions of records at a time (when doing data intake, a gigabyte or more is generally the minimum loading size for optimum performance).
- Delete – hides a record from view. It's a "soft" delete. The physical disk space still belongs to the table and appears as part of the table's footprint of used disk space. Example, if we delete all rows in a table, the table no longer contains visible data, but all the space used for the deleted rows is still being used. The nzreclaim utility recovers this space.
- Update – executes a delete/insert cycle, deleting the *entire* row and inserting it with its new version. No matter how many columns need to change, we get a *whole* new row. It still has the same problem of empty/unused space as delete (above) because it includes a *delete* operation for free. As with the delete, the nzreclaim utility recovers this space.
- Select – will not by default return any rows already marked for delete
- Recovery – the good news is, if you accidentally delete a bunch of rows, you can get them back if you haven't yet performed an nzreclaim or truncate.
- *nzreclaim* - a utility that reclaims the disk space used by deleted records, (akin to a disk defrag). Expensive operation.
- Truncate – zeros out the count of records and recovers the space of the deleted records. Executes in relative moments of time.

Consider the flow (on the next page) and understand what it means. In most cases containing old and new records, we'll need to update the old and load the new. We'll also note that the update row count is most often miniscule compared to the insert row count. Update operations will use a transactional mode, where insert will use a bulk-load mode (five to ten times faster than the transactional mode). We should not enslave the majority of the work (inserts) to the slower constraints of the update flow.

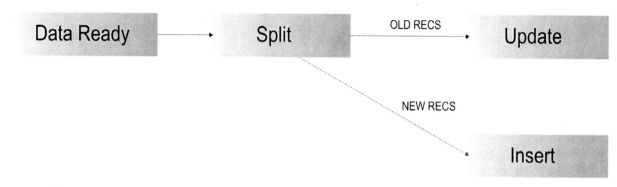

We then separate the updates from the inserts, pushing them into the Netezza machine on separate threads. This works perfectly for the standard RDBMS, and is perfectly *necessary* to get best performance. But as noted, I prefer an insert-only model because we don't have to deal with jumping through such hoops. In an insert-only model, we would insert all the records and then mark the "old" records (we just updated) using a companion filter table or other anti-join filter. This effectively creates a slowly-changing dimension for free, but because it uses a filter table, we don't have to do any engineering on the master table. Updates are a thing of the past, and we never run the risk of overwriting existing data (critical in high-audit situations such as financial services).

Here's a test of our counter-intuitive intuition.

Table A contains three billion records, representing three days of data
We need to delete the oldest day of data and append a new day's worth.

Do we:
- Delete one billion records, leaving two billion
- Perform nzreclaim to recover the missing space
- Insert the new one billion records

Or
- Build a temporary table with the new one billion records
- Copy the two billion records we want to keep from the old table
- Drop the old table, effectively deleting the oldest one billion records
- Rename the new table with the old table name

Which one of the above is the most effective way to execute the operation? It certainly seems like the first option is the simplest one. For the second, why would we copy two billion records from one table to another? It sounds insane.

Yet if we benchmark these two options (even on a 10200), we will find that the second option beats the first one in sheer time. The reason is that for a table of this size, the delete and nzreclaim combination are more expensive than a copy/insert. We mitigate their expense by using a different approach. However, do we *really* need to do this? Can't we just delete the records and allow the deleted space to accumulate, recovering it all at once on a weekend? Yes, we can and we should pursue this. A major reason is to support incremental backups. If we copy the data around all the time, it throws away our ability to reference "what is new or changed" for incremental backups. So for the sake of a *little bit more tactical turnaround*, we've thrown away something valuable. And that's not a good trade-off (see, *trade-off* isn't so bad when it buys us something good!)

So to conclude the above, use the machine in the standard, most obvious manner and don't engineer. The first option is the most viable (and I say this for non-continuous models, which are the majority of Netezza installations).

Here's another test for contrast:

Table B contains three billion records.

We have incoming operations that will require deletion of one percent of the three billion records on any given cycle. Do we:

- Copy the 99 percent of records-to-keep to a new table, leaving the deleted records behind?
- Actually delete the records from the table?
- Insert the identifiers of the records-to-delete to a filter table, such that we can join "where not exists" against the filter table?

Each of the above options is functionally correct, but option 1 may have no viability in our solution. Depending on how "big" the one-percent actually is, option 2 is not as viable, either. We have seen, for tables of any kind, the third option is always viable - it's an insert-only model.

Why not viable? Keep in mind, the word "delete" in its truest sense is *verboten* in many data warehouse shops, likewise with updates, because they are destructive operations. The word "delete" can send visceral, almost contemptuous shockwaves up the spine of a business analyst. Even a soft-delete like Netezza's is unacceptable for many audit-sensitive environments, especially financial services systems. So the question is not really one of whether we can functionally delete the records and perform the attendant housekeeping, but whether we *should*, or whether policies will even *allow* it. In this case, *only* the third option is viable.

Here's another test for contrast:

- Table B contains three billion records, distributed on random
- We have incoming (1 million) records to update Table B, based on a key called TID;

What will the machine do? We will find that due to the random distribution, these million records can take somewhat longer that we expected to find their homes and update their designated records. Why is that? Of 108 SPUs on the system, and a randomly distributed table, the designated records could be anywhere.

If we simply change this scenario to distribute Table_B on the TID, we will find that the machine will hash the incoming data on the same key, and the data will intake in mere seconds. Intake is not the issue in this case, but in whether the table is ready for the given operation.

This now raises an issue of distribution. Will we now have to choose between the distribution key we want for *intake,* and a different one we want for regular *query*? What if the TID is what we really need for intake, but when the user queries the data, TID is never used, but something else entirely?

If we don't perform an update at all, but rather tag the old and new in a slowly-changing dimension scenario, we don't have to worry about it. We can likewise use work tables and other intermediate scenarios to cover the difference in post-intake processing. What we must understand is that several factors are in play here: What will we require for proper loading, query consumption and maintenance? Are they all the same? If we use an insert-only model, what will it buy us, and what will it look like?

Case Study Short: The user had forklifted a star-schema from an RDBMS to a schema in Netezza. Each of the dimensions was distributed on its primary key, so loading and updating them was a non-issue. Unfortunately, the primary fact table was actually a summary-fact, and remained static in size from load-to-load, and the processes would simply update any changed entries instead of adding them to the end. We likewise had no good way to distribute the data to make an update work correctly. A good way to optimize this is to remove the update requirement entirely. We would push the data to an intermediate work table, itself distributed on random, then truncate the smaller summary fact table and remanufacture it from the work table. This intermediate table eliminated the need for any updates at all. Later we removed the summary fact table completely with no penalty.

Insert-Only – Whether we want to commit to this model now, or later, is only of consequence *later*, when we might have *to do it anyhow*. People who work with the Netezza technology for any period of time, sometimes gravitate to a model that embraces insert-only for everything they do. Here are some good reasons why:

- Avoids updates and deletes, and reclaim overhead (not always for housekeeping reasons, but for functional and policy priorities)
- Provides a forward-looking, non-destructive traceability for data processing
- Eases our implementation of process and data audit
- Eases implementation of information management (record rejects, errors, duplicates, etc)
- Eases implementation of checkpoint-restart
- Eases implementation of slowly-changing dimensions
- Aligns with Netezza's filter-based architecture

This last item, *aligns with Netezza's architecture* is critical, because we will get the automatic lift of the machine's architecture with no additional effort. Here's how it works:

If we need to perform an update to a table, is there a way to achieve the same functional outcome without updating, but only inserting? (Recall that updating a table will be executed by Netezza as a full-row delete/insert combination anyhow).

If we need to perform a minor delete to a table, is there a way to achieve the same functional outcome without deleting, but only inserting? How on earth, one might ask, do we delete records from a table by using an insert? It's *counter*-intuitive. Filter tables are the key.

We will also find that leveraging additional filter tables to achieve these goals is actually right underneath our fingertips. We don't have to fear the RDBMS penalty of manufacturing a temporary table or filtering table. The index structures alone would preclude such insanity. Indexes in Netezza are non-existent, and filter tables are massively parallel and an excellent way to process data. Those of us currently enslaved to an RDBMS will likely not favor the use of intermediate tables for multi-stage work products or filters. As Netezza users, however, we should embrace it.

For Actual Deleting: Insert-only models work for "deleting" records. We've already offered a couple of clues above. When we delete, we will see one of several baseline problems within which we must apply this action:

- Available duration window for the operation
- Intermediate and temp-table
- Deleting twenty-percent or more of the table (high-percentage delete)
- Deleting less than twenty percent of the table (low percentage delete)
- Frequency and circumstance of the delete (interday versus intraday)

The available duration window – might be something we want to gravitate toward just for the sake of making sure things happen in the shortest *available* timeframe. A short word to the wise (which we cover later in a case study) – don't over-focus on squeezing the performance out of the machine if there's no real need. We can always over-engineer, even on high-powered systems. But if the system already provides enough power, we can forego the over-engineering and leverage the power toward more functionally useful ends (like operation and troubleshooting) rather than just shortening the duration. Our solution will have lots of operational and troubleshooting eyes, not just those consuming the end-product data tables.

In short, burn some of that processing power to support the admins, operators and troubleshooters. We may not have had the power before, because every last ounce was required for the data processing mission. Budget the extra for something we've *always* needed.

Back to the problem at hand – deleting large-scale information from a large-scale table – and the most effective way to make it happen. Let's examine the mechanics of each scenario. Typically the "interday" frequency means we have a downtime window in the evening hours, a very common setting for data warehousing. The "intraday" frequency means we have little to no latency and we need to turn something around quickly. Someone is waiting on an answer, or our processing cycle appears in limited waves of duration. The intraday frequency requires more infrastructure, so we'll deal with it in the next chapter, *Continuous Stuff.*

Deleting is always destructive - in financial services warehouses, I've seen people almost jump across a table when the word "delete" was used in *any* context. We have to use careful language like "remove from view" or "filter" when we were really rolling the data out of the warehouse completely. We weren't truly deleting anything, just doing housekeeping to get it out of the way. So in this context, *true* deletion may not be an option at all. We have to soft-delete ourselves without using an official Netezza delete. And this means using a filter table as the lowest-impact model. If a record's identifier appears in the filter table, is it "logically deleted" because a query using "where not exists" will never let the "deleted" record escape.

Intermediate/temp table operation – whenever we do a multi-stage operation (discussed later) we will sometimes create a temp-table inside the transactional context. As a holding place for some necessary quantity, we may need to perform further operations on it to completely prepare it for work. Lots of reasons exist to instantiate a temporary table, just as lots of reasons exist to modify or enhance it after creation.

People then institutionalize table management governance for both temporary tables and their persistent tables, as if the same priorities apply to both. But they don't, because when the transactional context closes, the temp table evaporates with it. So don't get wrapped-around-the-axle on managing the contents of a temp table the same way we would manage a persistent table or final work-product table. We can and should update, delete, truncate etc. as necessary on a temp table - with reckless abandon - while in the context of the transaction.

So as we continue the discussion, separate (in your mind) the transient context of the temporary tables versus the persistent context in the following sections.

Interday options – deleting less than twenty percent – In this scenario, when we have the luxury of time, the delete/nzreclaim is usually the most effective. If we must remove a small amount of data, then the delete operation will return quickly. Likewise with nzreclaim. We should *always* perform a baseline test to understand how long the delete/nzreclaim cycle will take (so there are no surprises). We can optimize nzreclaim (blocked mode) by targeting the upper or lower section of the table. So if the data we've just deleted is in one of these zones, the block-reclaim will return even faster.

When deleting a small number of rows, it is often *not* as effective to nzreclaim and clean them up right way. We can delete a small number of rows and allow these to accumulate to another triggered boundary, such as twenty percent of the table, then we can invoke the next option. Accumulation will eventually raise our total deleted records to a "critical mass" above the twenty-percent mark, justifying a more dramatic event.

Interday options – deleting twenty-percent or more – In this scenario, we've either executed a big delete operation, or allowed a lot of little ones to accumulate to something big. Either way, a big chunk of usable space requires recovery, and we need a way to clean up the table as quickly as possible. The *nzreclaim* utility will always help us here if all the deletions are at the top or end of the table. If this is not the case, shoot an nzreclaim to get a feel for what it actually costs. If it fits inside our batch window and is likewise infrequent, we have no issues. As noted prior, we don't perform an nzreclaim every time we delete data. We wait for an appropriate housekeeping boundary, which may be far more infrequent than our daily execution. Still, if we delete more than twenty-percent at a time, we might need something in addition to simple deletes, because the frequency of cleanup might increase on us and we need to prepare for it.

It's when the available time window starts to shrink or the frequency rises that we need more options, discussed in *Continuous Stuff.*

Insert-Only for de-duplication, reject/error tracking, and other tricks

As an extension of the prior section, the insert-only processing model, we need to think carefully about what *else* this can buy, in more ways than just the primary tables, and more functions that just delete-management.

In practically every environment, we need a way to audit our work. In most flow-based solutions (such as Ab Initio) we have the ability to peel off bad records-on-the-move and drop them off in an administrative zone for later oversight. The luxury here is that the records are already in memory and we simply dispatch them. Peeling them from the original flow is relatively easy.

In Netezza however, to physically peel the records from the table, we would pick up the table as a *select*, then drop it into another table as an *insert*, transforming or filtering on the fly (if we want to physically remove the data from the table). If we really embrace the insert-only model, we can mitigate the issues associated with missing records, changed records, the necessary overhead to track them, and *still* align with Netezza's architecture.

ID	Content	Created		ID	Err Code
1001	21	Jan 1		1001	4500
1002	21	Jan 31		1002	3134
1003	38	Feb 1		1005	2130
1004	31	May 31			
1005	21	May 31			
1006	45	May 21			

Depicted left is a primary table and an error table. When we fetch records from the primary table, we do so with a "where not exists" against the error table, using the record id. If our record id's are globally unique (ideally), we can just join without regarding the primary table name in the error log itself. This makes the error log cleaner and completely decoupled from all the structures - and a reusable asset structure for *all* error and exception reporting.

In the depiction (above) we have a decoupled way to use an insert-only model to track error-records in the master table without having to move the record out of the table. This "tags" the record indirectly, in the error log. We can always remove it later in a regular housekeeping sweep, but for now this allows us to track the error, regard-it-or-ignore-it without having to physically remove it from the master. Think about what this buys us when we think of *scale*. We don't have to peel the records off or manage them in a flow-based form, but instead mark them for later action without having to do any work on the master record. We don't tag the actual record (this would be an update, requiring a delete-insert cycle - and an insert-*anyhow*). Instead we insert a reference to the record in the error log, and this effectively tags it *indirectly*.

In the section above we mentioned the "filter" table as a means to get things done, so here is a simple but robust way to implement the filter. If we set up a "filter" table alongside our primary tables that records all-the-errors-all-the-time, then we have a one-stop shop to find our error log for all processes, all tables. Elsewhere in this book we talk about audit-id's and checkpoint processing.

If we have the following in our hand: *audit-id, table-name, record-id, error message* – we can record any error in a central error-log table and it will "impute" the error to the *actual* record in the noted primary table *without having to stamp this status on the record with an update*. How is this?

By using the error table, we only add the primary table's identifiers and the error information, and we do it in-bulk-on-the-fly without dealing with individual records. We apply a transform rule in-bulk and those that don't pass-the-business-processing-test have their identifiers added to the error table *in-bulk*. Everything happens in-bulk here, not peeling off individual rows-at-at-time as-we-encounter errors. We cannot hope to capture errors correctly unless we plan to capture them in-scale and track them in-bulk. Within these constraints, we likewise cannot afford to go back and update the rejected/error records themselves with a status. We need an insert-only model to track these issues on-the-fly, and a filter table works great for this.

This also aligns with Netezza's filtration architecture, and will guarantee that the given exception records will be excised *on the output*. Operationally, if we need to know why a record did not pass our business transform logic, we can get a simple error report for each job (record and audit id) and each table and affected row. You will likely find ways to extend this structure, but here's what it will buy us:

- We can use a view on top of the primary table that regards the error table as a filter, consumers don't need to know the error table even exists
- Errors recorded for any table, any message, centrally managed
- Error written insert-only
- Errors not physically included in primary table, non-invasive to its structure
- Errors can be corrected later, and keep the audit trail of the error
- Error table can be audited per-job and per-table
- Error table can be purged periodically (and automatically) by using it as a filter for purging master tables.

What kind of errors can we record? We know that we'll find errors in a record's columnar data, perhaps key mismatches, even for tagging duplicate records, integration errors, such as unused join-keys or other set-based anomalies. The list is practically endless. What it does *not* do, is create a huge overhead of infrastructure for the administrators to bother with. What it provides the business analysts, is a one-stop shop to learn what errors happened and why, and if possible to work toward their correction with high traceability and visible lineage.

In *scale*. Let's not forget that such constructs are not as valuable unless we're churning data at the rates, volumes and sizes hosted by Netezza.

We mention in another section how some data processing people think in terms of "percent error". Unfortunately, the people engaged in administrative error reconciliation think in terms of error-*count*. Thinking in terms of *percent-difference*, is akin to saying that because a watermelon and a cloud are only 3 percent different in composition, that somehow there's no "real" difference.

Our business analysts are our number one constituency and potentially our biggest fans. If we want to be a rock-star in the data processing world, we'll need an entourage, and we need the business analysts as our number-one-fans, not spend endless hours complaining about, or propping up, or defending, the broken parts that never get fixed or even addressed.

An error log and error control structure like this will provide everyone with *objective* visibility to what's going on with the data and the machine, so everyone can proactively assist in making it better. The error log records won't get written without some controls in place to write the data, so the developers must pitch in. The error log won't have value unless the business analysts review the issues, review solutions with the developers to provide a transform or fix, or punt the problem upstream for a fix elsewhere. The operators can see that errors are happening even during the run, and can stop things if the error log goes into runaway mode (or we can build-in a threshold that does this for us, and alerts the operator). Anyone can also review the log to determine the health of the warehouse. No errors is a good thing. Lost errors is a bad thing.

Summary Tables

Summary tables are only handy (really) if we have a lot of processes that hit the database and constantly ask for the same summary data from a very large table. As noted in other sections, we have a responsibility at each stage of processing to make things easier for the next downstream process Here, if our "next downstream process" is a component, system, user, reporting tool etc. that requires a summary as its primary data point, then we really aren't doing ourselves any favors by re-summarizing the data on-each-demand (that is, if we really have many thousands of "demands").

A better approach is to manufacture the necessary summaries so that the *hard* work is already done. Okay – this is nothing new, right? We make summary and aggregate tables all the time, don't we?

But in other non-Netezza technologies, the summary table is *required* for significant performance gains *even for the first query*. A summary table also requires a lot of computing power to create. We might desire to capture back this computing power so the user has a good experience (Jurassic Park Model). The pitfall here is in assuming that the existing summary tables are a target for elimination. After all, they only existed to boost performance, and now we have Netezza, so we won't be needing them any longer, right?

What if the existing summary table is actually a good user-facing optimization. What if it supports a critical downstream functional purpose, regardless of its performance? We've just been taking-the-hit in building the aggregation for so long, that we'd rather get rid of it entirely.

But hold on – we have Netezza in the shop now. We can do *really* large aggregations in *minutes*, not hours. Now we have the power to shape an environment for the downstream consumer, rather than just brute-force the structures because we're running out of power.

Balance is the key – if aggregations assist the downstream and take the on-demand performance issues down to a minimum, *and* we can build them in a relative fraction of the time it took before - then embrace them and run with them. Otherwise we could be guilty of throwing out good ideas with bad ones, and this is no longer necessary, either. Keep what we need, or even what we like. The power is there to help us.

The question then becomes, if we don't really need the summary for performance reasons, what good is it? Well, whether we need to physically summarize or not, it's a safe bet that the business rules applied to make the summary are non-trivial. They may be hard-won rules that we don't want exported to the client level. If we remove the business rules of the summary, provide raw data and tell our BI environment to incorporate the logic that was once centrally hosted, we'll get some resistance from those who want to centralize those rules. Again, not to worry - just manufacture the summary, for now exactly like it used to be, and put a view on top of it.

The manufacturing cost of the summary is a nit compared to the functional and *political* resistance we'll get for removing it. Later, when we see actual usage patterns emerge, we can refactor the summary for a better fit. The consumers ultimately won't care because they enter via a view, not direct-access. All underpinning changes will be transparent to them.

Slowly Changing Dimensions

I'm almost always loathe to speak of these, simply because each time we're asked about them in a consulting interview context, it can go two ways, and one of them is always bad. I cannot count how many times we've had direct or sideline conversations about these oddly complex animals where people wanted us to solve their problem without paying us for it. In short, we're asked for a white-board session under the guise of hiring us for real problem solving, but in the end we're just one in a list of "appointments" they have that day with other consulting firms to pick their brains, too. Seems like a lot of overhead when the TDWI website is just a few clicks away. Forgive me for oft-smelling a rat, it's almost Pavlovian by now.

Case Study Short: I went on a consulting interview with a group asking about my general skills to come solve their problems. One of their folks started drilling me on SCDs at a very detailed level. It was almost surrealistic, because the person asking the questions had another motive. If I could give him enough information to help him solve the problem himself, he wouldn't need my firm to help him at all. Such are very nervous conversations. I want to pursue business with them, but they are asking me to give them the solution for free. Why would I do that?

How does Netezza help us with SCDs? Actually Netezza's insert-only architecture *beautifully* covers SCDs with no additional effort, and no special structures. Recall that when we update a record in Netezza, it will perform a delete/insert combination even if we are only changing one column. The SCD on the other hand, wants to *preserve* the original (and most recent) information while accommodating the new.

This plays into our favor in an SCD context, because now we don't really care what we update, or what version the update might be, or whether we should add another row to the table, or to a secondary table, whether we index the version or not, compound-index the version, or any other hoops we have to jump through to make the SCD viable.

ID	Store	Effective
1001	21	Jan 1
1002	21	Jan 31
1003	38	Feb 1
1004	31	May 31
1005	21	May 31
1006	38	May 21

OldID	NewID	Expiration
1001	1002	Jan 30
1002	1005	May 30
1003	1006	May 20

In the depiction (left) we version by date. Note the additional "audit trail" of the NewID. We don't need this for SCD, but for reconstructing an audit trail, is mighty handy.

Each time we enter a new primary record, we record the old record's ID, the new ID and the date of expiration.

We can have lots of variations on the above structures, but the takeaway is simply this: The slowly-changing aspects are managed in a separate, non-invasive filter table, not embedded in the master table itself. I've seen various organizations struggle with the most appropriate or most effective SCD paradigm, creating havoc whenever they want to install the "next best thing". With the filter table scenario, we can apply what we want in the filter table itself, and don't have to settle on one particular form of SCD or another. We can likewise experiment with other forms of SCD without disrupting an existing one, because we would just manufacture a new filter table to experiment with, and not disrupt any existing structures.

Mechanically, all we do now is *insert* the latest version of the row and apply the new version number to a version identifier (in the above case, the new Effective Date is the version, and the Expiration Date can be the Effective Date minus 1). Whether we actually change *one* column in the row, or *all*, it matters not. When we want the version back, we will filter on the version table, *as just another filter*.

And since Netezza's architecture is geared for filtration-based retrieval, the versioning table plays directly into our hands. We don't have to manage it or otherwise deal with it. We just ask for it by name and Netezza's power delivers the goods.

Consider that we have a table *my_dim*, defined with an ID, and with my_exp, an expiration table with matching IDs in it:

```
select * from my_dim md where not exists (select me.orgid from
my_exp me where me.orgid = md.id);
```

The above notation will return all records in the dataset that are non-expired, the most-often executed query on the table. Note that if we want to just publish these results to a downstream schema, we simply do so and leave both primary and filter structures behind. The dimensional mechanics remain localized, under control, decoupled and invisible to the downstream.

But what if someone wants to see the dimensions "as they were" on "a given date" where all the "active, non-expired" records are visible only in context of the date-in-question?

```
select * from my_dim md where not exists
(select me.orgid from my_exp me where
(me.orgid = md.id) and
('${mdate}' > me.exp_date and  '${mdate}' >  md.eff_date ))
```

Note how we have parameterized the date to return the state-of-affairs of the given master table *on* the given date. We could just as easily modify this to serve up records that were viable within a date range, etc. The date-style versioning is very popular in retail. The incremental integer versioning is seen smattered about in some financial services environments, or document-maturity environments such as loans and mortgages. We're not suggesting that you switch-over from one method / approach to another, but highlighting the simple fact that versioning can be handled with a **filter table** in multiplicative approaches, *without affecting the master data record structure.*

Case Study Short: Some information architects wanted to add slowly-changing-dimension (SCD) capability to their tables, but had not yet done any version ID manipulation. They wanted to add this and several other attributes to the noted tables. In Netezza, we cannot simply add columns to a table by altering it. Instead, we have to remanufacture the table into the target table with the new columns in it (this step is often a nit, even for very large tables, so not to worry). But in configuration terms, adding columns could be a significant issue for other consumers of the table. And what if we want to extend it to lots of tables, or all of our dimensions? Adding columns to tables is almost always a high-inflection-point event, with very high visibility and scrutiny where good governance applies. In fact, the more mature the governance, the more initial resistance we'll receive for this proposal, coupled with the need to have thought it through carefully. In typical (RDBMS) systems, experimentation is usually not encouraged when we have billions of rows.

We've noted earlier that surrogate identifiers provide us with options in Netezza not normally available in an RDBMS, and one of these is identification. If all we need is an additional version marker, such as an effective-date, it's simple enough to justify this for business reasons completely outside the need for SCDs. Once installed, we use it in tandem with the expiration date on our version filtering table, and we have an SCD that will function for more than just one table. This approach gives us the freedom to experiment without having to hack the primary structures.

The external filter table also provides us with a means to "version" our Reference Data. For example, if we record all IDs of all records in all tables we want to version, and save these identifiers in a "release" table, that operates in a similar manner, we have effectively recorded a state-in-time of our entire reference data database without having to directly touch the individual records. This would not be a viable approach in an RDBMS, but is a natural fit in Netezza.

One might see the shadows of an object-relational model brewing here, and this is partially correct, if we're talking about the freedom to connect information in creative ways without having to deal with indexing and the usual relational constraints.

From here, even if the reference data changes the next day, we can still faithfully re-publish the *originally* published version of it simply by using a versioning filter table, joining the original publication to the record ID's stored there, and reproducing the original information.

This kind of wholesale versioning is cumbersome (actually, impossible) in RDBMS solutions because of the index maintenance and other overhead required to maintain the table. Not to mention that the version table maintains, in row count, the same number of rows as the table it is versioning, times however many versions we might have. Big deal for the RDBMS, but no big deal for Netezza. In essence, our version reference table will contain the non-invasive construct that allows us to version the data in a primary table without having to stamp the version ID in the table itself.

Which brings us back to the original point, the filter table is where the volatility is managed, not the master table. It remains stable and unchanged.

Carving Out Smaller Tables

While loading up our larger tables might help us keep things all in one place, that "one place" might not necessarily be the *best* place to plumb and process the data. Especially if we have to churn the same table multiple times for multiple answers. What if we only need to join against some fraction of it? What if we have to perform a number of slice-and-dice operations?

Example – we loaded one table with a running 2+ billion records, to be processed each evening. Most of the joining/integration we required, was of records that were inside the same table, a self-join. For any given join, we weren't actually joining the *same* data to itself, but data to another set of records co-located in the same table. The joins were dynamic enough to discourage separate tables for the baseline storage, and had the self-join requirements of a topology model.

We would have to perform three different joins on "similar" information. Performing this very complex operation against the primary table required some eight minutes to complete each individual operation, meaning that all three would require over twenty-four minutes.

So in this case, we carved out one "side" of the join into its own smaller table, likewise with the other "side" of the join. Now we could join the two "sub" tables with the same functional effect. Once we completed all the work and got the required results, we truncated the two sub-tables. Truncation is cheap (sub-seconds even for the largest tables).

The total duration to carve out each sub-table was less than sixty seconds total. The time for each of the three joins instantly reduced to fifteen seconds total. Combining these operations into a short series, the mission was consistently completed inside of *three* minutes. Twenty-four minutes reduced to three minutes. It didn't really cost us anything, did it?

Conclusion- carving out the workload into smaller, manageable chunks actually gives us some of the pipeline effect noted in a previous chapter, and reduces our overall duration as a sum-of-smaller-activities rather than a single, monolithic one.

And note - this option might not be as viable with some of Netezza's competitors, because they have higher write-penalties for data, *so* high that the time required carve out the tables might actually negate any benefit. *Benchmark* with care.

Pre-Calculations / Avoiding Inline (Where-Clause) Calculation

It's very common in data warehousing to see RDBMS joins operations appear in multi-page form. Apart from insert/select or just the output columns themselves, we see multiple tables and the wildest forms of filters, left-outer-joins, correlated sub-queries and all manner of calculations *in the where-clause* to zone-in on specific rows.

The where-clause calculations look similar to this:

```
select * from m, a, where m.col1 > a.col2+5 and
    m.col2 < a.col3-4 and m.trandate+12 < now()
```

See how the where-clause must calculate the columns with each new examination of a given row? We can apply some optimization, but not very much. The where-clause has to pull the records, perform the math, then do the comparison. This will steal egregious amounts of energy because it requires the machine to examine data a row-at-a-time. *We don't want this.*

If we should physically count how many times these calculations occurred in-line while processing two tables in the billions of rows, we would not hesitate in finding another way to streamline how much energy they steal. It is *dramatic*, and we should not take it lightly.

In an RDBMS, the above inline calculation is a common performance problem as well. It puts all the "business-logic" into a single statement. It keeps the RDBMS from having to "touch the same data twice" (for the sake of efficiency and performance). It attempts to apply any-and-every rule it can to the data while it has the data *in its hands*. This is why we see page after page after page of SQL syntax in an "ugly" RDBMS join.

However, if we were to take the known values, precalculate and persist them in *anticipation* of their utility in a later operation, we can buy back a lot of wasted energy. Review the following;

```
Insert into temp_a select a.col2, a.col2+5 as col25,
    a.col3, a.col3-4 as col34 from a;

Insert into temp_m select m.col1, m.trandate,
    m.trandate+12 as trandate12, now() as nowtime;
```

Note how we've now persisted the inline values - *in bulk* - to the intermediate tables as pre-calculations. Now we can apply the desired query in much more efficient form, because the columns are precalculated for immediate inline-comparison in the where-clause:

```
select * from temp_m, temp_a where
    temp_m.col1 < tempa.col25 and
    temp_m.col2 < temp_a.col34 and
    temp_m.trandate12 < tempm.nowtime
```

The above are rather simplistic examples, but see how the pre-calculation in the *upstream* has removed the need for inline calculations in the *downstream*. What we've actually done is broken the query apart so that it actually has a more granular upstream/downstream rather than a monolithic process. By carving out intermediate tables with the desired quantities, and then joining on the two without any *inline* calculations, we reduce the overall time for the operation without much effort.

The difference is *dramatic*, reducing the time-to-result by *ninety* percent or more.

Our initial variation on this theme, might be to enrich the base tables with such precalculated values when the data first undergoes intake. It just depends on how many downstream consumers will need it and when. In short, doing the pre-calculation in the right place is key. We may not need to carve out additional tables at all if we've already applied the calculations upstream in another routine intake process.

Of course, in many cases the above pre-calculations might find their way into a more persistent table. In the case of processing equity trade records, we might find that the trade order's date/time has a bit of drift across participating brokers (the SEC allows for 6 seconds of drift in their clocks). This provides us with the need to create two additional columns, one for the date-time field *minus* 3 seconds, and one for the date-time field *plus* 3 seconds. Now in the downstream, rather than performing plus/minus inline calculation in the *where* clause to match this "fuzzy date", we simply check for *between* the transaction dates. This simple approach bought back ninety percent of the processing time, all attributed to the drain of dynamic calculation versus pre-calculation.

```
Where parent.trandate between child.trandate_minus_3 and
    child.trandate_plus_3
```

SQL statements (plus UDFs) are our only support for integration and transformation. A transform in Netezza is essentially one or more insert/select statements. Even a user-defined function operates within the boundaries of a SQL statement. This means all of our integration or transformation operations must fit inside a SQL statement.

So the temptation is to place dynamic / inline calculations in the body of the integration / transformation. Such calculations might go across columns, or compare a mathematical formula to a column's value (or the outcome of yet another function, etc).

The point, however is this: In traditional RDBMS scenarios, adding (or carving out) these extra pre-calculated columns is rare to non-existent in the open range of data warehousing. It's not a new idea. It's been around for decades, so why do people look askance when this is suggested? Ahh, the Lost World of bulk processing.

As with all things, the proof is in the benchmark.

CONTINUOUS STUFF

SOME SKEPTICS out there imagine that the Netezza machine is designed purely for overnight batch work. You know, when we kick off work at midnight and all that. If you're one of them, you might imagine that it sits on the tail-end of the Jurassic-Park flow model (like it's query-acceleration competitors). Can't and won't do anything continuous with it, they'll say. Fine. This section is not for them. Skip right along to the next section. Off you go.

How to leverage a Netezza machine in continuous form? It's an appliance, right? Shouldn't have any constraints to speak of, right? Absolutely right! In fact, you'll find that the continuous implementation for Netezza is even more powerful, because we can leverage all those SPUS for both inbound scrubbing and outbound streaming effects It's cool stuff.

Let's get some definitions out of the way – "continuous" in this regard is still flow-based batch/bulk, but on a more frequent and scheduled basis. It is *not* transactional-style snippets of work. We've spoken to people who, once hearing of Netezza's derring-do in continuous applications, immediately begin thinking about how they can mothball their transactional environments. Hold on there! We should not process transactional-style streams into Netezza. Our transactional environments still serve this purpose and likely always will. Let them do what they do best - store and manage those transactions. Let Netezza do what it does best, intake those stored transactions on bulk intake boundaries, and convert them into actionable enterprise information.

We mentioned elsewhere that one of our Netezza groups needed to get bulk data in and out of an RDBMS. Rather than to it with bulk extracts (painfully slow with many RDBMS platforms) they could benefit from a continuous model we're about to describe. After all, if the data is available (and in RDBMSs like SQLServer and Oracle, data is available incrementally throughout the day) what is to stop us from forwarding it on a schedule that keeps from overloading the RDBMS with an egregious batch extract?

We also must honor the simple fact that the business day is protracting and the luxurious batch windows we current enjoy are shrinking. We will (like soon) need an effective means to spread out the workload so that we don't take a massive hit all-at-once. Perhaps this hit isn't so massive if we have a Netezza machine, but as we scale, the business window evaporates and people really want 24/7 support, we'll need to find a way to make thing happen more creatively, perhaps more continuously.

Loading Up

A significant consideration in the continuous model is the data transport protocol into the Netezza machine. I've mentioned elsewhere that Netezza has a minimum / optimum load size of about a gigabyte. We can functionally load less than this, but it's not as efficient, and the smaller / more frequent we go, the less throughput we get. Note- if a small amount is *all* we have to load, then load it.

But in a continuous model, the data is *streaming* in, so we need a "fan-in" collector function that will make the pipeline more efficient. Thus we tank-up the data, then burst-load it on frequent intervals rather than just streaming it into the machine. This is necessary no matter what the receptacle is, whether Netezza or one of its heel-snipping competitors. If someone says they have this part squared away, make them show it off, and in a way that lets us know there's no effort on *our part* to invoke it, because otherwise it's not really *provided* by the product, eh?

We do have a lightweight option here, in that we can stream-load an instance of nzload on the client facing the Netezza machine. As long as the nzload is open, it can actually write to an external table on the Netezza machine, not the SPUs. So if we have a means to periodically close off a given "streaming" instance of the nzload, it can commit to the SPUs on this closure boundary. We would simply open up another instance of nzload and start the collection process again. The objective here is to avoid opening up a streaming (dribbling) ODBC write directly into the SPUs. We can use the nzload to "tank" the data into an external table's flat file, and when it closes, we bulk-load the entire file into the target table.

If we want to go with something deeper, like named pipes, many transactional publishers are *invariably Windows machines* and do not speak to Linux (Netezza's operating system) through named pipes. We can set up a socket protocol with inetd (discussed later) but some folks aren't comfortable with this. If we only had access to named pipes we would be far closer to our goal. Just as if we had access to the flat files themselves, provided we can convince our often flat-file-phobic Windows developers to make one for us, much less institutionalize it. The *horror*.

In a prior section I mentioned embracing flat files. Just swallow the pill. It won't hurt you. We can stream flat files into any receptacle we choose, then perform a bulk intake on a regular boundary. We can provide several different approaches and frameworks for this, but the objective in all of it is to actually *serialize* the inbound feeds into a *critical mass*. Once we hit critical mass, we load the data into the SPUs.

If we have multiple small feeds, where do we land the feeds? In many cases, these don't ever appear as flat files, but as real data flows coming in from ODBC-enabled servers. The developers on those (usually Windows) servers will gasp dumbfounded if you ask them to make a flat file for collection purposes. Our ETL environment *could* make us a flat file, but we *know* that ETL's should do, well, *ETL*. They should pull the data and push it via connection. So we're back to that pesky data transportation problem again. And the intake. What to do about the intake?

If we have a Continuous Flows environment for Ab Initio, hey, it's just a point-click away. Ab Initio manages continuous flows through Compute Points, behaving as collectors, which we can program to get the right Ab Initio *outbound* effect, in order to affect the right Netezza *inbound* effect. Only a relative handful of groups have this luxury, so what of the rest of us?

How to collect the data? Is it flat file? For all we know, the data will *only* arrive via ODBC, and when it does, do we have any choices as to delivering it to the SPUs? Well, strictly speaking, we do have a choice.

Let's take a look at inbound flat-file collection, a very popular way to drop off streaming data. We would suggest that total aggregate size of the file feeds (greater than a gigabyte) is a good start, but we need at least three more thresholds. The second is the total count of collections (or rows in those collections), a third is a timeout, and fourth is the maximum amount we want to deal with at a time.

Gigabytes - we can generally find this just by doing some file-size math on the incoming file sets. We don't need to open the files and count. We can examine the system files sizes and make some estimates. This is quick and cheap, and BASH shell will get us there. When we reach a known aggregate size, trigger the load. And while there, take *all* of the data, not just the stuff that triggered the threshold.

Total file count – likewise a fairly cheap operation with BASH shell. Not a lot of overhead in this. When we reach a known count, trigger the load. And while there, take *all* the files, not just those that met the threshold.

Total Time – let's say we're on a down cycle, perhaps late in the evening when the gigabytes don't show up as quickly. Rather than wait for the gigabytes to show up (it might take awhile, you see), we could just pull whatever we have on a given timeout. Determine what this would be and just do it. Five minutes? Fifteen minutes? Whatever makes sense to "empty the tank".

Maximum amount - what is the *maximum* data we want to intake all at once? I've seen cases where the intake environment might have to go offline for servicing, and the assumption is that when it comes back up, it will just *catch up* with the workload. We need to be careful that we don't saturate our systems in doing this. If we've been offline for several days, or have several times the normal data to intake, it won't hurt us to intake the load *several times*, effectively biting off the elephant in chunks. It may be that we can intake no less than a gigabyte at once, and we plan for it. But what is the *maximum* we are willing to process? We should plan for that, too. In one particular case, we had allowed the system to go offline for several days and when it returned, the total count of files exceeded the ability of the networks and external source systems to manage them as we wanted. So we broke off the total file count at a max-threshold and it executed several back-to-back intakes with no issues.

Most continuous environments don't have just one source, they have dozens of streaming sources, and in retail environments, may have thousands of them. How to support these streaming sources without some level of middleware to fan-in their feeds to a more controlled intake? In these cases, the sources are usually deliberately configured to formulate a file and deliver it to a repository. So the above protocol rules dovetails directly into this.

Some environments have a transactional staging platform that receives and collates all the inbound feeds. If we have a mature continuous environment, some degree of control already exists between the feeds and the Netezza machine, because many of these environments are already doing some portion of fan-in. Measure what they are doing and examine it for a fit. We might find that we're closer to a fit that we think. The point is - we still can't stream things into the Netezza machine like transactions, but the chances are very high that they are not physically arriving this way anyhow, *somewhere* in the environment.

Imagine executing the above protocol where each streaming load only has a few hundred records at a time, arriving at the rate, of say, twenty streams per second. These streams are too small and frequent for *any* appliance, including Netezza, to manage at a most-efficient peak. We can intake all these directly into the SPUs, but only with a bundled fan-in intake.

As noted earlier, a common streaming configuration is to set up an intake schema per upstream subscription point, because then it's just a matter of schema configuration if we need a new upstream point. A separate schema is useful for a variety of reasons, but some folks like to set up an "intake" schema and use it for all intake, all sources. This can create configuration problems, in that each intake source will invariably have different needs. If we accommodate these needs into one schema, the schema over time can become brittle. If we have one-schema-per-source, we can accommodate the exceptions in isolation without disrupting the configurations of the other sources. This also simplifies secure-access, so our administrators would rather have a separate schema for each one. B2B sources will require a separate, secure entry point, best supported with a dedicated schema that faces the publisher. In short, they will understand it, and it simplifies things.

For the record, a '*source*' is not a server, but a role. If we have five thousand retail stores trickling a feed to us, this can be regarded as one source, not five thousand. If our accounting system or internet aggregation system have clusters of servers, each *system*, not their servers, represents a source. Most environments have a simple handful of sources, so giving them a dedicated intake schema provides isolation and manageability for each source. Some DBAs read this and say they don't need it, but we're managing sources that are delivering *scale*, not simple loads. Breaking apart a problem into manageable chunks is a key to attacking *scale*, and dedicated schemas will help.

If we have fifteen upstream disparate sources, does this mean we will need fifteen schemas, one for each upstream source? Think about this: constantly modifying a single intake schema to add more upstream feeds is problematic for configuration control. It also constrains our ability to do more agile things, like shadow tables or special services that face the specific subscription point. A cookie-cutter schema is cheap. Maintaining one schema for all - is *not*. Over time it will take on the brittleness we find in organically-grown systems. For example, if we need to add one more upstream source, we only add one more cookie-cutter schema, not disturbing the schemas that are already in place and working nicely. If we need to add a feed to an existing schema (a new feed in an existing source), the dedicated infrastructure helps us to assimilate it quickly without fear of breaking the other source configurations. Once the given flow is functional for a given server/schema, leave it alone. Does this sound like cut-and-paste of a reusable capability? Well, we don't have to cut-and-paste the whole schema, only the parts that face the subscription point, like the intake and other source-facing tables.

One of our clients has eight fully mature operational systems, each of which has ten or more specific pieces of master data that are oddly similar in names and meaning to each other, but likewise oddly disconnected. Do we commingle all of these deceptively named tables into a common schema, or give each source its own schema and likewise a discrete, manageable table set?

Remember, we are not defining the final consumption point inside Netezza, but a dirty landing zone to perform high-octane *intake*. Once inside, we crunch the data in other ways to make it consumption- ready. In a continuous environment, the first operation is getting past the intake.

This also allows us to mix-and-match intake scenarios, where some bulk loads might arrive in large quantity while others might trickle down to us. Each schema can have attendant supporting processes, easily manageable and maintainable, like a component.

Let's say we have a cluster of servers that handle internet loan applications. It has ten servers (A-J) that all send data to the Netezza machine on arbitrary, streaming boundaries.

So let's say Server A lands a file to eventually fan-in to the host Table_A. We'll call it

```
server_a.20080401.09:18:04.345678.dat
```

So we see a pattern here. Each server in the LOANs cluster will land its data for Table-A into a common directory, and each file will be uniquely named based on its upstream source so that we don't lose track or lineage.

Over some period of time, we examine the path and find the following files in the location `loans/table_a_data`:

```
server_a.20080401.09:18:04.345678.dat        81410
server_c.20080401.09:18:04.418971.dat        22410
server_d.20080401.09:18:04.558910.dat        98410
server_f.20080401.09:18:04.778967.dat        398410
server_j.20080401.09:18:04.987490.dat        31410
server_e.20080401.09:18:05.114190.dat        55410
server_c.20080401.09:18:05.224370.dat        989410
```

Note that the data files all face the "table_a" data structure (and reside in the table_a_data directory), and all arrive on arbitrary boundaries with arbitrary sizes. Do we have enough files to load? Are the tables of sufficient size that they can justify a session of nzload? Have we crossed a time threshold and need to take everything anyhow?

Threshold-triggered intake – Now we need a way to check our thresholds for a triggered intake. We can check the thresholds on any particular time boundary, but it's best to check it when we are ready to perform a load. If we're not ready to load why bother checking it? This means that the time-boundary is an important arbiter. If we know that we must perform the intake at least every fifteen minutes, does it really hurt us to check every five minutes? What if we can execute the entire intake and processing cycle inside of four minutes? On a fifteen-minute boundary, we now have eleven minutes to sit and do nothing. What if we checked for thresholds every five minutes? We discover that one of the size or count thresholds is exceeded and we can start processing now. Otherwise we can go to sleep for another five minutes and repeat the cycle. We will "for sure" take everything with us on the next five-minute boundary (fifteen-minutes has expired), but we didn't have to wait. If the data is ready and there's nothing else to do, let's take it and process it.

One group has traffic-light scenario where it sets a "red" light condition in the box when the machine is in a high-intensity processing cycle. When it finishes the cycle, it sets the conditions back to green. If the threshold monitor happens to launch during a red-light window, it simply goes back to sleep. If during a green-light window, then it checks thresholds and potentially launches the work. It knows that it cannot launch during a red-light window or within the thresholds. It also sends status to a log that the operators can review, allowing them to see when the box was busy, how much work was in queue, etc.

If we should trigger our intake on file count or size, then this should likewise reset our countdown clock for the time threshold. Keep in mind that this will create a nuance in our scheduler, such that triggering a process on an off-window boundary might cause our time thresholds to be offset and not on exact boundaries. These will typically reset to a default boundary when we are in off-peak, meaning of course that we maintain high flexibility and throughput during peak times also.

We have several ways of handling a timeout check, but in Linux the most straightforward means is with a simple file timestamp. Set up a file with zero bytes in it that our triggered function will "touch" each time it performs a load. Likewise, the triggered function will check the difference in seconds between the last load (the last time the file was "touched") and the current time. If this time exceeds the threshold, execute a load with all available data and "touch" the file as normal after a load.

The intake protocol is very simple, and here is an extended variation of the framework noted in the chapter *Loading Up With Stuff:*

- We go to the holding tank and get a list of files (manifest) through the simple Linux directory "ls" command.
- We then instantiate a local named pipe and use nzload to listen to a local named pipe while its load target is the given SPU-based Netezza table.
- We then use "cat" to simply concatenate the manifest into the named pipe. The "cat" command is safe since the data isn't moving from disk-to-disk but from disk-to-pipe, so data will come off the disk drive and remain in memory until it finally lands on a SPU.
- Once completed, the "cat" will quit, the named pipe will close and the nzload will wrap its final commit.
- We then delete the named pipe, and use the manifest file to mark or delete its files This means that only the files that were loaded will be removed, while ignoring any other recent arrivals.

What do we need for all this?

We'll need some infrastructure inside the Netezza machine, including intake schemas, intake directory paths (whether onboard or external mounts) and some processes to circumscribe them. Overall, it's still a cookie-cutter infrastructure that we can easily describe with metadata, and thus extend for more external publishers without doing much more than simple schema configuration and logon credentials. Of the following capabilities, we're talking about a page or two of simple BASH script, *not an operating system kernel!* Infrastructure looks like:

- Intake schema definitions
- Intake file repository
- Intake file-copy
- Intake thresholding
- Intake assimilation

This intake protocol provides a simple framework that all trickle-feed upstream publishers can use to get their data cleanly into the Netezza machine without any issues, and also not swamp the Netezza machine with onesy-twosy load requests that "cane" the SPUs.

Truncation vs Delete

I'll discuss this scenario in detail in several other places, so forgive the repetition, the applications are varied.

We previously described how the delete operation takes time to execute and also leaves holes in the table structure that we will eventually have to clean up. Truncate is practically instantaneous, but removes all the data from the table and also recovers all used record space. In a *Continuous* environment, the *truncate* is clearly faster than the *delete*, but it gets rid of all the records. How can we keep a continuous flow of data in and out of the table, perform the necessary *continuous* housekeeping and not break any dependencies - or lose anything?

The *truncate* is the only viable option for high-intensity continuous-model housekeeping, but if we use it, we need a way to preserve what we want to keep *before* we actually zap the data. We also need a transparent way to execute this preservation/truncation cycle without breaking any dependent processes or consumers. If we logically separate the data, even using zone maps, it doesn't get us out of the pesky issue of delete-and-reclaim.

Case Study Short: The customer has a 24x7 continuous model and has to keep ten days of data online. Rather than put all the data in a single table, they put the data into ten *identical* tables. One of the tables is always "active", receiving the data for the current day. At the end of the day, the table containing the *least-recent* data is truncated and the system starts pouring information into this newly truncated table. This maintains a rolling-ten-days of information and the customer never has to worry about delete-and-reclaim. Truncation is nary a blip of time on the radar, so the customer's processes continue unabated.

Partitions and views

While the Netezza platform doesn't have the formal concept of "Partition" like some RDBMS, the functionality of a partition is not very far away. In a continuous environment, we need to pull data into the machine, manipulate it and prep it without stomping on the data that's already in-use. We also need to protect our consumers from accessing the information while we're in the midst of prepping it.

Another reason for partitions is maintenance. If we have a continuous environment, it's practically guaranteed that our older data is getting stale, and we need a way to dump it without disrupting the consumers or the data processing flows. We also need to avoid the housekeeping problems associated with a "delete-reclaim" operation on the tables. In most continuous environments, the luxury of downtime, even to execute a simple reclaim, is not available.

We have two basic models of partitions that have interest for us. We could probably think of others, but these two keep rearing their heads, so we'll deal with them one at a time. They are the *two*-partition model and the *multi*-partition model. But first, I'll describe two other important points, the nature of a *view* and Netezza's *concurrency* rules.

Netezza Views – In order to provide consumers with a consistent experience, we will leverage Netezza's *views* to steer consumer traffic to the appropriate partition. This means that for any given customer query, it will access table(s) that are visible to the view. If we want to include/exclude tables for the consumer, we do it under the view's umbrella. Keep in mind that a view-mechanics in Netezza is simply a single *select* statement. It might contain *union*s and the like, but it has to fit into a single *select* query.

Concurrency Notes – It is important to note several concurrency rules that are of extreme importance and interest here.

- If a view is pointing to one table, and we change the view to point to another table, any active or pending queries on the view's former table(s) will *not* be interrupted.
- If we want to truncate a table, or drop a table, this operation will *block* if any read queries are active or pending on the table. So it won't execute until all the existing read operations are completed.
- We cannot read from a table where a destructive operation (like an nzreclaim) is underway
- Likewise destructive operations such as delete or update, will *block* while a read operation is active or pending on the table.
- We cannot *write* to a view. The structure is read-only.
- We can change the view to consume different tables using the create-or-replace view, without disrupting any existing read operations, while blocking all incoming read operations for that view.
- We cannot afford the time for common delete nor an nzreclaim. A truncate is quick and cheap. Even the largest tables will truncate in split-seconds.

Two Partitions, One Active, One-Inactive – This is the simplest model. It is basically a double-chambered buffer to handle continuous intake-and-consumption. Let's say we have a table structure called *mytable.* We would represent this table with two physical tables and a view to consume them. Both physical tables are identical in the columns and distribution.

Structure Type	Name	Role
View	v_mytable	Read-only Consumption
Table	t_mytable_P0	Partition
Table	t_mytable_P1	Partition

View

P0   **P1**

Active   Inactive

In the depiction (left) the View points to the P0 partition while the P1 partition remains inactive. This is a typical dual-partition management concept, easy to understand and implement.

We can load and setup P1 without disrupting the continuous-and-or-user experience on the View. When the time comes, we swap the View to point to P1 and begin the data processing cycle on P0.

All external consumers will perform a *select* on the ***v_mytable*** view, effectively decoupling them from the underlying table that *v_mytable* is currently consuming. When we need to change the view, we execute the create-or-replace view command, which will reset the view from one underpinning table to another using a single, *uninterruptible* operation. This is key, because we will not have to drop the view and rebuild it, risking the possibility that a consumer may need it in this delicate interim. The view is always visible, and any consumer coming to read it while the create-or-replace is underway, will block. Any consumer currently reading the former table will not be interrupted either.

The following is a pseudo-configuration where the *v_mytable* view is consuming the 00 partition:

Partition	Visible To	Role
t_mytable_P0	v_mytable	Read-only
t_mytable_P1	Loading, processing	Read/Write/Truncate

Likewise here is the configuration when v_mytable is consuming the 01 partition:

Partition	Visible To	Role
t_mytable_P0	Loading, processing	Read/Write/Truncate
t_mytable_P1	v_mytable	Read-only

Which One: We know that by setting the Netezza *view* to a given "partition" table, we can automatically guarantee that the external consumers will read from the correct one.

Let's say some new data comes into the machine and we need to prep it. We load the data into the inactive table, process it and otherwise make it ready for consumption. First, how do we know *which* table is the inactive one, so we don't stomp on the active one while consumers are reading it? More importantly, how do we switch the view and the loading functions to point to the correct one?

For this, we'll need a metadata file. In this file we'll keep the names of the partitions and which one is currently active, and which one is currently inactive. If we use BASH Shell, we can further enhance our functionality into a supporting framework with:

```
export ACTIVE_PARTITION=t_mytable_P0
export INACTIVE_PARTITION=t_mytable_P1
```

Now if we need to switch partitions, we just read this file, swap the values and write them back. Any BASH shell script or other functions that need to know the score, will simply *execute* this file and the correct values will automatically export-and-instantiate into the shell's runtime.

Now we know that if we have a simple loading or data processing script, we can run this file and understand that we should load-and-prep the INACTIVE_PARTITION, in this case t_mytable_P1. Once completed, I'll run another script with the responsibility of (a) switching the partition tags in this file and (b) changing the view. We can then do anything we want with the view's former table.

- Discover the INACTIVE partition
- Intake data to the INACTIVE partition
- Perform any prep, transform etc
- If we need to carry-over data from the ACTIVE partition, select this data from ACTIVE partition now and insert it into the INACTIVE partition
- Change the View to start consuming the INACTIVE partition, now the ACTIVE partition.
- Truncate the formerly ACTIVE partition, now INACTIVE partition
- Repeat from the top on the next intake cycle

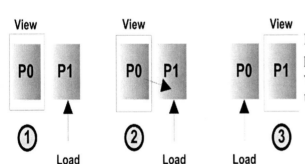

In the scenario (left), the P1 is the focus of all loading (1) where the View accesses the stable P0 partition. During the update cycle (2), the loading wraps up, we take what we want to keep from P0, then switch the view (3) to point to P1.

Using simple Netezza command and script statements, we can manage all of the above in less than twenty simple lines of BASH shell. It's actually easier to make your own and tailor it. I say this because I have some shell script that does the above, and each time I'm at a customer site it's just easier to set up this simple script *in situ* than it is to copy our own stuff and retro-fit it. The point is – it's simple to implement and very effective.

To take it one level higher, we could also put some shell script in place to manufacture the partitions and do some other housekeeping, but sometimes these are unnecessary. We generally like to install some additional metadata functionality just to get some reuse, but this is personal preference.

We will find that the above structures and process will give us a hot-swappable table structure for continuous operation. Now, do we wish that the "partition" was more formal? Yes and no. We like the flexibility of simple, programmable script to make these things operate. It keeps them visible with no mysteries. If Netezza engineers back in Marlborough should bind them into a more formal structure, we'll use it without looking back.

But for now, this is a functionality that is useful only for continuous environments, which is (today) a smaller (but growing) part of Netezza's overall user base. Not to worry, these structures are *easy* to put into place.

Multiple Partitions, One-Active, None-Inactive – This scenario is identical to the one above, with the exception that we have more than just two partitions and none are inactive. Think of it as a rolling-active-partition. Mechanically we will still have one active (for filling with most recent inbound data). But in this structure, *all* of the partitions are visible to the *view*. All partitions are available for internal data processing consumption. But only one is available for writing in any given interval. The *active* structure is simply the current loading/prepping target. We define the logical and physical boundary for the partitions, and simply change the load-target on the boundary.

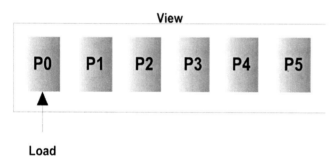

In the depiction (left), we actively load one of the partitions, designated the active partition during our operational cycle. *Active* for loading and assimilating information. The other partitions are quiet, having completed their physical loading cycles.

Note that in the depiction (left), if all partitions are full, P1 contains the *oldest* information of all the partitions.

For example, let's say that today is Friday and P0 is actively receiving Friday's data. Yesterday our P4 partition was active, receiving Thursday's data. Likewise P3 for Wednesday, P2 for Tuesday and P1 for Monday. When Friday closes at midnight, the new Active partition will transition from P0 to o P1, where we will truncate the existing data in P1 and declare it active. This keeps five days of history and one active day, all visible to the View, which has visibility to all the partitions. As noted in the depiction above, P1 contains the oldest data for this cycle. We will always transition from the most-recent to the least-recent partition.

I've seen people set this up primarily to handle some time-boxed portion of work, usually a day's worth at-a-time. In one particular case, the 'active' partition was targeted for the "current day's work" while the other partitions kept "prior days' work". So at the end of a certain cycle of days, the oldest partition would simply roll off, effectively maintaining a rolling-active window of time.

So how does this work, exactly? Firstly, the view is set up to consume all of the partitions in a *select* that uses a "union". Secondly, we put in enough partitions to handle the proper time-boxing.

In our case, we'll keep five days of active data. When the fifth day rolls off, we'll truncate the next rolling partition in the list, make it the "active" day and the load functions will target it.

- Declare the active partition
- Load data during the time-boxed cycle
- End of the time-boxed cycle arrives
- Truncate the least-recent partition's data
- Make this truncated partition the now-active partition

Creating the view: Making a view that sits on top of all the partitions requires a simple select from each table, coupled with a *union*. If we need to exclude a partition on each cycle, we use the create-or-replace view and Netezza's concurrency model will protect us from any disruptions.

However, because none of the partitions are offline in the default model, we can see that this is simpler than the dual-partition in the prior example. All partitions are always visible, so we don't have any issues with concurrency or view-maintenance. In this case, we would set up the view once and only revisit it when we need to add or subtract partitions.

Operationally, we have some additional overhead in keeping up with the "order" of the partitions to determine which one is "next". We can do this with naming conventions or metadata. In the end, we simply rotate the partitions so we can truncate the least recent data, and load the data to the currently active partition.

Creating the partitions: One of the ongoing maintenance issues we may see with this approach, is the necessity to perform intermittent table maintenance on the partitions. If we need to add/drop a column from one table, it's a pain, but from ten or fifteen is quite tedious. One approach is to simply keep a "template" table in a master configuration schema that serves as the "source master" DDL for the partitions. With this, a simple script can manufacture the partitions with:

```
Drop table partition_x;
Create table partition_x as select * from
    masterschema..table_x limit 0;
```

This repeating pattern (the above is pseudo-code) can manufacture the partition tables from a master table's DDL (replacing "_x" with an incrementing numeric value), guaranteeing that all of the partitions will be identical. So even table maintenance is straightforward and simple.

We will find that the need for *lots* of partitions, even for continuous operations, is somewhat rarefied. It is handy to know, however, that Netezza's basic structures easily support it and we can get there without much effort.

Case Study Short: One client decided to keep thirty days of data in thirty rolling partitions. With each new day, the least-recent partition would be truncated and all new intake operations start to use it. Over time, they realized that in their continuous model, on a statistical basis, no data older than fifteen days really mattered to the business because in their model, after fifteen days it would be processed by another system entirely. So they dialed it back to fifteen days and fifteen partitions. One of their analysts then looked deeper into the data. Over the prior two years, no continuous operation had touched data that was older than five days. So they dialed it back to five days and five partitions.

The point being, the partitioning model should be extensible and adaptable, and provide a means to determine how to right-size our model for computing power.

In this case, pulling the data size back from thirty days to five, provided them a means to reduce their batch window from a ten-minute model down to less than two-minutes. Netezza now provided a latency of less than two minutes, with incrementally scalable power, in an environment that had never experienced a latency below half an hour in its prior technology.

Socket-Loader from Windows/inetd

When at one customer site, one of their sharper engineers reminded us that the *inetd* protocol could be useful in allowing their Windows servers to speak to the Netezza machine, effectively opening up a Windows socket to load data into the Netezza machine via the Linux host *inetd* utilities.

We had seen this protocol used (by a different name and for a more oblique purpose) in the past, and upon examination of his implementation, we thought it was a very creative and solid piece of work. While we can't mention his name here (it is the underground after all) if he's reading this, he knows who he is, and this is the closest we can get to a shout-out and stay under the radar. There you go.

Inetd, on the surface, simply listens to a Linux socket address and when things arrive on the socket, it launches a pre-designated script in context of the socket's I/O. It can then *read* from the socket address like any normal file or named pipe. The *read* can stop normally when the sender transmits an end-of-file marker.

The inetd protocol is well-documented so we won't go into any rehash here. If we implement the simplest example found on web sites that talk about it, we're already about 99 percent of what we need on the Linux/Netezza side.

Some notes for the Linux side:

- Either keep a reusable pool of named pipes, or use a mechanism to dynamically manufacture a uniquely named pipe and then toss it when done
- When transmitting data from the Windows machine, send a header containing the target table's name.
- When the socket signal arrives, open the socket and read the header information. Keep this header handy.
- Open the named pipe and launch the nzload utility to read the pipe and load the target table found in the header

The remainder is identical to the intake framework noted in the chapter *Loading Up With Stuff.*

- Now perform some housekeeping by comparing the nzload's log statistics (records loaded) to the record count noted in the header.
- Report any errors to whomever wants to know.
- The *inetd* protocol will launch multiple threads for each server that wants to send data via the protocol, so it won't get confused
- For the target table, this may well be a partitioned table, so snap up the appropriate target partition name and load-away
- We might need to initially load a "dirty" temporary table (see *Loading* elsewhere in this book) and then copy the dirty table to a clean table, cleaning up the nulls and such in the copy.

Some notes for the Windows side:
- Use a simple utility or even a simply-configured .NET program.
- Open a Windows socket (connecting to the socket address listened-on by our *inetd* listener)
- Open the file to be transmitted
- Concatenate the appropriate header on it
- Send the data down the socket with simple writes
- Perform block-reads on the file, with block-writes to the socket
- Try to block up as much data as possible to maximize the socket packet
- If possible, set it up to load as many files as possible, so we don't need multiple socket instances

This protocol is intended to create a named-pipe effect between a Window server, which understands sockets but not named pipes, and a Linux machine that has gone the distance to support named pipes, but needs something like *inetd* to interact with the Windows sockets.

In the end, we will find that this protocol yields *network speed* in its loading results. Here is a summary (records are 50 bytes wide), Netezza system is 8250z

Note that in the tests below, the loads are coming from multiple disparate servers and leveraging both of the IP addresses on the 8250z's dual gigabit network card.

Parallel nzLoads	Million Recs	GB Input	Secs	Raw MB/Sec	Million Recs/Sec	Million Rec/Instance
1	10	0.5	10	50	1	1
2	20	1	14	71	1.4	0.7
3	30	1.5	14	107	2.1	0.7
4	40	2	20	100	2	0.5

So we can see, that we have 40 million records (2 gb) in 20 *seconds*. But our sweet spot looks like 3 simultaneous loads, with 1.5 gb in 14 seconds, maintaining two million records per second, over 100mb per second. This translates to 6gb per minute, or 360gb intake per hour. Look, however at some of the overhead numbers. We know that we have to expand the data sometimes to fit it into the tables. So while the system pulled 107 mb/second, it also created 163 megabytes per second. This translates to almost 600gb per hour laying down on the SPU drives.

Considering that the Netezza platform can intake over 600gb an hour, the Netezza machine was actually *waiting* on the network and Windows platform to complete its work.

Your actual mileage may vary. Get Netezza on the horn for a proof-of-concept. The 8250z is now operating under the call-sign of 10200, with greater speed, compression and capability. Ask for it by name at your friendly neighborhood Netezza dealer.

Named Pipes

The *nzload* utility does not accept multiple input files. It loads one file at a time. However, if this "file" happens to be a named pipe, we can stuff as many files as we like into the pipe. The vendor's competitors operate this way, too, but they might wrap theirs with a little more magic. Under the covers it's all the same and simple to operate.

Leverage named pipes when doing either socket or file-based loading. We will invariably find a reason to concatenate multiple files together. We will never want to use the *cat* utility to simply slam files together on the disk. But if we can use *cat* to pull multiple files from a disk and stuff them into a named pipe, we have effectively made a collector "fan-in" function, read many files into memory, without writing them back out to disk again.

If on the other side of the named pipe we have an *nzload* utility waiting to receive data on the pipe, we have effectively given *nzload* a means to do everything in memory, without any contact with the file system at all.

The *cat* utility is ideal for this. It will take an arbitrary file specification, read all of the files according to the specification, copy each to the named pipe *without its end-of file marker*, and send the end-of-file only with the last file in the specification. This is an appropriate use for *cat*, primarily because it is *writing* to a memory-based pipe rather than back to the disk.

Manifest File

One of the things we like to do for loading, is to create a *manifest* file, a list of files that are to be part of a given load. This allows us to audit this list later. It also provides us with a recovery scenario (just restart from the same manifest file). So rather than just using an arbitrary file specification on the *cat*, we would perform an "ls" with the file specification on the file system itself and create a text file containing the full path of the files to be included in the *cat*. This means we can designate load-ready files from various mount-points, create an inventory of files in the manifest, then start working with the manifest. It also means we can *limit* the total count of files in the manifest file, a very important loading aspect.

Once completed, we then use the manifest to mark the files we just processed, and now we are ready for the next processing cycle with a new manifest.

Another benefit of the manifest is that we avoid choking the machine, and choking *cat*, with too many files to intake. We can throttle the total count of files in the manifest, allowing *nzload* to get some breathing room. Why do this? What if our intake protocol is down for a day or two (it happens)? And when it comes back up, it has some *catch up* to do. Would we choke the Netezza machine in trying to catch up, or would it be better to bite off the load activity in manageable, automatic and relatively risk-free chunks?

By using *cat, named pipes, nzload* and a *manifest* file, we have effectively created a very robust but simple intake protocol. I've seen this sort of thing get put in place within weeks of the Netezza machine's arrival. We can simply and effectively load files into Netezza in a relatively *lights-out* manner.

Rather than cobble together several components or utilities for spot-application or minimal capability, what we should be doing is resolving an overall *capability inventory* for our machine. We can then leverage the capabilities without having to build-and-rebuild them as intermediate or secondary functionalities.

For Updating

If we need to update in *scale*, then we find the same issues as arise in deletion. An update is a delete/insert cycle. So we will take the hit for the insert either way. Only now we'll take the hit for the delete as well.

A caveat of bulk-updating, and bulk-deleting, is that we will *always* do this on a key-based protocol, meaning that the target intake table itself *must* be distributed on the update/delete key. If the table is not distributed on the update/delete key, we can sometimes see significant performance issues. Does this update-facing distribution affect the downstream consumption-point queries? Usually not (99 percent of cases), but evaluate as necessary.

We also have the same issues as in a ETL flow, where we have large group of records and will update some and insert others. Statistically, the count of update records is always much smaller than the inserts, so it's actually better to bulk-copy the insert-records and then bulk-update the update-records. It is this bulk-update cycle that seems to be different, but it doesn't have to be.

If we get the insert-records into the table, then identify the update records into an update filter table, like a slowly-changing dimension, we can then simply insert all the update records without deleting their prior versions. At least, we don't have to delete them quite yet. At some appropriate housekeeping interval, we can delete them later.

But in a continuous model, we don't really have the luxury of time to update, any more than we have the luxury to delete, and this would be true on any appliance technology. By using an update-filter, we embrace an insert-only model both on the primary table and in the filter table. We can blast data into these tables on-the-fly without any hiccups for the continuous operations.

Here's an easily implemented scenario that is perhaps the most complex of anything we'll try, and is akin to a slowly-changing dimension. We can always back down from here.

Solution A
- Identify the to-be-updated records.
- Identify the to-be-inserted records.

- Copy the identifiers of the update records into a "filter" table. (Recall, a filter table is a physical table we will use to perform an exclusionary (where not exists) join.
- (We'll talk about row identification techniques elsewhere)
- Then insert all of the records, both the updates and the inserts.
- Leverage a view that will regard the "filter" table to perform a where-not-exists for all table retrievals.
- Now when we retrieve data, we will get all the inserted records, all the recently updated records, and filter out all the records we don't want to see anymore.
- When we have a slowly-changing dimension scenario, the filter-table supports it very well.

Solution B
- Identify the to-be-updated records
- Copy the identifiers of the to-be-updated records into a filter table.
- Perform the update by inserting the update records into an intermediate table.
- Perform the insert with the to-be-inserted records into the intermediate table.
- Copy all records from the main table that are not found in the filter table, to the intermediate table
- Drop the main table
- Rename the intermediate table to the main table's original name

Why do this? Again, we are embracing Netezza's natural operation but getting a little more visible control over the actual flow. We would perform Solution A if the update operation was relatively small. We would perform Solution B if we had a large number of records to update. We would also perform Solution B as a cleanup to the gradually accumulating values in the "filter" table.

Of course, Solution B has implication for incremental backups, so choose with this priority in mind.

These steps may seem a little out-of-place and certainly counter-intuitive. Isn't there a simpler way to cover all this? If our batch window is shrinking, our options for *complete* simplicity shrink with it. Still, the overall power of the box means that - even with the above scenario - the solution is relatively simple, visible and easy to maintain. We can always implement something simple today, and as our window shrinks, consider our options and grow into it slowly.

PUBLICATION AND DELIVERY STUFF

DATA WAREHOUSE environments have a number of different constituencies and consumers of our work products. The ones we will personally interact with the most, are the operators, administrators and ad-hoc data consumers. The ones we will interact with least are the downstream system consumers, or those who consume "burst" or parameterized reports. These folks often sit in faraway places and are a faceless mass. We must, however, remain ever mindful that someone, somewhere has an opinion on the information we're producing and how we're producing it.

Apart from the metadata associated with data processing and publication, which could be the subject of another entire book (and likely is) let's examine how Netezza supports data outtake in large quantities. In context of an upstream and a downstream, we will extract from an upstream and our consumers will extract from Netezza. When we say publication, we don't really send anything anywhere, we just package it for extraction.

Firstly, I'd like to make sure we're level-set on what "extraction" means to the average data warehouse. Usually an ETL product will pull from a database with a SQL statement. If we violate Rule #10 with this SQL statement, we will invariably include a join, aggregation / summary or other operation that requires the RDBMS to get involved. We don't want the RDBMS involved!

Netezza is different in that practically any query we issue will enjoy the massively parallel power of the machine, so on a Netezza extraction, does Rule #10 apply? Could it *ever* apply?

Indirectly, it can apply if we submit an overly complex query to Netezza *for the purposes of extraction*. If it has a lot of sub-queries, correlations, filters and whatnot, it is actually doing data processing *as part of* the extract, when it *could* be simplified. In short, if we have to do anything additional as part of the extract, then the data wasn't *quite* extraction-ready and we've required the downstream to know more than necessary to get their data. The time for complex data processing is always *prior* to the extract, otherwise our external consumer must accept it as an on-demand performance penalty. Not only that, if the extracting process has to know a lot of this logic (the complex join has been exported to the extractor after all) we've not done a good enough job in balancing the power *and* decoupling the two environments.

So we have several broad categories of automated consumers we want to deal with, but when we talk about "publication", it's always in context of a downstream *system*. An example might be a web site that hosts customer reports, or an accounting system, or even another more formalized business intelligence environment. We could have multi-variant targets, all of which want an *automated* bulk extract.

Decoupling the extract simply means we must serve up an interface, with some content behind it. The consumer does not and should not care what is *structurally* behind the interface (be it a view or a published file format). But according to the rules of publication, once we publish the interface it will take a life of its own. We must remain mindful that others will create downstream dependencies on it, so decoupling the output from our internal warehouse, structurally at least, is a best practice.

A good way to decouple is to make the data *extraction-ready* in the same sense we would want inbound data to be *load ready*. After all, one machine's extraction is another machine's intake. We should take the extra steps to reduce the extraction query's content by re-factoring the data into an outbound publication form. Whether this takes the shape of a regular Netezza table or a Netezza *external* table, is largely a function of the user base and the machine's availability. We just need to think in terms of making the data ready for plain-vanilla extraction, so the work to extract is minimal and the logic to form it is locally owned. We want to minimize the outtake overhead, so want to minimize or eliminate any outbound/on-demand integration, processing, enrichment or the like in the actual outbound request.

We will provide a notable exception here, however, as Netezza's User Defined Function (UDF) capability is leveraged, we will see more inline power for a variety of user types. The UDF can be applied inline, on-demand at extraction time. However, we don't need complex joins and integrations to enjoy the power of UDFs.

The point of all this is – make the data *extraction-ready*.

Extracting Bulk

Typically when we reach the end of a processing cycle, we have some options for delivery, including:

Dashboard – a canned, static presentation appears, on demand. The user simply requests it with no other parameters than what it takes to recall the report itself. These parameters are usually associated with the unique individual, such as embedded userid, cookie or other, and with limited user input (e.g. Viewing American Airlines AAdvantage miles or Reservations). May provide for *some* canned drop-down style parameters, such as date ranges and the like (online banking interfaces). Represents widest majority of users.

Parameterized – exemplified by desktop BI platforms such as Business Objects and Microstrategy, these will allow the user to select from complex drop-downs, edit-checked text or canned entries, then formulate and submit a query. The requests and results are usually packaged in their actual return contents. Often represents a large number of users, but relatively small compared to the dashboard user base, and are usually all internal.

Ad-hoc – the user is given free reign to issue any read-only query they desire. In most systems, these will go across all columns and tables. Because of the intensity of their queries, ad-hoc users typically need their own systems (although they don't always get one). Generally used for analytics and information profiling, patterning and the like. Ad-hoc users identify opportunity and risk. Represents fractional minority of users.

Extract – the 'user' is actually another system that will perform full unload of an information store. External tables (next) provide some significant lift here, but extracts in general are something that the extractor likes to shape to their own liking. Formalizing it with a view or external table is sometimes problematic, but desirable nevertheless for purposes of decoupling. Represents the tiniest minority of users, but those that require the data in bulk.

How does Netezza support these?

Knocking off the top, the dashboard and parameterized query, these are perhaps the easiest for any storage system, including Netezza. Even if we *must* create an aggregate or special table, even materialized view, these are just minutes if not seconds away from instantiating, so we can always, easily support external users with high scalability.

How many such queries can Netezza handle at once? This might be a shocker, but as of today there's not a known upper limit. If any Netezza owners have reach an upper limit, contact The Remediator at ITToolbox and we'll post it! The reason, however, that we can't tell how many queries that Netezza can handle "at once" is because it's impossible to feed it queries fast enough. In one shop with hundreds of users, the various desktops and dashboard were firing queries into Netezza with abandon, each one receiving a sparkling user experience. Yet on the Netezza side, we never saw the "high water mark" of total query count go above 25, and even this one spiked and evaporated, so fast are the query turnarounds in the machine.

We know of several sites that have ten thousand users or more, with thousands of concurrent users. Mythology: Other systems support more concurrent users than Netezza. Busted: This is nonsense. Practically and empirically disproven. Get references from the vendor.

Ad-Hoc support is always an elusive animal, but not in Netezza. The main reason is that we have no index structures. If the ad-hoc users get together with the DBAs and lay down some data with zone maps and the like (you know, simple sorting) we can get even more filtration power. Netezza derives much of its searching lift from what it *doesn't* have to examine versus scanning for things it *does* have to examine.

What does this mean? Think about any other relational environment. When the ad-hoc users need more power, they either ask us for a summary data view or a new *index*. The index will then affect our loading intake time. The summary will affect our SLA, and either way the flow-time takes a hit. Not so in Netezza. We have no indexes to worry about, so every column on every table is fair game from day one. If they want to examine this column or that, search that table or those, the response is always *knock yourself out*. We won't hear from them very often.

Extraction likewise benefits because Netezza is able to execute queries of any magnitude and practically any complexity with mind-bending speed. We say "practically" any complexity because the last thing we want to get into is dog-piling a bunch of query logic into a single query. If we're doing this for the extraction, then the data wasn't quite as "extraction ready" as we may have thought. Perhaps a couple more internal churns will do the trick, to shape the data such that when the external extract fetches the data, it's just reading rows and not much else.

External Tables

I've already mentioned how external tables can help us turn the Netezza machine into a *chugging engine* platform. The external table can be seen as an *input buffer* or an *output buffer*. In this section, we'll examine the output buffer aspect.

An external table is simply a flat file with a Netezza table façade on top. The table itself is seen in the Netezza catalog as a regular table. We can internally query the table in a similar manner as other tables, but this has performance caveats. The primary reason being, once we're in an external table, we're serialized. And that's the bottom line. If we think we need to query on it with filters and the like, we really need to consider taking it to the SPUs for this activity, not an external table.

So what does an external table buy us? Basically if we've done all the data crunching in the system and the information is ready-to-go, it is almost guaranteed that we will have a good idea of what our downstream processing system wants to see. For example, we might need to produce a final report for a downstream accounting system, a marketing system or campaign management system. We might have a need to burst customer or account-holder-facing reports and statements, etc. Each of these will require a bulk extract of some kind, and it's invariably a bulk extract with consistent parameters, content and boundaries, and one that spins the SPUs quite a bit.

So for this kind of extract, we might pre-extract it into an external table. When the consumers come to get it, they access a table *which happens to be an external table* (the consumer cannot tell the difference) and pull their content from a pre-processed serialized flat file off Netezza's host disk drive, not from the SPUs. We anticipated what they needed, pulled it from the SPUs and served the content through the external table. Now when the external system comes to pick up the data, it just extracts the serial information and the activity does not access the SPUs at all.

Why do this? If the Netezza machine is still underway with data processing operations, and is actively using the SPUs to complete another ongoing SLA, then our downstream consumer performing an on-demand extract against the SPUs during this time will create some degree of drag in both the processing and the extract operations. By publishing to the external table when we know the data is ready, any consumer can come pick it up without touching the SPUs. Of course, if the Netezza machine is largely quiet when we request the data, just grab-and-go straight off the SPUs. Why over-complicate?

Some shops start their *global* processing cycles on different time-zone boundaries. in trading systems, some users start the daily processing for Singapore when the Asian markets close, then several hours later roll to London to process data when the UK markets close, then roll to New York, then the West Coast. Four sweeping processing cycles, all performing the same functions for each time zone, yet running in time-offset.

This is just one of many examples where pushing data to an external table will make it extraction-ready and *non-invasive* to the high-intensity processing about to follow in the next cycle. If the prior cycle's consumers are a little late in retrieving their data, no worries. They pull from their designated external table while the existing SPU-intensive processes chug right along.

Think about how a competitor would respond to this approach, especially if the competitor eschews in-box data processing (ELT) and serves the exclusive purpose of query acceleration. For them, we would never create an external table. We would always pull the data from the core system at extraction time, no matter the degree of query complexity. With Netezza, we can mitigate the complexity without having to re-engineer the tables. We have more options than those query accelerators, so let's examine them, quantify them and use them.

And of course, for continuous environments where the batch cycle is even shorter, the external table serves as a "component output buffer", so we can pull data into the machine, crunch it and push it out in sweeping waves of work, regardless of whether the external (continuous) consumers are on time, early or a little behind in their data pickup. More advanced forms of this scenario may have need for an external table *queue*. For example, let's say we produce the external table for Monday's nightly run. Unbeknownst to us, the consuming system is offline for some unpredictable reason, and misses its retrieval window. Do we

(a) overwrite Monday's data with Tuesday's data
(b) append Monday's data with Tuesday's data
(c) create a separate Tuesday external table
(d) fully externalize the output

The easiest thing to do is to (a), but methinks our business users would take issue. The next option is (b), but this takes some under-the-cover work to create the external file to handle both days worth of data. If these are very large, it will eventually become too cumbersome, if several days accumulate.

Option (c) requires us to maintain a queue of the external tables that we've produced and are awaiting consumption. This is a bit more complex, but if the external consumers are themselves automated processes, it's easy enough to shape the queuing to the expectation of the consumers, and make it virtually transparent. Another reason to use a queue, is if we have multiple identical "robot" consumers and we want to dedicate a throughput thread to them, with their own table.

Option (d) means we have an external volume mounted to the Netezza machine, and the external table's underpinning file actually exists on this external volume (which could be a SAN, NAS device or anything else external to Netezza) You see, for an external table's file we don't necessarily have to be on the local Netezza host, we just need a mounted file path. If we use our internal processes to define a flat file, then instantiate the external table as any arbitrary temporary table name, we can then publish to this table with simple SQL commands and the data will physically land on the external volume filespace. When complete, we drop the external table from the catalog and get on with our other business. The file we just published on the external volume is now someone else's problem to manage.

We've not really solved the problem completely using Netezza, but we've taken it as far as Netezza can go. Likewise many environments already have file and site monitors that can detect the landing of such a file, and process it when the event happens. Our options are wide open.

An external table has all the primary trappings of a regular table, but includes a file path as well. The file path is the location of the flat file containing the information represented by the columns on the external table's catalog definition. For any other regular table, the source data is in the SPUs. For the external table, the source data is in a flat, serial file on given file path.

Here's the important part: If we want to completely get rid of the table and its data, we simply drop the external table, but we must also delete the file under its covers as a separate operation. The *drop* command will remove the table definition, but not the flat file. As noted above, an external table is one of the most effective ways to manufacture an outbound flat file. There will be times when we want to manufacture an external table *for the purpose of* creating the flat file itself. There will likewise be time that we want to instantiate an external table *for the purpose of reading an external flat file.* These are very common usages of external tables.

So now we have yet another issue. If we need to queue-up the external tables we've been manufacturing, we also need to provide a way to clean up the external tables once we're done. Otherwise, the external tables will clutter up the catalog space and will clutter/eat up the disk space. Here's a thought – if we put the external table management into one place, as a Netezza *component*, so to speak, we can then manufacture, deliver, and housekeep all our outbound data automatically. Does this mean instantiating a separate publication schema and directory structure for this? Why not? If it's a component or capability for use by all our data processing applications, why would we bury it across various or particular application streams or schemas? Centralization leads to consistency, in the spirit of an appliance.

Incremental Stuff

One might think that incremental things are in the past when we have a machine like Netezza. We can intake data like breathing, output data like rushing water, so why would we need anything *incremental*?

Well, just because we *can* boil the ocean doesn't mean we *should*.

Most infrastructures are simply not geared to keep up with Netezza, either in delivering data to the machine, or receiving data from it, and this includes the downstream processes expecting bulk outputs, not just the ad-hoc or other query users. Within an enterprise, data moves like water under the raised floor, through networks and over the waterfalls of our enterprise interfaces. If we choke these interfaces with too-much-data-in-too-short-time, we simply frustrate the owners of those systems. It is incumbent upon us to leverage Netezza's intake and outtake control to throttle ourselves, rather than just showing off!

We can always open up the valves at a later time, but for now we need to think about interacting with our slower-moving brethren on the raised floor. They are *all* slower-moving, and this doesn't have to be an issue, does it?

If we use the aforementioned external table publication scenario, creating incremental files out on an external volume, we effectively publish the work products on an acceptable time boundary and provide a more incremental means for downstream consumers to assimilate the information. All we have to do is throttle the output content for any one file.

Aggregation

In traditional RDBMS systems, aggregation is a key performance booster – for the *downstream*. It had better be worth the effort, because building up an aggregation on an RDBMS is very time consuming. The alternative on the RDBMS, having people attempt to run the aggregation on demand, is even worse. So our engineers will pre-aggregate the data and "bring it closer" to the reporting infrastructure. We sometimes see this in the form of cubes or marts, whatever it takes to push the data a little smaller, a little cleaner, and a little closer to its constituents.

In Netezza, aggregations like this only serve a functional purpose, like data consistency.

Typically an aggregation will apply some inline formula to the data, and we'd rather have it applied in one place rather than submitted by an external BI platform. We don't really need it any longer for performance, just for serving up "a version of the truth". The luxury here is, that we can manufacture an aggregation on Netezza in a fraction of the time it would take on an RDBMS. So we can actually sit together at a white board, discuss what the answers should be, then implement them without fear of "dimming the lights" when the aggregation process kicks off, or for that matter, having to spend huge cycles reproducing the results in case of failure. Success is a relative minutes away.

Also as noted earlier, if we're migrating from an existing environment where the downstream has hardwired dependencies on the aggregations, it won't matter how many white-board sessions we have with their consumers, if we say that the aggregations are going away, they will kick and scream and make all manner of political hay. To avoid pain (and political injury) just pump out the aggregations!

Case Study Short: One client had three downstream consumers with published, mature interface expectations. While these consumers were automated and could be reconfigured to access the data rather than their summary data, the re-integration curve was too steep. It was just easier to remanufacture the original "ugly" outbound summary tables than to refactor the downstream to access the data without a summary. In this case, keeping the summary helped to avoid downstream destabilization.

Incrementally speaking: Since most aggregations deal with rolling up "most recent" activity and combining it with "least recent" activity, incremental aggregations can take on a lot of subtle issues, both solving and creating them. For example, if we have a report that needs year-to-date sales, do we really need to "boil the ocean" (summarizing all prior days) to get the same incrementally different answer each day? Or is there a better way?

Case Study Short: In one solution, a reporting structure required the day-of-week view along with a week-to-date summary. This was easily accomplished by summarizing each day's work to its daily value. At the end of the week, we would summarize all days into one (the week-to-date) and then start the daily summary over again. So for any given summary group, the most records we would ever see in a given year would be one for each of 51 weeks, plus the days of the final week (6 days) before it got summarized to the 52nd week. This means a high-water-mark 51+6 or 57 records, with the final of 52 records for the year. A max of 57 records is more efficient than 365 records, and the summary answer from totaling the records, is always the same. At any given time, we could get a "running total" by capturing all the days' work, and all the prior weeks, and summarizing it.

What if we really need to get some incremental, day-bounded summary from prior history? The details remained in the base, and the ad-hoc users could always execute something like this anytime they wanted. The point is, for most of the users, a week-to-date summary minimized our overall data footprint and provided them with a consistently functional, precalculated, consolidated and *fast* view of the data.

Summary data is ideal if it serves a functional purpose, not necessarily because we're artificially boosting performance.

Case Study Short: In another solution, we saw daily accounting feeds delivered from the primary repository to the accounting system. The feeds did not regard incremental changes, but rather bulked-up the entire accounting history each evening and shipped this massive file to a drop-off directory. From there, the accounting system people had also done something very interesting, they put business logic on the *other* side of this file, so that as it was extracted from disk, it would only take the *changes* from the prior day.

In essence, the publisher was artificially inflating the file, requiring the consumer to artificially *deflate* it.

When we first arrived on site, our mandate was to provide a better way to perform change-data-capture in this massive intermediate flat file. The answer was not in the file itself, but in the file's construction. If we could make the flat-file's construction incremental, there would be no need for a file-level change-data-capture. They wanted us to negotiate for a smaller, incremental file with the downstream consumers.

Ironically, no sooner did we begin discussion with the publishers of this massive file, that we heard all the complaints *from the downstream consumers* that the file was too big, and *why do they need to send us the whole thing anyhow*? Wouldn't an incremental extract be better? Go talk to them. Make them understand, they're *choking* us. And all that. This was an easy resolution.

One problem remained, in that another downstream consumer was also dependent upon the massive flat file, and needed for it to remain whole. Not to worry. For the most recent execution, we just left the current file in place. It held all the aggregations for all prior history. For the following evening, we dropped the next incremental delta. Each evening we would drop another incremental delta. (The "total" file then became a "virtual" quantity, found in the baseline plus all incremental deltas). The accounting system was pleased with the deflation of their data load. The publishing system was pleased with the recovery of their resources for More Important Things. The secondary system did not experience any issues either, since they could consume the baseline aggregation and the incremental deltas as one complete source.

Upon further investigation, one of their own downstream processes was also sifting out the changed records as the accounting system had done. We helped reconcile that problem, too.

The final conclusion in all this – incremental output and aggregations are often used to enhance performance, but sometimes they are *functionally necessary* for a downstream consumer. We need to make sure we meet their needs in the right way, continuing to treat the data as a functional flow across all systems, so that no upstream or downstream suffers in supporting the other, or in propping up the apparent weakness of another.

Analyze the entire flow, not just part of it. The intake *and* the endpoints will both benefit.

10

LURKING STUFF

WHEN FIRST approaching the Netezza platform, people have lots of questions. *Lots* of questions, mostly dealing with the mystery of implementing a bulk processing platform. After a proof-of-concept, they see the benefits, the power, the possibilities. It's just so mysterious. They want assurances, confidence, all that stuff. A lot seems to be riding on the decision, and it feels a little like walking out onto thin ice.

Trust us, the ice is solid. Just having a Netezza machine in the shop means success should be a clear target in our cross-hairs. Apart from the mystery as to how it can be implemented, or even should be implemented, they want to roll it out *exactly, perfectly* right, the first time. Well, "getting it right" the first time and "delivering it perfectly" the first time, are two contradicting goals. We can definitely get a good, productive start, heading in the right direction, but keep in mind that it's a journey. Perfection is a distant goal, but we can deliver excellence along the way, and this is what we want to aggressively pursue.

So just load up the data and start working with it. There's nothing like actually wringing out the data itself with a machine that can do it, and do it *easily*. The power and turnaround time we get back, lets us gain rhythm and momentum like no other platform we've ever experienced. If we *accidentally* paint ourselves into a corner, we actually have the luxury to completely toss the approach, even *all* the prior work and start all over. It's a learning experience, so *learn*. We have the luxury of inline, on-the-job training because the machine is so powerful.

Either way, the problems before us have very little to do with Netezza. We can master it as a weapon in the fight for good data processing, as long as we keep in mind that the fight is not with Netezza, or even within Netezza, the fight is with the information itself.

Netezza lets us harness the data, even if the data resists the yoke.

There be dragons

In **DMReview** not too long ago, entitled *There Be Dragons*, was a cheeky article on warehousing and the propensity of dragonslayers to believe that the data warehouse (dragon) can be *slain*. Sort of a shot-across-the-bow to folks who want to treat a data warehouse like a project and not like an environment. But more for those who believe that the warehouse is something that we can build and leave to itself. In the article, the dragon is the information and its propensity to do evil things. It likes to offer wrong information, jump out of its cage and breathe fire (at least, create a fire-breathing environment).

The dragon is *immortal*. Nobody can slay it. That's why we have *dungeons*. We lock the dragon down, and keep the keys close to us. We feed it, avoid its foul breath, hose it down with an upgrade every once in a while, but we never let it *out*. This is the spirit of harnessing (and containing) a data warehouse into a living environment. And before we go off thinking about our data being in a dungeon or prison (no analogy is perfect), we need to think about what things would be like if it ever got loose. A data warehouse out-of-control is no different than the dragon blasting fire at the hapless villagers. The villagers (end users) want to consume clean, healthy data for their decision-making processes. If we deliver bad data, the heat they feel will come from a different quarter, like their customers, or their boss.

Because the dragons we harness are the *chaos* wrought from poorly managed data, the *misinformation* delivered by mishandled data and the *distrust* bred by a consistently poor user experience. These are the dragons we really, *really* want to keep in the dungeon.

Dragon *Chaos*: The master dragon, *Vermithrax Pejorative* in the movie *DragonSlayer*. This dragon has an easy job, as it turns out. Chaos can find a natural home just about anywhere it goes. All it needs is a lack of attention, or a complex of neglect. Either way, works just fine for him. He grow *without* our effort. A very dangerous thing.

"So then neglect becomes our ally..."- etched on the wall in the prison Chateau D'If, *The Count of Monte Cristo.*

Complex of Neglect - Assuming that the *obvious* is under control. People walking past, browsing past or otherwise ignoring something open and obvious, because it's not their problem, not their expertise, not their business, and they are certain that someone, somewhere is taking care of it. That this Very Important Thing is being ignored. and that this Most Obvious Thing belongs to nobody's care, is a complex of neglect.

Make no mistake, neglect is the *ally* of the Dragon Chaos. Just because we think we have it in a dungeon and *think* it is unable to escape, looks are deceiving. Escape is the only thing on the dragon's mind, 24/7. He looks like he's given up, accepted his fate, and will live out his days in the dungeon.

All the while, he plots his escape.

When we neglect the dragon, one day his cage door will be left open. He'll be out. In his weakened state he might not be too much danger, so putting him back inside won't be hard. The longer he's out, the stronger he'll get, and the harder it is to put him back.

I've already mentioned **logistical capacity**. Chaos loves a place where the principals have no clue as to the logistical overhead required to keep their businesses running. The more people, the more confusion, the stronger the dragon grows. People will abate their confusion with workaround processes, things they can touch, taste and handle. The more workarounds, the stronger the dragon grows.

THE NETEZZA UNDERGROUND

We experience logistical capacity issues in our workforce when one of our haggard workers asks for a raise, that they are doing the work of five people and should be paid for it, etc. A myopic boss sends such an impudent worker back to their desk, consoling them with platitudes. When the worker suddenly evaporates because they actually found another company that appreciates them, and our hapless manager finds that it really *will* take five people to replace that person, the logistical issue is clear. A simple raise would have solved the problem. Now it will cost the manager five times the original amount if he wants the same logistical effect.

Our platforms are a lot like this, where we offload and cross-load our capacity onto them, not realizing that as they run out of power, our dedicated work forces are on-the-job, propping up their weaknesses with brute-force logistical prowess and engineering derring-do.

We might call them tiger-teams or strike-forces – but all they're doing is putting the dragon *down*. For a *day*. It will be back to play tomorrow. We might call them dragonslayers. They think they're killing the dragon, and that each new day is a new dragon. But it's the *same* dragon.

It's immortal, you see.

Case Study Short: When installing a data processing environment for a client, two members of a larger team darkened our doorstep with a request.

"We need a development area for fifty applications," he noted.

"Fifty?"

"That's right, fifty."

"Not forty-nine, and not fifty one. Not *around* fifty but exactly fifty?"

"Yes," he said nervously, feeling like he'd crossed a line.

"Why *exactly* fifty?"

"We have fifty files and fifty tables," he responded, "So fifty applications."

We stood quietly for a moment, allowing the silence to sink in as we stared at each other, "You don't need fifty applications. You need to invoke one application fifty times."

He stared back at me, realizing that he was now standing in a school, and suddenly I was the teacher. Very awkward, considering that he worked for our competitor. Off he darted to make his *application* go, but no sooner had he gotten started than he was back.

"The data has junk in it," he lamented, "So I'll need to transform the stuff, too."

"Where did you get the data from?"

"The other group across the hall."

"That *other group* is your team, from *your* firm," I reminded as gently as possible, then said as lightly as possible, "You really mean, your *team* is producing junk."

He laughed, "Well, not in so many words, but yeah."

No, *exactly* in so many words.

So we took a short walk down the hall to speak with the *other group (wink!)* who were busy slinging code with reckless abandon. After a short conversation, We learned that their application had been configured to go through a series of steps, actually *too many* steps, to deliver the fifty files of tainted nectar. We asked one of them if we could spot-check a sample of their code.

This revealed all, and I've mentioned a similar effect earlier.

Riddled throughout their business rules were scrubbing "wraps" such as "if is-null() then this stuff else that stuff". As we examined the code, with each component doing check after recheck *on the same columns*, We asked them why they had not fixed the data once, at the first of the stream, not allowing the dirt to simply pass through?

They hadn't thought about *that*.

The entire application was *over-coded* for these redundant error checks by fifty percent or more. In the end, the output result was *still* junk that couldn't be loaded to a database. *Data stewardship*, recall, is about making the data *better* every time we touch it, not just allowing it to pass on.

And what was the result of this neglect?

Chaos.

The dragon lives on.

Dragon *Misinformation*: A minion dragon, *Smaug* in Tolkein lore. A dragon with the ability to manufacture enough stinging smoke in the eyes of our users that they begin to wonder if the information is broken, or just broken for *them*. They'll help us chase down the right business rule, get it installed and validate the outcome. Then they'll expect it to *stick*. Forever and ever. If the information doesn't stick, they'll start to ignore it as either useless, unstable or simply unreliable.

"If it's not useful, they won't use it" - *Unanimous*

We've actually sat alongside end-users who actively and enthusiastically described all the things they wanted on their new reporting system, using older reports as a baseline. We would indicate this data point or that, and would get a functional answer or the response "We ignore that value. It's always wrong."

"If it's always wrong, then why is it still here?"

"It's still there for the same reason that it's wrong."

"What reason is that?"

And then we're treated to a rant on the incompetence of practically everyone who provides information to them. They will forgive small errors as long as the error eventually disappears. What most technologists don't realize, is that it's better to have no functionality than broken functionality. No functionality can be taken several ways, including a promise of later fulfillment, or an admission of inability.

Broken functionality is an advertisement - of our shortcomings. Something we'd rather keep in the dark, if it's all the same. Better to remove that broken piece of published information rather than continue to publish it, knowing that it's broken.

Case Study Short: In a retail environment, the company published weekly reports to their store managers showing their sales staff's productivity numbers. The total hours worked were listed alongside the total revenue sold. Unbeknownst to anyone, the stores (nationwide) reported their employee times in *1-week offsets* to keep from overwhelming the timekeeping system. Half the stores reported in one cycle while half in the other cycle, with no apparent logical consistency as to what constituted one group or the other. Also, the sales data was only completely in sync for all stores at the *first* of the month.

Meaning - this particular report (aligning timecard hours with sales revenue generated) was only accurate once a month, at the first of the month. The remainder of the time, it was misinformation. Yet managers across the country used this report's *weekly* output to manage their stores.

Even more scary - people's *careers* relied on the accuracy of this information. This is a scary dragon, indeed.

Case Study Short: One national appliance rental company had a number of highly mature operating environments. These included product delivery, warranty service, product control, customer service, advertising, marketing, accounting, store operations, vendor management, human resources, investor relations, and many others. Interestingly, none of these environments talked to each other, *at all*.

We asked some simple, highly impertinent questions like;

- If a product comes in for a lot of warranty service, would you consider replacing it with a more reliable product?
- If one of your stores is in a market for a specific type of product, are you geared to over-stock it for times when the market spikes? (e.g. ethnic holidays)
- How do you know how profitable a product is?
- How do you know which vendors are your best? Your worst?
- How do you measure "same store sales"?
- If you have a backlog at one store and a surplus at another, how do you reconcile this to get the products into the hands of your customers?

Their environment had become so filled with misinformation that the whole idea of actually leveraging the existing data, to make the business better, was a completely foreign concept. Capitalizing opportunity. Minimizing costs. Reducing overhead. Controlling risk. Protecting consumer loyalty. Moving our products. Isn't this what we're in business *for*? If the systems aren't helping us do this, what good are they?

Netezza's power allows us to converge this information into a common platform, cleanse it, integrate it, reconcile it in ways that don't currently exist - on all those distributed stovepipes. We could pull the same information into an RDBMS, and we'd still have the same issues. How do we affect the data after it arrives?

Recall that in a real warehouse, the stuff arrives on a loading dock and we then apply forklifts and logistical rules to intake, organize and logistically manage it under one roof. What if we established a number of places for our vendors to put their stuff, and each day the vendors show up with their own trucks and forklifts, unload their stuff and put in their *own* assigned places? We arrive after all this activity and find the stuff in its place, but it's too big and too heavy to do anything else with it. We have to leave it where it is, in the receiving zones, and deal with it directly from there.

This doesn't sound like a workable warehouse does it? We want to deal with stuff, organize it and redistribute it inside the warehouse for the best, most useful (and most manageable) effect. In an RDBMS, the data lands in a table, and there it shall remain. There's not enough power to move it around or re-process it once it arrives. Not a very workable model, either.

Case Study Short: One financial services firm had allowed its internal business units to commission their own "personalized" data warehouse environments. By the time we had arrived, fifteen fully mature warehouses existed, covering hundreds of server devices with information in various states of flow and process over the weeks and months of its lifecycle.

The people in the middle of all this, were some sixty business analysts, who knew the exact state of the information across the entire environment. Because this knowledge was largely the function of mentoring and tribal storytelling, these analysts were often called the "tribal priests and priestesses". In essence, the information we might want was dependent on the day of the week or month, and the nature of the question itself.

Q: Where is the loan boarding information?

A: Today?

Q: Does it matter?

A: Today it's in cluster four, but tomorrow morning it moves to cluster five. Unless it's the West Coast information. We don't move that until the day after tomorrow.

Q: Why not?

A: Their data only synchronizes on Friday, so we'd just have to move it again.

Q: Why not move it all at once?

A: People over here need it now, every day.

Q: Why?

A: Weekly reports

Q: Oookay, so where would we find new customer loan applications?

A: The master application system. But we're not allowed to access it directly.

Q: So how do you look at it?

A: It's downloaded every night to cluster seven. We're always a day in arrears. Unless it's the tenth of the month.

Q: Why the tenth?

A: They do monthly reconciliation and we don't get a download.

Q: What about accounting updates?

A: For revenue or costs?

Q: Why does it matter?

A: Costs are handled in cluster eight. Revenue in cluster nine.

Q: They're separate?

A: We reconcile them on Wednesday.

Q: Why Wednesday?

A: Backups are finished by Tuesday night on cluster eleven, and they share disk space.

Q: What's on cluster eleven?

A: Human resources

This conversation continued for over two hours as we weaved and "porpoised" through the systems. More than just thought-experiments, this was tribal knowledge, and *very* valuable to the company. They had hired enough people so that if any one were to get hit by a truck, hired by a competitor or other problem, the company would still be covered.

In a follow-on interview, one of the business leaders told us:

A: I needed the latest revenue numbers for my region, so I could do budgets.

Q: They could not provide them?

A: Not on time. But here's the funny part, they provided the numbers on time for my peer departments.

Q: But not yours?

A: No, mine were late. More importantly, I missed the deadline to get budgets into the system, so I did not get enough money for my projects.

Q: What happened to the money?

A: One of my peer departments got the lion's share of it.

Q: Why is that?

A: The head of the department had several of his family members hired into the analyst group. They always do stuff for him first.

All things being equal, if the information in the system is pure as the wind-driven snow, all of us have an objective touchpoint from which to make decisions and derive more answers. But if the *gathering* of the information requires another *human*, we have the potential of the injection of error, or nefarious activity, or political favoritism, an ever present problem in any business domain. (see Dragon Chaos above). We also have the potential of personal bias, and even the deliberate injection of error to cause harm.

The mere presence of chaos provides the temptation and offers the opportunity for advantage - by those who see its potential as *misinformation* –to their own gain.

In the above case, the chaos only *appeared* under control. It was actually a smokescreen for *misinformation*. And we can see how, politically speaking, some people would be predisposed to resist changing it, especially if maintaining the chaos is to their advantage.

Honest human error is one thing, but we should also never underestimate the subtle power of deliberate human avarice to capitalize on chaos for its own benefit.

Dragon Mistrust: Another minion dragon, this one rules after the other two dragons have scorched the Earth. Once this dragon is ensconced, he is practically impossible to dethrone. The users have lost confidence in the data, the ability of the people who provide the data to do it correctly, and have formed, matured and leverage their own workaround and backup processes to make sure their own workday isn't a bad one.

One day we look around and see this teeny-little computing center with its paltry computing engine. We look out over the business and see people on roller skates trying to keep the business alive. Not only are they on roller skates, but others have formed cottage industries of roller skate rental, cleaning, repair and sales – all as satellite activity within our walls to support the derring-do of our data-warriors. Our people speak fondly of their roller skates. We have roller-derbies, trade skate-keys and might even have x-treme skating invitationals. When at first they were only a workaround for underpowered and ill-designed systems, now the roller skates have become part of the culture. Replacing anything that supports the roller-skate culture will be met with resistance. The roller-skate supporters want to keep their jobs and don't want to be re-tooled to use something else. They really like the roller-skates.

We can see this dragon often when we enter a shop and the business users have nothing good to say about the data, and their departments are overstaffed and over-loaded with manual workarounds to buffer themselves from its ills. Once overstaffed, they have a built-in reason to keep things like they are (staff development and accumulation). Likewise the IT group leaders have thrown-in the towel on the ability to fix the problem with any kind of confidence. The risk of trying to fix it is higher than the risk of remaining in the malaise.

Why is this? If we attempt to fix it, some would argue, we admit that a problem exists. If we fail to fix it, others would say, it means we are incompetent. If we deny that a problem exists, says another, it simply means we don't understand. If we were never hired to understand, people will forgive us. We get to keep our jobs. The minute we say that we understand, says the others, we admit that we have a shortcoming. We get it, but we can't fix it.

Somehow, the darkness of "not getting it" just seems safer to some people. Were they hired to "get it" or were they hired to just keep it running? This is why the phrase "neglect becomes our ally" is so dangerous to us. The people who we really need to fix it are hiding in the darkness. We cannot ask them to come into the light, because they fear exposure and a loss of their job.

This is also why the concept of an Underground is both dangerous and tongue-in-cheek (for us, anyhow). We know that the underground is a real place, trading Dark Secrets about Important Things. But these things only touch on Netezza at the periphery. The true darkness of the Underground, is fear.

Without information, the fear grows. Mistrust grows. The dragon grows stronger.

Dragonslayers Unanimous: Netezza is a dragon-hunter's weapon, a dungeon and dragon-keeper all-in-one. So for all practical purposes, our dragon woes are over right? No, the dragon is still immortal no matter how many pieces we chop it into. We need a stronger dungeon, bigger chains and thicker door on the castle keep, but never forget that the dragon never dies. How to cope?

Netezza will first harness these dragons. It will step into the computing enclosure, take a bow, say in a guttural voice while its lips are out-of-sync "Your Kung Fu is not strong!" Then it will boot the dragon from its throne, perform a full-contact takedown on the raised floor and rip out its heart of stone - while it's still beating. A little grisly, we understand, but Netezza doesn't mess around. Its Kung Fu is strong.

But rather than just put the dragon into the dungeon, now we'll install a device (Netezza) that captures the dragon's strength and uses it *against* him. What if we were to come down into the dungeon one evening and see the dragon running on a treadmill, his wings flapping to power wind-generators, and his fiery breath used to power steam turbines – all to generate power for the castle?

Now the dragon's earnin' his keep, no?
It's a beautiful thing.

People Pitfalls

The primary pitfalls in assimilating a Netezza machine are really no different than the pitfalls of any other appliance or utility, and are mostly in the realm of helping people understand the machine, where it fits and what it does best. For example, the propensity to want to leverage Netezza for all computing, including transactional, which would be an incorrect path.

We'll need an operational framework, lightweight though it might be. Netezza runs under Linux, but nothing about Linux automatically guarantees flow-based application architecture. This is a synergy of mind and machine. Even though it's an appliance, it's a highly adaptable one. Just don't imagine that the adaptability is completely automatic. Operationally, our environment is not hard to build. But build it we must. Commodity parts combined with Linux can make it a professional rollout quite easily.

We should not assume that our DBAs will just "pick it up" without some orientation. While we can easily train a DBA on the appliance, they will likely map it what they already know. They will call it a relational DBMS because superficially it behaves and interacts like one. They will find it mysterious and an object to be pursued and tamed. Netezza doesn't need any taming and it doesn't need engineers to keep it going. This won't lead to complacency on the administrator's part. The machine, while quiet most of the time, still needs attention even though it's very light. Administrators realize that with a machine of this power, they need to take it seriously, even if only part-time.

Engineers who start working with Netezza sometimes undergo transformation. An engineer is a skeptic one day and totally sold the next. They immediately want to eat, live and breathe Netezza. It's the platform they trust now. It does things right, and right quick! Well, that engineer or admin still has other servers to take care of. The developer and tester working with the machine sometimes act as though a drug has taken over their brains. Just short of getting an *Apocalypse Now* message saying "Sell the car. Sell the kids. I'm not coming home," you'll find that the admins will get addicted to the speed and want nothing more than to hang out with the new kid, the little black box.

Not to worry, after the honeymoon, the leaders will see promise and a deep well for creative thought-experiments. *Onward and upward* will take on a new meaning, one of hope-realized rather than capacity breached.

So now we move into another phase of existence, that of expecting far too much from the Netezza platform's functionality. A good governance model will help Netezza find its place in our enterprise, and become the gravity-bending appliance it is designed to be. We still must protect the machine from ambitious do-gooders who want to use the machine to solve World Hunger and bring about World Peace.

It's an *appliance*.

EXOTIC STUFF

FORMAL ENCOUNTERS with Netezza, whether their user's conference or in presentations, include a common banner headline:

We are different.

In every foray into new and interesting technology, we have opportunities to see things a little differently than before, and in this respect, Netezza is no different! While this chapter does not attempt to capture the essence of why and how Netezza is different (hey, they just are, in so many good ways!), offered here are some simple examples of implementations, proofs and such. They show how using Netezza in oblique but useful approaches, yields sophisticated capabilities and results that are not even possible nor feasible in traditional RDBMS platforms.

An Application Example

Many years ago we worked deeply with artificial intelligence and its more applied form, expert systems. One of the engines we constructed was for Value Health Sciences in California for a medical-claims processing application. As a background, whenever we visit a doctor, on our way out, they give us a sheet with various codes and items marked on it. Those codes are actually part of a formal code manual and the doctors agree with insurance companies as to how they will use them for identifying their activities, and bill their patients accordingly.

At that time, a favorite practice of some (mischievous) doctors was in "unbundling" the codes. In short, where one code might represent a group of procedures, the doctor could make more money by claiming them separately.

The expert system engine's responsibility was to take some 40,000 rules of billing and apply them to the claims as they passed into the system, "rebundling" the codes, changing the claim and resetting the effective dollar amount for payment. On proof-of-concept sales calls, this application was applied to six months of *prior* claims history to "get a feel" for how much it *could* have saved an insurance company had they applied it some six months prior. The answer was often in the millions of dollars.

Sales of this product were brisk.

Inside the engine, in order to optimize the searching for claims, codes and the like, we used C-language and constructed some memory-based cross-reference structures using linked lists and binary search trees, a pretty vanilla, bread-and-butter approach to this sort of problem. The power of course, was in having these exotic, oddball structures in memory so we could slice-and-dice the data and intersect it in creative ways. We could use all kinds of vectors, vectored structures, spider-webs of memory-based navigation that allowed us to do things in memory that were not feasible in a relational database.

For context, the *original* application had been built in context of what a relational database could do, but it could never get off the ground. Because what it really *needed* to do, a relational database *could not* accomplish. Functionally the RDBMS and COBOL could make it happen, but not with any viable performance. In fact, if the application had to depend on a relational model and a traditional database approach to process claims, we could possibly get the claims themselves in and out of the system, but applying 40,000 rules to each claim would take months to process even a single day's worth of claims. Clearly not viable if the insurance company needed to meet its financial obligations to the providers.

Likewise the application development team was immersed in COBOL and structured business processing, and unable to understand how we could leverage mass-memory to affect the application of these highly complex rules. One of the tactics was to take the entire rules database, pull it out of the RDBMS, reduce it to a high-performance memory-based structure and then save it as a flat-file to disk. We would only have to perform this reduction whenever the rule base actually changed, which was rare. At run-time, the application would load this rule base into memory and leverage it there. I still recall a conversation with one of the more experienced developers, who objected to how much memory this rules base consumed. I had it in my mind that, when running on the mainframe (where this batch application would reside), the difference between CPU cost versus memory cost (at run time) required me to quip "Memory is cheap". When we think about it, if we can load memory with data to shrink the total duration, and since we are charged for duration and not memory utility, seems like a valid tradeoff.

This particular application developer, in a nutshell, *didn't get it.*

Within the hour, he returned to me and said that he'd just had a conversation with one of the mainframe engineers, querying him on the cost of memory. This person had told him that their memory cards for the mainframe were extraordinarily expensive, and that anyone who suggested they are cheap is just a fool.

Perhaps they are expensive to *purchase*, but not expensive to *use*. CPU cycles were charged to the project, and to the client. Memory utility was *not*.

To my point: For our purposes, *memory is cheap!*

And to another aspect of this conversation that we should not miss: An aversion by an application developer to leverage the physics for higher performance. For many application developers, their trust is *solely* in the software, never in the physics.

Back to the original problem, which architecturally remained an *entity-at-a-time* processing model, applying forty-thousand-rules-per claim, rather than finding a way to apply only the rules that counted *for that claim,* and no others. The model we centered on, in *memory*, was one of "We know what we don't need, so give me the remnant and we'll work with that". Essentially, we know where *not to look*, which is, of course, the theme of Netezza's anti-filtering model to find data.

Had we been privy to Netezza's technology way-back-when, we probably could have leveraged it for the VHS engine without nearly the fuss that we went through to make it happen in a carefully engineered, memory-based model. Large-scale bulk processing, rather than surgical claim-at-a-time processing, is a better fit, hands-down. But no matter.

The point is, those odd and exotic memory structures were *just data structures.* Anyone with a mastery of basic data structures could do the same thing. The constraint of course, is that the RDBMS doesn't give us any structural power, only structural *constraint*. If we need some exotic, oddball structure, or if we need some real structural (or inter-structural) power, the purveyors of the RDBMS will point us to a memory-based application environment. It is not their job to provide such capabilities. It's what *applications* are for.

But not anymore. Netezza's got the stuff.

Intersections

One of the more creative ways to integrate data, is *not* in actually merging it together, or even linking it directly with a formal primary and foreign key relationship, but in using intersection tables. In an RDBMS, we incur a penalty for indexing these, but not in Netezza, opening up an enormous canopy of opportunity. A more advanced form of this approach follows in *GROKs*. We don't always want to move a lot of data around, nor do we want to form invasive row-level relationships. What we want is to connect two data points together, provide some metadata to describe the connection, and then use the connections themselves as a point-of-entry. The traditional fact table, but more.

In the aforementioned medical claims processors, we took the memory-based rules database and knitted it together as a structure in memory, with various forms of circular linked-lists to navigate the structure. If data needed sorting, we would sort the linked list, not the actual data. The linked-list references would be rearranged into their proper collating sequence, and when we needed to consume the data in that sorted order, we would simply traverse the nodes of the list, each one maintaining a reference to the static members of the memory-based database. But we never moved the *data*, only the pointers to the data. Once again, a vanilla, remedial concept to some, but *not to those* who are accustomed to facing an RDBMS, and *only* an RDBMS for these kinds of structures.

These structural gymnastics are sometimes egregious in large-scale systems. In transactional systems, the most agile way to put it all together is to build the relations into the schema, with hard connections between tables. Even these don't always work.

But for large-scale data, even for simple intersections, the *index* overhead makes it impractical (but as Netezza has no indexes, the door opens for us).

Case Study Short: In one transactional environment, we were charged with providing a browsing window that allowed users to drag-and-drop artifacts from other windows onto a main canvas. The canvas captured the relationship in a tree-like structure, allowing the users to drag-and-drop into tree structures no differently than we'd see in a common Explorer window on our desktop. The problem here – these units of work joining the tree were actually complex objects themselves.

We had one of two options. We could extend the individual objects to make them polymorphic onto the tree structure. Or we could treat the tree structure as an intersection table. One side of the intersection anchored the object to the tree, while the other side maintained a reference to the object. This effectively created a tree-centric architecture where the participants (the disparate objects) were largely along for the ride. In such a (relatively) simplified transactional environment, such intersections are creative and useful, and provide far more functionality. For example, if we need to add another object type for management within the tree, we only have to provide a means to identify the object. The tree infrastructure already exists.

But for large scale data processing, such a structure would be in our way, wouldn't it? We would have to join and re-join, perhaps recursively self-join until we found an answer. Does this scenario scale to hundreds of billions of rows in a common RDBMS? Think for a moment about the indexing *alone* for such an intersection table, not just the data it contains. The overhead becomes untenable.

Yet in Netezza, this is *exactly* what the doctor ordered, and actually provides additional lift to the queries. Why? Recall that the Netezza machine is geared for filtration, that is, what to *ignore*. Any additional filter we can provide, squeezes down the total workload coming off the SPUs. Thus an intersection table, especially with no indexes, behaves as a filter and actually *accelerates* the query.

This is a complete shift in thinking for most data architects, the idea that adding a table to a join actually accelerates it. Welcome Aboard!

What else does this buy us in Netezza? In another chapter, we talk about the "insert-only" processing model. What if along the way of crunching data with sweeping transforms, we discover errors? Do we mark the data itself with the error (an update), or do we insert a record in an error log, with a reference to the erroneous record? In the first case we perform an update. In the second case we perform an insert, but can only realize the error-log's effects (to exclude the bad record) by joining it to the primary table with a "where not exists". Not to worry, since we have seen (above) that this filtration scenario fits in with the Netezza architecture.

Give this a try: Add one hundred million rows to a table, where fifty million of them have a switch set to "0" and the other fifty million have a switch set to "1". In another table, add fifty million records, each with an identifier for the records in the first table that contain a "1". Now perform the select count(*) of all records with the switch equal to "0" and check the time. Then perform the same select count(*), this time using a join to the second table with the appropriate "where not exists" clause. Check the time on this. We will find them to be *very* close. If the filter table is distributed on the same key as the main table, we will achieve this result in *seconds*. In fact, while the first query will likely come back slightly faster than the second, the difference is negligible. This gives us the impetus and permission to build filtration tables rather than modify the original structures with a range of disparate switches and filtration columns. *Not* to forsake the filtration columns, but to assert that we can freely choose between the two with no penalty.

In many cases, our table-level filtration columns are necessary and required. But when it comes to general information management a the capability level, like audit, error control and the like, we can share a common operational framework for all, with all the benefits of the framework and no data processing penalty. A beautiful thing.

GROKs

Talking with a friend who does highly complex XML manipulation, he used the term *grok* in context of decomposing an XML document into its various parts for action, examination, dispatch, etc. In his case, *grok* was a verb.

In our case, GROK is a noun/acronym, and for the record, we were here first.

Another friend is a big genealogy fanatic. While some might think it strange to search out one's ancestral roots, it often leads to fascination and sometimes obsession. Our conversations are interesting romps in using computers to connect disparate information instruments, tracing lines of ancestral activity. For example, answers often lie buried in court documents, family Bibles, birth and death certificates, marriage licenses, divorce decrees, adoption papers – you name it. The real trick is to connect these disparate sources by intersecting them in a meaningful way. The actionable information – the ancestry - is in the *intersections,* not the raw data in disparate documents.

Moving to another place and time, so to speak, in Operation Desert Storm. Reconnaissance and field operatives had standing orders: *immediately* report enemy activity, no matter how minor. Information collectors then filtered the reports through connectivity algorithms – *intersectors* if you will – integrating disparate sightings to form a meaningful pattern. After all, each sighting had common information, like what was sighted, location, time etc. Individually, the activity was really nonsense noise. Taken as a whole and connected together, the leaders could see whole troop movements and make deliberate and highly effective decisions. The actionable information was in the *intersections,* not the raw, disparate sightings.

In a renowned, UK-based law enforcement organization, systems analysts asked their experienced detectives to list every nefarious character they had ever encountered, their known aliases and their acquaintances, accomplices, associations, etc. Basically anything connecting one criminal to another was fair game. Once again to find meaningful intersections. A pattern emerged, that about *ten people* were primary conduits for all crime in the UK.

These weren't the traditional crime lords, but *fences and facilitators.* In a sweeping motion, detectives arrested, charged and removed them from the criminal equation. Practically overnight, the UK criminal element felt the tremor of their absence. Thieves couldn't move their stolen goods. Drug traffic stood at the ready, willing but *unable* to proceed. The crime rate fell like a rock. Of course, new facilitators moved in on the open territories to fill the vacuum, but it gave law enforcement a powerful tool and strategy. Once again, the actionable information was in the *intersections,* not the criminals in particular.

In our current war on terror, don't imagine for a moment that people aren't working diligently with similar intersection algorithms, no doubt with more breathtaking breadth and impact than those noted above. And no doubt we'll never understand their preventive effect. Meaning that we'll sleep at night without fear, while the algorithms chase down and capture the dragons. The actionable information is in the *intersections,* not the raw, disparate data. In fact, the hit-TV-series *24* uses this aspect of counter-terrorism – intersecting people, places and associations - as a transition mechanism for the entire flow of the television season.

Important note: these are *not new* applications. They are *concept maps* and as such are part of a larger discipline called *Graphical Representation of Knowledge* (GROK). Some of you Robert Heinlein fans will appreciate the linkage to *Stranger in a Strange Land.* In Heinlein's context, to *grok* means "to reach a level of understanding so thoroughly that the observer becomes part of the observed – to merge, blend, intermarry, and lose identity in the group experience".

In our context, a GROK is a solution approach connecting disparate elements into a useful pattern, such that the pattern *emerges* from the applied connections. All anecdotes aside, how does this play out in our world?

Invariably in our data warehouse endeavors, we end up with similar but distinct data types, sources or record formats. We might have ways of identifying the types toward a common center, but not *directly* with each other. We might have "fuzzy" relationships requiring derivative comparisons. Do we perform these comparisons *each time* we access the data?

The real issue for resolution: Can't we form an intersection table that connects the disparate elements once and for all? We can find the interesting intersection points, form a "hard lock" between two elements and then sink a record containing the unique identifiers of those elements, side-by-side in an intersection table. Alongside with the identifiers, we can mark the intersector with metadata, such a information for the rule that formed the "lock", and we can add other metadata to give us context as to why the intersector exists at all.

From here, we no longer navigate the raw data. We navigate the *intersectors*. This is where the real information is. Does this sound a lot like a *fact* table? If we only had facts, perhaps this would be the case. But we don't. All we have is the intuitive, perhaps fuzzy rule that says these various elements have an interesting relationship. It's not particularly based on any event or transaction. The elements may themselves be transactions we are trying to connect. Sort of the facts-of-the-facts.

The takeaway, is that the relationships exist. They are objective and discoverable, but sometimes only intuitively. If we can reduce these relationships to a hard-lock in a Netezza intersection table, we can present the relationships as more than virtual. More than conceptual.

Thin/deep for XML

We had a long chat with a chap named Graham who lamented that their data storage needs had escalated completely out of control. He said their environment contained an enterprise storage device that could hold 200 terabytes of data, and recently learned that this had "topped out". So after ordering a brand new upgrade of this device, with nearly 450 terabytes of storage, it already approached saturation even after only six months. We checked in with him a year later, and they had purchased yet *another* machine with over 500 terabytes of storage to *stand alongside* the first one.

He'd told us what they were storing, and at the time we had no answers for him. Their environment fielded a lot of e-business data, so was very XML-intensive. Many of their transactional information sources were XML and many more required XML as a transmission protocol. It seemed like XML was everywhere.

Now, the big deal with XML is in how we *exchange* the data, not in how we *store* it. At the time, Netezza did not have the capability for storing XML.

Yet, Graham said, almost one third of the data arrived in an interesting but non-actionable form. Hundreds of meta-tags arrived with the data streams, all of it containing marketing or other kinds of valuable information. They were certain that the data might be of use, if they could ever find a way to harness it. They felt that tossing it was like throwing out the gold mine before ever sifting for gold, and this just didn't seem right.

Their problem however, lay in the actual storage of the information. They used XML to receive, transmit and *store the data,* giving them an egregiously steep incline on their ongoing storage needs. They were about to explode from the inflation of the data. And that's all it was, really. Data artificially inflated from the largesse of XML tags.

We suggested something completely radical. We would take their ETL environment and pull about a terabyte of XML data off their servers. We would then strip off the tags and store the data in a Netezza machine. The data would continue to maintain its record identifier from the original source record, and then two varchar() columns to hold the data. It looked like this:

```
org_ID BigInt
org_xml_tag Varchar(50)
org_xml_value VarChar(50)
```

In the above configuration for an RDBMS engine, the *index* on the org_ID alone would choke most database engines. (Netezza has no index structures, so no issues!) For the single terabyte of XML data, this wasn't so bad. Once stripped, it reduced to eighty gigabytes of data, represented in a billion rows.

Within this table, we did some profiling and discovered additional patterns, of interest to the marketing staff. They asked us to divide these into ten separate categories of visibility, essentially ten tables containing the same three columns.

We then went about converting the several more of the incoming terabytes, likewise reducing them in size simply by stripping the tags. In this first experiment, we loaded 100 terabytes of XML into just over 8 terabytes of actual storage, distributed via their patterns across these ten tables, and now many billions of records.

The marketing staff thought that these kinds of stratospheric storage numbers would bring the box to its knees. But for Netezza, a terabyte is a terabyte no matter how it's configured. The ad-hoc users started running their queries against these tags and were stunned at the overall turnaround time. With no index structures, and these thin-deep tables, the SPUs could sift and rip through the information like a hot knife through butter. It was actually faster than their highly optimized and summarized data mart down the hall, the other one created from the core XML but having thrown away the detail. This new structure had all the spare data and was far faster than its over-engineered and over-muscled RDBMS-centric brother-down-the-hall.

The best part about the Netezza platform is the rate at which it scans data. No matter what the size of the table, the scanning time is very deterministic and reproducible. We knew, based on the turnaround times of these initial queries, that we could load all of their current XML information, stripped down, into these tables, eliminate the need for the monstrous enterprise storage system, and enable the users to query the information with common SQL. A beautiful thing.

A thin-deep table like this in any other technology would be laughable - three columns and (before we were done) all those billions of records in their monolithic tables. Then performing self-joins and self-comparisons, summaries and zoned aggregations just as though the data was *much* smaller, and getting better query results than a high-powered, engineer-tuned mart. With no additional configuration effort. We just loaded the data and cut the users loose on it.

The conclusion of the ad-hoc users, after a week of detailed profiling, surprised everyone: *There's no value here. Let's get rid of it!*

Well, at least now they *know.* Consider the storage systems they were investing into - based solely on the fear of losing something valuable. The principals of the environment decided they would continue to monitor the information, sampling a terabyte here and there *just in case.* Imagine! The nerve of wanting to use *samples* in terabytes! The audacity!

And this was just a proof of concept. A profiling exercise. None of this ever made it to production. After the profiling, they were glad it didn't have to. The Netezza machine remains ensconced to provide them with the necessary profiling power for all their other data, actually serving as a means to qualify information before committing to long-term storage and management.

The summary is – the Netezza platform allows us to treat the data like it's liquid in a pond, rather than like sand in a box. With sand, we need ways to shovel it out, store and carry it. With water, we need only attach a pipe. Gravity and hydraulics do the rest.

It's physics after all.

User-Defined Functions (UDFs)

As noted earlier, we could (and likely will) make a whole book on UDFs. We're putting some more notes on them in this chapter to round out the information.

Many years ago, a salesperson (of another, unrelated product) told us that he liked to sell a product to a customer by learning a little bit about the customer's business, problem domain, etc so he could speak the customer's language. Then he would use a *cultural analog,* sort of like using a cultural or language bridge to help the customer understand things.

For UDFs, *there is no cultural analog.* UDFs extend Netezza's power in ways that eclipse our ability to fully explain them. Like a butterfly might try to explain to the caterpillar what awaits it, if it will only incubate for a wee spell, the caterpillar has *no* capacity to understand its future as a butterfly, so the average developer has *no cultural analog* to understand how massively-parallel UDFs will likely change history as we know it. Not that a the average developer *couldn't* embrace it to fully understand it, there's just no semantic bridge.

Alas.

But we'll give it a go.

The mechanics of a Netezza SQL statement execution, described earlier, leverage compile-on-demand for a variety of reusable operations, and keeps them around for reuse. The stream will access these compiled snippets in-line with the SQL statement's execution. Some of these are the regular inline SQL formulas such as max(), min() etc. Others assist the operations under-the-covers, understanding that the functions run at the SPU level, and are therefore massively parallel when invoked.

Netezza has exposed this capability to the end user. Many end-users today are software houses, integrating their products into the Netezza appliance. SAS Institute is one of these, building their componentry to reside in-part at the application layer where it always has, but now with components down on the SPUs that work with their regular components. This allows them to push their analytic power-formulas into a massively-parallel execution stream for truly phenomenal performance boosts.

The implementation of the UDFs is straightforward. Using the Decanter environment (Netezza provides), we form a C++ program that can perform row-level, inter-column calculation, but also load and leverage in-memory values and lookup tables that persist across SQL statements.

This has far-reaching implications, especially for those groups with advanced-science or advanced-algorithmic requirements. Invariably, such applications leverage in-memory databases and structures because the algorithms are very intense.

Those readers immersed in (or familiar with) advanced-algorithm environments will recognize the breakdown of a multi-stage resolution process. Essentially, the algorithm consists of a series of small operations that bubble into a final resolution. It behaves a lot like a tree of activity, where the leaves are the smallest parts (usually containing the variables / polynomial elements) that enter the equation at various levels as it resolves.

```
( (a + 1) + (b * .07) - (sqrt(c) * .8) ) * (d * .91876)
```

In the above (simplified) equation, we resolve each element, then perform the final operation.

(1) PlaceholderA = a + 1
(2) PlaceHolderB = b * .07
(3) PlaceHolderC = (sqrt(c) * .8)
(4) PlaceHolderD = (d * .91876)
(5) PlaceHolder E = PlaceHolderA+PlaceHolderB-PlaceHolderC
(6) Result = PlaceHolderE * PlaceHolderD

We can see how this would shape up if we had the right memory-based objects to take our column-level variables (a, b, c, d) and just "do the math". But what if we're processing in breathtaking *scale*? Like the telemetry records coming from a satellite or deep-space probe? Or the tag-value pairs streaming off the internet, the geo-spatial data in an oil-and-gas survey, the claims flying through an insurance processor, the loan qualification algorithms leveraged for an internet applicant - the possibilities appear endless.

In the above calculation example, would the developer find solace in using an RDBMS for such things? Only if invoking the MISD model (Multiple-Instruction-Single-Data), which would:

(1) Read a record in cursor-based form, capturing the columns a, b, c, and d
(2) Apply the given calculations
(3) Resolve for the result
(4) Store the result
(5) Repeat as necessary
(6) Spin, rinse, etc.

Notice how we read the data in MISD form, a unit-at-a-time, apply all rules, and return the value? We know this approach won't scale, especially as we increase the algorithm's complexity. We've also seen in another chapter how to resolve this *in scale* with Netezza.

- Read the entire data set, calculating on-the-fly the values for PlaceHolderA, PlaceHolderB, PlaceHolderC and PlaceHolderD, storing them in an intermediate table.
- Read the intermediate table, Adding PlaceHolderA to PlaceholderB, subtracting PlaceHolderC, and storing the entire result (PlaceHolderC) in an intermediate table.
- Read the first and second intermediate tables, multiplying PlaceHolderD by PlaceHolderE and storing the results in a final result table.

Using the above approach, we can apply the noted algorithm with high visibility. But what if the algorithm is wildly complex, as are most environments leveraging them? The above (more simplistic) approach would become tedious and difficult to maintain. We need simplicity in all areas, so we can both understand it and easily extend it with no mysteries.

If we defined the calculation in a UDF, we could call the entire thing myCalc() and it could look like this:

```
insert into final_result (myresult) select myCalc() from myTable;
```

In the above, the calculation is completely harnessed by the UDF and we don't need the extra intermediate steps. Or do we?

What if the above calculation is simply the one we need for the given rows of a *single* table? Perhaps we have one table we need a pre-calculated advanced-algorithm on, with five or six other tables also requiring some form of algorithmic outtake. We then use their results as intermediate results into a larger one. What if the final calculation was called MeaningOfLife()?

```
insert into biology_result (key, biology_meaning) select key, myMeaning()
from biology_tab;
    Insert into physics_result (key, physics_meaning) select key, myMeaning()
from physics_tab;
```

```
   Insert into chem_result (key, chem_meaning) select key, myMeaning() from
chemistry_tab;
   Insert into paleo_result (key, paleo_meaning) select key, myMeaning() from
paleo_tab;

   Insert into final_meaning (meaning) select myFinalMeaning (b.biology_meaning,
p.physics_meaning, c.chem_meaning, pl.paleo_meaning) from biology_tab b,
physics_tab p, chemistry_tab c, paleo_tab pt where a.key=b.key and b.key = c.key
and c.key = pl.key
```

and finally:

```
select sum(meaning) from final_meaning;
```

Whether we receive the usual result (*42*) or another, we can see that the flexibility remains to solve a highly-complex, multi-table problem using the same methods we would use on the whiteboard - that is solve for the parts and summarize into the whole. We've used these simplified examples above to draw insight *only*, not to provide a hard-and-fast approach or methodology.

The takeaway here, is that the Netezza platform provides the same scaling power in its parallel data structures only previously available in advanced memory-based structures, themselves enslaved to a multiple-instruction-multiple-data model.

In our existing underpowered environments, we might see flavors of these algorithms in specific systems or software packages, perhaps separated entirely into their own functional and physical stovepipes. One group hones its proprietary formulas for its user base, while another group carefully shapes its algorithms for another user base. Somehow we instinctively know that these two (or more) stovepipes should integrate, and if only we could integrate them, we might find yet another set of algorithms on the horizon. We might *already* be there, unable to proceed because the stovepipes prohibit us.

Without Netezza, our primary roadblock remains the lack of power, sheer *physical* power, to rise from the miry clay. Netezza's internal physics allows us to move these domains closer to each other, within the same physical platform and certainly within logical striking distance of each other. Armed with this kind of processing power, we can take our information to the next plane of existence. Perhaps not *quite* to infinity and beyond, but on a path in that general direction.

Solid-State Storage

Okay, it's all the rage. We all have a flash-stick with huge amounts of memory on it, why not have a SPU that is fully DRAM or some other form of high-speed memory instead of a lowly disk drive? Seems like the next level of product development, right?

In the prior discussions, we've talked about using temporary storage for workspace, including temp storage for intermediate results rather than solving the problem in entity-at-a-time form. This means, in no uncertain terms, that we could leverage memory for our temporary table space. Considering that it will evaporate the moment we exit our transactional session, everybody wins.

What would this look like? Well, the vendor freely admits to toying with this scenario, but also notes that the cost is currently prohibitive for a completely solid-state (memory-based SPU) architecture. This could and may change in the next three to five years, so we will stay tuned.

What could we expect until then? We dare not second-guess the vendor's engineers, but we'll offer a simple scenario to show how one might *imagine* extending Netezza's architecture to support this. Are we having fun yet?

Recall in Netezza's "create table" we have the option of making a default, SPU-based table or an external table that uses flat files for its underpinning storage. Since the only difference in the two statements appears to be its storage location, how easy would it be to make a create-table statement that simply uses memory for its underpinning storage.

```
create table xyz
create temporary table xyz
create external table ext_xyz
create memory table mem_xyz
```

We could see this memory hosted on the SPUs, or perhaps on a separate SPA rack entirely. No matter. This would allow us to transparently manufacture a temp-table, use it, form a solution set, then toss it. Or in our diabolical plans, create a persistent table, form a solution set, and keep leveraging it in memory.

The cool part about this is that we'd have memory for our temp workspace rather than a SPU or even an external table. If we were to load such a structure with an intermediate filter table or other filtration construct. If it is physically co-located with the data on the SPU, we can only begin to imagine how much power we could derive from it.

In any case, this is just one scenario and we know of many others. The takeaway, is that if / when Netezza starts leveraging solid-state memory on the SPUs, we already have a use for it, and will expect phenomenal lift from it.

No pressure there.

Stored procedures - no, not that again!

Well, the vendor recognizes that even in bulk-processing scenarios, some SQL-centric looping and procedural control is highly desirable. What if we need to perform progressive linear analysis, churning one set of data into another, and yet another, cascading the activity and iteratively boiling the data down to a kernel of actionable stuff? You know, like a refiner boils the impurities out of gold?

While the vendor has yet to release, I'm hoping that the vendor puts some constraints on the functionality so that nobody is tempted to use it in an entity-at-a-time looping operation. It's bulk all-the-time, folks, even when we're looping.

When we think about what we need in stored procedure functionality, it really reduces to the basic language constructs like conditional/nested branching, looping and yes, even subroutines. What does this buy us? The ability to keep more of our logic inside Netezza's control and less of it outside in ETL-style drivers or BASH script. Lots of blazingly powerful efficiencies arise when we can loop down on the SPUs instead of another, externalized mechanism.

However, we will not retract our prior statements as to the banes of stored procedures. They ensconce us into the technology and bind us deeper. Of course, we don't particularly *mind* it on this go 'round, but the effect remains.

Libraries of Congress - or...

The ANSI-99 SQL library supported by the Netezza engine has the expected complement of built-in functions. The more exotic part is that the User-Defined-Function capability allows the vendor and its third-party partners to develop whole libraries of algorithms and functions for various uses. This extends the appliance-nature of the machine and takes it to a completely different level. Mainly because the libraries don't just run on the machine like a vanilla suite of functions, they run down on the SPUs, in *massively* parallel form.

For example, if a given customer is a retailer, how about a library of retail-facing functions. Or if a financial services firm, equities firm, pharmaceutical, building materials or - you get the picture. Rather than boiling the most-it-can-for-all, we really only have to leverage these plug-in packaged libraries, effectively customizing the box as a retail-box, a pharma-box, or whatever.

This capability has far-reaching implications, not just for an over-the-counter custom purchase, but for third-party resellers that want to sell their own Netezza-branded appliance.

Actuate recently announced a branded form of the Netezza machine. Think about how branding works in most marketing scenarios: We understand the generic brand, call it Netezza *Classic*. Then we might see a group like SAS come out with the SAS Netezza appliance. You think I'm kidding? Expect to see a lot more custom Netezza-centric products and applications hitting the market.

This is what the vendor calls the Netezza Ecosystem, and is exactly where any vendor wants to take their product. It gives the vendor the right kind of product control, the right level of user feedback for product improvement, and fulfills (at least part of) the dream of open-system scenarios. People contribute because it's fun, and they fulfill another very important aspect of open-system collaboration - they can make some money at it, too. Everybody wins, at so many levels, as a functioning ecosystem should be.

OPERATIONAL STUFF

12

OUR OPERATORS always hunger for more operational information, logs, progress reports, visibility to the actual activities on the machine. Some of this, Netezza provides right on the *nzadmin* panel. Other parts such as application logs and alerts, we will build into our application levels. With an enterprise environment such as Ab Initio (or an ETL environment) to drive the Netezza machine, it would simply fire one Run SQL component after another to invoke Netezza's internal processing, and likewise provide operators with the logging and visibility to what's-happening-now.

We can also set up simple BASH shell scripts to launch our required operations, and it's very easy to drop the logging results of this activity to a common logging zone for the operators to review. It's Linux after all, and has a lot of built-in stuff we can leverage for reporting.

A suggestion however, if we want to go the route of shell script, is to set up a simple shell utility/framework that the shell-based operations run under. This allows the framework to invoke logging and error files and generally provide a backdrop for our application-facing script. We're not talking about a lot of work here. A reasonably savvy programmer will see the common operational patterns emerge and can write up a simple shell framework. It's easy to do and worth the time, primarily because all of our shell-based SQL statements will run under it, and have a common place to log their results and errors. The operators will love you.

The second option, running our shell scripts "as is", is simply too primitive for enterprise processing. Don't be surprised if the operators, upon delivery of said simplistic model, express their disappointment. They expect a consistent operational framework, not separately delivered application operation instructions.

Cherish their feedback.

Intersystem Replication and Disaster Recovery

One of the questions people ask in the scheme of things is – what's the deal on real-time replication? Another question is akin – that of Disaster Recovery (DR) and backup/restore.

Backup/restore capabilities of Netezza are very robust. Recently (Spring 2008) the vendor has announced an integration partnership with EMC whereby an EMC *StoragePad* component will interact directly with the Netezza frame for high-speed backups in a hardware-to-hardware backplane operation - physically onboard the Netezza frame. This will effectively hard-line the machine's backup to our enterprise storage and make it virtually transparent. Note also that this storage component also serves as an onboard staging area. We interact with lots of customers who want to bring the data to the box as staged/flat-file form, but lack the enterprise storage capacity to support it. This option puts the storage right on the box, no mess, no fuss. In addition, the Netezza platform can interact with this storage at the rate of one terabyte per hour *per frame*.

It's important to understand the implications of this. One terabyte per hour per frame means that an eight-frame Netezza configuration (10800) can load at *eight terabytes per hour*. This utterly eclipses every other enterprise platform.

Disaster Recovery is a more complex animal, because we're talking about the capability to bring up another machine in the case of the destruction of the first (e.g. fire, flood, earthquake, etc).

The Netezza platform is internally ruggedized with all kinds of failover characteristics for its own use. It has dual redundant power supplies, hot-swappable SPUs, dual-host failover and redundancy kung-fu all over the internal architecture. So for the machine itself, we're covered against failure.

But what of the data center? What if our environment is hit by a tornado, fire or any other natural disaster? What if a terrorist understands the value of our carefully crafted algorithms and detonates our machine? (The visual alone of such an act is traumatic for me, so I'll take a moment.) Can we bring up another Netezza environment to support the same operations as the first? The answer is unequivocally yes, and the Netezza machine, because of its ability to reload its information at such high speeds, is likely the *least* of our worries.

Most DR plans allow for any number of hours to restore the operating environment to nominal if not full strength, with the consideration that the initial hours of operation are for critical items. Data warehouse operations are typically on a back-burner, so aren't really the topmost priority. Not to diminish their importance, but for many environments the data warehouse availability can lapse.

Should Netezza rely on this latency? Of course not and it doesn't have to. Since we're talking about recovery of the most recent loading of the information on the Netezza machine, we have to ask ourselves several questions about this kind of recovery. The first question is – are we running in a continuous model? If not, DR is not as much of a hot-button.

Why? Because in nightly-batch-cycle model, we have the option of processing all of our data, performing a snapshot backup and providing the information to the user all within the given batch cycle. It means our most recent work is already secured to backup, ready for restoration. If the environment fails between the current cycle and the next, we simply re-load the current cycle's information and proceed normally.

In a continuous model, we have a bit more to do. Many shops will perform double-loading of the same information to two separate sites, and likewise perform the same data processing operations on both sites, but only publish from one. They will also switch the sites on a regular basis for maintenance, keeping two separate "hot" environments that are constantly running as though one is "on deck". This is a necessary quantity of many continuous models, one that is already embraced and operational for many mature continuous environments, so Netezza just plugs right into this.

Data Replication is similar in construct, except it assumes that the data has been first hosted on a local Netezza platform before forwarding it to another. This allows the first platform to distill the information so that what is later transmitted is the clean, tight version of the data, and the business rules to clean it are only applied in one place. Replication then, means copying *processed* data *in bulk* from one Netezza machine to another using some automated utility.

Other vendors provide this automated utility as part of their package, where Netezza provides the raw hardware hooks but leaves the actual control to a third party utility. This is actually a very shrewd approach, for several reasons:

- What do the other vendors offer in this same capability that is *actually in use*? The answer is usually *not much*. People don't like the *secondhand* technologies that the other vendors bolt-on to their core technologies as an afterthought. Replication utilities fall into this genre. Rather, our engineers go with a more robust enterprise tool, usually a programmable backup/replication product with features that deal directly and *homogeneously* with *all* their servers and systems, not just one vendor.
- Why should *any* vendor provide a backup/replication automation controller if nobody will use it? (any more than they use what the *other* vendors supply for this same capability).
- Netezza does not supply a controller function, but supports all the major enterprise tools that do. Meaning that it will plug directly into our enterprise. Like an *appliance* should.

As a note, see the section *Information Theory* on why plain-straight replication is a dangerous animal. What we actually need is a data transportation environment that will harness the information, extract it, move it and load it *in better shape* than where it came from. Simple replication forfeits a grand opportunity for stewardship, in that we can do something *with* the data while it is en route to its next target. It is never the best stewardship model to carry junk, vestigial or unused information from the source to target (as with blind replication). Tailor the replication for the target, and use a data-shaping tool that will make this happen. Simple data copy is not an optimal data transportation practice.

In addition, *real time* replication smacks of *transactional* replication, which Netezza does *not* do. We cannot expect a bulk processor to respond in real time to transactional information, when the machine itself is *not* geared for transactional processing. We can, however, configure the machine to deal with *continuous* operations. This allows us to collect/accumulate inbound information and to publish/reposit outbound information in consumable, time-boxed chunks (like a mini-batch). This give us the ability to harness our scale with *reasonable* latency. When it comes to processing in scale, we need to think in terms of scaling the *latency*, not the individual transactions.

An external replication mechanism (enterprise data transport environment) can easily broker Netezza's workload into the machine and broker its output to the rest of the world. We would simply schedule these operations on boundaries that provide the best overall Netezza performance. Smaller, more frequent batches, but batches that are large enough to efficiently invoke Netezza's intake and outtake cycles.

Which machine(s)?

In every first-purchase scenario, people ask which machines they should buy. The larger Netezza machines can feel like overkill and the smaller ones seem, well, *small*. So what is the functional balance?

Each "frame" is essentially a 10100 machine configuration. It has 108 available SPUs, 4 spare SPUs, 12.5 terabytes of storage, and a single internal host. If we move to a 10200 machine, we double everything, including the internal hosts. However, the 10200 internal hosts are bound in a failover coupling, so that if one host dies the other one automatically picks up and keeps moving. We also have the benefit of a doubled-network intake, with bound network cards running at twice the intake speed of just one.

Note that we don't get this internal failover with the 10100, having only one host. So often people ask – *which machine should we buy?*

You're gonna hate me, but the answer really is – *it depends.* Some environments just don't have a need for the internal host failover capability. If the box dies, they'll call for service, and service will be restored in short order, but the only people inconvenienced are internal users who will "understand" the outage and plan their day accordingly. Other environments are high-availability, and cannot tolerate longer outages. This is what the 10200 buys us, but some folks still might think it's overkill.

Buy the machine that suits the *operational* priority.

Likewise, the data *storage* capacity on a Netezza machine arrives ready-to-use, but can remain under administrative lock-and-key until we need it. We can get a 10200 with 25 terabytes of storage, but only license it for say, 6 terabytes. Later when we need more, we shoot an invoice to the vendor, they shoot back a license key, and we unlock more storage with the license key. Thus adding storage is an *invoice* event, not a *hardware* event, and we only pay-as-we-go for what we want to use (capacity-on-demand).

We can also do something creative with this approach, in that we could add more frames before we add more storage, essentially beefing up the processing capacity before adding more room to store the work. We don't have to wait for a machine to fill up its storage before we add more SPU power. Once again, it depends on the operational priority.

Which certainly makes capacity planning more interesting. It also causes us to review our options differently. We can get a 10200 and have all the power (216 SPUs) without having to pay for storage that we might not need (right away!). We can reach each level above the 10200 simply by adding another frame to the mix, each time appending the full power of a frame to the existing frame(s).

Which machine do we need to buy? Talk with the Netezza vendor and get it tailored like you want it. You can always add another frame later. We don't say this dismissively, only that in an initial purchase we might be unsure of how much we need, but we have not painted ourselves into a corner. Adding another frame literally doubles the power from a 10100 to a 10200 and may, depending on our data configuration, reduce our processing time by *more than half*. So if we're uncertain as to how much we need, we get what we know, with the understanding that we can add more later with no programming or configuration penalty.

And to reiterate the response to Netezza mythology, adding data to the machine does not slow it down. In one of the Dilbert comics, the boss comes to Dilbert and asks for a plan to bolt down the desktop workstations so they can't be stolen. Dilbert suggests that they just load up the workstations with data so that they are too heavy to move, and the boss likes the plan.

Saying that the Netezza machine gets slower as we add more data is akin to saying that the workstation will get heavier as we add more data. We can always *deliberately* configure a Netezza machine to tank its performance, but why would we do that? What's the point?

The point: The Netezza physics harnesses the data, not the other way around.

In-box Processing (ELT)

When performing in-box Extract-Load-Transform operations, we have several options for in-box transformation. One is to drive them with internally launched scripts. Another is to drive SQL statements into the machine from an external environment such as a formal ETL / data processing environment.

Either way, our operators will want some visibility to what's happening inside the machine. One way is for them to pop open the *nzadmin* utility and watch the queries running in real-time as they execute. Another way is to keep logs via the internal scripts or the external driving mechanism. By default, the *nzadmin*'s active query display only keeps about fifteen minutes of work in memory, but some simple scheduled activities can periodically offload this information and save it to disk for the operators. We don't have to keep a log like this running full bore all the time, but it's handy when the operators need to turn it on for their own work.

Whichever method we choose in this regard, we need to account for the simple fact that operators cannot tolerate "driving blind".

With the traditional RDBMS stored procedure, the procedure kicks off and starts slinging SQL statements with abandon. Some procedures may be short, some long and some in between. A single RDBMS "black boxed" stored proc can run for hours. What does the operator see? The stored proc is running and the disk lights are flashing. The operator has no other status as to what the proc is doing, how far along it is, if it's bombing off or anything. The operator just has to wait and hope for the best.

We've seen such RDBMS stored procs run for hours only to finish with empty tables or no work output, because early in the cycle a preliminary temp-table errored-off on its creation, causing every subsequent operation to join-on-nothing and end up with zero results. The operators *could* have restarted the job at the point of error, *if only they had known.*

When the operators complain about this black-box effect, the developers just roll their eyes, because without a commonly accepted reporting protocol for these things across *all* stored procedures, they are loathe to install one for the special case. They know that one special case often metastasizes into multiple disparate cases, and soon the end is worse than the beginning. If they form a committee to build a governance standard, this process quickly devolves because they don't know how to build a governance standard. It's not something they've ever done before and are daunted by the potential pitfalls and permutations. After weeks of exasperating work, they give up on a standard, and likewise give up on supporting the operators. This cycle continues, year after year.

Netezza has the right capabilities to make these problems non-issues, but we still have to embrace some kind of formal standard. Thankfully, the Linux environment has everything we need to script and manufacture logs without major overhead. The ETL/processing environments likewise maintain operational logs and information. Embracing either of these environments automatically provides a higher degree of visibility. Standardizing the outputs and their formats, naming conventions etc, is relatively simple as well. We don't have to build a standard from scratch, just around the chosen utilities.

But we need to commit to its construction, and not stop until the operators are getting what they need.

In-box processing, for the average technologist, smacks of mainframe computing and the days of yore that he/she has been trying to escape. Alas, it is bulk processing and *requires* the knights of the round table, not rounds of nightly batches with tables, to complete a data processing mission without killing the machines, the systems and our personal lives.

Before we jump into processing *everything* inside the box, with scripts and such, just recall that every environment needs some kind of governance standard. A suggestion, since with Netezza we are in Linux, is that we embrace a Linux-friendly governance standard for all Netezza internals, and this is relatively simple to do.

Checkpoint/auditing

One of the most pernicious problems in database-side transforms, especially multistage transforms such as those we'll do in Netezza, is being able to restart from a checkpoint, or for that matter, audit the work we've already done.

From an operational standpoint, the human user needs something that is *foolproof* to restart and recover a given flow of work. The best thing we can do for them is, at the beginning of the execution, manufacture a run-time script file that is fully self-contained for restart. It will hold all of the original run-time parameters for the current instance of the script or program, and it will likewise pass the run-time *and* restart context of the failed instance to the next instance, to insure proper restart.

Example: if we pass three parameters into a given script or program to initiate a run, we will want to capture those same three parameters. If during the run-time we intend to fetch a unique audit_id or job_id for the work, we will need to capture this for a restart as well. Then we push the physical restart command into a file, the *whole* restart command, long before we'll ever need it. We hope that we never need it, and it's just throwaway. But if we need it, the operator knows exactly where to go, because we've prepared a simple way out for him that could otherwise be a maze. All the operator will have to do is launch that restart file. It's fully self-contained.

We're pointing this out in operational stuff, because we *really* need to support an effortless and foolproof restart for the operators. We cannot afford a misfire for no better reason than they misunderstand some exposed detail of the restart. Encapsulate all the details for them, and give them a single, simple, parameter-*less* command line call to make it happen.

Case Study Short: One group used logs to capture every step of the job's process. At the beginning, they captured the startup context and wrote the proper restart command directly into the log file. However, they took it one step further, in that the entire log file had all of its information commented-out (with a "#" symbol), *except for the restart command.* This allowed the operators to restart the failed job simply by executing the log file itself. All other lines, except for the restart command, were ignored. This approach fully-self-contained the restart protocol so the operator always had a one-stop-shop for everything.

We have lots of ways to support the operator, but we need to *reduce keystrokes* as much as possible.

Keystroke reduction

In one setting, the application administrator carefully set up an environment to automate the processes for tagging, promoting and implementing Ab Initio assets using the Enterprise Meta Environment (EME). For those unfamiliar with this process, Ab Initio provides the EME as a repository to check-in and manage the complexity of Ab Initio's various application assets. For our packaged scenario, all a developer had to do was tag the assets, which would produce a Tag ID. Then the developer would send this Tag ID to the Software Configuration Management staff through their portal. Then one of the SCM staff would simply execute a promotion script with the tag ID, and the promotion happened automatically. The promotion process would run on the target platform, reach across to the source platform, package up the assets, pull them over to and check them all into the next-level region. Neat and tidy.

Just one problem, though, the original form of this interface required a lot of keystrokes on the part of the SCM staff. We had several conversations with the application admin about simplifying the interface to its lowest, most keystroke-less form. He understood the need, but thought it was already simple enough for anyone.

We pulled several of the SCM folks into the room and asked them to sit down and give this original version a whirl. The first of them stared at the keyboard for a moment, then tapped a key. Then tapped another, and another. The application admin looked up at us and thought *why are they so scared of the keyboard? What is going on? This is so simple!*

But what he didn't realize, was that *all* the SCM folks were from a Windows world, and knew *nothing* about Unix. They were almost afraid to touch the keyboard for fear of breaking something.

The application admin *got it.* He further reduced the interface to its simplest, bare-boned interface, so simple the SCM folks could hook it directly into their web-level controls and work everything remotely, without ever having to touch a Unix command line at all.

Reduce. Simplify, Eliminate human error. Reduce keystrokes so the operator's success, and ultimately our own success, is just a *few* keystrokes away, if that much.

pLink launching

The *Putty* utility, which many of us adhere to rather than terminal services, telnet and other

THE NETEZZA UNDERGROUND

Unix utilities, has some interesting supporting utilities, including the *pscp* copy utility to transfer data to and from our desktop and the Netezza box.

A *very* handy utility, *plink*, allows us to initiate a command-line operation on the remote host. Thus if we have a script or framework entry point that we normally use to drive Netezza from the *Putty* command line, we can do the same thing with a Windows / DOS command line in *plink*.

```
C:/>plink -pw nzpw nzadm@192.168.1.209 pkg/nzf APP_DIR=powerbatch
```

The above is an example of connecting to the Netezza Linux host located at the given IP address with the given username/password (nzadm/nzpw). The Linux host will automatically navigate our default directory associated with the *nzadm* user. From here, we have a subdirectory called *pkg* and a launching point called *nzf*. The *nzf* is simply our lightweight framework of Netezza utilities and Linux utilities. It's easy enough to make one of these to one's own liking. In the above notation, we also tell our *nzf* that the application we want to run is the *powerbatch* application. This is a parameter for the *nzf,* because *plink* does not care about it.

Basically, all we need to do is open a command line "hook" with *plink* and we can then invoke any Netezza-side script or operation we so choose, on a Windows command line, *just as if* we had launched it directly from the Linux command line.

This utility is *very* handy for troubleshooting, but can also prove useful for restarting or even remote launching of internal scripts such as housekeeping and the like. If we're launching internal Netezza work from an external scheduler, the *plink* will allow our testers to launch the same work just as if the scheduler had done so.

ADMINISTRATIVE STUFF

SO WE'VE just delivered a shiny new big black machine to our administrators. We've put the *nzadmin* utility on their desktops and dropped a copy of the Netezza Administrator's Guide in their inbox. Off we go to play with the machine while they muddle through the foreign technology issues, right?

Uh, slow down a bit.

The Netezza vendor support does on-site training for the administrators and can quickly bring them up to speed the necessary things. Now, if Linux is a foreign animal to them, there might be a *slightly* steeper curve, but seriously not by much. Most of what the admin *initially* needs to know can be easily handled in the *nzadmin* utility. The vendor's own support engineers bridge the gap with their own activity (all part of the customer experience) so let's not fret about it.

No doubt that as an administrator, or someone who wants to make sure the administrators are supported, we might have some questions on the application or usability side, or in what to expect from how the users will actually leverage the machine.

But a word about Netezza administration - we won't be doing admin of pages, tablespaces, disk striping, index maintenance or any of the other object-level or system-level maintenance activities required by the traditional 'Orrible RDBMS. Some admins see this as a threat, others as a blessing. It's an appliance, and the vendor has taken this to an extreme level, packaging anything and everything out of our view, so all we really have left, is to do "good data warehousing" with a product that is about as reliable and consistent as the sunrise.

Following are some tips and tidbits, and are by no means exhaustive, but just a few extra things we've seen along the way.

Alerts and Implementation stuff

Our access into the heart of the machine is the *nzadmin* utility. If you have one, there's not much reason to rehash the details here. One of the things that oft eludes the administrators is the creative use of alerts. Jump into the alerts section of the admin guide and then browse through the default alerts. Before we make our own alerts, think about something:

What of implementation? What happens the *next* time we have to service the machine for upgrade, or just add a new machine to the floor? Will we tediously review and *reinstall* the existing alerts? Manually?

No.

Alerts are installed through the command line as well as *nzadmin*. One does oneself many favors by placing the customized alerts into an executable file, so they can be reinstalled from a script. Like an implementation script.

This allows us to have common machine implementation scripts, plus scripts that take parameters, even subscripts for our different configuration regions (Dev, Test, Prod) or the machine types. It also provides us a starting point to install implementation directory structures for our applications, the implementation schemas, etc. to provide a script-driven implementation scenario that is foolproof (largely) for production implementation.

Considering that just about everything in the implementation of an initial environment, the applications running on in and the supporting scripts – are all basically simple scripts themselves, it behooves us to start treating the configuration seriously from the administrative panel and on into the machine.

Make the configuration repeatable.

Governance is good, but we need real development and implementation protocols to realize a production delivery. Administrators will *really* like a lights-out, black box (for them, at least) implementation.

External Tables

What's an external table? In the prior *Publication* section we dealt with them for application outtake, but administratively we have a concern only in their housekeeping.

The external table appears in the database catalog like any other database table (it is, however marked as external). The primary difference is that it does not talk to the SPUs, but to a flat file. If the flat file is located on the local host drive, we must be careful how we implement it. We don't want to eat up the local drive space.

We *could* mount an external SAN drive and point the external table to that. It's a handy way of publishing data *out* if we want to avoid the outtake protocol of having someone come to get it. Keep in mind that we can make as many external tables as we like, pointing to as many files as we like, but each external table can only point to one file at a time. Don't go wild with this, because it can become a configuration and housekeeping issue both for the external-table entries in the catalog and the proliferation of files.

Also, we can drop an external table from the catalog *and it will not delete the underlying file*. For administrative purposes, this can be a serious issue if a given application is manufacturing external tables, pushing data to them and then not cleaning up completely. It is, however, quite handy when we want to publish a persistent file. We can insert to the table, thence create the file, drop the table, and move on.

The Netezza catalog is accessible with some very simple notations against its system tables, described these in another chapter. From these entries, we can discover *exactly* which underlying file the external table thinks it's talking to. We can also use this information administratively to remove the file (when we drop the table) or deal with the file in another way.

For example, if we have a outtake protocol that is publishing information, once we write to an external table with an *insert* command, we cannot write to it again without Netezza automatically truncating the table's information. It actually zaps the file on the next insert.

However, if we simply provide the external table with the name of the file we want to write, we don't have any worries that it will truncate our prior file. We can likewise move the filename from view with a rename, and then the next insert will create (rather than truncate) the file. So external tables are one part catalog management and one part file management.

Hidden Columns

At a customer site, one of the engineers ran up to us and said "We're in trouble, we just deleted five million records from the database. We don't have a backup to restore them from because it's the development machine!" Okay, chill, it's not a problem as long as nobody truncates the table or otherwise tosses the data. It is *possible* to restore these records to the table, and do it rather quickly. Before we share any operational secret on this, give a shout to your Netezza product engineer. He/she can execute some very simple operations right away to get you back in a good state.

Recall in another section we mentioned that the *delete* operation does not physically remove the data. It merely marks the records for deletion and they will be automatically filtered from all subsequent queries. To assist us, all operations in Netezza have a transaction ID (hidden column *createxid*) applied to a given operation, and the *delete* operation is no different. Every record touched by our inadvertent *delete* will be marked with a common createxid. Likewise the deleted record's marker (hidden column *deletexid*) tells us which ones we can restore the records from a deleted state.

As hidden columns, they never appear in a "select *" and we have to ask for them by name in the select and where clause. One of the more remarkable things about these (and the hidden column *rowid*) is that the vendor has the freedom to apply other forms of row-level identification and attribution as a data-architecture practice, that we as users can leverage for higher value, and that third-party vendors and suppliers can leverage for data control (for such things as incremental backup and restore).

Some of the practices mentioned earlier discuss additional data warehouse attribution such as audit_id and the like. The objective with all these additional hooks, is to provide a stronger harness on the data and the processes touching it.

Mythology

Another area of mythology is in Netezza's backup-and-restore capabilities, which are reknowned and robust. If as an administrator you have doubts, deliberately drill the vendor on this topic. Backup/restore at speeds of 1.5 TB per hour, using common enterprise backup technology. The Underground's myth-mongers will tell us differently. Believing the mythology is no different than trusting a leprechaun, or explaining to your boss after a "careful investigation", repeating what the leprechaun told you.

In the Spring of '08 the vendor announced a partnership with EMC, noted elsewhere in this book, seamlessly installing and interfacing up to 10TB of *onboard* EMC storage per frame (for staging etc) that directly and transparently interacts with our existing EMC installation.

Reduction

The vendor has an aggressive and passionate mission for reducing the repetitive and mundane maintenance and administration, pushing it under the covers so we deal with it less and less. Even things that were regular maintenance activities when the author first encountered the technology, have since been optimized and pushed out of view. We never have to worry about them again. This includes everything from generating database statistics to simple table creation. One glimpse of the extraordinary maintenance and overhead required by the average RDBMS, compared to the equivalent in Netezza, and one will never wonder why this is important.

The mission of your operation is to manage the data, not manage the hardware that manages the data.

Short Chapter

We kept this chapter short for a reason: Administration of a Netezza machine is found in the Netezza Administrator's Guide and apart from this, regular admin of a Netezza machine is a short and inconsequential affair. We won't need a gaggle of people on it, and there's not a lot to talk about.

It's an *appliance*. Put it in the corner and let it work.

14

STRONG KUNG FU

WE'VE RIPPED the gift wrapping off our Netezza box, offered an ecstatic, albeit professionally awkward, hug to the managers who count the most, and a friendly and amazingly knowledgeable guy named Ray, Ralph, Paul or Jerry (or the equivalent) has given us onsite training, and shown us how to get around inside the box. We're sitting at a desk, staring at *putty* window, the blazing future in our view and the malaise of the past in our rear view mirror.

What's next?

We've no doubt got a big system we need to move from Point-A to Point-B, and regardless of what Point-A looks like, we have a nagging, perhaps sinking feeling that while the functionality may be identical, it just won't look the same in Point-B, the Netezza machine. Surely there's a path, a way to get us from Point-A to Point-B without guesswork?

You could hire someone like us, but if we're busy and those like us are indisposed, what then? You'll find that the Netezza machine is not really all that hard to master. The speed at which we will move will be largely determined by our ability to *adapt*. To a new way of thinking about problems.

"You must think *differently*, grasshopper," said the old man in the television series *Kung Fu*. And while this process is in no way akin to Zen, and you might not see a book called the *Zen of Netezza*, you will understand something when you start to port your first functionality into the machine, especially if your data warehouse kung fu is not strong.

"Easy for you to say, old man," grasshopper retorts, to the old man's astonishment, "I have fire-breathing users on my back that make a Chinese dragon look like a plush toy. I have all these transactional systems I have to forklift using a shell game that looks like the Towers of Hanoi, and if you don't help me I'm gonna snatch those pebbles from your hand and feed 'em to you – *without* the soy sauce!"

To which the old man replies, in true Chinese Mafioso fashion, "Shuddup."

Many years ago I was required to go through the Evelyn Wood speed reading course. My cruising speed on a book was already pretty fast, but this course was necessary so I could get through technical volumes, reams of data and otherwise perform a higher volume information intake – maintaining high comprehension. Not to say that my brain actually assimilates and catalogs every last ounce of information, but my brain is one of those oddball anomalies that seems to *snap* on patterns. Problem is, the patterns don't emerge until enough data shows up to quantifiably separate the noise from the reality.

Wood's method is interesting, in that all the principles center on keeping the eyes from going backward on a page and actually pre-processing words before they arrive on our eyeballs. By assuming that we're actually reading several lines at a time, our eyes have this uncanny ability to assimilate words that are several lines ahead of the line we're on, almost like pre-processing.

Our eyes also have this odd habit of back-tracking on a page, where we will get to the end of a line of text, and our eyes will arbitrarily back up several words before proceeding onward – a highly inefficient but almost reflexive activity. The method to enhance the first as a strength and eliminate the second as a weakness is to use something (like waving our hand on the page) to help our eyes track.

The takeaway here is that *mass intake* is about anticipating future work and about constantly moving current work in a forward direction (like an insert-only model).

Our current environment, the Point-A we are moving away from, probably isn't doing any of this. Its activities likely solve a single problem without care for anything 'downstream'. Its flows work in terms of *read/update/delete* while the *insert* is usually something saved for error records or initial intake. In a traditional RDBMS, it's just too much hassle and a wasteful to use inserts for *everything*. Updates and deletes seem so much more efficient.

In fact, *lots* of things inside an RDBMS seem the most efficient, so why is it running out of gas?

Standing the problem on its side

When we consider a typical bulk-oriented stored procedure in our Point-A architecture, we will see a common pattern of activity.

- We select one or more units-of-work
- We begin with one of these units of work
- We apply business rule A
- We apply business rule B
- We apply business rule C, etc.
- We update the unit of work on the database
- We start working on the next unit of work
- We continue until no more units of work

The above describes the aforementioned MISD model, where we take a unit of work, beat the daylights out of it, and put it back. I mentioned in another section how in a similar scenarios we converted hours of work into minutes of work simply by converting this unit-at-time application to wholesale-units-at-a-time.

If we want to invoke the SIMD model (in Netezza), the process would look a lot like this:
- Step 1 - Read, Filter and write out the records we care about, to tempT
- Step 2 - Apply business rule A to *all* units of work, writing tempT to tempA

- Step 3 - Apply business rule B to *all* units of work, writing tempA to tempB
- Step 4 - Apply business rule C to *all* units of work, writing tempB to tempC
- Step 5 - Throw away tempT, tempA and tempB
- Results are found in tempC

We *can't* pull off the above scenario in an RDBMS because the write-times to the *temp* tables would kill us. The build-times for indexes (to support the next rule) would likewise ruin us. In Netezza however, these are *parallel* tables with *no* index structures. More importantly, the *actual* data workload will almost invariably look like this:

- Step 1 – filters and cleans the data into a *subset*
- Step 2 – works only on the new subset, creates *smaller* subset
- Step 3 – works on smaller subset, creates *even smaller* subset
- Step 4 – works only on the smallest subset, to create *even smaller* subset
- If we organize the data correctly, it never leaves the SPU, because each SPU is moving data from table to table in its *own* domain.

Now let's examine the difference between the Point-A solution and the Point-B.

Point A (Original)	Point B (Netezza)
one unit of work at a time, all instructions	deals with one instruction at time, all work units
applies all rules to all records, regardless of whether they are truly necessary	applies the each rule only to the records that count for that rule (via filter)
has to process the entire workload end-to-end	can cascade the solution into smaller, more efficient subsets of work
timed based on its ability to run once for each unit of work	timed based on its ability to run four (and only four) end-to-end bulk processes
takes 30 seconds to run for a given unit of work, and has 20,000 units of work, it will take many hours, perhaps days	for 20,000 units of work, it can apply one whole instruction set in seconds, with only four instruction sets total – finishing in minutes

The effect of this approach is ideal - and something we want to capture - for each kind of flow. We start out with a lot of data and *reduce* along the way. Each subsequent step is more efficient with less data, cleaner data and a smaller product. We should think of this as "standing on its side" the original stored procedure, such that when standing on its head, it will process one-record-at-a-time through all rules. Where on its side, it processes *all* records through *one rule*-at-a-time, reducing along the way. For those who rarely work with bulk processing, it's a different way to solve a problem.

And *very* strong kung fu.

Patterns

I'm a big fan of design patterns, and may I say, the design patterns we are accustomed to in software development have their counterparts in data warehousing. Unfortunately, we usually have to profile the data to get something of *applicable* value. For those who don't find any value in profiling, keep in mind that profiling-style activities is just about *all* our ad-hoc users ever do. They grind and churn the information to find the *business operational* patterns. What we need to be mindful of, is that the data is *supposed* to reflect the business operation. *Our* business operation. Our ad-hoc users can often show us things about our data that we never knew existed. It's worth forging and maintaining a relationship with such users rather than making it tense and tenuous.

So the patterns we can expect to detect in the data, has everything to do with the process to 'get it there'. In essence, we have a starting point for the data and the end point, and the 'what happened' is where we're losing energy and time, often to redundant and weak processing components.

First pattern we want to find is the core flow path, sometimes called the "***happy path***". What is supposed to happen to it after entering the environment, never encountering an error and landing in its final state? More importantly, what are the core processes to make this happen, and do we have any exception processes that look strangely *like* these core processes? In other words, is our exception processing *actually* the happy path? Why don't we re-characterize the happy path and make the exceptions part of another pattern, like a reusable capability of exception processing?

And in so doing, make the exceptions, you know, the *exceptions*, not the *rule*.

Case Study Short: Our team was asked to forklift and realign an existing data warehouse to eliminate its thousands of tables and thousands of stored procedures in a traditional RDBMS. Our analysis team approached the stored procedures as patterns, because they all ultimately flowed into the same downstream location. We bundled the stored procs into several major units of work, trimmed the redundant operations, intermediate tables and squeezed out the unnecessary fat. We replicated those units of work with a relative handful of lightly parameterized SQL statements in Netezza, and our work was done. Takeaway: Our existing organically grown environment has a lot of fat to trim. Trust me on this.

Case Study Short: One environment had so many servers, flows and systems that the sheer logistical complexity had everyone in a state of half-numbed catatonia. They answered simple questions with broken sentences, their voices trailing off as if living and breathing in a funerary procession. Surreal and macabre.

The principals had collectively made a decision to bring in a highly complex environment, and wanted us to assess its viability. Our report basically told them that they had a simple, straightforward processing model, but the existing implementation had grown out of control. Their approach should *not* have been to build a more powerful and complex solution without first understanding the overall process model. After examination, it turned out a lot simpler than they originally thought.

Instead of addressing the actual problem, a fairly vanilla input-process-output model, they had bought yet another underpowered environment, one that came with a lot of white-paper kool aid, and merrily proceeded down the shining path towards tomorrow. Only problem is, tomorrow never came. That was two years ago and they are *still* not in production, *still* myopically transfixed on their chosen technology.

If it *could* have solved their problem, by now it *should* have solved their problem.

"Know when to hold 'em, and when to fold 'em," Kenny Rogers in *Big Unit Gambling*.

Flow-based Thinking

When developers typically examine a problem, some tend to approach the problem they *see* rather than the problem as it actually *is*. This is cause-versus-symptom thinking, and is a form of intellectual slavery.

Some developers and application engineers live within the confines of their own systems and environments. They optimize what they know and don't usually consider integrating with other systems. Those things are so far away, and so complex, and their walls of protection higher than any English castle's, the prospect of integration seems daunting.

What if our problem not only exists within one of those systems nearest us, but *beyond* it? Many times we've dogpiled a gaggle of engineers into a conference room to talk about their issues holistically. It never surprises me how many times eyebrows are raised across a table like this. When our groups devolve into stovepipes of activity, they often form their own center of gravity. Worlds beyond their own become strange, and they don't want to meddle. It's political, you see.

A guideline of engineers is that we allow every other engineer to solve their problems in their own way. While we might be required to review their work, we won't necessarily volunteer for the duty. After all, many solutions look the same, feel the same, and the details are largely a function of comfort rather than a best-practice or compliance issue. We often fall into the trap of expecting everyone to "do the right thing" when in many cases they've been adjured to simply "get it done". The "right" way to do something might fall into the realm of ideology or personal taste.

Without hopping back on our *can-do* versus *should-do* soapbox, we need to grasp something about intersystem integration that many tend to ignore.

Data warehousing in general, but *large-scale* warehousing requires a *flow*. From the time it enters our environment until it finds either (a) a final resting place for consumption or (b) exits our environment to a final resting place – the daunting middle between the two is constrained by the rules of *flow*. It must be regarded in end-to-end form, not a series of flow components. Some environments, such as Ab Initio, allow us to put flow-based components on a graphical canvas and run the application in graphical mode. Kind of like assembling a VISIO diagram, and then punching the "go" button and watching the diagram activate *as the application*.

If we think of the Netezza appliance in this manner, that the data must move from its original location in order to arrive at our big-black-box's front door, then we have an issue regarding robust data transportation. It won't matter one whit if we can process the data *inside* Netezza in a matter of minutes, if it takes *hours* for the data to actually arrive.

Case Study Short: The data flowing into Netezza was a mere fraction of the data actually flowing out. Upon exit, it was spirited into a relational database where the results were finally derived from some high-intensity joining and summarization. While the data arrived to Netezza in relative minutes, was processed, enriched and exited also in relative minutes, the final platform took half an hour to load, another hour to process and another fifteen minutes to extract for the *next* downstream consumer – still on average a 2-hour process.

We worked with the engineers to pull these post-Netezza RDBMS integration points (largely reference data) into the Netezza machine. Once hosted, we loaded all the data within minutes, did its normal preprocessing in minutes and then executed the integrations normally done on the RDBMS. These took a grand total of *eight minutes*. We then transported the *much* lighter resulting subset to the downstream, bypassing the RDBMS altogether. The downstream was suddenly receiving its data in less than eight minutes instead of two hours.

This highlights the need to optimize the *entire* flow of data, not just the parts visible to us. The systems are supposed to work for us, and not us for them.

Do a little flow-architecture. Pop open the VISIO and draw the data's **"happy path"** – the path it normally takes when nothing goes wrong. Verify that we're doing the heavy-lifting in the right place at the right time. What's more, get *all* of the heavy-lifting into Netezza. And make sure when we're done, that only the *necessary* data has to exit the Netezza platform, and that *all* bulk processing is completed on-the-inside.

On the flip side of the flow, many data processing environments, most especially those with Ab Initio as the core processing pipeline, should seriously consider Netezza for the heaviest of the lifting. Imagine pumping data through a 32-way machine running Ab Initio, itself arguably the most efficient, high-powered SMP-based software product on the planet. Once completed, we pipe the data into Netezza and within a relatively short period of time, it is ready for consumption simply for having been loaded, and nothing more.

Then we consider what Ab Initio actually does for the application. We learn that a particularly steep curve is encountered with a Sort and Rollup operation. The sort must organize a 10-ways parallel flow of three billion records, drive this into a Rollup that will produce some two billion records of output (a "light" summary) and then forward the results to Netezza. The entire operation takes about 65 minutes to process in Ab Initio, and another 80 minutes to load, being some 700gb of data.

What we *could* do is push the entire load of 800gb to the Netezza machine, costing us some 90 minutes to load. Then perform the same summary of the data in less than ten minutes of processing time. Grand total for this flow of work is now 100 minutes, down from 145 minutes. If we were talking about a few minutes or even a low percentage, this wouldn't be worth the effort. But we've saved forty-five minutes *and* reduced the cycle by almost thirty percent. Simply by shifting the workload from one environment to another. Rebalance the power for the right fit. Some things Netezza does well, and some it doesn't do at all. Many things Ab Initio does well. In fact *really* well. Balance the power so that your Ab Initio environment and Netezza machine are partners in the tug-of-war, moving in *synergy* and not competition.

As for the lower-scale ETL environment such as Microsoft SSIS, DataStage, Informatica and others, break the workload into row-level transforms in the ETL, and then heavy-lifting in Netezza. Both environments will give high payback and the whole flow will stay healthy.

Analyze the *entire flow*. Don't imagine that any environment we have is more efficient for *very large scale* operations than the Netezza machine. As in all cases, benchmark to your own satisfaction.

Just don't *assume*.

Sweeping movement

We've noted in other sections how we will process data inside Netezza rather than just using it as a repository, or a receptacle for pre-processed information. In fact, if all we really want is query acceleration, why are we using Netezza at all? Any of Netezza's would-be competitors tout query acceleration (using the Jurassic Park preparation approach, of course). Even though the Netezza query acceleration itself will be faster than the competitors, it's always tempting to consider one.

Of course, with one of those other technologies, we won't get the robust loading of the data, and we'll need our own data processing environment (pick one) to get the data in shape for the final consumption-ready state, but no matter, our ETL application experts have this part covered (don't they?). We can load data into a competitor, even if the load is slow, and not worry a bit afterwards because the user will have a robust query acceleration experience, and that's what all of us want (don't we?)

Really?

What happens when we really need to take "one final step" inside the machine? What if the data has to be enriched with other large-scale data sources stored on the same machine? How will it fit for enriching Master Data, Reference Data, and *Whatnot* Data? Will Netezza's competitor handle integrating or enriching the incoming data with these values? Or will we need to extract them into our ETL environment for the mass integration exercise? These are all significant questions and demand an answer.

Like, uh, *now*, before we commit resources and cash.

To start, let us just say, please review Rule #10. If our final target is a system like *Oracle, Sybase, UDB, Informix, Sybase IQ,* or *SQLServer,* these platforms can perform well as *query accelerators,* if we take the time to *engineer* the schema and/or platform correctly. Star schema, snowflake, index management and housekeeping, all under our control, such as they are. The primary use-cases (we've engineered those, too) can get to the data just fine. Ad-hoc users are pretty much on their own.

If we have an competitor's technology, we can expect some degree of lethargy in the loading processes (three to four times slower), but usually quite a bit faster than their relational counterparts.

Once our data is inside, what options do we have to *process* the information? That is, perform *even one* large-scale transform? This entails invoking a SQL statement with the "insert-select-from" syntax, effectively building (either a temporary or final target) table from the contents of another.

How do any of our above non-Netezza technologies fare in this sort of endeavor, and more importantly, do they actually *need* to? If our ETL/data processing environment is feeding the storage environment, and its responsibility is to do these big-league transforms, why would we care about such things?

We spoke to some proponents of a Netezza competitor once who claimed, in a competitive POC, that if we planned to transformation inside-the-box, we should just stop there. *Everybody* knows, he claimed, that we should do transformation in the ETL layer (hence the T in ETL) and that doing it inside-the-box is not the "correct" way to do it. And it goes without saying (so he didn't say it), that if we don't do transformation in the ETL layer, it won't get done - *if we purchase his competitive product.*

So clearly, he has made his product (an SMP-based software product) such that it is dependent upon the presence of an ETL layer to perform the heavy-lifting of transform and integration.

But Netezza, as an MPP platform, has no such constraint.

We asked him whether he wanted our group to turn the project into an *ETL project,* rather than a database-centric "ELT" project. Because he was proposing that our sponsor shift the architecture so that all the integration would take place in the ETL layer. So this would make our project an "ETL Project". And if it's an ETL project, what the heck do we need their competitive database platform for? Any database would do, if the heavy-lifting is to happen in the *ETL layer*, after all.

He suddenly found himself sawing off the limb that was holding him aloft. It's always humorous when someone is selling a product, rather than a solution.

So this is why we're not part of the Netezza sales cycle, or anyone else's sales cycle. We really like what Netezza has done to solve the problems at hand. But we really liked all those other products when they were the only game in town. We have to remain product-neutral. It's the way of things. Can't you tell?

Back to in-box transformation and integration.

It is invariable, inevitable, inexorable, immutable and undeniable that we will *absolutely* need a transformation capability inside-the-box. We only kid ourselves when we imagine that we do or will not. With an SMP-based competitor, we will likely commit to the required engineering in the honeymoon phase of the original implementation. Once implemented, we will quickly bore of the tedium required to keep it running. Others come after us, perhaps wondering what we were thinking in constraining the machines to such functional, engineered rigor. As any machine *under-*performs in its assigned role, engineers will swarm. As tribal knowledge and reasoning is lost, the engineers will compromise to meet a deadline.

And the slippery slope is beneath us. It was always there, from the time we inked the contract for the non-Netezza technology. We will then start processing the data inside the machine – doing ELT-style transforms. It was never designed nor selected for this activity. Woe is already upon us, from the point of purchasing an SMP-based RDBMS to do what it was never designed to do.

Bulk transformation is about *sweeping motion* over the data. We execute a single instruction that is blasted to all data points. We have the massively parallel power to embrace an insert-only model, preserving the state of the original data and everything we did to it along the way (and embrace persistent traceability). The machine must support the integrity of the mission and its steps, otherwise we are buying into expedience, rather than the robust problem-solving and troubleshooting capabilities that Netezza provides.

Simply by turning on its power-switch.

Think about sweeping blasts of data processing, each one doing less than the one before it, but each one leveraging the results of the one before, and supporting the one after.

Stewardship in *motion*.

Testing in Peking Opera

In the movie *Kung-Fu Panda*, the master, voiced by Dustin Hoffman, challenges the main character, voiced by Jack Black, simply by saying "You are free to eat". The ensuing melee is perhaps the most entertaining Peking Opera one could ever witness, all executed with chopsticks and imagination.

While watching this, only a geek's mind would drift to what it would take to actually test this scenario against *real* martial artists. When in college, we used to watch the Saturday afternoon Peking Opera flicks, where the lead martial artist would jump from a ten-story building, fight fifty guys including a big fat guy twice his size, get shot and knifed ten times, run eight miles to the beach and repeat the scene, half of it in the water - *whew*! You get the picture.

Of course, while this is one superhuman guy clearly dealing with a problem of *scale*, how can he really pull it off on talent *alone*, and where does martial-artist talent end, and the movie-magic and choreography kick in? And how do these fellows fare within the boundaries of *true* martial arts? Jackie Chan is the king of this genre and himself is a blackbelt many times over in more than one discipline. He would *have to be*, to make it look that good, and that authentic, and *still* be acting all the while!

So when we think about testing, we need significant power when testing results of *scale*. Like Jackie Chan is able to rise above the simple fight and into choreographed entertainment, we've never had the power to do this before. We were always in the thick of the fight, very often the size and complexity of the data just kickin' our tails and takin' names. We really wanted some strong kung-fu to beat back the data.

Rising above it like Jackie Chan, to another art form, probably never occurred to us. While we're thinking about the problems in a different way, we have to think about the testing in a different way, too.

A data warehouse project is practically *all* testing. And when we're facing *scale*, with fifty virtual martial artists with guns - or just a hundred million rows of data, we either want some *power* or some *choreography*, but if we have both, it's the best of all worlds.

In practically every environment we're in, we have an original machine hosting the solution that we're migrating into Netezza, and someone will suggest that we set up a process to get all the information ready inside the Netezza machine, then package it up, push it to the original machine and test it. Over *there*.

THE NETEZZA UNDERGROUND

Uhh, isn't that where all the black-belt dudes with out-of-sync dialog live and play? Isn't that platform where our skills are a lot like a mouthy schoolkid - and we *always* get our tails kicked? But over here on the Netezza machine, we're Jackie Chan. All those guys get to come over and play in our sandbox, while we stand at the ready with two simple words.

Bring it.

No really, bring it - over here. The data. *All* the data.

We snapshot the original platform's existing source feeds, its reference data and all other resources, and copy them into the Netezza machine, to a read-only testing schema. We then take another snapshot of the existing platform's final, polished outputs, one that was produced from the source feeds we just copied and all the original platform's internal processes, and likewise host this in the Netezza machine. Now we have the source content, the target content, and all we have to do is bring them together, reconcile these two data stores and we go home happy.

Now when we produce any outputs, we can compare it using the high-speed parallel power inside the Netezza machine. The data came from the same sources, fought its way through the same reference data and error-control sieve, and we introduced it to its new master, the Netezza machine.

And now we're ready for the final test. We will pit it, in bulk, to the parallel snapshot and learn just how strong the data's kung fu really is. We can compare whole terabytes in minutes compared to the hours we would spend just porting the results to the original platform, not to mention the time to actually execute the tests.

It's kind of scary, to think about column-for-column comparison on terabyte-sized tables on an SMP-based RDBMS. That's like moving from Peking Opera to Fright Night Theater. The *horror*.

One might well ask, and appropriately so, why we don't have an entire chapter devoted to testing our data warehouse? Such information would be redundant, because as noted in the Boot Camp and introductory material, the Netezza machine wraps and circumscribes the highly mature discipline of data warehousing. The testing practices of bulk data processing are legendary and likewise mature, and don't need any additional fluff from us.

But we will provide a simple word-of-warning for any doubters out there - testing accounts for over eighty percent of our work in deploying the data warehouse. Give this area short-shrift to your own peril. The 80/20 rule applies here, in all its glory. For every 20 percent of development effort, we will spend 80 percent testing. That means for 1 day of development, 4 days of testing. We might not see it in "waterfall" form, where we spend one day in hardcore development and then spend the rest of the week testing. But it will eat away our time, we add a change here, and test it. Add a change there, and test it. Make no mistake, the agile, iterative methods are not available to us when we need to test things in scale. We will have to exercise the same patience as with any development model.

Thankfully, the Netezza platform gives us lightning turnaround on the testing, meaning that we can go much further, much faster, and with higher quality. But as we look back, we'll find that we still spent 80 percent of the time testing it. We just tested more. And better, and are more certain of the quality of the work products.

Or at least, we *should* be.

Wrapping it up

We intake staged data, marking its work product as part of a stream of work with our Audit_ID. We then perform some transforms, enrichments, integration to create new tables, not update the existing ones, so that we preserve our flow's contents and we can recover from failure. We then land the data to its final location. But wait, we're not quite done. Along the way, we discovered dirt or bad records, and likewise sank an error record into an exception or audit table for administrative review. The record we sink isn't the original data record, but contains all the information *about* the data record so we have traceability to it. On the outbound publication, we can trim these housekeeping values as the data exits.

If we need to back-out some information, we can use the Audit_ID to *retro* a data processing stream to a known state, up to and including backing out the entire work product stream.

When we need to perform wholesale cleanup – in an environment that gives us a batch window for it – we can easily clean up our target tables by remanufacturing them while using the error/audit filtration. If we need to cleanup in a continuous environment, we need to think about partitions and truncation.

When pulling data into the machine, we have lots of freedom if the intakes are each larger than a gigabyte and come all-at-once (batch style). We have to be a bit more creative if the data arrives more often and in smaller chunks (continuous style).

Before long, we'll find ourselves wearing a black-belt, and we will have strong kung fu.

MIGRATION STUFF

COMMON QUESTIONS for new Netezza customers often revolve around migration from an existing platform to its new intended home, the massively parallel quarters of our Netezza machine. Perhaps the customer has carefully executed a Proof-of-Concept, compared Netezza to the marketplace and for a fit in their enterprise and is running headlong toward the next step - migrating an existing platform to Netezza.

In fact, for many new customers, by the time the Netezza platform arrives, one or more of their existing platforms are already in their cross-hairs, targeted for replacement or redeployment in another role. They have plans and want to execute on them, and those plans might be perfectly viable. Still others have questions as to where to start and what their priorities should be.

We will plumb the prior chapters for answers in this regard, since we've already touched on all the aspects that will make the effort initially successful. The first of which is the most important, so we we'll go there first.

It's requirements-driven. What are our requirements right now? Simply to migrate the existing functionality? How will we know the scope of the effort, or when we're done? These are not particularly complex or daunting questions, but we need to ask them now. We need answers for them now.

We're probably inside of one (or more) major categories of situations.

1 - We have a need to build out a new reporting warehouse. One does not yet exist.
2 - We have an existing reporting server that we want to replace.
3 - We have an existing (formal) ETL or transport mechanism.
4 - We have no existing (formal) ETL or transport mechanism.
5 - Our reporting server receives data and is a query accelerator only.
6 - Our reporting server does post-loading data processing (in violation of Rule #10)

The more our environment grows, and runs out of power, the more we will organically nurture the elements of the above. We'll start out slow, then start to grow. We may never have gotten a chance to do #1 above, because the other situations just crept up on us. What is the most direct and risk-free path?

What dreams may come - uhh - what were those dreams, again?

What mires the migration into the weeds is the too-long pondering, perhaps perseveration, on the *existing* functionality. This is the worst phase of the migration, and is often characterized by "some professionals" as something we need to analyze into the ground before we start the process itself. I've seen people suggest months and months of analysis before tapping out one, thin line of SQL.

As noted in the book's first chapter, and later in *More On the Rules*, we can avoid this paralysis by simply committing to the idea that: What we're about to embark on is simply the next phase of work. Make this decision now - it goes like this:

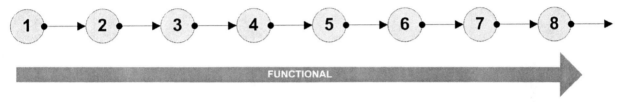

In the depiction (above) we see our development/construction process following a line of functional analysis. We iterate from the first phase, to the next, in rapid-fire iteration until we reach a conclusion. This process may take place over months, days, or even hours. What does it mean? That we gladly, perhaps gleefully threw away hundreds, perhaps thousands of lines of code, components, and ideas in favor of our new-found, hard-won functionality.

The problem is - the functional line and the technical line are married, so they appear to be the same work effort. And we worked so *hard* to achieve it. The only tangible evidence we have of all the hard work, is the final results (above) of *iteration number 8*. This is what we've delivered to the end users, it's what we've been bonused for, and it's what makes the environment be all-that-it-can-be.

And now it is out of gas, and has fulfilled its *functional* mission, but has fallen short on performance. We might fear that moving our iteration-number-8 to another platform actually throws away something, so we want to preserve it. We've been told, even assured, by our consultants and gurus, that we need to carefully re-analyze everything. So we lose nothing.

But wait, how much have we already thrown away in moving from iteration-number-1 to iteration-number-7? We don't miss any of it.

Do we?

Conversely, we know the *real* effort was in boiling down the functional path, so throwing away the only tangible result of all that work *seems* like throwing away something valuable. Our consultants have *told* us that we are throwing away something valuable, and it must all be carefully analyzed and inventoried to make sure we don't miss anything. We're convinced that we must take this course. It's something we must do.

Do we?

We have another problem, in that the engineering on the existing system has kept us running for quite awhile. We've forgotten when it was, that we stopped our development and entered the performance-engineering phase. We've worked so hard, had so many meetings, and been beaten up so many times, that the effort we've put into the most recent phases of work, has eclipsed all the hard work that ever came before it. We feel we must defend it. We simply must.

Do we?

The functionality in our environment, now that it's run out of gas, has another problem. Its *true* functionality was last seen around iteration number 5. The following iterations were all engineering exercises - rework, tweaking, tuning, etc that have led us to iteration number 8.

But how much of it is real, and how much artificial, just to support the performance needs?

The functionality is now so dense, and so tightly packed that it looks like a black hole, an object so dense that no additional functionality can escape. When we attempt to take it apart, the functionality looks more like a hairball than what we thought it was. Again, how much is real, and how much is artificial?

Our wunderkind consultants have told us that unraveling this black hole, without their assistance, could create a rift in the spacetime continuum, unless we follow their carefully crafted analysis-paralysis methodology to catalog and inventory *every single hair on the ball.*

"There are 5149 strands of hair on the ball," said Edmond Dantes, long-time prisoner.
"You've *counted* them," said the second prisoner, "But have you given them *names*?"
from *We Count the Monte Cristos, Too*

What isn't obvious, because it's largely a function of the Underground, is that we don't have to regard the artificial complexity as *real*. The hair is a *symptom*, and what's more, if we try to cut the hair to find the ball, we might go all the way in and find that there *is* no ball. It's *all* hair.

Now what?

"There is no ball," said the hairless kid with a spoon - *The Waitrix*

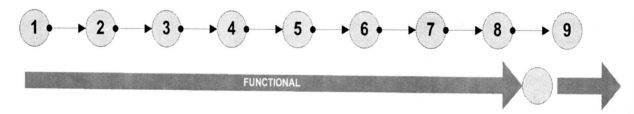

So now we're ready for iteration number 9 (depicted above) and there *will* be a functional analysis, albeit a brief one, before proceeding. The analysis should not immediately involve HOW we're currently providing WHAT the users want to see. We already know *what* they want to see, because we've already provided them with a published interface. You know, the data mart or the output target tables that we've been loading all those lonely nights and weekends, and the ones we talk about whenever someone suggests we've missed an SLA.

But consider what we've really done. Functionally speaking, we've moved from iteration-number-8 to iteration-number-9. We may have taken a new phase to make it happen, but it's just another phase, and we should treat it this way. In fact, we should embrace an iterative model to rollout our new environment. Soon, we'll wrap iteration number 9, then 10, 11, etc and we will have long forgotten the *artificial* finality of the iteration number 8. We won't miss it.

Will we?

The best example of this project effect is in the "airplane analogy," which in a nutshell, is how we treat our projects (as airplanes) and our requirements (as passengers). When we first start the project, we load the requirements onto the airplane. When it pushes off from the gate, we discover (or are given) more requirements, so we put these passengers in a jeep and run them out onto the tarmac to load into the airplane. When in flight, something more is needed, so we helicopter the passengers onto the airplane, and before we know it, we're adding passengers to the airplane *even as it is rolling up to the gate.*

A better way: schedule multiple flights. This is the essence of iterative development.

Here's an example: Let's say I roll out iteration 1 of a production environment, with the plans to roll out iteration 2 rather quickly behind it, and iteration 3 quickly behind that. If we push out one iteration after another, with planned releases and a solid delivery highway (configuration management) for our work products, we have effectively set up a delivery-based architecture that is responsive to change. If we find that some change is needed, or even a change in direction, this may only constitute iteration 124 of all the iterations that came before it. The releases become a regular, automatic backbone operation of the environment. Nobody fears change. The environment is responsive to change, it exists with the *expectation* of it.

What do we need up front?

Firstly, commit to some basic componentry and capability maturity inside the Netezza machine. Spend a little time setting up an intake capability that will serve for more than one application or source. We might need a simple staging/intake schema (for now). We might need a more advanced intake strategy, like multiple cookie-cutter intake schemas that face multiple, disparate sources. For intake, start out slow and bite off what we can chew in a single swallow.

Once inside, the data lands in an intake (staging) schema for data-inventory assimilation, then undergoes set-based transformation on the way to its home in one or more schemas representing

(a) Master Data
(b) Reference Data
(c) Operational (single-day-integrated-but-unfiltered) data
(d) User-centric consumption points (marts).

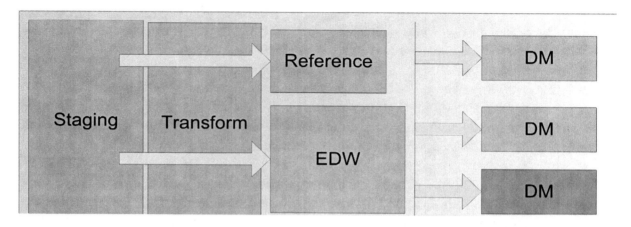

The depiction (above) is only one possible configuration. We might have multiple intake schemas to face multiple disparate sources with distinct, non-overlapping needs. We might have additional temporary work tables in the Transform schema that persist for a given day or time period. We might have additional user-facing tables in the marts that serve user-application needs but do not interact directly with the upstream flows or schemas. The configuration is flexible and malleable.

What we should not do, is by default manufacture application-centric flows inside the machine, unless we intend to roll out a separate machine for each application, which is often not the case.

If we don't have a formal data transportation and/or ETL environment, all we need to do is get the data within lasso-distance of the Netezza machine, either by directly landing it into a flat-file located on a mounted volume within the Netezza Linux host's visibility, or we can follow one of the several intake scenarios noted in *Loading Up With Stuff*. Likewise if we have systems that can understand ODBC/JDBC to push data into Netezza, we can mix and match any of the intake protocols noted in this book to affect the data assimilation.

If we already have formal ETL environment, we need to make some strategic decisions as to how we'll leverage it in the future. Likewise point it to our intake schema - with a caveat. How much set-based processing in the ETL environment is better-hosted inside Netezza? If we have a high-powered bulk environment like Ab Initio, it's probably not worth an immediate review (unless this system is running out of hardware power and we're at a strategic decision-point juncture already).

If we have a lower-powered environment, we need to review the implementation to discover (a) row-level cleansing and (b) set-based transformations. We will want to separate these now.

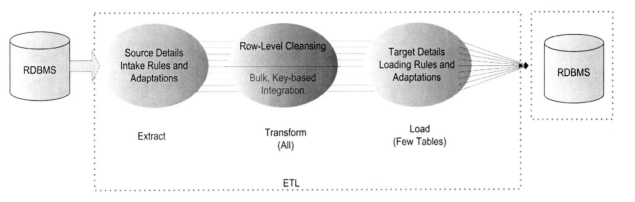

In the depiction (above) we see a common ETL configuration with the data transportation, row-level cleansing and bulk-integration happening prior to arrival on the RDBMS. Upon arrival, the data is load-ready and by definition consumption-ready, since we don't plan to do any additional processing once it lands.

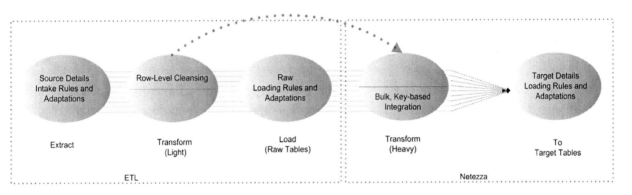

In the depiction (above) we have extricated the bulk integration from the ETL environment and placed it inside Netezza. We then have data transportation and row-level cleansing on the ETL side, taking a large load of work from the ETL and moving it into a massively parallel platform. For the ETL-side migration of set-based or key-based transforms, these are typically very mature and visually obvious. Simply move them into the Netezza machine and replicate their functionality with common SQL-based joins.

Can we pull apart the row-level cleansing from the set-based bulk operations? If we can, we should do so and leave the row-level cleansing in the ETL environment. We would then reconstruct the set-based operations inside Netezza. What is the scope of this? *Anything* that does a key-based transform. This includes lookups, cross-reference scrubbing, Reference Data enrichment and most importantly - anything that deals with Master Data or integration to larger data stores.

THE NETEZZA UNDERGROUND

The Happy Path

"Find a happy place. *Find A Happy Place.* **FIND A HAPPY PLACE**!" - Peach the Starfish, *Finding Nemo*.

Whenever we're unraveling the hairball and re-implementing it into our new machine, we'll find that what we *thought* was functionality is *really* a lot of performance tuning and engineering that wraps *around* our functionality. These will include exception processing as well as performance compromises. We must strip away all this and find the happy path.

What is the happy path? It's the path our data would normally take if there weren't any errors, performance problems or other issues. When data arrives, where is it *supposed* to go? What is our operational mission? This is the happy path, where we expect the majority of our data to travel and ultimately land in its end state.

Then we find exceptions, and harness them. Any performance issues, we deal with them, as optimizations, not as engineering exercises. When we do this, we'll find a repeatable pattern. Intake, Transform, Publication. In the Transform section, we'll find opportunities to peel off erroneous data (into an administrative harness). We'll then correct, integrate and perform any other set-based activity we must.

I've seen developers say they'll never load and process anything unless they can load and process *everything*. In processing *scale*, such sentiments are only naive musings. We cannot easily explain to our users that we decided not to process a few billion records for the sake of a few thousand. It doesn't wash on paper or in the status meetings.

Carve out the exceptions. Deal with them administratively. Harness the exceptions with rules, instead of allowing the exceptions to *become* the rule.

More Power

Likewise with the advent of Netezza UDFs, we'll find additional candidates within our advanced algorithms. Whether these appear as row-level calculations, or as inter-row mathematics and logic, we should review them as candidates for moving into Netezza so we can execute on a larger scale. After all, the UDF can execute for row-level or inter-row / set-based calculations with greater power than the common ETL platform. It scales faster and with more consistency, too.

Does this mean we need to re-host our Master and Reference data into Netezza? It definitely means we'll need a *copy* of it in Netezza. Whether we periodically refresh it or re-host it entirely is a matter of degree. We know of one shop that performed copies of their Master and Reference data into Netezza. At first these were full copies, then incremental, and then someone realized that the only place they ever *actually* used the data was inside Netezza. So they re-hosted it and stopped worrying about its regular replication.

The question arises then - *where* are we managing the master and reference data, and is this the *right* place for it? One shop decided to ensconce a master data management system, and had all the strategy worked out until someone asked the simplest of questions: Where will we store it? Who will need to use it? What are the mechanics of its outtake? In each case, the consistent answer was that we should store it where we will use it. Since "using it" means set-based integration and validation, the RDBMS was the wrong place to put it. Netezza was the right place to put it. Logic and math will drive us to this inexorable conclusion.

So in reviewing data transportation, examine it holistically. Are we already punting data around inside our system enclosure in a panting effort to keep up with under-powered resources? Stop the madness, push all the integration data into the Netezza machine once and for all and give our networks some breathing room.

Before jumping directly into the bulk-processing, we need to consider the outputs. If we have no existing warehouse or downstream dependencies, then publication (today) is no more than white-paper expectations of our users. If we have an existing constituency, we cannot afford to break their stuff. We should start with their outputs and work backward toward the sources. It is easier to do this than attempt to drive the sources toward the outputs, because the outputs already serve a purpose. If we have a purpose-in-place, we need to build out the warehouse to serve it. We shouldn't necessarily build it *only* to serve those outputs, but we should keep those outputs in our headlights as a priority. Shortchanging them is a bad plan. If the purpose of the warehouse is to toss and replace a bunch of broken outputs, then don't give them a first thought, much less a second thought.

As for what's in the middle, we have the situation of simple query acceleration (#5 above) or we have some internal data processing (#6) to migrate. Query acceleration is easy to put in place, because we're simply landing the data. We can structure the information with distribution keys or other optimizations for a best fit. Migrating stored procedures for internal data processing requires a little more effort.

For the stored procedures, we usually have two flavors. One is a series of insert/select statements that drive toward a conclusion. Migrating these to Netezza is usually only a matter of syntax for a straight conversion. The second is a cursor-based scenario that reads from one entity, sends it through a series of rules, and puts it back. In the *Boot Camp Stuff* - **SIMD** section, we laid out the differences between this model and the MPP model we're shooting for. In Strong Kung Fu, we talked about **Standing the Problem On Its Side** section. Both of these sections have the necessary insights to help us take cursor-based operations and convert them to a stronger, set-based form.

However - for *both* of these stored-procedure scenarios, as well as the ETL re-host, take a few steps back and review the happy-path of the flow. We need to capture what the core data flow should look like rather that just re-hosting the existing flows.

Case Study Short: We reviewed a set of over one hundred stored procedures, each with a subtle difference. What this process revealed was that over half of the procedures had been cut-and-pasted from a common stored procedure. They were completely redundant except for some basic parameters, so we consolidated these into a common procedure. Then we examined the remainder and discovered that only three of them handled the actual flow of data, and over half of this logic was redundant between them. We also discovered that within this flow, the majority of the other stored procedures were being dynamically identified and invoked - only for exception processing.

In essence, the vast majority of procedures were snippets of code to support exception processing. We then consolidated and simplified all of this logic into a single flow with an exception-capture capability. We reduced hundreds of stored procedures into a single, manageable and visible flow of work. It likewise removed hundreds of intermediate temp-tables and supporting structures.

Artificial complexity evaporates with Netezza in the house.

The point of all this, is that we need to review the entire environment, its intended purposes, goals and priorities, and reproduce the *functionality* in the new environment. We're not porting stored procedures and ETL operations. We're porting *functionality*.

As the functionality emerges, we'll want to focus on building capability assets as mentioned in *Data Warehouse Stuff*, concerning **Rule #10.** These include (or grow into) Transportation, Intake, Transformation, Integration, Publication, Error Control, Data Versioning, Housekeeping Operational Reporting and Control, Metadata-based management, to name a few. None of these are trivial when dealing with large-*scale* data. We need to develop capabilities around them so that our environment starts out in an adaptive mode and drives toward adaptability as an architectural priority.

By architecturally separating our **capabilities** from our application **functionalities**, we effectively allow our applications to become *consumers of capabilities*, with still other capabilities available to support, administer and oversee the applications as a whole.

As we're building all this, we need some ability to test our work. We strongly suggest that a snapshot of the preprocessed data be hosted on the Netezza machine in a separate, static schema. Likewise (in this same schema) put a static snapshot of the output results that would be produced by the existing system, given the same snapshot of the inputs. All these should be stored in common SPU-based tables, so we can leverage their parallel power.

Now our job is very objective. All we have to do is take the snapshot of the inputs, run it through our new processes, and produce the same outputs. Once we produce these, also into a parallel Netezza table, we can now compare them (column for column) with the snapshot of the outputs. We might need to add some more intelligence to the test cases, such as sequencing and the like, but either way we will test the outputs on the Netezza machine itself, and will not port the test results back into the existing environment to compare the results there. If the existing environment is already too slow to compete with Netezza, why would we enslave our testing processes to it?

Once we have a clean bill of health on this initial set of tests, we need to pull yet another snapshot of source data from the existing system, along with a snapshot of output results, and host it in yet another schema, preserving the original snapshot. Then we re-test our work on these new data stores. Once these are solid, we can open up the pipeline for an actual feed of data, in the same intake-form that we would experience in a live environment. We then test the outcome against this feed.

The tests themselves are very simple to setup and execute. What is not obvious, is that we will spend the majority of our time testing the outputs. It is best to have a correctly-powered system for this activity.

A pitfall exists here that occurs in all new data warehouse implementations, not just those with

Netezza. Many shops will purchase a high-powered Netezza machine for production (like a 10200 or above) and then get a 10100 (or two) for development. The 10200 will sit in the production enclosure, humming with all that power - but nothing to do - while the developers work on the smaller machines to produce the functionality. While the power of the 10100 is significant, it is still quantifiably half that of the 10200. This is a common scenario in data warehouse development, as the people spending the money on the systems want the power focused for their production environment. It does not serve the initial development work, however, because of all the Netezza power available in the house, only one third of it is being leveraged for development work. (e.g. 2 parts in the 10200 and 1 part in the 10100).

Another sticky issue arises in that the production machine is installed inside a protected enclosure while the development machine is "where the action is". But the developers also need the ability to configure the production machine for later implementation, and to shake out their assumptions on how to properly package and deliver their work products. This is much more difficult to validate with the target machine sitting behind the firewall.

To mitigate this situation and to accelerate development, we should *initially* install both of these machines into the development environment in order to get past the first-push development curve. This also allows us to set up an implementation and configuration protocol between the machines that will serve as our work-product delivery highway for the future. Once the configuration is in place and the majority of our testing is behind us, we can deploy the larger machine as our production machine, knowing it is properly configured to receive our work products.

In Configuration Stuff, we provided some insights as to what it means to deliver once, then keep delivering, because we have set up a process for rapid delivery, not just rapid development. This moves us past the *common* developer agility so coveted by tactical technologists across the globe. This sets us up for *architectural agility*. Is it harder to do? Sure, but not significantly so. The investment in time and effort now is worth the payoff we receive each time we meet a deadline without fanfare or grief.

The Target Rules

Whenever we migrate, we have one and only one primary priority, that we don't disrupt the experience of our existing targets. I've seen whole methodologies focus heavily, almost myopically, on the processes, components and artifacts that drive toward the conclusion, that is, the target tables.

May I say, *forget all that stuff*. For now, anyhow. We have a functional specification in place, it's the target tables. Replicate their output, and we're done, or at least mostly done. *Why attempt to do it the same way the former environment did it?* We want to do it another way now, the Netezza way. So for all those who would claim that we need to focus on all the little parts that "get us there", I say *poppycock*. And for good reason, because in case we missed it, *many* of those little parts are artificial enhancements to the core functionality that were put there only to prop up a performance weakness in the old system. And no, we don't want to take any of that stuff with us.

What we want to do, is simply this:

characterize the targets and work backwards, toward the source

It is the most effective way to guarantee that everything we build will have a purpose, and will fulfill **what** the users want. The difference here, is in **how** we do it. We don't do it the old way.

Think about it. If we start from the source, we might throw away the majority of the data. If we start from the target, we must map how every column arrived - in flow form. This is the most effective way to know that every target column has a place, and when we can leave source columns behind rather than carrying them forward only to throw them away later.

Steps to a happy migration from an existing platform:

Inside the new machine, set up a configuration control environment, possibly including separately configured schemas for hosting the static snapshots of test data, intake, transformation, reference data, master data, operational data and application/consumption marts.

Such a configuration will set up the schemas so that we can host both development and quality-assurance versions of them, understanding that each schema represents a decoupled component asset or capability that can be separately tested and promoted.

Review the existing outputs. **Work backwards from there.** We have to support existing outputs, and these may be the only reason for the *warehouse's* existence.

Set up test cases on the Netezza machine. From the existing environment, we capture a snapshot of the source information and the final outputs. Hosted on the Netezza machine in its own schema, our testing will execute in massively parallel form rather than on the original platform.

Review the data transportation mechanism. Either setup a simple intake protocol or point the existing ETL to the Netezza machine. Ideally intake to a schema that is dedicated to the source.

Without an ETL environment, send the data raw to the Netezza machine, into the given intake schema. Do *both* row-level cleansing and integration it inside-the-box.

With an ETL environment, break apart the row-level cleansing and the bulk integration, and re-host the bulk integration inside the Netezza machine. Keep data transportation and row-level cleansing inside the ETL environment.

Regard data transportation holistically. Copy (or re-host) any data that is part of the integration stream (lookups, cross-references, master or reference data etc.) into Netezza for this purpose. It is better to plan for how these schemas will look now, because we'll need to focus a deliberate set of housekeeping and reconciliation functions on these data stores separately from the primary flows of information.

For continuous operations, setup the appropriate Netezza data structures to support frequently arriving inbound information per the insights in *Continuous Stuff.*

When converting ETL-based bulk integration, initially replicate the functionality of what it does today. Then refactor the work for a more holistic approach to all internal "ELT" flows.

When porting the functionality of stored procedures, refactor cursor-based operations into set-based operations, and test their outputs against the baseline snapshot. Likewise take serial SQL-statement sequences of insert/select functions, consolidate and port them functionally into Netezza.

Do not knee-jerk port any cookie-cutter or cut-and-paste procedures. Find the common pattern and functionally reproduce it.

As this is moving, take the time to refactor the rehosted ETL integration and new stored procedure functions into a holistic flow, trimming the fat and redundancy.

In the final analysis, the above refactoring can occur with incredible speed and turnaround, so it is important that this activity be executed by a smaller, focused team rather than a very large one.

Once the flows are smoothed out and the patterns captured, delegate any additional conversions or testing and push the functionality toward closure.

The migration to Netezza is often a very short ride if all we do is fire-and-forget. The problem with such an approach is that we miss extraordinary opportunities to install the things we really want out of the environment, such as operational control and architectural resilience, that are elusive in an underpowered environment.

We can certainly capture and deploy all the prior system's functionality, and then muscle past the sticking points, but this is no more long-term than what our prior environment offered before. Amazingly, even though Netezza offers us the power to accelerate into the future, some shops prefer to slowly stride, or even stumble.

Our clients ask us in no uncertain terms to help them Get Things Right the first time. But it's not really a good formula to get things right for the *first* time, because this implies that the first time is the *only* time that counts. What about the *next* time, and the next? Don't we want to get things right for *those* times too?

Laying down some infrastructure, like a delivery highway, goes a long way to make sure that our first delivery and every one to follow - is as good as the first, if not better. So as we analyze our existing environment and move toward Netezza, let's be good stewards of the opportunity and make things better than they were before.

We have the power now.

Let's use the power for the *best*, and not just for the "acceptable".

"Sounds like migration is a lot of re-engineering work," said the Netezza tire-kicker.

"No, it's actually *de-engineering* work," said the Enzee.

- Overheard in the Underground catacombs just outside the entrance to the Enzee sanctuary.

OF ALL THE things one might take from this book, we would hope that *more* knowledge of the vendor's product would be one of them. As we noted in the front-matter, people who don't already own a Netezza machine probably wouldn't get much out of this book anyhow, but if you're really looking to kick the tires, it can help. People have many questions about the technology and about data warehousing in general, and appliances in particular. It feels a lot like an underground. We might walk around in the dark tunnels by firelight, hoping to find answers but find only clues, glyphs on the walls, or red-herring warnings placed on the bricks over our heads that say "Turn back!" Of course, Netezza's competitors put those red-herring warnings up there. Didn't they? Or did they? The underground is filled with mystery, isn't it? Even people we trust, and trust a great deal, might align with the red-herrings because it's safe to do so. It seems safe. The underground is a scary place.

Also in case one hadn't noticed, it's a fun technology to use and just as fun to talk about. I'm a big fan, but I also have other vendors that I mix-and-match in the data processing zone. For us, in the large-scale-data business, only handful of vendors play in the space, and of those a whole network of information is available.

But of those, a whole host of information is also *missing*, because the people who use these products are relatively rare and intentionally silent. Their data warehouses compete in a niche that has very high stakes. Using a high-powered product like Netezza is a competitive advantage. They won't readily admit to their competitors what technology they use to compete against them.

This is another factor that makes the underground a quiet place. Eerily quiet, sometimes.

But the big black box is still a rising star in the marketplace, and while we certainly don't mind giving it a lift here and there, we also don't mind folks calling up and asking to solve their big-data problems, because it's what we do. If you bought this book because there's a Netezza machine in your shop, think about what the appliance genre means, and where Netezza fits.

Storage - we can store data just about anywhere right? But can we store it *fast*? Pound-for-pound (or is that pound-sterling for pound-sterling, and dollar-for-dollar?) nothing beats Netezza's intake speed.

Query acceleration - we can get data back out of the box *en masse* at network-choking velocity, so it handily competes with any other appliance or software product that does query acceleration alone,

Very large-scale bulk integration and data processing - yes, mainframe-scaled processing power with a fraction of the footprint. Massively parallel machines solve problems in ways that are unavailable on SMP platforms.

Creative data structures - we can actually apply and persist exotic data structures that add extraordinary value, navigation and integration to our otherwise disconnected data stores

Scalability, adaptability, stability - in short, *capability* to solve large-scale problems in record time with little overhead and high confidence, with long term resilience.

Architecture-centric performance - where the appliance architecture does the heavy lifting that our overworked engineers do today.

Enterprise interoperability - with our existing systems, storage, backups, you name it.

Low-to-no administration - relatively speaking, of course, our primary administrative problems will be found in our applications, not the machine itself

Seriously powerful visibility - to the patterns in our sea of data. In ways that we could never harness it before.

Of all the things that the appliance does well, it definitely does well what it was designed to do, and that's circumscribing decades of hard-won bulk-data processing, data warehousing and business intelligence capabilities into an easily configured, highly powerful platform. One has to merely browse the TDWI site or visit a shop with a mature data warehouse to realize that many complex and daunting patterns repeatedly emerge - all of which require strong capabilities that are already available inside Netezza when we flip the power switch.

Okay, enough hype and all that. People ask what the product does and we say it solves your hardest problems. If they then define their hardest problems as thus-and-so outside of Netezza, so be it. They don't need Netezza.

But if they have large-scale information problems, Netezza really *does* solve their hardest problems. Once an enterprise goes large-scale, there's no turning back, and the horizon looks more like a precipice without some real processing power. Who wants to buy a mainframe? Or jump into another *highly* expensive SMP platform that only *promises to approach* what Netezza delivers on day one?

Very often when we realize that we've grown into a big-data shop, it really is too late to turn back. The engineers have worked diligently to prop up our underpowered and overwhelmed technologies until they have officially and completely run out of gas. The time to have made a proactive decision is long past.

But will we make a reactive decision in the wrong direction? Will we throw more tactical money down a rabbit-hole to support the underpowered technology? Or will we just make the commitment, embrace the problem for what it really is, and run with it?

It is the pain of this decision that sometimes paralyzes people, because the consequence of failure is so high, and the consequence of doing nothing is even higher. A misstep could mean millions of misplaced dollars right away, and much more over time, and nobody likes to make that kind of decision in the dark.

And nobody likes to get their information from the underground.

So here's to those who need a little more info, and hopefully you've found a little more here. If you've found too much, we didn't mean to overload. But hey, that's all part of the spirit of the outtake.

We've also called the machine a "big black box" from its outward appearance, and some might take this nomenclature to the next level, saying that it's *internal* stuff and implementations are so mysterious that "black box" takes on a meaning for the inside of the machine as well. Not so, and hopefully even *less* so after reading this book's contents.

Many years ago, the discussion of cathedrals and ivory towers versus farmers markets and bazaars was all the rage. The *cathedral*, one argued, kept things close and dictated to its user base what they will get, and be *happy* with it, doggone it. The *market* model, on the other hand, has a lot of contributors and interactions, leveraging the collective strength for a broader base of lift.

"I've entered the Collective and shan't return," Jean-Luc Picard, *Data Trek, Last Contact*

The drawback of the cathedral, is the artificial illusion of control, forsaking true user loyalty. People love to hate the ivory tower. When the users ask for more stuff, the people in the tower hold a meeting, sip Scotch and announce, "Let them eat cake," or perhaps, "Let them drink soda."

One of the drawbacks of the vanilla *market* model is its lack of purpose-driven goals. After all, the people just sort of, you know, *collaborate* on *stuff* with no particular direction or deadline. Without purpose and accountability, the ivory tower says, the people cannot have hope. Without freedom, the market-mongers say, there is no progress. In the *market*, therefore, things arise on their own time, if at all. It does not by definition or requirement embrace the spirit of capitalism, therefore doesn't capitalize on anything. Many proponents of the bazarre-model live a life of vicarious idealism, "taking one for the team", but not taking any money home for it. But in a capitalist marketplace, an unfunded idea is a non-viable idea. It will die on the vine, starved for attention because nobody works for free.

We see this effect in major service providers who attempt to build internal products to support their business focus. An example is a major service provider attempting to build an application development environment for internal and external use. Since this product was not the focus of the service provider's actual marketplace presence, its project managers had a tough time staffing it and keeping it staffed. The good developers were always called away to support clients, causing a natural gravity of the bad developers to work on the product. In the end, the quality of the product suffered. No money, no sponsorship, no traction. The project invariably dies.

Netezza's version of this situation is *very* different, in that it actually *elicits* the primal force in the business and technical mind, that is to be a part of something that is bigger, that is real, and that naturally engenders a sense of belonging. In addition, we see this elastic, slingshot effect of delivering value to the open market, generating a value-added revenue stream while entering a circle of support and camaraderie. One can step into the public eye while remaining a part of the whole. The whole gleefully cheers the successes of its own.

Yes, this EnZee ecosystem is an interesting place. An environment where the users really love the product, embrace like family those who have joined their clan, and really like to talk about what they're doing with it.

"When the moon hits your eye, like a big pizza pie, that's amore' " - *Dean Martin.*

I recall the CEO of a product company saying almost wistfully that he wanted his user base to *love* his product and *love* his company. This desire for marketplace *love* seemed so odd, perhaps even arrogant to place as a bullet point in a corporate goal, whether unstated or not. In fact, this particular sentiment and strong *desire* to achieve it, caused the sales staff and leadership to do strange things, such as being marketing-averse. Keep in mind that in a marketing model, one must generate a dissonance, even a dissatisfaction in the heart of a potential buyer. To the point that we cannot live without their product, even if we've only heard of it five minutes ago! It's this "creation of discontent" that is anathema to someone who deliberately wants to elicit love. We see this as no less unseemly than the college jock who sets his eyes on a pretty, but elusive, girl and states that he will "get her to love him" as though it's an achievable goal.

But if the love just *happens*, if for no better reason than the object of love is worthy, nobody has to state it as a goal. What *makes* the object of love worthy? What about a Netezza machine, just metal, disk drives and firmware, could possibly elicit *love*?

The EnZee community is a lot like this. People are loyal because it's fun to be loyal. They love the technology because it's loyal back to them. It doesn't break, complain or betray them. It is consistent, deterministic and keeps its promises. On the people side, the vendor's employees, from the inside out, carry a contagious enthusiasm.

Where's the love? The EnZee ecosystem is really about the people, and the spinoff products are simply an effect. This isn't odd when we consider that in reality, the community is loyal to the success of the whole, and the spinoff products are their contribution, an expression of that loyalty. Does it have to be all that touchy-feely? Nahh. People participate for their own reasons. It's just great that the participation has its own reward.

As for the little eyes and ears at the end of each chapter, we're adjured to **look**-and-**listen** in the underground. It's awfully frightful in the catacombs, especially when the firelight is dancing on the walls, making all kinds of scary shapes.

Was that a dinosaur over there? It's awfully *blue.*

Not to worry, as your guide to shine light in the darkness, rest assured that this book has intended to bring stadium-strength sodium-vapor lamps to illuminate the problems and their solutions. Keep in mind, however, that such lamps have a kind of ramp-up time, so they might not be full strength by the time you finish the book. Ideally, thought, the lamps will continue to gather in strength long after the reader has put the book down.

Best of luck in all you do, and keep the pump (of data flowing!)

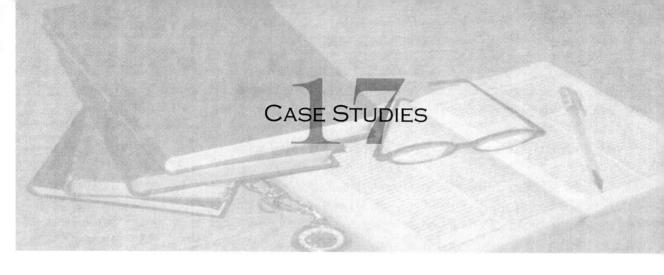

CASE STUDIES

THROUGHOUT THE prior pages, we continually promised some case studies and deeper dives, so here we go. The Netezza-based case studies are so labeled, while the others use various technologies as a backdrop to make a point. Otherwise, what's the point?

All the case studies are real, but as noted before, the names and scenarios have been changed (or modified enough) to protect the guilty. The innocent are mostly in witness protection programs.

Netezza Case study – Proof Of Concept (POC)

Part 1: At one client site, we worked out a competitive proof-of-concept between Netezza and several other competitors. We focused on the principles suggested herein, that we should minimally focus on the processing needs that client was using today, and additionally focus on those the client desired to use tomorrow. By forming the POC rules around this, the other vendors thought we were shaping the protocol to favor Netezza, but after review with the client principals, they discovered the truth - the POC rules really were in place to find the right fit, so put up or shut up.

Ahh, well, the nature of a competitive POC brings out the - er - *competition* in all of us, no? So this POC reduced to what could be described as a "hosing down the raised floor with testosterone" in no uncertain terms. It was strange to see grownups trying to engage in a footrace rather than a technical, thinking exercise. There's simply no accounting for the nature and outcome of a competition.

After the smoke cleared, the results were in, and while the Netezza platform had all the best results, the other two had results that were still acceptable to the client. One problem remained, in that we had proposed that we could get the Netezza environment up and running for them, with a working prototype of their warehouse, in about two calendar months. Our experience with the other two platforms revealed that a timeframe of three calendar months was more appropriate. The client asked us why this was the case.

On the Netezza platform, we explained, one of the test-runs would take about 5 minutes while on the nearest competitor it would take about fifteen. If we multiply this by say, 100 cycles of iterative testing, we could show that the Netezza testing would complete in one day, where the competitor's testing would complete in three days. Multiply this by the many threads of work, plus the conversion of a number of stored procedures, and this inflation is pretty consistent. The one-to-three ratio is an *inflation* of the timeline from the *inside out*, not bolted on to the end.

We're not altogether certain why this needed an explanation. We have here a fast platform, and a slow platform, and there's a question as to whether this factor would affect the project's delivery timeline?

Seriously?

We could offer several other examples, such as two long-distance runners, one is three times faster than the other one, and will finish the marathon in one-third the time. We're not talking about bolting additional time or mileage to the slower performer. His performance will be evident with each step he takes, and for each three steps the faster runner takes. It's just math, but it's an analog-stretch, not a bolt-on.

The takeaway here, was that we did not stretch the timeframe or cost by a factor of three, but by a factor of fifty-percent. In other words, we were willing to split the difference and work harder to close off the time frame. With Netezza, we still would have worked hard, but we could have performed more testing in more ways with the additional power. As it stood with the slower competitor, we performed the standard tests and did a standard delivery. It arrived on time, on budget and in ship shape. The users loved it.

Within six months, the client called us back for performance tuning and engineering. We're still working with them on it. We know that if we had installed Netezza, we would never had heard from them again, or at least not so soon.

One may well ask of us -

"If the time line is longer and you will make more consulting dollars to install it, why wouldn't you recommend the slower technology anyhow? It seems in your best interest as a consulting firm?"

"And with that, if you will be called back sooner to engineer and tune the slower technology, it seems in your best interest to recommend it, seeing that you will get more consulting dollars for this activity?"

All of the above are excellent questions and betray a pervasive industry truth. Believe it or not, some people actually *do* champion inferior technologies because it will allow them to charge more for their installation, implementation, maintenance and troubleshooting. Others who champion superior technologies, will also champion inferior *methodologies* for the same reason. One can make more money doing a so-so job over and over. At least, so I'm told. So why wouldn't *we* recommend the same? Aren't *we* interested in making money, too?

This is a question we would find asked in the Underground, where purveyors of various technologies sell their wares with a variety of agendas in mind. Some of them align with their customer's actual data processing needs. Some do not. The Underground is a scary place.

Part 2: At one client site, a group called us in to review their environment. Running on underpowered technology, also not optimally configured, their people swarmed around the systems to keep them operational, and barely fulfilled their SLAs, re-living one breathless, white-knuckled weekend after another.

We suggested that their environment needed reconfiguration, which started the whole process of discovering what technology might serve a new configuration. The client had heard of Netezza, but feared that the internal technology-approval uptake for the purchase would kill their delivery timelines. They needed answers soon. And fixes soon.

This might sound like your shop. It is a very common state of affairs. "Soon" is rarely Right Away and never Soon Enough. The question I could ask anyone in this condition, "If you knew it would take you a year to get into another technology, would you have taken this path a year ago, and if so, what would be your expectations today?"

This might sound like a "time machine sales technique" but it's really not. People rarely think in terms of how much time things *actually* take, only how much time they'd *like* it to take. People who start adding up the numbers realize that any solution is months, perhaps a year away, so they never engage the process at all. Too much time, too much money. Life's too short, and all that.

As it turned out, another division had recently completed a proof-of-concept where Netezza had wiped the floor with its nearest competitors. Hands-down it had cleaned the clocks – literally – of the other appliance offerings, coming in at less than ten percent of the overall clock times of the next-fastest, hot-on-the-heels competition. Can you imagine browsing a spreadsheet of queries, loads and extracts, where Netezza is measuring in (low) minutes and seconds while the other competitors are measuring in *hours*? I made a reference to Jurassic Park earlier, and trust me, this differences in clock times *felt* like geologic-scale measurement.

The outcome of this POC was the dramatic selection of Netezza as the "preferred" technology. All this was happening in parallel to our current effort. When we found out about it, everyone in our client's department was excited to see something new, *really* new and different enter their shop.

More interesting, was the drama around the POC exercise. I did not understand why so much emotion interlaced their review of the numbers. Actually, that's a lie – I *did* understand it. Down the hallway from this POC group, in the prior year yet *another* group had completed a POC with the same technologies, and had not chosen Netezza. Rather, they chose the Jurassic competitor. I wondered why this was the case, when I realized that perhaps they were planning on using the technology *Jurassic Park style* – hours and hours of crunching to coalesce the results into a nimble cube or mart.

But after listening to their conversations, it became clear that this second group had not asked the right questions on the POC. They had only asked the questions concerning *query acceleration and no further.* A word on query acceleration – *all the technologies do it.* With a little engineering we can make practically any RDBMS a hot competitor. Not *holistically*, of course, just the query acceleration. The second group really needed a lot of crunching, but had not leveraged or planned on their ETL environment to do so, and the more they backed this stuff into the ETL environment to get the necessary lift, the more they realized that they had under-specified the ETL environment's hardware. The ETL is a software product too, and it needs hardware, lest we forget.

In the end, it's still just engineering. The hard part (that's *really* hard part) is getting the data into a consumable state of existence. This requires two major powerhouse capabilities – loading and transformation. Without the ability to intake the data, we have a bottleneck. Without the ability to transform and integrate the data quickly, we have an even bigger bottleneck. For those of you with Ab Initio, the data movement, transform and integration stuff is under control. But attaching a racehorse like Ab Initio to a poor performing technology (for database loading) completely dishonors our investment in Ab Initio. In fact, the rabid evangelists of the poor-performing database solution will invariably blame Ab Initio for our data loading woes. We know this is impossible, of course, but it won't stop the mud-slinging. And this is where it crosses the boundary of the technical to the political, and sometimes to the surreal.

In this particular case, the political heat was like a furnace. We discovered, once the smoke cleared, Netezza was chosen, a contract signed and hardware on the way. We also learned that a catalyst to this outcome was the state-of-affairs of the "second team". They had already installed the slower competitor into production. And *from day one* were not meeting their SLAs. Now that's a hard pill to swallow, especially when another technology was reviewed alongside it, and now all is revealed that the first POC did not ask the right questions. And even now wasn't getting the right answers.

In fact, they weren't getting any answers at all.

What are the right questions? I've already mentioned it before, but the first questions out of the gate had better be centered on the subject matter of *how does it handle what we're doing right now?*

This seems like the simplest question to ask. Why would we buy a product that cannot do the things we're *doing right now*? More importantly, why aren't we asking the questions akin to what we want to do in the *future*, but don't have the power? Why drink the white-paper kool aid? Ask the tough questions. Get the solid answers for them. It's a business.

No sooner had all these political hijinks come to light than we found ourselves immersed in a POC with the same technologies. Incumbent upon us was to write a POC protocol that would focus on what the current technology was already doing, just not doing it very well. In the end, the POC was very bulk-processing centric.

We had tests for loading the largest of the tables. Followed by simple read-queries, then complex read-queries. Then transformations, where we would insert-into a table based on the selection from another table. Keep in mind that in ELT space, the machine executes a transform while reading from one or more tables to create another one. On an RDBMS and even in ETL, this means leap-frogging on and off the local disk drives, and I personally despise this method of processing. It's viable on Netezza only because its SIMD model is wildly more efficient doing it this way.

Here's an example – on a single 108-processor 10100 machine, we loaded 20gb of data in about 7 minutes. It's nearest competitor did the same load in 50 minutes.

Another example, we did a transform of data, pulling information from the largest table (200 million rows) to create it *into* another one. The competitor pulled this off in 93 minutes. Netezza in 10. We followed up with a complex query, joining two of the largest tables. The competitor did it in 480 seconds, Netezza in 19 seconds.

In all this, the competitor cried "foul" at this test, with the disclaimer that "nobody processes data this way" and that "everyone else uses the ETL environment for this stuff".

Yeah, yeah yeah, whatever.

The simple fact was, the potential customer *really was* processing data this way, and did not appreciate the vendor pooh-poohing the POC protocol so that their product would not look like such a loser. The customer likewise did not appreciate their almost knee-jerk offloading of the solution into a completely unrelated solution domain (the ETL environment) to further rarefy the stakes of the POC. But the stakes remained. The problem-at-hand did not go away just because the vendor simply waved their hand. Come to think of it, they did a lot of hand-waving during this exercise.

"You cheated," said the Vulcan officer.

"I improvised," said Kirk - from *Data Trek, The Wrath of Con*, where Kirk explains that in order to beat the unbeatable *Kobayashi Maru*, he reprogrammed the computers to let him win.

Sometimes, in a competitive POC with Netezza, the competitor sees the writing on the wall, so to speak, and their fate is sealed. They cannot win, so they pull a *Kobayashi Maru* and change the rules of the game. In the above case, by offloading the problem to another domain (ETL), this looked a lot like *punting*. What they did not realize, was that the customer had no desire whatsoever to invest in an ETL environment *and* a query accelerator. The Netezza machine could do both inside the box. In fact, what the competitor looked like it was selling, was a dessert topping. You know, query acceleration to feed the user's immediate needs. But *not* a floor wax, something for heavy lifting and cleansing. The customer needed a floor wax, and the competitor hadn't brought one of those into the arena.

Back to the POC, the client decided to triple the data in Netezza, then make five times, and ten times the data. For the transform above, Netezza did the 10x version, over 3.6 billion rows, in 94 minutes, just a minute longer than its competitor on *today's* data. Likewise the complex query for 10x completed in 256 seconds, about *half* the competitor's time on *today's* data.

Interestingly, the *query acceleration* turnaround for simple queries was practically identical on both machines. If we were to measure query acceleration alone, the difference between the two - would reduce to haggling the purchase price more than anything else.

In our POC protocol, *bulk data processing* was at the top of the list as the primary *gateway* of tests for any technology selection. We assumed *a priori* that the product white-sheets were not lying concerning the given product's *flagship* capability, that of *query acceleration,* and we suggested that testing it *first* was a waste of time if it *couldn't* do the bulk processing. So the bulk processing became the priority of the tests. The competitor cried foul, because (as noted in Part 1) this felt like the POC had been geared to keep them from succeeding. Actually, the POC had been geared to *keep posers at bay*. The most professional answer to this objection came from the client - the POC rules *are* what we're doing *today* - put up or shut up.

It is also important to get a technology that we *know* will grow with us, hence the inclusion of the metrics on the 3x, 5x and 10x. We could have just shown the 10x and been done with it, but this would not have shown the linear scalability. What could the client expect from the transform

test above?
- 1x = 10 minutes
- 3x = 22 minutes   (but about 2.2x time)
- 5x = 36 minutes   (but around 3.6x time)
- 10x = 94 minutes   (but around 9.4x time)

Can we detect a pattern here? The scaling is *linear*. The difference to complete 5x versus 10x is about 2x, which is exactly what we would expect, and only if we *stayed* with the 10100 machine. But what if we simply upgrade to a 10200, boosting our CPU power from 108 to 216? Do you believe that the numbers above will reduce at least by *half?* You'd be right, and this is the kind of scalability we're talking about.

With the competitor, the scaling is also found in the hardware, but more with engineering the schema itself so it will properly take advantage of the hardware.

What we also learned with the competitor, was that their scaling was not linear. The performance fell off with the first test and got progressively worse.
- 1x = 94 minutes
- 3x = 280 minutes   (more than 3x time)
- 5x = 540 minutes   (more than 5x time)
- 10x = 1510 minutes (more than 15x time)

Note how the difference between 5x and 10x is not only significantly longer than Netezza, but the scaling is not linear. In fact, the time to execute against twice the data takes *three* times longer. This is exactly the effect we are trying to negate. The competitor is an SMP-based platform, and is unable to scale by design. It has hardware constraints that do not appear in the Netezza machine.

The next thing we did is to "show the machines in their best light". One might think that this means all of the players in the POC get their "best times" reported. And that's *exactly* what we did – run the same tests multiple times on the machines to get their "best" times.

But we must be careful. People see numbers like the above, and their first reaction is -- *you're lying*! I'm not kidding about this. At one client site, a leader got wind that the algorithms we had put in play actually reduced processing time from ten hours to fifteen minutes. No magic necessary, the hardware did all the work. His response was that we were *lying* and he wanted his own people to test the work. They did so, and his people reported metrics within less than *one percent difference* of what we had reported.

The reaction of this leader was to push back from the table, slam his fists into the table top and shout *"It's a LIE!"*

Well, as a I noted before, confusing your leaders with the facts can be a very harrowing affair. With numbers like Netezza's performance provides, we might want to keep a fire extinguisher or a defibrillator nearby. You never know.

So how best to deliver Netezza's amazing performance numbers and still show them in a light *better* than what the numbers can provide? The answer is rather ironic - the "best time" for the competition is the *fastest* time. The "best time" we reported for Netezza was the *slowest* time.

Now, that's sounds a little odd, but some of you may already realize the wisdom in displaying the results this way.

As one of our UK counterparts noted, *"Netezza is positively caning the competition!"* That word "caning" anchors in my mind sort of like "paddling" or "spanking". And for the sake of good sportsmanship, it was best to show the numbers this way. After all, why show a load time for the competition in fifty minutes, when the Netezza time is around ten minutes? We could afford to report a *clunky* fifteen minutes (fifty percent higher than the actual number) and still make Netezza look *stellar*.

Can you imagine being in a board room, relaying your findings when you finally reveal this truth? The Netezza numbers that beat the competitor, by a factor of five, are the *worst* case, where the competitors are the *best case*. This sends a message loud and clear to the decision-makers. It goes like this:

While we could have spent some time in tuning Netezza, this would have sent the wrong message. The real message is that Netezza doesn't need a lot of tuning. We can set up the database structures in their most efficient – but simplest – form. We don't have to embrace tuning, engineering and complexity to get the performance from the machine.

This kind of message speaks *volumes* to the decision makers, and as I noted, actually shows Netezza in the *best* possible light. An appliance shouldn't need a lot of care and feeding to get the performance it already promises. Netezza delivers, even in the worst case.

And that's a compelling story, indeed.

And now – once the smoke clears on the proof-of-concept, take a little time to examine what the most efficient Netezza-centric model might look like. We're not really far from it already, but it's important to take this critical post-POC step seriously. We don't want to use the existing model "as is" unless we can verify that it's the *right* one. I mention elsewhere that it's really tempting to leave the bad model "as is" because we have *all that power.* But a bad model arbitrarily steals energy, and we don't want that. We should spend some time fixing and shaping the model into something that is understandable by the users and most applicable and useful in the Netezza machine itself.

Then do like the movie Mafioso types do, and *fuggedaboudit* (forget-about-it).

Something to take very seriously in all this, is how we intend to get the data into the Netezza machine once the machine first arrives. I have a number of war stories in this regard, but if we imagine that the data will just copy-right-over in a weekend, we really need to rethink.

Moving data from our existing environment has several major "long poles" - these center on technology, policy and people. When we think the technical problems are a nit, the policy problems can be our major hurdle. Since we need people to make it happen, who's to say that the one person who can make this happen isn't on vacation or otherwise indisposed? In some cases, it's designed this way, because policies are meant to protect the data, from people with nefarious purposes, by people who are authorized to keep us from taking it, and we're about to find out just how effective those policies and people are, aren't we?

A few paragraphs back, I noted a couple of questions, along the lines of: Why wouldn't you recommend inferior **technology** if doing so brings you more consultant dollars? Why wouldn't you recommend an inferior **methodology** if doing so brings you more consultant dollars?

The answer is already given in the story above. Those who work with the champion technologies like Netezza really want them to shine. Loyalty to the product is not the same as loyalty to the mission, which is to make our clients as successful as they can be.

And this is the most transparent agenda. If I have been hired to make your company successful, I could say that I'm just doing my job to recommend the best. More importantly, it's my job to get as much realistic information into your hands as possible, so that you can make an *informed* decision. Once the decision is made, we run with it. The objective, in all this, is to make you successful.

So would I fulfill this objective by selfishly recommending inferior technology? I certainly wouldn't be doing so to increase your success, but as noted, to line my pockets. These things have a way of coming back to bite a person, in often the very worst ways.

Also, there is a spirit in the Enzee universe that keeps bubbling up. Enzees want their customers to experience wild success, and know that the Netezza product is a catalyst for it. Like I said at the first, it's like a drug. It feels good to hit the ball out of the park over and over and over. Why *wouldn't* it?

Part 3: One group wanted to move its data from one system to another. No worries, said the technologists as they set about to make it happen, and promised to get it done before close-of-business that same day. Our principals were excited and hopeful. but we neither rejoiced nor held our breath. As it turned out, the source and target systems were in different data centers. Ahh, well, they said, still no worries. Then they discovered that the data centers were in separate *countries*, one in the UK and the target in New Jersey, and only a very thin network pipe between them that nobody was about to let them saturate with a bulk transfer, especially one that could take many hours.

So someone suggested that they cut the database to a tape, put it into a FedEx container and ship it. This was already underway when a policy person put a pile of paperwork on a principal's desk to make sure all secure protocols had been followed, filled out in triplicate, especially since the data was traveling between two separate divisions of the company, between national boundaries, and overseas at that!

"You'll need the *blue* form," said the Vogon wonk to Arthur Dent, *Hitchhiker's Guide to Data Warehousing.*

The entire process took over *six weeks* to get any data in place for testing, **and** at the outset it certainly *seemed* like an easy chore. The issue at hand: our data has never left its home before now, and people want to keep it that way, and may have made it both technically and politically difficult to move it, whether deliberately or indirectly.

Moving the data out in bulk was never a priority before. Nobody had ever asked.

THE NETEZZA UNDERGROUND

Part 4: In another environment, the data and the Netezza machine sat on the same floor, but had a thin network pipe between them. What seemed like an easy move, really wasn't. They decided to make a cross-network transfer, but the regular users complained about how this saturated their network bandwidth, so they decided to export the data to flat files. Once exported, they started loading data, and all seemed right with the world. Until they got to the largest tables, and then the export choked and failed. Considering that one export could take eight hours all by itself, to have it die in the middle meant a lot of lost time. Also considering that they were kicking off in the afternoon and their failures weren't discovered until later the next morning, more time was lost.

After three failures, we suggested that they export this stuff in smaller chunks. They thought for sure they could make it work, and tried one more time, but it failed again, We then exported the data to multiple smaller files and then imported them into the Netezza machine. The entire export scenario alone took over a week. While any one part did not seem difficult, the systems simply choked on moving it because they weren't prepared for it.

Actually *loading* to Netezza was a nit.

Moving your data from its ensconced home will be *difficult*. Brace yourself.

Part 5: We worked diligently with a client on a proof-of concept. In the final state of affairs, Netezza was the hands-down winner. The competitor was a software product running on a really souped-up SMP platform that had been *specially* jacked-up to perform the proof. Once all the numbers were in, even though the SMP platform product had not performed well, the internal case was made based on *cost alone.* The internal proponents of the competitor solution showed the project principals that the cost of the software product, plus a system to host it on, was about half the cost of the Netezza platform.

These numbers were shared with us, and when we saw the specifications, something was noticeably missing.

The cost of the *storage.*

The POC had been run on very high-end enterprise SAN equipment, but the cost of this had not been included in the specification. The project principal had made his decision on the *cost alone*, so was completely aghast that the cost for storage, a *significantly* high number, had been inconveniently excluded from the specification and cost summary. The principal felt that skullduggery was afoot, and was on the warpath for answers!

Our team would need at least six terabytes of storage for development, perhaps more, and at least four terabytes to support the first rollout. The cost of this on the enterprise SAN storage was *four times* the cost of just one of the SMP systems. This additional cost, coupled with the fact that we would need not one, but two of these jacked-up SMP systems, escalated the overall hardware cost to almost double the cost of the equivalent Netezza platforms. With Netezza, the whole thing is self-contained, storage and everything.

What stunned the project principals was that in the final analysis, these jacked-up machines *plus* high-end enterprise storage were *still* no match for the strong kung-fu of the Black Box. As noted in the opening chapters, we must compare and contrast *all* costs, not just the most visible ones. In this particular case, the project principal had already given the green light to the proponents of the

280

competitor solution, and had to spend the next three *weeks* reeling-in the discussion.

The original POC was in February of that year, and by December, they *still* did not have a solution in place because of the internal technical and political wrangling. It is virtually guaranteed, that had they chosen the Netezza platform after the closure of the POC in February, our team would have had them in production before Summer. Counting the cost, they lost the *time*, and lots of it.

Part 6: In yet another environment, we were testing the ability of the SAN to store data, while pulling it from the SAN and into the Netezza machine with a simple transfer. We were load-testing the environment when the performance just dropped off to a crawl. "It happens," said a developer, "The network notches down automatically."

"Really?" we asked, "So we're trying to get the best bandwidth possible, but the network perceives the load and it automatically ratchets down the bandwidth?"

"How is that possible?" said another engineer, "None of our switches have that capability!"

What we discovered, was that when the network started running slow because we were bulk-loading data to the Netezza machine, one of the *operators* would see this happening and then *manually* ratchet down the network switch on the Netezza machine, because he knew that the Netezza machine's loading was causing the slowdown! Once the traffic cleared, he would *manually* ratchet the switch back up again!

Technology, policy and people. It's rarely about the technology alone.

Proof of Concept Notes:
- Plan ahead. Getting the data from your existing systems into the Netezza platform can take as long as 4 weeks or longer
- Don't ship your data to Netezza Corporate offices for a preliminary proof. You will only have to do another one on-site. The only value such an activity has, is to "see things for yourself" – but you can do that with fabricated data too.
- Address your hardest problem first. Low-ball POCs only make the low-ball players look good. This is enterprise computing. The products should put-up or *fuggedaboudit*.
- Use queries and capabilities you are already using. Don't save them for later.
- Don't focus on query acceleration. All the main products do that. Focus on intake and internal data processing. Not all the products can do that in *scale*.
- If necessary, seek external assistance to shepherd the POC
- Define the parameters of the POC before you start, complete with example queries
- Perform the same tests on your existing systems. You need a comparison for what you are leaving behind versus what you are approaching
- Compare features first, cost comes later
- Compare cost-for-cost – meaning that Netezza is a self-contained system, so we need to consider all the other "equivalent" parts and their costs (system, CPU, SAN) to understand the total cost of the product
- Ask around. Most product vendors will give you references. If the reference tells you they have discontinued working with the vendor's product, be *impertinent* and ask *why*.

In the end, we always need to stay neutral on the issues at hand. After all, if the customer sees all the data, all the numbers, costs etc and still picks Netezza's competitor, who are we to argue? They have made an *informed decision*, have examined all of the data and put ink-to-paper on what they really believe will take them into the shining future. They wonder if we will still be there with them, since our so-called "favorite son" has not won the day. Mighty Casey has struck out, and all that.

Solutions are solutions, and they take on a lot of flavors and technology bases. You are reading this and may have a Netezza machine and a lot of other disparate technologies, all working in happy integration. Solutions are often comprised of components that interoperate.

As a consultant, I help people make informed decisions. I don't nip at their heels for a favorite. I am a big fan of a wide variety of technologies. I can champion most any of them in the right context. Netezza has a context, and it gets things done. I never have to worry about things getting done. What's not to like?

With other technologies, more work is involved, whether in integration, engineering or whatever. For those, I have to ultimately put in place and test, what Netezza delivers at the flip of a switch. I can do all that for you, and train your people on the new environment, and make it manageable, operational and everything else you want, *and* help you hire and train more people to keep it going. We'll help you contain your additional costs. Just let us know what you want. Not to worry.

Wait, you just raised your eyebrow. Why was that?

Case Study – Science and Engineering

This case study is something that Netezza is perfectly suited for, and we are actively in a proof--of-concept preparation for a Netezza-based solution. The purpose of this exercise is more to fit the single-instruction-multiple-data model to the problem domain. If it's a fit, we'll consider technologies to support it. Netezza is a front-runner, as are others that the client has already identified.

The problem domain consists of five memory-based data stores, each containing some form of pre-calculated seed data for an advanced engineering application. The current application renders superimposed text and graphical image overlays on a large monitor, combining geo-spatial, database, geological and physical maps, to name a few. It is not an oil-and-gas scenario, in case the reader wonders.

For processing, the underlying data stores had been divided into several stages. To kick off the process, the user selects various parameters from drop-down menus, which create steering metadata for the memory-based access. Then the user selects a particular geographical area, which leverages the pre-calculated mapping data-stores to produce basic mapping images and information overlays. The memory-based stores are then integrated to the map using geocode-styled keys, cascading the participation of the other memory stores to render more overlay information on the screen. In essence, the user hits several touchpoints and the memory-stores drive the final renderings.

While this may seem acceptable for a single-user in the office, it is entirely unacceptable for dealing with issues of *scale*. The users now want to query the data-stores for *which* particular geo-spatial areas match to a given set of criteria. In the existing application, the selection criteria was already known, but now they wanted to perform comparative analysis to gain insights on similarities in various geographies.

The memory-based stores would not support this activity. We would have to first apply the criteria to gather insights in each memory-based store, connecting them to find the correlations. This is very intensive process requiring literally millions of permutations and combinations for any given search, many of them currently keyless and Cartesian in nature. Before committing to a key-based search, they needed to know if a database, with key-based power, would do this for them. Preliminary functional tests revealed that the chosen RDBMS could not meet the performance requirements even with the smallest test-case data. It was out.

Applying the key-based operations to their existing memory stores, their initial tests had turnaround times in the multiple hours, prompting them to move the activity to a larger SMP server with more memory and CPU. This shrank the search times by some percentages, but nothing acceptable for their desired turnaround.

The first query typically returned a large set of candidate data that the user would like to drill into. Browsing the entries, they clicked on several of interest, effectively kicking off the entire comparative process again. Each successive turnaround is over an hour in duration, and unacceptably slow. The breadth and depth of information is significant, and their engineers exhausted every possible means to make the memory-based stores work correctly.

Another portion of this operation included packaging the search criteria to deliver the same canned reports to various constituencies. As each report cost hours, the overall report delivery time required daily static outputs rather than on-demand, and they were still too slow to be viable.

After review of their implementation, we identified the opportunities to reduce the entire throughput to a Single-Instruction-Multiple-Data model. In fact, as we go to press with this book, the user has already completed the case-studies and examples to show how each of their on-demand report requirements could be supported within SIMD. In addition, all of their algorithms are ideally suited to Netezza UDFs.

We put the identified functional model on a SPU-box, one of the 4-SPU mini-boxes that Netezza announced last year at the '07 conference. This allowed us to test out the proposed data structures and algorithms as Netezza parallel-tables and UDFs. Once in place, we took all the algorithms through a functional evaluation, with the expectation of linear scalability. The potential is profound - we could easily produce an on-demand model, with almost instantaneous turnaround on the most complex queries. Likewise their pre-fabricated reports could enjoy on-demand without all the pre-calculated data, memory-based integration and cross-referencing.

Case Study – Anatomy of a Re-Platform

Underway as I write this is an assessment of an existing data warehouse currently using a competitor. If we compare the functionality of the competitor offering with Netezza, we will find that the competitor does more stuff. Whether it's "cheaper" is usually a function of contract negotiations rather than list price, no? Whether each machine can do what the client needs today, or in the future, is a function of assessment. Data warehousing circumscribes a set of core capabilities. Everything else is nice-to-have, but is it *necessary*?

These were the questions on the minds of the people paying the bills, but not the technologists. They had long-ago successfully campaigned to get their high-powered technology ensconced before there were any competitors on the market. Now that competitors existed, and the disparity in what they had been paying was a lot more than what they would pay if moving to another solution technology, the bloom was off the rose. The technologists told every consulting firm up front. "We have a say in who we work with, and if you say that our technology is the wrong choice, we will kick you out." Hmm. well, such situations eventually reach a critical mass. And in our case, we were entering the environment when the critical mass was already realized.

The person calling us into the assessment was not the technology staff, but from the senior business staff. Their primary issue was not the capability of the competitor technology, but whether it was overkill for their needs. One of them asserted a common analogy, that if we want to take a jaunt around town, we can walk, bike, take a bus or ride a car. If we choose to ride a car, do we need a Compact, a Cadillac or a Ferarri? A compact car won't cut it, a Ferarri is overkill, but the Cadillac is looking good.

This simple analogy appears in many forms and in many ways. I wrote an article over ten years ago for DMReview online called *Beware the Eccentric Innovator*, coming down from an environment where the principals were frankly acting in desperation. In this article, I suggested a way to steer a principal's understanding between a dream home, a family-builder-home and a starter home. Most people do not deliberately choose an extreme, unless their financial situation steers them this way.

For this particular client, the competitor solution was considered the "dream home" by the principals paying the bills, because they could not see the value in paying the extra money for the machine when they weren't using, or needing, the extra stuff. The technology staff made an objective and impassioned plea to keep the machine(s) and not throw the baby out with the bath water.

Enter *moi*, between these two groups, to provide an assessment delineating actual needs versus desires, and navigating the mine fields of both arenas. Don't imagine that technologists misunderstand such politics, but in the end, someone has to pay for it. And in the end, someone has to pay us for our opinion, and typically it's the same person paying either way, so the technologists already felt like the decision was "in the tank" in favor of the people who were paying the bills, and not in the favor of the Technical Experts, who are collectively Paid More-Than-Me to Know Their Stuff.

Those readers who understand these equations, often wonder why the upper crust of the company can send mandates down to the technologists for the technology they are required to use, largely based on matters of financial cost and not technical capability.

Uhh. It's a *business*.

So this is the primary minefield I find myself navigating, and some would even call it a tightrope. The client had already invested lots of money in their existing competitor environment, found, hired and/or trained resources, and have some degree of infrastructure circumscribing the technology.

In this particular case, however, the competitor platform had been cast as an Active Data

Warehouse, and it just wasn't working out for them. The answer from their *vendor*, as to how to make their performance issues abate, was to upgrade to More Vendor Stuff (imagine that!). This decision had an accompanying price tag that warranted replacing all the batteries in the office defibrillators, which was the last thing the client wanted to hear. Isn't it true, though, that when we purchase a machine for a smaller need and then starting using for a larger need, we must embrace the necessity to upgrade in support of this direction? Of course, this is perfectly reasonable.

But with people in place who already have doubts about the original decision, the situation clarifies itself. The principals doubted the necessity of the vendor platform because it appeared to be overkill.

The point is, we already know it will work, because it's already working in so many other places. The challenge is, to re-educate the users and technologists on the product placement, not the capabilities. Once people are embedded and committed to a given technology, especially one that invites a cadre of specialists, the tendency is to protect the (often hard-won) specialization for fear of losing staff. Or at least of losing morale.

Are technologists so arbitrary and capricious that they will abandon us if we change out one technology for another? Yes and no.

Yes in that some feel that their skills are marketable and pricey, and they chose those skills toward this end. Our choice of a not-so-pricey platform places their career plan at risk.

No in that some technologists are self-styled generalists and welcome the presence of a new technology. Especially if the new technology is one that serves them. I know several "family guys" who aren't really interested in new technologies for the technology's sake, but welcome any technology that does not enslave them and chain them to a desk, away from their family.

I also know companies that made decisions about their technologies, rolled them out to the corporation, only to realize that it was the wrong technology, or at least one that was not optimally implemented. Such leaders then feared for their jobs, so would not arbitrarily abandon something they once championed, in this case at an extraordinary sunken cost. This would be suicide.

In this particular story, the Active Data Warehouse was looking good until it started to run out of gas, and then came the more serious questions, the *money* questions. On the grill – the implementation of the machine to perform transactional activities along with its data warehousing role. The transactional activities were swamping the box, affecting the experience of the data warehouse users, who wanted resolution of this problem, and *quickly*!

Someone on the data warehouse team made the incomprehensible suggestion to move the transactional portions to a lower-powered commodity RDBMS, which they could cluster up for scale, then connect over the network to the vendor warehouse machine for any required drill-through. Whether this was the best suggestion within their heated political climate, you be the judge, but it brought even higher scrutiny to the viability of the vendor machine. Because if the transactional portion could be covered by an inexpensive commodity environment, with clustering for scale, what of vendor's data warehousing capability? After all, they bought the machine because it could do *both*, but now that it really shouldn't do one, why do they need it only for the other? All interesting questions, and a quagmire for all.

Back to the original summary. The competitor looked like overkill for what they actually needed: simple and scalable data warehouse power.

Hmm, I know where I can find simple and scalable data warehouse power, it's called Netezza, and yes, it costs a fraction of their existing vendor environment. Once the vendor heard that Netezza was in the running, they magically changed their tune on licensing costs. I wondered that the vendor wouldn't start doing door-prizes and free vacations for technical staff. This cost-shifting somehow re-balanced the equations and stopped the bickering. The vendor remains installed, not deposed by Netezza, but we'll see if the vendor remembers all these hijinks when the next license contract comes due.

While our client has sunken all that cash into a competitor machine, there's still hope for you. The point is, review technologies for how you intend to use them, and don't buy things you don't (and won't) need, or that you can fulfill with another product. It may well be that the same vendor is in your future, and that's great. *Bon Apetit* and all that. It's a fine, high-functioning and very powerful platform.

Another example: I once had to perform an assessment for product selection on analytical tools. I asked the business users to give us a list of all the functionalities they expected to see in such a product. I then received a multi-page specification listing dozens of capabilities, I called one of them and asked if they were really using all this analytic power, and they said emphatically *yes*. After reviewing the marketplace, I discovered something interesting – that one particular analytic product listed exactly the same features, in exactly the same order! It was as if they cut-and-pasted the product sheet from the vendor's web site.

So I asked them if they were partial to any particular product, and they said yes, *this particular product*, hands down. Well and good, since this particular product is an excellent product and can do a lot of stuff. We purchased it, and they were happy as clams.

Why tell this story? What if we ask someone what they need in a data warehouse and the list of functions looks strangely like a specific vendor technology? What if we find that they have specified their needs toward the purpose of acquiring a *specific* technology? I appreciate the fact that people have certain preferences, and like to work with familiar technologies.

But we're not talking about a Blackberry versus a Palm, we're talking about cost-of-ownership in the *millions* of dollars over time. The decision is an important one. Should we make it within an agenda-driven context? If we perform an honest discovery and market survey, we can come to a conclusion quickly. Will this process always favor Netezza? Who can say – but if approached honestly – the Netezza price/performance profile, plus its extraordinary capabilities and architecture, make it a highly *viable* choice.

Would our environment be happy with RDBMS clusters as the transactional environment, and Netezza as the bulk-processing environment? Will our users be happy? The answer is *quite possibly*, but you should examine them both if you want the most objective, *informed* opinion.

Case Study - Dogfights and Other Corporate Drama

Often performing assessments for data processing firms, invariably I'm asked to give a white-board session on the problems within a client's environment. The following is a composite of at least four of these sessions, for those who are in the middle of a decision-making process, or just coming out of one. Perhaps some will find shadows of reality here. I have deliberately scrubbed the parameters so that nothing resembles anything that anyone can personally recognize, and our attorney agrees!

Our first stop was in the descriptions and roles of the systems themselves, the general configuration of the hardware and what they contained. People often view their environments in terms of functionality, or the business processes. And often in context of what the systems should do, or were designed to do. So we always have to ask, *Is there anything else the systems are doing?* Invariably, most systems *organically* acquire roles and responsibilities for things they were never *originally* designed to do. Then we look at the people-interaction with these systems. After all, the systems are *supposed* to support the activities of the people, not the other way around.

We see something typical in organically-grown environments. The functionality grows over time, undergoes various forms of rework and spot-refactoring, the greater functionality attracting more business, inviting even more functionality. These are all healthy cycles. So what we have here aren't signs of sickness but of *growth*, and now we need to consider what will help it *continue* to grow. It feels right *now* like its growth is stunted, because it's not meeting the goals we'd like it to.

Let's start with how the systems actually operate. We have a transactional system that provides us with all the transactional functionality we'll ever need. While we see some minor opportunities for change here, they are not pressing or urgent for new *technology*, and are usually centered in the implementation or governance of the technology we already have.

No sooner was the transactional environment in place, then someone needed a report. The report requests kept coming, and soon the system was swamped with supporting two critical roles – transactional activity *and* reporting. At some point we moved report processing to after-hours activity (if we have this luxury), so we don't ruin the experience or performance of the transactional environment. This helped, but the system continued to run slower, encroaching upon (or breaching) its SLA boundary. We threw some hardware at it. We upgraded a number of things. It helped incrementally, but something was gnawing in the intestines of the leaders. They were approaching a hard wall, and something had to happen *before* they hit it.

So now what we really saw, are two functionally separate roles inside the machine. They fight each other for resources and time, like two dogs in a cage. The dogs are growing but the cage is not. One dog is growing fast, while the other dog isn't. Our reporting environment and its throughput needs - the sheer processing power and bandwidth to get things done - currently *eclipse* the transactional environment's capacity needs.

Our only effective path right now is to put the two dogs in separate cages. Considering their very separate talents – one is a retriever and one is a shepherd, we might consider tailoring their cages to the dog's classification as well. The shepherd will need a different class of cage, configured for a dog that deals with large-scale problems. The retriever might need a different kind of cage, one that faces it's ability to chase down and retrieve things one at a time.

As I noted, the cage for our smaller retriever dog is just fine for now, but the cage for our larger shepherd dog needs careful consideration. If we were to take a step back, would we buy another cage *just like* the first one? If the dog really is bigger, it needs a bigger cage. Do we go for physical upgrade, logical upgrade, or a different technology altogether?

We need to consider what the dog needs in order to be healthy and grow. And do it in a way that won't have us shopping for a new dog cage every couple of years. On the short list are dog cages that are suited for shepherd dogs, the ones that deal with large scale problems. It's a rarefied list, and if we know what we're looking for, the answer is under our noses.

And while all analogies are ultimately flawed, and this one has probably run its course, the composite of the environment is still applicable. We have different processing needs for different machines with different roles. We should not be afraid to push back on those who would arbitrarily circumscribe these functional roles and data processing missions with underpowered, inappropriate or inadequately tuned equipment. Especially not if the decision is made on getting a bargain for the technology. Nothing is for free. You will pay now for the hardware, or pay later in labor costs to keep it viable.

The machine should run when it arrives, and meet our capacity needs *and then some* right away. We should *not* fear having to re-address the capacity needs before we've even gotten our feet wet. We should *not* fear running out of time-to-market for core operational and business needs. And we should *not* expect to have engineers swarming the machines to keep them from melting down.

A lot goes into a decision like this, but the outcome of the decision is what we will live with for many years to come. It is important not to let *fear* (in any form) drive the decision. Appliances like Netezza are a step-into-the-light for the vast majority of environments that are starved for power.

Case study – SAN with no Power

I've already mentioned that when examining enterprise processing equipment, the storage systems are a very high ticket item. We can often find our storage devices costing more than multiple system boxes combined. For good reason, it's where the data resides. As we add the bells and whistles, each bell costs some bucks and each whistle costs some more.

Our client had some interesting issues. Seems that all the systems were running out of power simultaneously. Upon investigation, we learned that the SAN was the actual dragging point, and nobody could understand why we would make this assertion.

"We've striped the disks and volumes," said an engineer, "Each of the production servers has its own space, and so do the development machines."

"The development machines share the same SAN?" I asked impertinently.

"We didn't have the money for a second one, but no worries," said the engineer, "I can guarantee no contention on the disk drives. We can logically and physically partition them so there's no conflict."

He showed us a detailed map of the servers, their assigned space on the SAN and how the SAN kept the disks physically separate. It all seemed so simple.

"The production guys say that whenever the developers are testing," I noted, "That the production systems slow down. Quite a bit."

"It's not the storage array," the engineer assured, "There's no contention on any of the drives."

"Can we do a simple test?" I asked, "Just monitor the activity when the developers kick off a test. Then we will know for sure."

"We've done that test a hundred times," said the engineer, "I know what the outcome will be."

So I asked him to humor me, we set up the tests and watched the systems take off. Something was very strange in the I/O pattern, but the engineer did not notice it. He was focused on the spinning drives to make sure they didn't cross over. I wasn't watching the drives at all, but the I/O points from the systems to the SAN. Seems the servers were constantly waiting on the SAN regardless of contention. Pending queries were not arriving immediately on the disk. Something was holding them in queue, or throttling them.

The engineer announced triumphantly that the disk drives had behaved as expected, and showed us the system stats. We did not disagree, but asked why the systems spent so much time waiting on the SAN. The engineer did not have an answer, and felt he did not need one.

We called the vendor. All was revealed.

A SAN is simply a CPU-array sitting on top of a storage system. The more CPUs we have in the SAN, the more responsive the system. The balancing point should be the ability of the storage system to store and retrieve, not the ability of the SAN CPUs to manage things. Many environments have up to 32 SAN CPUs to support their smallest development environments. Production environments often have 32 as a minimum.

For this client, the SAN they had purchased, some years prior, was running on *two* SAN CPUs to support the entire storage array of over fifty terabytes. Moreover, these two CPUs were supporting production, development, testing and everything else going on!

The vendor noted that for the kind of I/O our client had implemented, they should have had *sixteen* CPUs or more on the SAN, minimally two CPUs for each connected server. The engineer was shocked as to this revelation, and immediately went about procuring a remedy. He put in a request for more CPUs for the SAN, along with the justification. Although the request was met with resistance at first, the leaders finally loosened the purse strings to buy the necessary hardware. Success was now in their headlights!

A follow-up call to the vendor revealed something more disturbing. Back when their SAN was originally purchased, the agents within the client's purchasing department did something dastardly. To save ten percent off the cost of the SAN, they purchased a version of the SAN *that could not be upgraded with more CPUs!*

The engineers and the decision makers were completely flummoxed as to how this could have come about. The purchasing agents had not been authorized to reduce the system capabilities. Yet here they were.

Upon examination of what was required to resolve all this, the fact remained that the 2-CPU-SAN was not much more than a doorstop for enterprise computing. The principals drafted another purchase order for another SAN, this time with 10 CPUs expandable to 32. A principal confirmed the purchase with the vendor and then carefully shepherded the paperwork through the process. After several days, the principal called the vendor to confirm the order, and the vendor reported that the order they had received was for *another* 2-CPU, non-expandable system!

Well, after reducing some drama, getting all the guilty parties together, and some innocent ones too, they finally got it straightened out and moving forward. I suppose we can never underestimate the power of bureaucracy to shoot us in both feet!

The point of all this is simply: we are only as strong as our weakest link. When the data is running slow and the breaks are beatin' the boys, the culprit is always right under our noses. Don't make any assumptions. Follow the path of the data through every system and every layer it touches.

Of course, Netezza's storage, CPUs – and the works – all arrives in a self-contained appliance unit. Drop it on the floor, plug it in and it's ready to go. And then say to yourself, *I'm glad I have a self-contained Netezza system!*

And if you can't say this, why not?

Case study – Gaming the System

A major national retailer measured the time duration from when merchandise arrived on its store docks, until it found a place on the sales floor, until it was actually sold. This supply-chain measurement helped them evaluate vendors and store operations to maximize the intake of goods - ultimately to maximize sales.

Oddities in the data arose, in that some vendors received higher ratings than others, and when the slower vendors stepped up their efforts, they fell further behind, potentially jeopardizing their relationship with the retailer. After enough heated vendor calls, the retailer realized they were actually incurring the ire of their most cherished vendors, not just the ancillary ones. This would not do, since the retailer had contracts in place and could not sacrifice these valuable relationships.

The information oddities seemed to say that while the vendor claimed to have shipped and delivered the goods on time, they weren't making it to the sales floor until some time later, protracting the overall cycle of vendor-to-floor. The vendor manager couldn't accept any vendor excuses, and was certain that nothing could be broken on his end. To placate his own curiosity, he made a visit to a local store's loading docks, where all was revealed.

Upon arrival, he noted palette after palette resting on the loading docks, ready for store intake, but with nobody in sight to actually move the merchandise. He found a dock supervisor and inquired as to when they would move the merchandise to the sales floor.

"Anybody's guess," said the dock supervisor, "There's no room on the sales floor to put any of the stuff. So when the sales manager clears enough of the merchandise, we break the plastic and move the stuff from the dock into the store. We don't break the plastic until we need to."

"So why does the system show that the merchandise makes it to the sales floor within hours of arrival, if the stuff actually stays on the docks for indefinite periods?"

"Oh, that's easy. We only clock it into the system when we actually break the plastic," the dock supervisor said, as though this was etched-in-stone policy, and obvious to the most casual observer.

The manager was stunned. "You mean that a vendor could have shipped this stuff here last week, but it won't actually be clocked into the store system until it's time to move it?"

"Well, it's how we're measured, right?"

"How do you mean?"

"Our people are measured by how quickly they move the merchandise from the dock to the floor, so we never break the plastic until we're ready to move it."

"What?"

"If there's no room on the sales floor, why should we be penalized? Heck, the store managers over-order most of the time so there's always a surplus, anyhow."

"There's a surplus because the orders aren't arriving on the floor in time," the manager shot back.

"We get the merchandise to the floor when the managers ask," he said, "All they have to do is ask."

But the manager knew that the policy was for the floor managers to simply order the merchandise and expect its arrival, never inquiring as to its delivery status.

Well, the operant factor here was that the dock workers were doing their jobs, in letter, but not in spirit, and had found a simple way to "game the system" so they could look good. But this tactical approach to the supply chain, with no visibility as to where the breakage was, had actually delayed delivery to the sales floor and affected revenue. All because the dock workers didn't want to take a hit for a delay that was out of their own control.

"We get what we ask for" and "we get what we measure" take on different meanings if the measurements and the requests inadvertently elicit behaviors that are incongruous with our business mission.

Case study – My Operations, not Theirs

We had the occasion to review an environment that, like so many organically-assembled environments, was rapidly running out of gas and regularly missing its deadlines. On several occasions of *spikes* in the business transaction activity, the systems almost popped their seams.

After some initial interviews, we found things even more awry. The business users were unable to access the daily business information. They had each been given IT "liaisons" through which they could post their requests for data – through email. The liaison would review their daily email requests, execute the queries and return the results in various forms. Many of the business operations, especially for daily processing of transactions, were also living behind an artificial firewall, almost like the entire data processing environment was a black box. This artificial firewall was a function of a poor design and a circle of people protecting / propping up its deficiencies.

The operators wanted more visibility to the data as well, and to the processes that actually created it. But the processes were all RDBMS stored procedures. The processes would normally initiate, run as black-box operations for *hours* and finally come up for air. If they ever errored off, they would require restart, from scratch. This happened a lot.

The business users had tried to put a reporting environment on top of the data structures, but to no avail. The structures were simply too complex-and-unknown to harness with a commodity product.

And we wondered why this was the case.

Way back when, the firm launched itself and the primary data source was an external vendor. This vendor would receive the firm's daily transactions, process and enrich them, then pass them back to the firm. Oddly, the data was always transmitted back in these *strangely* normalized flat files. One file in particular, was over-normalized into several files. The primary reason for this was in the vendor's support protocol. They would transmit the data in its original form and format, per their original publication rules from days of yore. If they needed to transmit more, even if on the same file, rather than change the existing publication interface, they simply provided an entirely new file. This is a very typical protocol for long-term service providers.

But the service provider's expectation, you see, was that they would transmit the additional files and the engineers on the receiving side would re-assemble them into *their own* operational form. This was the vendor's assumption, and a valid one. It's what all their other customers did. However, it wasn't what our customer had actually done.

Rather than take the vendor's files and re-shape them into an internal, business-facing set of data structures, the engineers had simply assimilated the vendor's data structures "as is" and institutionalized them. Thus the only data structures available to the internal business users was in the format (and not a pretty one) *of the external vendor*. Not only this, external subscribers to the firm's information were likewise exposed to these structures, further propagating the dependency.

The primary reason for doing this was in no wise a function of sloth in the engineers, but a lack of power and functionality in the IT environment. Given the right tools and properly powered systems, the IT staff would have happily converted the data to an appropriately structured internal form. Where was the funding? Missing - and not for lack of inquiry, either.

Without the transformation and data processing power, the *entire* environment, from the internal business users *all the way out to external subscribers* were beholden to the *vendor's* data structures!

How such environments come to be is quite simple – the principals who must commit resources to the data processing environment somehow believe, in the face of all evidence, that businesses can be operated on a subsistence diet of commodity, underpowered products.

But engineers must make up the difference. With underpowered machines and critical business problems, we give the engineers *de-facto* permission to innovate. We honestly expect their innovations to be competitive and not eccentric. We will nevertheless find some eccentric innovation, and that our critical business needs are being met by it.

For this particular organization, the primary reason they called us in, was because new leadership with serious concerns *clearly* understood the problem and wanted it fixed.

How to fix this problem? The business should create its own internal data structures that represent its own business operation, not the arbitrary interface characteristics of a third-party vendor. When the vendor data arrives, it should flow through a transformation process, conforming it to the firm's internal, proprietary structures. When the firm must publish the data to the vendor, it reverses this process and transmits it. This harnesses the immediate effects of Information Theory's chaos, and gives us direct control over the information.

Most people involved in data warehousing would not think of doing it another way. Likewise, people who are forced to do it this way, because of a lack of funding to do it right, sometimes have a tense and unhappy existence. They take a lot of heat for the system's shortcomings.

Where would Netezza play in all this? Get the vendor's structures directly into the machine, stage them and then launch some transformation and integration statements to drive them into a consumable form. Success is only minutes away. What are we waiting for?

This client is actively involved in a POC with Netezza, and some of their principals are virtually euphoric.

Netezza Case study – Load History On-Demand

One of our client liaisons described an interesting need. Each day saw a new influx of data to process, yet the history was only valuable to the ad-hoc users, and those who needed to browse history for legal / compliance purposes. Without the freedom to throw away data, keeping it online was daunting as well. The daily business users did not need it all that often, really only every once it a while. How to keep the data "usefully available" without resorting to common backup and restore scenarios?

For any given day, they had about a terabyte of inbound data, a need to keep thirty days on tap, and a need to keep several years of backlog. The data requirements were enormous, easily exceeding the capacity of the environment that the customer was willing to invest in.

Based on a white paper offered at the Netezza '07 conference (not by the author), one of their in-house engineers tried an experiment, in that the historical data was offloaded in flat-file format to a SAN. The (one-time) write-cycle of the storage to the SAN was pretty egregious, but afterward they could read the SAN at network speeds. They organized the data on the SAN by an easily loadable logical interval, and provided the ad-hoc users with the ability to load-on-demand with some simple parameterized web pages.

This would allow the ad-hoc users to load-on-demand the data associated with a given time interval, intake the data into a Netezza table, query it on the SPUs and throw it away. On average, no two files would ever be accessed at the same time, since their access was already intermittent and infrequent. Total cycle time was less than two minutes.

This load/query/toss scenario was later embraced by several of Netezza's *much* larger customers with good success. This made the data readily available to a larger user base without the expense, overhead and lethargy of tape-based systems, and without having to keep it all online within Netezza.

It seems that when we have a machine that can inhale data, the ad-hoc experience feels a lot like a breathing, or a breathe of fresh air.

Netezza Case study – Where's my data?

After many frustrating days, perhaps even months, of attempting to optimize an environment, one of the leads finally threw in the towel and started asking hard questions.

"We've been chipping at the edges," he explained, "And getting an incremental boost here and there. I see the developers' eyes light up when they squeeze a little more out of the systems. The problem is, we're only processing about one percent of the overall data stream, and this means we need orders-of-magnitude change, not just these incremental improvements."

We asked him to provide us with a roadmap of the data's path through the processing cycle, but he could not. The more people I asked, the less anyone knew. After a day or so of fruitless gleaning, we finally called a mass-meeting of all the players to talk about what actually happened to the data as it flowed through the systems. I wanted the **happy path**, and wasn't leaving without it!

Over twenty people showed up, each one looking as tired as the next, clearly wanting to get the meeting over with so they could go back to the optimization fray.

From the primary servers and into Netezza, everything seemed fine. But when it exited Netezza, things started looking strange. The post-processing environment was pulling over a million rows from the Netezza machine, then comparing them to the data in *another* machine. In fact, this was a lot like doing a common Ab Initio *Join* operation, where two sources were pulling and joining in memory to get a final, filtered result. Of course, they weren't using Ab Initio, but C# in .NET! In fact, each of the million records was being instantiated as a .NET dataset, then joined in memory to the secondary data set. This process was so egregiously slow that it had never *once* met an SLA. In fact, this was the portion of the processing that they had spent months trying to optimize, with no fortune. Interestingly, this model is exactly the MISD model we're trying to escape, and yet they were building one.

What I found interesting, was this second data source that they were joining the Netezza information into. After all, it was still just a join, and I wondered why they were doing it in memory. I asked how big it was. Seemed like a simple question.

"Huge," said one of the developers.

"Really huge," said another.

"It contains *years* of business information," said a third.

Around the table, each one agreed that it was enormous, ginormous, humongous, but none could say exactly *how big* "enormous" might be. In fact, nobody knew the actual row count of this secondary source.

While everyone was busy debating how many teeth were in the horse's mouth, someone at the table decided to open the mouth and count them. He logged onto the secondary source and performed a *select count(*)* on its main table. The Really Huge one. He did not expect an answer back right away, and the answer he received actually stunned him. He repeated the query, just to make sure he hadn't made a mistake. He verified the name of the main table with several of those around him.

Forty-four hundred records!

Not only that, but only *five* of this table's columns were actually necessary. This revelation was a shocker to almost everyone in the room. All this time, they had assumed that the secondary environment was too big to deal with, but now the ideas started to flow. One the them – *why are we joining all this in memory? Why don't we download this table into the Netezza machine and perform the joins inside?*

Why not, indeed?

By the end of the day, their DBAs had downloaded the secondary table's contents into the Netezza machine and performed the join-filter on the outbound *select*, deriving *exactly* the same filtered result as the painfully and tediously optimized .NET code. In this one experiment, we effectively eliminated the need for the majority of the .NET code layer.

The system was suddenly processing the orders-of-magnitude the original engineer had lamented was so elusive. In fact, this simple fix not only blew past the 100% mark of their processing demand, it reached *Eight Thousand Percent* of their processing demand.

Plenty of room to grow before entertaining an upgrade.

In every environment, we need visibility to the entire flow of the data, and an inventory of data locations, sizes and roles. Lacking this, we need to avoid and eschew false assumptions, artificial constraints and fomented chaos about something we are trying to harness, clarify and gain greatest control of.

Lastly, *get all the data into the Netezza machine*. It's the center of gravity now.

Netezza Case study – To and From Underpowered Tech Pt 1

I had an interesting conversation with the leader of a financial services group. Seems his transactional environment had grown incrementally and organically over the past several years, and the entire platform was running out of gas. Oh, *transactionally*, it was doing fine. No worries at all. But the reporting environment had gone completely out of control. In such environments, people report off the primary tables until it becomes untenable. Then they make separate tables and start dumping. When reporting runs out of gas, they start *aggregating*. It never ends.

It contained over three hundred million rows in one of the reporting tables, and another one hundred million rows in the second largest table, with several more tables in the twenty- and thirty-million row range. It was bulk-processing *inside* the RDBMS, so we're already in violation of Rule #10.

We suggested that they move the reporting environment out, completely out. We also suggested they select an environment that was more suitable for handling report tables of this size, and report outputs in the quantity, magnitude and tight time lines that seemed to get tighter by the month. The engineers and DBAs held *daily* meetings to discuss SLA encroachment and breach, none of which were happy conversations. The environment was constantly tense, with the principals running about trying to get their new functionality in place, all the while knowing that their old functionality was unstable, with the trepidation that the old functionality was the *foundation* for the new functionality.

Ugliness ensued.

Their proof-of-concept with Netezza and another competitor told the tale quite well. Not only could they reel in their processing durations into a time frame of less than forty-five minutes (compared to the current eight to ten hours), they would have room to grow for many years to come. The three-hundred million records threatened to become three *billion* records within the next four years. We strength-tested the initial solution on a 10100 (108 SPUs), and found that the solution could go to *20x* without breaching a 2-hour total duration. And this *without* upgrading the machine to a 10200!

Netezza has the power to transform the data, but it also has the power to transform how we do business. No sooner was the POC put to bed than the leaders starting thinking about which other mountains they could conquer. Mountains they passed every morning on the way to work, they could see from their office windows, mocking their inability to execute within their own business operation, much less take on more.

The leaders started dreaming again.

Case study – To and From Underpowered Tech Pt 2

In an RFP review, the client lamented that their RDBMS environment was running out of gas. Their business model was simple – download stock index, equity performance and risk information, seed the database with seven to ten years of data, then pull the updates regularly from the market.

At regular intervals, they ran risk-related, time-series analysis of the data. If the data did not have seven or ten years of information (as a new ticker symbol on the market) they would take a snapshot of the most recent activity and *replicate it backwards* to simulate the information *as if* the equity had been around all that time (artificial data inflation).

One of the users said that the system had worked great once-upon-a-time, but now their time-series execution would take days to setup, and weeks to execute. They had beefed up the SMP platform environment to its maximum capacity. It continued to run slower and slower.

An engineer then realized that the stored-procedure-centric nature of the solution was *possibly* dragging the system into the mud. He decided that it would be better to surround the database machine with external satellite servers that would fire asynchronous queries to the RDBMS machine. This would take the processing load off the database server and spread it out among the various satellites. The cost of this endeavor was extraordinary to develop, test and implement.

In the end, they actually realized some reasonable degree of lift. But within a year, the system was further behind on the processing time than ever before. They really were out of gas and ideas. This was an eccentric innovation, and someone should have stopped them before they killed (another system) again! This was a case of instantiating asynchronous, and *calling* it bulk.

As noted in the first chapter, adherence to Rule #10 will keep us away from this sort of malaise. The RDBMS is the wrong technology for bulk processing. Engineering around (and propping up) the wrong technology always leads to artificial complexity, and eccentric innovation.

We assessed their overall processing environment, their processing model and needs, and determined within a matter of days that their needs were entirely bulk-related. Why had they embraced an asynchronous model for bulk processing? Wrong technology often leads us down such paths.

After a review of their data sizes, we determined that the initial implementation of a Netezza platform would involve three sweeping data processing activities. The first would be intake, which for them had become laborious, tedious and time consuming. The second would be an initial cleansing and reconciliation. The third would be the actual time-series crunching, requiring table-scans of five or more terabytes at a time. We also determined, based on this analysis, that they could be producing a *daily* time series update to their risk systems, with processing room to spare.

May the metrics be with you.

Case study – To and From Underpowered Tech Pt 3

A colleague of mine provided this interesting anecdote, so with his permission on file and the attorneys all happy, I share it now with only minor editing.

"Working with an overworked application development team. I noted that their development time-to-completion was starting to slow down. We had completed the majority of the core application and complexity, and all we had remaining were the one-off "leaf" dialogs and screens that seemed, by comparison, to be a piece of cake. While everyone committed to completing all of these screens by the end of the week, we had no idea what the *true* problem was. We were about to find out.

In the middle of the week, realizing that the teams just weren't going to make it, I took a walk around to chat with the senior developers, sort of over-the-shoulder to watch them work.

What stunned us was that, while each of these small screens was simple in nature, the developer had to navigate through the more complex screens to get to them. This meant waiting for each screen to tediously load its grid and functionality, then drill deeper. While any one developer could experience a quick turnaround, it always depended on how many other developers were working at the same time. Because even though they each had their own power-center desktops, they were all using a central, underpowered database. It was so underpowered in fact, that I started doing some productivity metrics that brought some attention.

The average developer would need several minutes to review the next step of development, several more to make the fix, compile it and run the program. I judged that for even the most complex fix, the turnaround time should be no more than five minutes, but for the simplest fix a turnaround of less than a minute was not uncommon. So we averaged the total round-trip time for a developer to review / fix / deploy was around three minutes You can see that our developers were *very* focused.

Well, nobody would accept a constant turnaround of three minutes, but five minutes seemed a bit more palatable. Rather than be challenged on this number by people who made money decisions, I upped it to ten minutes.

Because here was the stinger: any given turnaround was *actually* twenty minutes or longer because of the slow database response, a completely unacceptable number for such miniscule functionality. I wondered at that point why we had not performed some productivity metrics sooner. Doing a little math, including the total function points we planned to produce plus the turnaround time for each one given several iterations, we would not be finished for *months*.

I asked the program director for permission to put local versions of the databases on the users desktops, but was told that this was against company policy. I asked for more power in the development and test database platforms to get more productivity. I shared the numbers with him. No sale. Get back to work and stop whining.

Not surprisingly, we did not meet the end-of-week deadline, but the total functionality produced actually tracked to our productivity metric. At this rate, we would wrap the functionality in about eight weeks. I reported this to the project manager, and he actually thought that the developers were sabotaging the effort in order to "justify more toys"!

One of our senior developers, upon hearing this, flew into a rage, ran down to the project manager's office and, in no uncertain terms, "administered feedback" on his strange and unproductive stance. His appeal was simple – if the company was serious about finishing on time, it should provide the correctly powered environment, or quit complaining about missed deadlines.

Such tirades are verboten, however, and the project manager was about to make an example of our tired and overburdened hero by firing him, but I and two other leaders let him know that the entire team would commit mutiny if that happened, because all of them actually agreed with our hero. In fact, now he really *was* their hero!

Then I heard something totally unexpected, that the project manager now firmly blamed me for the malaise of the situation, because of all my metrics and meddling. He had already called his boss, who was due to arrive at any moment to give us all a talkin' to!

With the metrics still in my frontal lobe, the manager's boss asked me about them, considering that it was a charge against me now laid at his feet to deal with. I explained that since in any given day, the developers could only pull off three iterations per hour (twenty minute intervals) that this meant only thirty per day (in a ten-hour day). By allowing the developers to have a local version of the database, or a more powerful central database (just more CPUs and memory mind you), we could double if not triple the productivity of the entire team. Two months for one month, all that stuff.

The project manager's boss liked the idea, and could not imagine what all the fuss was about. He'd found himself approving such upgrades all the time, and all our project manager had to do was ask. So he told the project manager to get the request for upgrades to him immediately, and he would expedite.

Excitement ensued.

Except for one problem. Our project manager fancied himself a modern-day Captain Blighe.

That evening the project manager called a meeting and told us all that he had sent over the request for the upgrade, but it had been denied. Unbeknownst to any of us, the project manager's boss was sitting quietly on the conference room's phone (on mute) during the entire meeting, as the project manager carefully explained how he'd put in all the paperwork, but his boss had rejected the request. For lack of funds.

But the boss had done no such thing. The next day, the project manager was no longer."

Do we really need this kind of corporate drama in our development projects? It seems like the thing to do is provide our teams with the tools they need to succeed, rather than giving them underpowered or stone age tools, and expect them to build information-age functionality.

Netezza Case Study – The Cruncher

Several years ago, I spent significant time immersed in an equity-trading organization with a strong need for compliance with OATS (Order Audit Trail System). Some of you may recognize OATS as the FINRA (Financial Industry Regulatory Authority, formerly NASD) standards and compliance reporting model. Like FINRA, this client's member-firms generated equity trade order reports into the client's core compliance processor in OATS format.

In all this, member firms issue orders across and among each other, creating new orders, desk orders, routed orders, canceled orders, execution orders – yes – all the order types noted in the FINRA / OATS implementation requirements, and all of it ultimately converged into a collector front-end in raw, disconnected form. One firm could initiate the given order, pass it on to other firms and so on. Each firm ultimately passes their records to our client, which ultimately merges and sorts out everything, then forwards it to FINRA for dispatch and compliance.

For those of you aware of OATS rules, any given firm can split up a trade into smaller parts and route them internally or externally to other member firms for final execution. For each member touching the trade, they must manufacture an event record and pass it on to the compliance environment. Later, the compliance environment will match the disparate-but-connected trades together into a chain of events to make sure that all players did what they were supposed to do. Any missing information constitutes a trade break. Any out-of-compliance information has to be fixed or escalated. The SEC is watching.

So by definition, the connectivity patterns exist in the data, but are only applicable after *all* the data *arrives*. To add further complication, these order types have disparate information, upstream/downstream connection points and fuzzy matching criteria. They reference each other like a chain or tree of activity – a *concept map* - each member of the chain pointing to the one above it, perhaps near it or following it. The data elements defy, for functional and performance reasons, traditional RDBMS index-based joining. The data itself *utterly* defies traditional entity-relationship mapping.

In fact, *there is no inherent relational model – the data **itself** determines the nature of the relationships, and where any given row on one table connects to any given row on any other (arbitrary) table. The relationship is in the data, not in an identifiable key constraint.*

To get a picture of the scope of this trade-correlation effort, the system must match these incoming orders with intraday and interday orders, *four hundred million* daily orders, against more than *two billion* trade orders held in immediate seven-day history – all for the primary purpose of finding *a few thousand* missing or non-compliant trade orders.

The client has the proverbial *needle in a haystack* problem. Of the two-plus *billion* trade reports in play for a given period, it has to pinpoint the *mere several thousand* of those reports not in compliance. Not only those in error, but also those that are duplicates and those missing entirely (trade breaks).

In their original RDBMS environment, a brute-force correlation algorithm would seek the members of a chain of trades. It would start out at the lowest leaf "child" of a perceived tree of order activity – the Execution Order – and proceed up a "tree" via weaving (or perhaps porpoising) through the various "parent" order tables to *discover* the relationship. This process could pass through the same table(s) more than once. How else to solve this problem in a relational database setting? No other options exist – the RDBMS constrains the solution domain. Data retrieval is in the tables, marked by relational attributes but unable to leverage them. More unfortunately, this is also a *pure* bulk processing problem, not the optimum domain of the traditional RDBMS (Rule #10).

The client had already embraced the simplicity of a loose topological definition of the problem domain, that is, a given thread of trade order reports appear chained together like a topology tree (*concept map).* They started at the top of the tree in a hierarchical representation of initial orders (roots) with more parents and children to follow. Of course, nothing is perfect, and oddities in the rules allow for bunching, cross-referencing and other issues that "break" a pure parent/child tree model. Accommodating these exceptions, we could still drive toward a tree-based topology without any major issues.

In fact, a simple driving philosophy arose that cut through the "purist" mathematical chatter of a *comprehensively* representative model. Otherwise, the possible combinations and permutations of topologies approached mind-numbing proportions. However, considering the *business* and *legal* data processing rules of requirements-driven functionality, we needed some business and regulation-driven boundaries.

The business analysts stepped in to help us out:

- **Rule 1** - if the data itself cannot or does not represent the relationship but is otherwise perfectly valid, we are simply *unable* to take an action on it. Seems simple enough. And upon application, we would find data-related anomalies that were reasonable, consummately compliant but in no way represented a true tree topology. The key here is that they were *compliant*, so weren't on anyone's radar anyhow. In short, if the data is not in error, but the relationship are otherwise unknowable, then we are not on the hook for knowing it. How can someone be expected to know something that is objectively unknowable?

- **Rule 2** - If a trade order was outside of the OATS regulatory scope for any reason, but still inside compliance for all others, no action was necessary. The important factor here is "regulatory scope". Put another way - if we are not *legally* required to know it or harness it, we take no action. This is sort of like the IRS rule, if you don't owe it, you don't pay it.

To clarify, let's say we observe thousands of cars on the highway and know that one of them *might* be running low on oil. Running low on oil might be "bad". If, however we cannot *find* the car, and it's not *illegal* to run low on oil, we have nothing actionable either way.

These rules both rarefied and clarified the scope of topology mapping to a manageable number of concept combinations. We could always extend the scope later if regulations should change, but we needed to capture and harness the existing regulations and make them completely airtight.

The compliance environment faced an imposing problem: While the existing implementation seemed to work well in executing the agency's business rules, it was also slowly approaching capacity on its resident RDBMS, clearly the wrong technology to scale into the future – both for functional and performance reasons. The business and technical leaders wisely chose to address this before ultimate saturation.

If the topological approach truly defined the problem domain, the existing technology (a traditional RDBMS) could not support an effective solution with any scale. Once upon a time, when the RDBMS was the only *available* technology to address the problem, the engineers simply worked around its inherent limitations.

This technology weakness ultimately led this client's implementation into artificially higher solution complexity (i.e. over-engineering the environment *and* the schema). The *artificial* complexity gave the illusion of *true* complexity. When systems start to run out of power, the engineers are charged with abating the possibility of failure. So engineers do, what they do best. They engineer. This is when complexity artificially escalates.

Over time, the artificial complexity becomes indistinguishable from the core solution.

In our client's case, repeated tactical engineering exercises led to greater artificial complexity, such that several major tactical extensions were highly complex and over-engineered to the point of complete functional saturation for the *entire solution*. With more business and functional opportunities on the horizon, the existing system required review and re-factoring at the core architectural level.

This scenario is common in IT shops everywhere – the systems start to run out of power and the engineers solve the problem either by adding extra hardware to an existing design, or bolt-on tactical modifications to provide lift in perceived problem areas. The engineers then reach a saturation point where they can no longer get any more performance, and the existing functionality is inside an engineering "cage" that requires enormous analysis to apply the simplest fixes or changes.

Why do things "get this way?" The primary reason is because hard working people do the best they can with what they have. It's not like these environments devolve into some chaotic abyss because someone wants it that way. In fact, our engineers often work tirelessly to keep the environment viable. The best way to reward their labor is to give them the machinery and power plant to do it even better.

In discussion of their re-architecture, two paths arose. One path regarded the artificial complexity as *reality*. Another path regarded the artificial complexity as an *artifact* we should ignore and forsake altogether. The first path generated numerous proposed solution paths attempting to address both the scale of data and the artificial complexity, including a Java infrastructure and clustered/grid computing. Others proposed similar approaches, each attempting to express performance and functionality through harnessing size *and* complexity at the same time.

What we really wanted to avoid was *actually* institutionalizing something *artificial*. The solution was not complex *because it had to be*, only *because it was*. From a methodology perspective, we needed to express performance and functionality – period – disregarding the existing artificial complexity as an *artifact*, not a requirement.

Could we simplify the solution? Upon first examination, actually within only a few weeks of exposure and discussion, business analysts and our team members agreed – it was a straightforward bulk processing problem requiring a bulk processing platform. No complexity to harness, just complexity to unravel and eliminate.

Since the lion's share of bulk processing activity centered in the order audit correlation and trade-matching / trade-break detection, we attacked this as a centerpiece. After a number of deep discussions in topological concept mapping, it was clearly a perfect candidate for GROK. In fact, in the project's third week, this author posed a possible GROK solution to several internal engineers to hammer out a GROK approach to the topology -and found it practically bulletproof. I must repeat, the GROK intersection approach is nothing new, but it's application is easily recognizable when we are trying to connect disparate entities toward a common center.

While the client had initially settled on the Netezza appliance for storage and processing, they still needed to determine if it was the right choice. The agency was hopeful, we were hopeful, and engaged a prototype/proof-of-concept scenario.

The test platform was a Netezza model 8250 containing 216 active processors and some eleven terabytes of storage. The vendor now offers this machine as a 10200, with more power and storage (up to 25 terabytes).

Within a short period of development time (several weeks), we produced data structures and a correlation algorithm that could process four hundred million records in less than *fifteen minutes*. It could process the entire week's activity (seven days at over two billion records) in less than *thirty-five minutes*.

The platform and the GROK proved "practically perfect in every way" (with all apologies to Mary Poppins).

Our approach was a simple departure from how customers generally use Netezza. As a streaming analytic platform, customers load it up with consumable information. Once loaded, end-users then execute complex queries against its contents during a business time window, pounding the daylights out of it.

In our context, however, we would receive data raw, then pass through an intense transformation cycle – effectively leveraging Netezza as an "ELT" data processing engine. This approach used multiple stages of simplified SQL statements, the machine's massively parallel processing power coupled with parallelized intermediate tables. Any single point of activity was traceable, understandable and easy to tune and troubleshoot. It also embraced the data processing approach of Single Instruction Multiple Data (breaking up the problem into a flow of manageable, bite-sized chunks).

Another area of "reducing complexity" was in pre-processing all of the incoming trade orders (eleven separate and disparate entity tables) into a consolidated and enriched table containing only the primary workhorse attributes from all eleven tables. We leveraged a surrogate key to each order record in the consolidated table. We would further leverage the surrogates for the GROK intersections. The consolidation process took mere minutes and was well worth the extra step.

Initially consolidating the disparate trade events into a common table also gave us the ability to cleanse the raw information of null and trash values, enrich it with additional useful information and pre-calculations, and eliminate the need for joining across multiple raw order tables during the correlation cycle. Thus in a single stage of processing, we optimized and simplified all further downstream operations.

While the consolidated table held all the trades in one place, we could still perform selective "carving" of the information for further optimization. For example, only certain trade types appear as "parent" and certain types as "children". So we carved the potential parents and their parent keys into one table, likewise with the potential children and their child keys, then joined these two smaller tables multiple times, in criss-cross fashion, to derive the connectivity facets. This simple tactic reduced the time-to-conclude by *ninety percent* over directly joining against the larger consolidated table.

Other simple tricks included pre-calculating and integrating / enriching the trade order records as they entered the consolidated table. As a principle of pre-processing and data stewardship, the consolidated table represented the first best opportunity to make the data "downstream ready" all in one place. The objective? Anytime we discovered ourselves repeating a calculation, derivation, transformation etc in the downstream logic that *could have already been applied,* we would refactor the consolidated table, apply the logic in the upstream, and thus further simplify (and accelerate) the downstream.

Using a GROK approach, we could then apply intersections across the consolidated trade reports and then use the intersections to discover the patterns among the orders. This would allow us to join and intersect the data only once – at the time we create the intersections *en masse*. Then we could leave the order records in their comfortable, consolidated home and start crunching the intersections.

In building order intersections, we no longer had to deal directly with what any given topology "tree" looked like or how big it was. All we had to do was find each connecting relationship between any two orders in the consolidated table, and make an entry in the intersection table. With the primary trade order considered a "child" and its parent trade order considered a "parent", we could rip through all the information, applying the fuzzy keys *in situ* without regard to overall context. Once completed, the repository contained simple GROK entries: "parent_id, parent_trade_type, child_trade_type" and other correlation-centric attributes. From this initial cut, we could immediately know all possible one-on-one intersections – but we could also know all possible trade breaks (the records that failed to intersect), because they would be glaringly missing in the GROK table.

The decided-upon name of this intersection structure was *EventLinks*. It held all the topology trees for every trade activity, so a proposed name was Hierarchical Order Node Intersector (HONI) – you know - like *oats and honey*. Another name for the consolidated order table was Consolidated Order Management Baseline (COMB) – you know – *honey comb*. Okay, so perhaps we were giddy with superfluous creativity (high-powered hardware systems can leave one in a perpetually euphoric state). Either way, gleaning the data from the intersection table really was a lot like harvesting honey from a tree. We ultimately settled on the more professional term, *EventLinks*. Alas.

After filling *EventLinks,* we could take the next step – that of applying the one-on-one parent/child business rules. Simple things like "no parent trade should have a time stamp later than its child" and many others. We could *virtually* process whole terabytes of information in a smaller, more compact and agile form using *intersections only*.

As such, the GROK intersection proved the best possible springboard of metadata describing the context of every trade order type.

Some of you may want to liken this to a compact *fact table*. After all, isn't a fact table simply a useful intersection of keys from various dimensions? Perhaps, but this structure is different in that it represents a cascading tree of hierarchical information, primarily from the same source - the consolidated orders table. Considering that the orders *are the facts* – the EventLinks table is actually a *metadata fact table*. Also considering that the fact table has disparate attributes, now we're talking about metadata intersections *about* the facts – like a GROK.

EventLinks led to another opportunity, initially expressed as a goal by the agency business analysts. If we know an arbitrary number of orders exist as a connected "tree" topology, then why

THE NETEZZA UNDERGROUND

not stamp each intersector with a group ID? Later, when downstream systems want to examine trade activity for a given execution, they bring up all common group IDs and see the complete assembly and its trail of activity from top to bottom. With Netezza handling all the pre-process heavy-lifting, elements like this were only a few more cycles away.

But again, I must emphasize, EventLinks is not a new or innovative data structure or concept, but for this problem domain, it fit like a light bulb in a socket.

In the final analysis, the simplified structures and the power-plant to drive them led to an easily maintainable solution that could fully complete its processing day – against 2 billion trade orders – for consolidation, de-duplication, correlation, transformation, and publication in *ninety minutes,* well within the target of eight hours for only four hundred million orders. In fact, it takes longer to get data in and out of the Netezza machine (to / from the lower powered storage systems) - about 2 additional hours - than it does to actually process the data.

The salient takeaway here, is that many large-scale data processing problems are squarely in the domain of bulk-processing solution platforms. We *can* apply an RDBMS to a large bulk processing problem, but ultimately it will not scale. It will eventually run out of gas because it competes against its own engine's processing drag. In large-scale bulk data processing, we need environments that understand and best-leverage parallel *flow-based and set-based* processing rather than serialized, transactional-engine-based processing. More importantly, we need more than just horsepower, we need *efficient* horsepower.

An assertion which perhaps invites the simple question: *Couldn't my RDBMS get the job done if it had 216 available processors on its system like Netezza has?* And the answer is only "perhaps", with the additional question, *at what cost?* Seriously – how much would it cost us to roll out a 216-way SMP machine? Including per-CPU RDBMS costs? You see, in the end we can always make something *look* good with extra hardware. The real trick is in getting a complete system that is *most efficient and cost effective* for solving the problem at hand.

We also need focused, deliberate, applied physics to solve a physics-based problem. Large-scale data processing is borne on efficient, purpose-driven *physics*, not general-purpose commodity hardware and software and superficial functionality alone.

Without forethought, we might under-power our solutions or allow growth and time to over-power and overtake them. Our engineers will faithfully keep the engine running, even if it means over-engineering to extinguish the fires. One day we might look up and see more engineers than systems. More people working for the system than the system working for the people.

Some call it job security, others call it prison.

We will incur a cost either way – in the size of the system required to power our business, or in the labor hours required to shore up an underpowered, or an *overtaken* environment. The former leverages force-of-physics while the latter leverages force-of-will. Which model is more sustainable? What we'll find with technologies like Netezza is a consistent leveraging of physics over sweat to drive high-volume data processing.

This re-platform is a simple but repeatable example of an artificially complex environment ultimately approaching functional and processing saturation. If the principals embrace functional and operation priorities together, this necessitates selecting a platform and technology supporting operational, administrative, functional and performance aspects all at once.

Artificially complex solutions are simply bundles of under-powered or secondhand technologies masquerading as a powerful technology. The customer chose to leverage a truly powerful technology without the artificial bundling, juggling and additional moving parts. The decision fulfilled the pressing requirements. As a bonus, also provided high measures of resilience, adaptability and scalability.

Netezza Case Study – the Chugging Engine

Upon arrival at the client site, several of their leaders took us aside and told us the "bad news". It seemed that an architect had come and gone, had made a lot of purchases along the way, and left a mess in his wake. One of the "messes", they surmised, was that pesky Netezza machine that didn't seem to do anything right. In their minds, it was a high-speed processing server, but it was always slow and always having hiccups in every part of its technology base. They wanted to know if they'd made a mistake (or rather, the now-missing architect had made a mistake) in purchasing the hardware. It certainly wasn't delivering on any of its promises, they mused.

Or was it?

Upon a casual examination, we learned that they were using the machine transactionally, not for bulk processing. I asked them why they expected the system to behave in a transactional manner. *Hadn't they read the product label?* Of course they hadn't, that was the former architect's job. I kept getting the answer, "It's an RDBMS, what's the big deal?"

No, it's an *appliance*.

Upon examining the flow of their work, they weren't very far off the mark. They just needed a tighter configuration and some protocols around it. (It's always in the configuration and governance, isn't it?). When their data arrived from various disparate sources, they were using *nzload* to push the data to the machine immediately. Considering that any one push was fairly minor, they were swamping the box with high-frequency, too-small loads. By fan-in collecting the data for a single, less frequent load, we recovered the machine's operational breathing room.

We were also able to do something else rather unique in Netezza space. We were able to define a fifteen-minute batch window. Their batch cycle ran every fifteen minutes, 24/7 with no stoppage. Of course, many of you recognize this as a continuous model, which I'll bet some of you didn't think Netezza was up for.

The first operation after loading the information, was to carve out batch cycles of incoming work. Since the work appeared in ebbs and peaks, we could only be certain that the peaks were high-water marks, but no fifteen-minute interval passed without *some* data.

As a note, we tested having all the master data in a single table, joined to the table containing all batches. This join operation took roughly 300 seconds. We had to join the data three different ways in three different contexts, giving us an average of 900 seconds for the complete operation. Note how this 900 seconds *is* the total batch window time, with none to spare.

To refactor, once the batch intervals were known, we only had to carve out the most recent batches into a single intermediate table. This table was then used to join thirty days of history, with each day's data in a partition (see partitions elsewhere in this book). Invariably, the data did not join to all the information in one partition (a filtration effect), so many of these joins returned right away. (automatic zone maps are a beautiful thing).

By dividing the data into day-based partitions, and likewise carving the active batches into a smaller temporary table, we reduced the overall time for all three of these operations to less than two hundred seconds (on average about three minutes).

This left a total of twelve minutes in the batch cycle, at least two of which we would use for loading data and housekeeping, leaving ten minutes to prepare and publish data.

Rather than require the extraction process to pull the information by reading a table (and activating the SPUs), we already knew what information the external consumer process was about to ask for. We used part of the remaining time to perform the pre-extraction join of the results, into an external table. This meant that the external system only had to make a request to the external table, and the data was already prepped to go. Why was this important? If the next processing cycle was underway, we wanted all SPUs dedicated to processing the data, not fielding external query requests.

Some caveats of this scenario included automating the partitions so they rotated each evening at midnight. The oldest partition would be truncated, then made the "target" partition for all new data. Truncation (rather than delete) of the table's contents was critical for performance, because if we had deleted the data from a monolithic table, or attempted to housekeep the table with an *nzreclaim* operation, we would breach our shortened processing window and fall behind.

We also saw another interesting aspect of processing this way, that it took all the processing burden off the external systems, effectively converting them to data delivery and extraction models, rather than doing any kind of bulk processing on their own. So the external systems experienced enormous lift in their own operations, indefinitely forestalling an impending hardware upgrade to boost their own performance.

Some of the people around us asked, if we really can get things done in less than five minutes, why not just reduce the batch window to this and make it even more aggressive? This was an intriguing option, so some of them set about making a kind of accordion, where the processing would find the balance between how much data was actually available to process and how much downtime the system had to deal with it. Not to get too creative or anything, but stay inside the boundaries of your business requirements and don't give away precious processing window time for free.

Netezza Case study – Just Mix and Match?

I had a really animated conversation with an engineer who had built a set of status-monitoring tables. Their batch cycle would kick off and they would save a record to the monitoring table. When the cycle was done, they would update the table with the final status. Just one problem - this was a table in Netezza, and writing a single row to it was essentially a transactional model. It was also highly unstable. I did not particularly have a problem with them using the tables for status monitoring, but a flat-file logging (discussed earlier) would be more effective and not just spin-the-SPUs for a single record. It was the secondary update that was killing it functionally. It errored off a lot with conflicting writes and updates to the table.

Another group down the hall had done something more creative. In their status monitoring scenario, they were logging the status to a flat file, and at the end of the batch run, performed an nzload of the flat file into a status table. Now this was closer to the mark.

Funny thing, though, this group related "You know, we saw what the guys down the hall did. I think we want to implement one of those, and get rid of these flat file logs."

No. You *don't*.

Some of the funniest conversations we've had, were of people who had implemented things correctly in their initial round, and then re-factored to another solution that was the wrong direction entirely. In short, they had initially swerved into the truth quite inadvertently. And now, without knowledge of the right thing to do, were about to swerve away from the truth quite deliberately.

Know the product. Read the label.

Case Study – DAC Attack

Some of you have encountered the (former Siebel) functionality called Data Warehouse Administrative Console (DAC). As a background, various Oracle customers will purchase the ERP systems of Siebel, JDEswards, PeopleSoft, etc. Oracle has provided star-schema definitions and canned transforms for each of these sources, allowing a customer to install the given star-schema as a mart, and plug in the additional components to source-and-fill-it from the ERP system. This is all supported with a skinnied-down version of Informatica, plus a scheduler/handler package controlled by DAC. In addition, the DAC operation is pre-configured with the target table names, their index maintenance, mappings and loading order so that the dimensions are loaded before the facts, etc. So we have these pre-packaged pieces: the DAC config, the mart star-schema and the generic mappings from the ERP to the star schema. It's all a canned, configurable product offering.

The JDEdwards option selected by our customer was the General Ledger Data Mart (GLMart), a package containing source-target mappings for the DAC and the schema definition for the target mart database, also hosted in Oracle.

The end-game of all this, is to allow a user to connect to the Oracle-hosted GLMart through OBIEE, the Oracle BI interface. Whew!

The customer didn't want to point OBIEE to the Oracle-hosted mart, but to an identically-defined schema in Netezza. They also didn't want to export the data into Oracle's GLMart and then copy the data to Netezza, but to bypass Oracle entirely. The plan was to get the whole thing working in its original Oracle form, then replicate the structures and behaviors for the target Oracle environment down into Netezza. Of course, the DAC is a data-mart manager, so it "knows" that certain tables have certain needs, and allows the administrator to provide hints as to whether to handle, drop, create indexes and other supporting structures. The pre configured DAC comes with all this already set up, none of which is necessary for Netezza, so to use it we'd have to rip most of it out.

The problem at hand, was that the canned OBIEE reports for JD Edwards leveraged Oracle's star schema, *in Oracle*. So the customer took this canned star-schema, reconstructed it in Netezza, and *voila*, OBIEE could effectively read these forklifted, albeit empty table structures in Netezza.

That step in place, it certainly seemed easy enough to simply fill the Netezza machine with data from JDE. Unfortunately however, the DAC was doing all the data movement and transformation, so if this was going to happen, the DAC had to be reconfigured to source the JDE data stores *and* push to Netezza targets rather than the current Oracle targets - and would have to eliminate all the Oracle-facing activities, such as index maintenance.

The data movement involved only two flows, one to pull data from JDE and into canned Oracle staging tables, and one to pull from these staging tables and push back into Oracle for the final GL Mart. The DAC controlled the Informatica instances, their configuration and metadata to make all these things happen.

The customer had already worked with Netezza product engineers to convert and instantiate the Oracle Staging and GL Mart tables into Netezza form (is there *anything* those product engineers can't do?). Now to load them.

Couldn't we just tell the DAC to load Netezza instead of the original Oracle instance? We copied the canned DAC configuration for the JDE-to-Oracle flows and made a new application instance. Within this, we ripped out all the index references and other dependency overhead (Netezza has none) effectively burning this down to the core flow logic for table-to-table movement - and little else.

Finally, we tweaked the database connection metadata and redirected the DAC downstream connections away from the Oracle instance and into the Netezza instance. While I don't want to oversimplify this transition, these were the basic mechanics, with some minor tweaks along the way.

In the final configuration, the new DAC instance would pull from the JDE and pump directly into Netezza. It would then pull from Netezza, perform the canned GL transformations, and pump it into the GL Mart. No mess, no fuss.

Or was there? Well, there's always a catch. It seems that this original configuration treated the star's fact table as a summary-fact. This meant all the dimensions and facts could and would experience updates. Now, who implements updates for fact tables? Really? This requirement elicited the additional purchase of the Informatica PowerExchange module for Netezza, a necessary quantity to support this solution in a canned, non-engineered model.

But wait - there's more. Seems the original configuration of the fact table was a random/round-robin distribution. Many of you realize that this doesn't bode well for bulk-updates of any scale. Ahh, we had to but distribute the fact table on its update keys, and likewise the dimensions on their update keys. So what could have been a big deal, was no big deal.

Some of you may note that the DAC movement from-Netezza-to-Netezza doesn't leverage the table-to-table copy power of Netezza inside-the-box. Unfortunately on this gig, the time was short and the priority was to redirect the flow without breaking anything. In the follow-on, we decided to dive into the DAC preconfiguration and peel back the pre-defined transforms, moving these into the Netezza machine and eliminating this secondary DAC flow. Remember the maxim - Make it work, make it fast, don't break anything. Make it fast usually comes last, no?

For the client, the daunting part of this whole exercise was the black-box nature of the DAC, the skinnied-down Informatica instance and the whole issue of testing to make sure nothing was broken for the OBIEE users. Not only was DAC a mystery for the client, it was a mystery for the various vendor technologists who had arrived to install and implement it. Seems their job was just to show up and install, deploy and validate. Not to actually tweak or modify the DAC configuration for anything else. And of course, the final version of this was declared "unsupportable" by the RDBMS vendor, but you didn't see that coming, did you?

For our team, the daunting part was in the fear of having missed some critical piece of information that would rear its head and bite us. But no, the conversion really was that straightforward.

And this is a testimony to Netezza's ability to seamlessly dovetail into our flows, even with configurations that aren't especially friendly to the conversion, and declared "unsupported" by the people who originally provided them. Quite frankly, we didn't expect much help from Oracle, considering we were helping their client redirect their products onto one of their competitors. But Oracle was very helpful and professional in the conversion. They were also very experienced, as though they had already done this a few times?

Warehouse Case study – Projects vs Environment

We had an opportunity to utterly transform an environment from its stove-piped, user-centric data warehouse to a world-class, centrally governed warehouse with resilient capabilities, reusable components, a strong semantic layer and lightning turnaround for the user's daily-changing requirements. It all seemed so perfect.

Until it came time to pay for it.

Oh, the client had money, and lots of it. But it was all spread out over the stovepipes. With nearly twenty-million dollars in play on an annual basis, you'd think that a reduction in overall cost would interest someone, anyone? But of fifteen different warehouse threads, each with anywhere from one to two million dollars to burn, had no money to spare to make things right.

What they had instead, were *fifteen* completely mature data warehouses, each with its own staff and administration, all to support a business that could fit on one floor of a common office building. Why all the stovepipes?

We asked this question a lot. One of the most significant problems lay in the human resource model for the technology staff. Each of them was rated, measured and given raises based on their project-centric activities. Nothing about the environment was, well, *environmental*. It was all driven down to the tactical project level. The *fifteen* business leaders controlled their own fates, rewarded their own people, all that stuff.

Our proposal was very simple. We would reel these fifteen, largely redundant warehouse threads into a common warehouse. We would deploy a common semantic layer with a commodity tool, and use an enterprise-strength data processing environment for the backbone. We had an approach. We had a framework. We had a beautiful, industry-standard design. What could go wrong?

The first conversation we had with one of the fifteen business leaders, set the stage for the remainder of the chats. By the time we interviewed the fifth one, I could have written a script. "We have priorities, we have deadlines, we don't want to be beholden to the other business units." In essence, we have an issue of ideological, and even political *competition* between the business units, not a collaboration indicative of a healthy business model.

Our proposal would have reduced their cost by over fifty percent – ten million dollars – that we assured them could be used in any number of other upcoming ventures, including much-needed staff increases. Imagine the benefits of ten million free dollars (conservatively speaking). The possibilities were endless.

But none of the business leaders would budge, and the IT department was a strapped-for-cash cost-center (go figure). It seemed that nobody wanted to spend the money to make money back, or to control the costs. Keeping the engine running *as-is*, was a far higher priority. Yet here we have a quantifiable means to reduce cost, realizing an ROI within the first year. All of the business leaders understood the model and thought it would work, and had no disagreement with the plan.

But none of them were about to release any funding for it.

One of the most pernicious problems to overcome was their HR model – nobody understood how we would transform this model from a quantifiable, task-oriented and business-leader-facing model into a model that was environmental, governable and more resilient over time. We had a perfectly reasonable approach for this as well, but the commitment did not materialize.

This was over four years prior to this writing, and as of today the company has not budged from its original model. It continues to experience breakage, escalating costs, lack of visibility, unreliable sources, unreliable work products, difficulty in maintenance and extension and a revolving-door-turnaround in business and IT staff. Even in our initial interviews, the staff viewed the environment as unstable, brittle and *not* something they wanted to spend their careers propping up without improvement.

Can't say I blame them.

Netezza Case study – Migration Builders Inc.

We've encountered several situations now where the customer has plans to bring in the Netezza machine, but wants to test out a target data architecture on their existing RDBMS. What does this really mean? A launch, testing and tuning of an SMP-based *RDBMS project*. It will take just as long as any other SMP-based project, and the performance delivered in keeping with the SMP's capability. Yet, these technologists hoped their new architecture would offer the same functionality and performance as the Netezza machine they had yet to purchase.

We've noted the filtration approaches, oddball structures and wild creativity that Netezza offers us, and that such assets are impractical if not impossible in an RDBMS, if for no better reason than those pesky index-structures alone.

In a particular case, the architects wanted the topology, versioning and error reporting approaches (discussed in Bulk Processing Stuff), and to apply this to millions of records. What's more, they wanted to process fifty million transactions and thirty million other entity-based records on a 2-CPU prototype platform. The objective of the prototype centered on performance rather than functionality - *all on an underpowered SMP-based RDBMS!*

We were frankly troubled as to why they thought the RDBMS would offer the same performance inside its machine, using structures and methods that are only appropriate for an MPP machine. We worked diligently to wave them off rather than pursue this approach.

Whether it's a square-peg-in-a-round-hole scenario, getting an existing RDBMS data architecture to work inside Netezza is a snap, in fact nearly a nit. But getting a Netezza-facing data architecture working inside an SMP-based RDBMS, especially if already leveraging the core Netezza capabilities, borders on impracticality, perhaps impossibility.

Warehouse Case study – Requiem for Requirements

When I arrived on site at this client's IT division, I was immediately led to the floor where the data warehouse was under construction. Except, of course, it wasn't under construction. It was in an operational pause.

The floor was eerily silent, having been recently vacated by all the developers who had been working on it. Our client-side counterpart told us the sad, rather unavoidable tale.

"We'd been working on this warehouse for over a year, and there seemed to be no end in sight. We had sixty contractors and a small group of regular employees working like crazy on it. One of the leaders finally said. *This project has to be completed by July 31ˢᵗ of this year. Money will completely run out on that date. It has to be completed!"*

"How did that mandate work out for you?" I asked, already knowing the answer.

"It was devastating," said our client, "Rather than work hard to complete the tasks, they already knew that it could never be completed by July 31ˢᵗ. So, to a man, they all updated their resumes, found other work, and when the rest of us showed up on August 1ˢᵗ to continue like every other day…" he pointed to the empty cubicles.

"They *all* left?" I asked, incredulous.

"All of them. They were told the money would run out. They were contractors. Who works for free?"

"Can you get any of them back?"

"That was a month ago," he said, "And now here we are."

Yes, I thought. *Here we are.*

This wasn't the strangest conversation I would have. Over the course of the next two weeks, I interviewed various players in the process. One thing was for certain – nobody knew for sure what they were really trying to build, or what its end purpose was.

"We have some extract-tables," said the client, "They serve as a bridge between the data warehouse and the Business Objects desktops at another site. Those extract tables are a blight on the design. The BO clients should be hitting the data warehouse directly. That we have these extracts is a sign of a flawed design."

Or was it?

The more I interviewed the end-users, I discovered that the extract tables were, for them, the end-goal. *The* work product. The *meaning* and *purpose* for the existence of the warehouse. How strange was it, that the IT folks saw these artifacts as a tumor in the system, when the end-users were getting exactly what they had asked for? How much trouble would it have caused, do you think, to get rid of those extract tables? Heads would roll, I am certain of it.

This was also a case of where the end users actually formed the scope of the delivery. They managed the projects and the deliverables, and kept the scope-creep under control. I was taken somewhat aback by this scenario, because in most every other case like this, the IT people are the ones holding-the-line on scope while the business users arbitrarily dogpile one requirement after another onto the project's timeline. In this particular case, the users defined the scope and controlled it as well. More anomalous behavior.

I interviewed their data architect, also a contractor. This architect had chosen to make a very innovative and avant-garde data model. So innovative that it was useless. The end-users needed the extract tables because actually navigating the core data model was impossible. It had been third-normal-formed to death. And back again.

So this data architect had taken a lot of heat for the lack of functionality in his model, and his persistence as to its viability had actually caused several other more experienced architects to quit the company – so vehement had been their disagreements. Somehow this architect had gained the favor of someone inside the company, and had outlasted all of his pallbearers. All of them except for me. His last day was the end of that week, without us having to say a word.

My first clue that he was clueless, was when he explained to us that one of the main dimensions of the "fact" table actually behaved both as a dimension *and* as a fact. Upon first glance, it actually behaved as neither. This guy didn't know what he was talking about. Word to the wise – get a data modeler who has actually put a data warehouse into production and lived to tell about it.

This chap was just a poser.

What was worse, this model better represented what we would call an "Operational Data Store", not a data warehouse, and certainly not a data mart. The necessary parts, measurements and functionalities were completely missing. Hence the need for the extract tables. In fact, the extract-tables were a lot like a data mart feeding from the ODS. The patterns were there, all right. Had he built the model with mass-extraction in mind, it would have looked completely different. It's probably easy for a master, experienced modeler to review a bad model and poke holes in it. This is almost like shooting fish in a barrel if we are just bantering about at the lunch table. But this model had been (and still was) the centerpiece for a multi-million-dollar, enterprise-wide data warehouse implementation, and the person in the driver's seat did not have a license to drive. People lost their jobs, the company lost oodles of money. Someone needs to take this problem seriously and not worry about hurting someone's feelings. It's a business, not a playground.

Of course, I could further describe the overall malaise in this data model, but suffice to say that when I finally had to describe the model to the company's DBAs, who would be in charge of implementing it into production, I should have brought smelling salts and defibrillators. Need I say more? Another word to the wise: Get your DBAs involved for design review early in the cycle. They know what a database system can (and cannot) do, and many of them are well-aware of data warehouse-related issues, especially bulk processing and mass/ad-hoc query performance. Cherish their feedback.

In short, the data architecture is useless if the technology won't support it.

On a lark, we visited the end-user site to interact with their Business Object developers, the ones who were consuming these strange extract tables. They showed us how they pulled the extracts into the Business Objects client, then they showed us something else: how they pulled *five other feeds* directly onto the BO client desktop, and how they joined and integrated them to the extract-table contents, and how *slow* the whole process was.

Could we optimize Business Objects? they asked. Could we make the local network stronger so that the Business Object environment would run faster? We found ourselves sitting in one meeting after another discussing how to optimize the local user desktops.

Stop!

All I really needed to know, was *how* the elusive five feeds had not been considered when developing the overall data warehouse? It was as if they had never even existed before. It was the end-users' original intent, to get the main company data into the data warehouse and then they would follow up with integrating everything else on their desktops. I suspect that the person who came up with this underpowered and unworkable application architecture was either an analyst or a business user who probably understood the business and the data, but not *how* to make the technology parts work for them.

What they really needed to do, as painful as it seemed, was go back to square one and redesign the data warehouse to regard *all* these feeds. Integrate them and pre-process them each night into nimble, agile data structures that Business Objects could simply navigate with relative ease and minimal overhead – and no mass upgrades to the end-user's physical network or machines.

A universal theme rose from the smoke of this malaise. At every turn, from the leaders' announcement that money would run out, to the end-users' lack of foresight in the data integration, to the IT group's lack of visibility as to the nature and purpose of the extract-tables – was simply this:

People were getting what they asked for, but not what they needed.

A Requirements Analysis can be a tedious process, but it's a necessary step in making sure the architecture doesn't have a shortfall. We don't have to build to all the requirements at once, but we need to know what the end-state will look like, within reason.

Some takeaways of requirements analysis include some salient information from the end-users, including

- How they operate a business day
- What data they need when they arrive at their desk in the morning
- If they ask anyone for data, what do they use it for?
- What they expect from the information systems
- Is there a wish list?
- What data does their supervisor desire of them, what metrics and measurements, any statistics or operational health?
- Determine the end-state of the data delivery and work *backward,* for clarity. It's great to have a centerpiece architecture that can grow and scale, but if we miss the delivery to our primary end-point, all we have is data in a database. We built it, but they didn't come. Costner will be in touch.
- Don't innovate the data model. It's a floor wax, not a dessert topping. It's supposed to do one thing – integrate and synchronize massive quantities of data for reports. Dessert toppings don't do heavy lifting. Floor wax does that.

THE NETEZZA UNDERGROUND

What was the final outcome of all this? Well, it's a data warehouse environment. There is no final outcome. Once upon a time, we thought data warehouses were a project. Now we know better. In this particular case, the "operational pause" was seen by the business as an utter failure, when in fact, it was just another iteration step of many more to come.

The only failure is in *quitting*.

The above case study shows how a project can gain a life and identity of its own, complete with political and daytime drama machinery. Watch out for this. Data warehouses are not projects. They are environments. Those who want complete control now, will not want it a year from now when the warehouse is finally running, operational and only generating career boredom for them.

Fight the urge to get political. Get the work done and go home happy.

Or at least, go home *on time*.

MORE ON THE RULES

AT THE OUTSET, I provided some rules leading into Rule #10, but these were somewhat skeletal (since I was trying to get to Rule #10!). Here is more detail on some of those first rules.

Rule #1 – Everything is requirements-driven. Every environment finds itself replete with requirements, many of them deeply held but unspoken expectations. The business users don't really understand that when they left their former company, itself sporting a data warehouse that was driven by a former industry guru, they were taking a step down in functionality when they joined our happy clan. Yes Virginia, there is real data warehouse functionality, somewhere over the rainbow. If you liked it so much, why did you leave?

Now we have a different requirement - punting terabytes not gigabytes, and housekeeping, maintenance and administration in a *mansion*, not a two-bedroom apartment. Or feeding hordes of people in a convention center, not a local corner deli. It is a problem of *scale*, where the same duties have completely different needs.

A whole mental list of unspoken expectations await us – from the operators, administrators, troubleshooters and maintenance developers. In terms of science, and the scientific method, we would call these folks *peer review*. They know better than anyone else the true quality of the work products. Does it *produce* what it's supposed to produce? Fine – but *how* does it produce those things? The process is directly tied to the quality of the outcome. I'll repeat this another way just so it's not lost –

The quality of the outcome is directly related to the quality of the process it came from.

If you have any doubts about this, keep in mind how much we depend on process every day. We can visit a Burger King anywhere on the planet, and the burgers will taste the same. We can buy Campbell's soup off the shelf, and it will taste the same every time. Process control is quality control. Lack of process control actually indicts the quality of the product. We depend on it for simple things, too.

"While on a remote consulting gig I had to switch apartments. When I arrived at the new apartment, the person there seemed friendly enough, He offered me something to eat and drink, so I settled on orange juice and a piece of fruit already on the table. We chatted for about an hour on the move-in logistics, then when it was time to leave, he had to take a call. As I was gathering my things, I watched him become immersed in the phone call, then in horror as he went to the refrigerator, grabbed the orange juice carton and drank directly from it.

Ew."

We expect a certain level of quality and value about what's being delivered to us. Any perceived violations of those expectations can cast everything from doubts to aspersions, to outright accusation. Perhaps to avoid pain, injury and – er - food poisoning, we need to get to know the people who we deliver to, and determine what they expect *early on.*

With a flawed, untestable, unobservable, unauditable, unmanageable process – then who's to say if it's actually doing what it's supposed to, or it's just getting lucky? What if some pesky business users saw glaring flaws in our logic? What if they saw perfect business rules, but were uncertain if those rules were just documentation or real code? What if they review our logic and see something out-of-sync, or out-of-order, or some other functional anomaly?

What's worse, what if they review it, and it's so bad they can't tell what it's doing? Developers say, they wouldn't be reviewing it, if they *really* trusted us. Ouch.

How about this: Why not ask them, what they expect? Find out what they need to do their jobs better. Don't throw it over a wall and hope they figure it out. They won't. They can't. And here's a shocker – it's not *their* job, either.

How do we make our data warehouse offering a more pleasant experience for these people, who could end up being our number one accusers or our number one fans? (and let it be known, the difference in the two can be just *one* "bad delivery" away). Now that we have terabytes under our umbrella, the users still expect the same crisp experience, and won't take no for an answer.

Following are some of the first things that the system implementers will do or say that will tell you, the data warehouse is a non-issue for them. This is a running conversation, sort of a composite conversation lest anyone imagine these are real people.

Ten percent dissolution

Oliver is the data architect overseeing the flow of information in the enterprise, he asserts in a status meeting, "The transactional systems are up and running. We have had no problems with executing transactions."

Lewis is a business operations person, who is constantly correcting bad data, "What do you mean? Of the one-million transactions we processed yesterday, one-hundred thousand of them failed."

Oliver: "Ten percent is not so bad."

Lewis: "I don't see it as ten percent, I see it as one hundred thousand transactions that we had to manually examine and put into the system."

Oliver: "All of the transactions that the system can process, were processed."

Lewis: "So you're saying that all those failed transactions, the system *can't* process?"

Oliver: "If the system could process them, it would have, wouldn't it?"

Lewis: "We manually insert each row, applying the very same rule each time, each night. You can't tell me that there's no way to automate it."

Oliver: "I never said there was no way to automate it. Did they automate it at the company where you came from?"

Lewis: "We didn't have a hundred thousand failures every night, that's for sure."

Oliver: "How many did you have?"

Lewis: "Not a hundred thousand."

Oliver: "But you did have failures."

Lewis: "Yes, we did."

Oliver: "Then the environments aren't so different. One just has fewer failures. I bet they were processing less data than we were too, huh? How many transactions did they process each evening?"

Lewis: *(incredulous)* "Around a hundred thousand."

Oliver: "And how many errors?"

Lewis: *(gulping)* "About ten thousand."

Oliver: "Ten percent!"

Metrics man

Richard is a business user who needs metrics on all the daily operational activities.

Richard: So, how many did we process exactly?

Oliver: Everything that came through.

Lewis: *(glaring)* Minus a few.

Richard: How many of each?

Oliver: What does it matter? They're all safely inside.

Richard: It matters so we can measure the business.

Oliver: You measure the business. I process data points. The data points are not the business. We are not a data processing company, but an XYZ Business company.

Richard: But we process the data as part of the business.

Oliver: We process the data. It's not the business. Business happens whether we process the data or not.

Richard: We need a way to know what our capacity is. How do we know we can accommodate another big client?

Oliver: That's easy, we can't, so don't sell anymore. We've had hardware upgrade requests on the CIO's desk for months now. Don't tell me I'm not looking after the business. I see the danger and sound the warning. You bozos are the ones playing games.

Richard: (*aghast*) We would gladly justify the purchase of those things if we knew they were necessary.

Oliver: I know they are necessary. It's my job to know they are necessary. Is it your job to know they are necessary? I don't think so.

Richard: Are our systems about to *crash*?

Oliver: Our systems were about to crash months ago. You and I have had this same conversation in one form or another every week since then, and we're having it again now. I say the systems are about to crash. You seem to think that I'm "chicken little".

Richard: Well, it was months ago when you sounded the warning, and the systems haven't crashed.

Oliver: It's my job to keep the systems from crashing. Is it *your* job to keep the systems from crashing? I don't think so. The systems haven't crashed because I'm doing my job.

Richard: And when they do crash, it will be – because you failed to do your job.

Oliver: When the systems crash, none of us will have jobs. Except for me, of course.

Richard: Oh, how's that?

Oliver: I'm covered. Not to worry.

Unaware and loving it

Katie is a business user who needs to find a particular transaction to solve a customer service issue.

Katie: We need regular access to the business data for reporting purposes.

Oliver: That's a little vague. Reporting purposes. Big field of view there.

Katie: One of our customers called and wanted to know what happened to their order.

Oliver: Shoot me an email with the customer info and I'll hunt it down.

Katie: We need *direct* access to this information.

Oliver: In the time it will take us to have this conversation, I could have already given you the information.

Katie: If I had direct access to the information, we wouldn't have the conversation at all.

Oliver: We gave it to you and you never used it.

Katie: It took forever for a query to come back, if it *ever* came back. Half the time, it would time out and never give an answer.

Oliver: See why it's easier just to send me an email with the request?

Katie: Why don't you just fix the data?

Oliver: Data's not broken. Works fine for me.

Katie: But not for anyone else. It takes weeks to learn how to use the table structures.

Oliver: Once a week we have an 8-hour orientation session on the data structures. If you need to know how to use them, that's the best place to come. You need to start early, though, some of the developers take several weeks to master the knowledge.

Katie: Why can't you just give us a model that works for the business?

Oliver: I am unaware of any business need for more data or a different model.

CIO as GI-Joe

Jake is a developer, John is a DBA, both are sitting in the CIO's office awaiting his arrival. Minutes later, the CIO shows up, flustered.

CIO: Sorry I'm late, gents, duty calling.

Jake: We just need some direction on these new reports. The context is not clear.

John: Which tables do these come from?

Phone rings, CIO immediately answers it.

CIO: Yes? You need a what? *(starts tapping on his keyboard)* Okay, that's a summary column on Report Fifteen. I just added it. The next time you see it, the summary will be there. *(phone call terminates)*

CIO: Where were we?

John: The report format? Where do we get the data?

Phone rings, CIO immediately answers it.

CIO: You need a what? *(taps on keyboard)* Okay, it's there. When you run that report the next time, you'll get the additional totals at the bottom and three spare copies. Anything else? *(phone call terminates)*

This cycle continues for the next hour, with Jake and John barely able to start the conversation before another tactical report request arrives.

CIO: Look, guys, I'm sorry for all the interruptions. When you get to know the data as well as I do, then you can *really* be productive.

Both Jake and John exit, wondering why a person in the position of CIO is fielding tactical report requests.

Jake: (under his breath) He's doing *our* job.

John: Maybe we should *let* him.

Jake: Lunch?

John: Sure.

Moonlighting Inc.

CEO of MegaCorp has commissioned an assessment that Mike has just completed, and Mike is reporting his findings.

CEO: What do you have?

Mike: Well, when you first told me that you spent the first three hours of each Monday, assembling spreadsheets from latent data in all the systems, I wondered why this could not be automated for you.

CEO: I'm with you, what's the answer?

Mike: You're the only one who knows where the data is. We don't have any tools to perform a clean extract and presentation.

CEO: Hmm. What else?

Mike: The same problem persists all over the floor, in fact all over the corporate site. Your VPs get reports from their staffs, who in turn spend most of their business days extracting, merging and formatting the reports for their bosses.

CEO: Glad to see the VPs are putting their staffs to good use.

Mike: One of your VPs in marketing, has a lot of really great ideas for using data to penetrate new markets, but he doesn't know where the data might be. Nobody else does either. He said that he used to ask these questions, but eventually stopped asking because there was no way to answer them. He feels like it's his job to ask these questions, but he never gets answers, so he's stopped asking.

CEO: He's right, he's stopped doing his job. I'll fire him. What else?

Mike: It seems that you are running two distinct businesses here. One is MegaCorp. One is a data processing business. If I go to any given desk, of the two hundred people on this floor alone, I will find that half their day is spent in data processing, and half is spent running the business named MegaCorp.

CEO: What does it matter?

Mike: If you were to automate these highly repeatable tasks, you would buy back all those labor hours to use in pursuit of the business of MegaCorp. A rough estimate is about ten million dollars in labor. Ten million dollars will buy a lot of automation.

CEO: Or a lot of free time! How much are we paying *you*?

Taking it seriously

Nick is overseeing a large data processing environment that has failed to meet its Service Level Agreements for the fifth straight week. He is in a meeting with the CIO and CFO, wondering if they plan to lop off his head.

CIO: Fifth week straight, Nick.

Nick: Yes sir, I know.

CFO: My reports are required by regulation. The company gets penalized if we don't supply them. It costs a lot more than just time.

Nick: I know we talked about it last week. And the week before, and the week before. (*voice trails off*)

CIO: You seem to be making light of all this. That disturbs me.

Nick: No, actually you're the one not taking it seriously, that's even more disturbing.

CIO: (*incredulous*) What? I'm the one with fire-breathing users on my back!

Nick: (*to CFO*) Same for you. You're not taking this problem seriously at *all*.

Awkward silence as the two leaders assimilate this insolence.

CFO: Explain yourself

Nick: We have a environment that has flow-based processing needs. Data comes in, it gets processed, and goes out. It's a flow.

CIO: (*rolls eyes*) Here we go –

Nick: You can't process half a terabyte of data on these underpowered and antiquated systems.

CFO: We've been doing it for years. Of course we can.

Nick: No you *haven't*. The data sizes and administrative overhead have doubled in the last six months. We're so far past capacity that it will take us six months to right-size it for *today*. By then we may have already doubled again.

CFO: How does that translate to me not taking the problem seriously?

Nick: Invoices on your desk for the right tools and systems to make it right.

CFO: Nick, we don't just run off and spend five million dollars without good justifications.

Nick: Is staying in business a good justification? How big a justification do you need? Prophets carrying tablets from the mountainside –

CIO: Now just a minute!

Nick: You think I'm kidding? We didn't meet the SLAs for the past five weeks because we *can't*. We never *will*. We're *done*. *Cooked*. I'm through looking sheepish for something that can't be fixed. Neither of you will step up to the plate to fix it. Get a spine.

CIO: (*disturbed, then looks soberly at CFO*) Nick, will you excuse us? We need to chat alone.

Nick: *No* problem (*exits*)

Nick finds his desk, reaches underneath and produces a box. He rapidly fills it with his personal belongings, completely cleaning out his cubicle. He has another job awaiting. He will start on Monday.

CIO: (*exits his office without walking down Nick's aisle, finds the second-in-command under Nick, named Richard*)

Richard: What can I do for you?

CIO: We're having trouble meeting our SLAs. We need your help.

Richard: Upgrading the environment? Sure, count me in.

CIO: (*looks down, then back up*) Well, no, not to upgrade. We need to make it happen with what we have in place.

Richard: (*turns back to his computer screen, radiating disinterest*) I'll pass.

The CEO of the company learns of these games three weeks later when the transactional systems spike from a market peak. The entire environment is brought to its knees. CEO fires the CFO and CIO. Hires a consultant named Nick to come in and pick up the pieces. Unlimited budget, spare no expense.

Richard runs the project. Life goes on.

Drilling down

We have several sets of requirements – those that face:

(1) the application's work products
(2) the application's development, deployment and maintenance
(3) the people operationally supporting the application
(4) the people measuring the application's output
(5) the people managing the application's capacity requirements

The first is spoken, sometimes written in a formal functional specification. The remainder are largely unspoken and unwritten, but highly expected nevertheless. Some environments call these "non-functional" requirements. While this naming convention, juxtaposed with "functional requirements" seems to make sense, we see how awkward it looks when it's seen by itself.

Overheard at the water-cooler: That requirement is non-functional! If it's so non-functional, why are we still using it? You get the picture.

Some common complaints from the various intersecting groups include:

- *Developer*: (Using a Scottish accent like the nutty guy from *Star Trek*). There's not enough pow'r in the system! If we need to make a change, it might be relatively small. But we need to functionally test it, sometimes against millions of records in systems that choke on mere thousands. Who can get quick turnaround in an environment like this?

- *Implementer* - When we want to promote it to production, it's a comedy of errors. Nothing is under control. I get called in the middle of the night because someone missed a clearly stated implementation requirement. It's like we have to hold their hands *and* wipe their noses.

- *Operator*: The developers turn this stuff over as black-box. It kicks off but I can't tell what it's doing, how long it has left to go or if it's hung. It never comes up for air. If it dies, I have no idea how to restart it. We don't have any metrics for how long it ran, how many errors it produced or the health of the final output.

- *Administrator*: The thing chews up disk space like crazy and never cleans up after itself. We never know which tables are okay to housekeep. Some applications keep stuffing redundant data into intermediate tables without emptying the tables, and we have to clean up this mess every night.

- *Troubleshooter*: The solution is made from disconnected components like a bunch of spinning plates. There is no discernible flow or intermediate touchpoint to gather a health check of information. Each part is its own component, does its own work. Many components repeat the same work that other components do, unable to leverage the prior work for the gain of all. When a component dies, we have no visibility as to how to restart it, or restart the parts that come after it. Often its just safer to back out all the work and start from scratch, But we lose all the time in between.

We should not build a system we cannot operate, administer, test, enhance, modify, monitor, troubleshoot, recover, etc. *with the required agility of our business operation*. Processing the data to the satisfaction of the end users is only *one* requirement in a *broad* constellation. We need all of the above and perhaps much more.

The maxim is this: ***We are building a data processing environment***. It's a living environment. It needs operators, administrators and personnel who are responsible for it. There is no such thing as a lights-out operations environment. We might have a lights-out data center, but whatever is running inside it - needs to have a shepherd.

Request-versus-requirement - I have seen case after case of enterprise gurus building the most high-powered, high-functioning systems we can imagine. Once in place, the end user will ask a simple question that brings the engineer's dreams out of the clouds: "Can I get a report on thus-and-so?" Where the "thus-and-so" is a core business metric that they cannot live without, and should not have to. If the system does not provide the metric, watch the engineer scurry back to their desk and provide a tactical solution. To fulfill the *tactical request*.

Then something interesting happens – we suddenly experience a backlog of these requests and the engineer is hard-put to deal with any of them. He did not build it with these requirements in mind. Soon the running joke becomes "Does it do thus-and-so?" followed by the answer, "Was it *supposed* to?" In other words, the requirement was never specified, so no, it wasn't *supposed* to, was it? If the system isn't useful, people won't use it.

Back in the saddle: I have noted in another chapter that a special effect of requirements analysis is just this: We roll out the new solution and one of two things happens: they hate it or they love it. Either way, we are immediately back at our desk. We are either fixing what's broken or meeting the additional demand. So the "do-ourselves-a-favor" approach seems to be - make it as thorough as possible on the first go-round, and not just throw a tactical solution over the wall and hope for the best. In this case, "thorough" is good for the sake of defining an adaptive architecture, but lousy if we mean "comprehensively perfect". I've seen architects try to make things 100 percent comprehensive, so why did their architecture turn out so incomprehensible?

Any given requirement might be implicit – or perhaps never specified only because it was never garnered, elicited or regarded. The functional requirements necessary to run our business never go away, no matter how much we wish it so. It is far easier to get a strong functional specification from our users and build the system towards it, than try to retrofit their burgeoning list of requirements into our architecture. A request-driven architecture, that is about to be crushed, by the way, if it is simply not built with the power to change.

Build with "*the expectation of change, not the fear of it*". Requirements never stop coming, so don't imagine that we will ever have a break. Rather we can pace ourselves and manage the releases, if and only if we have built a system that gives us this capacity.

Rule #2 - simplify and clarify, rather than inject artificial complexity or engineering. Bulk processing is simple. While it might not seem "cool" or "sexy" to build an input-process-output model, it is what it is. If we build it right, we don't get calls in the middle of the night. Underpowered or secondhand platforms make it harder. Build it right, do it right, get it done and go home happy – at 5pm – without expecting a midnight call.

We saw in one of the case studies how a company almost veered toward higher complexity instead of simplicity. And another who had it right the first time, and didn't know it, and almost threw it away in exchange for the wrong answer.

Eliminate artificial complexity - For a legacy system with high (or increasingly high) complexity, we must *first* assume that the complexity is *artificial* – a product of engineering within an underpowered environment. We must attempt to define the problem in its simplest flow form, and then identify exceptions as "harnessed accommodations". Otherwise the exceptions will become the rule and the two are indistinguishable (see #3).

Refactoring or re-characterizing such a solution should regard the complexity as an artifact, not a driving requirement and certainly not a necessary reality.

One of our customers had allowed their machines to lose power, and allowed their engineers to run amok, such that the solution had so many "spinning plates" that the business owners just knew it was all about to unravel. In a simple examination of their business processing, something jumped right out – the complexity was artificial and the activities to support the complexity were futile.

One of the internal engineers had already come up with a plan to fix the problem, but the plan involved embracing even more complexity than what already existed. This engineer's assumption was that the complexity was here to stay, and had to be harnessed. This was a false assumption.

The complexity was artificial.

Your complexity might be artificial, too.

How easy is it? Really? When we deploy our Netezza machine, and ensconce it either in our data warehouse environment or a bulk processing role, what have we done to make life as easy as possible for those who will intersect with it? I'll pull no punches each time I say that the data and information output are produced to keep the *users* happy. But the data itself is a *work product of our work products – the applications and infrastructure.* Were we thinking that we would toss these over a wall and hope for the best? No – the operators, administrators, troubleshooters and the like – are chief constituents of our work products. We must support their needs, and what better way to do it than to make their lives simpler?

Wouldn't it be great if when one of our jobs failed, the operator would only have to roll their eyes once and within a few keystrokes, we're off and running again? It's late at night, they're minds are numb with boredom and disinterest, or they are busy fighting the fires of work products that are not as good as ours. How do we know they will follow our painstakingly documented recovery instructions? How do we know if they fat-finger just one part of it, and our whole world will unravel even while we are sleeping?

What do *you* want to wake up to?

One shop solved this problem in a very simple way. Each time one of their job streams launches, it writes a file to a recovery directory. If the application dies in the middle of processing, all the operator has to do is launch the recovery file. No parameters, no guesswork, it's all self-contained.

Compare this to another site that deploys its work products in a very command-line intensive manner. Not only do the operators have to recover one part of the job, they have to manually kick off the remainder, individually, because if a broken process stream. What's more, they have reams of documentation on what the operators should do in each and every case of failure, for each particular error code, for each particular application.

Come on, folks – this is *institutionalizing* something that we could, and *should*, eliminate entirely. Part of it is governance, but a bigger part is an operational framework that automatically captures these things and makes life easier for everyone involved. I'm not saying it's easy, I'm saying that the alternative – inviting chaos and complexity into our home, is *far* worse.

Case Study Short (from the oldies archives): My first introduction into massively parallel systems was in 1985 at then Martin Marietta Orlando Aerospace. We were making a target recognition system for the infrared vision pod for military attack aircraft. This little "block" of technology was a set of custom hardware, fabricated on-site, into a cube of about 18 inches or so. It had cooling pipes running into both ends, circulating a high-tech heat-pump liquid that was provided by the aircraft in flight. We had to keep a "cooling cart" next to the box, on and running at all times, because our little box could generate enough heat to cook, well, just about anything. Including someone's career.

The "hardware guys" – you've met a few of these – took us on a walkthrough of how to deal with the box and the cart. Always turn off the box, then the cart. And vice-versa. Okey-fine. I did this, being the last one out of the lab on that Friday. Killed the power. All lights were off. Killed the cooling cart power. Nothing amiss, I went home.

Later that evening came a knock at the front door, and one of my team members met me there, a hardware guy (who incidentally lived down the street). He asked me what I had done with the box that evening, and I explained. He told me "Several folks two labs down could smell the box cooking. You left the power on."

To which I was flummoxed. I spent the whole weekend in a stew and when I arrived on Monday, I learned something new. The power supply, its seemed, could only be turned off by *unplugging* it, something that the hardware guys had failed to mention, because they didn't know it themselves. It was a ticking time bomb, and I had stepped in it, or on it, whatever. The shoes *and* the fan smelled bad, in other words.

Feeling somewhat off-the-hook for the debacle (I *had* followed instructions after all), one of the other hardware guys, a more nervous chap, asked me,

"Weren't you worried that you would lose your job?"

"Of course."

"Then how can you be so calm about it?"

"It's already done," I said, "So why worry about it? There's nothing I can do about it anyhow."

"You can do better next time!"

"Do better with what? Following the instructions? What did I fail in?"

"You almost destroyed the box," he sneered, "And it would have cost us millions."

"Interesting you should say that," I noted, "The box has cost four million dollars in hardware alone, not to mention the labor to bring it to life. Yet there's no temperature breaker or surge protector on it. I have those in my house and it's not worth what that box is worth."

Before he could respond, I looked up and noted that the numbers on the box's power supply were blinking frantically, but the cooling cart wasn't turned on. Stunned, I gasped, "Is the – power – *turned on?*"

In that moment, my friend's heart must have skipped a beat. He inhaled a startled gasp himself, then a yelp of horror as two white plumes of smoke burst from each side of the box with a whining *pfffft!* sound. He bolted to kill the power and then I watched as he almost went into shock. These were the days before portable defib boxes – and I knew beans about CPR (what recent college grad does?). Alas and forsooth – *we are undone!*

What does it all mean? The box had a *single* point of failure that represented *true* failure, *catastrophic* failure, completely at risk to error-prone *humans.*

Whether Murphy was right or not – if it can go wrong it has the potential of doing so, and what will *we* do if it does?

Failure, and the propensity of failure, *hides in chaos.* The more complex we make the environment, the more we multiply our failure points. Once we reach a critical mass of failure points, it's only a matter of time. Failure is a mathematical certainty.

Do yourself a favor. Keep it simple.

Rule #3 – Use correctly powered and scalable systems. Underpowered systems require our staff to use engineering tricks, generally to optimize hardware and schema definitions. Once-upon-a-time-powered systems that over time become over-powered (or over-taken) with volume and workload, require regular review from top to bottom.

Stop applying tactical extensions for performance-related fixes. This only leads to artificial complexity creeping into the solution, where ultimately the artificial complexity becomes indistinguishable from the core.

But it's more than just the production environment. If we provide under-powered environments to our developers, we should not complain when they cannot meet deadlines. If we provide under-powered machines to our testers, we should not complain about the time-to-market, or the lethargy in our "agile" environment.

Agility requires power. (see Spiderman). The larger the data problem, the more power we need. Don't be naive about this. Take the problem seriously.

Rule #4 – Governance - Our entire environment needs some rules that set expectations of the participants. Do whatever it takes to build the governance model into the architecture. This doesn't mean draconian steps, it simply sets the tone that rules are in place with an expectation of loyalty to them. Otherwise the developers will sense the freedom to mutate the architecture, and will naturally gravitate toward, leverage, and even exploit this freedom.

With no rules in place, are they really *violating* anything?

When developers are in the heat of battle, we need something in place that will encourage if not require them to comply, even if it is not convenient for them to do so. In many cases, the governance constraints are in place specifically to control runaway rogue activity, so that things don't end up in production within the same hour they were created, regardless of the level of testing applied.

Active Rogue: the rogue that doesn't like your rules, likes his own better, and will consistently and rigorously apply them. At least we can remediate this rogue's work, if only because he followed some kind of standard.

Passive Rogue: the rogue that will follow your rules rigorously until it is inconvenient. The passive rogue will pepper his disloyalty all over what could have been a robust implementation. It is very difficult to remediate the work of a passive rogue. You cannot protect your environment from someone who is willing to break the rules.

Rogue control: is no further away than activating your governance model and a review infrastructure that can serve as a gateway mechanism. It maintains a *level* of quality, but does not guarantee an absence of mayhem, only a means to harness the mayhem - to mitigate the mayhem's damage. It gives us a common center of gravity, which is at least a common center to adhere to, or a target to remediate *toward*.

Architectural harness: One of the best ways, albeit the most challenging, is to set up an architecture that enforces governance and embraces compliance for each participant, *simply by participating*. Example: In our homes and offices we have power outlets installed at regular intervals on the walls. All we have to do, to comply with the original architect's plans for power delivery, is put an appliance plug into the socket and we (a) instantly have power (b) are in compliance (c) the boundaries for compliance keep us safe.

We did all this by passively participating within the environment's boundaries. Of course, the boundaries have to exist.

Otherwise, our alternative is to blow a hole in the wall, rip out the wires and rig it. This would place us, our family members and perhaps the home itself into peril. Do this enough times, and one would wonder why we ever paid an electrician to put outlets in the wall to begin with. Non-existent boundaries (especially of developer behavior) is no different than having a home with electrical wires snaking all over the floor. People participate by hooking into the wires, or they simply step over the obvious problems, unable to fix it whether they are willing or not.

Recall, a complex of neglect arises when everyone collectively ignores the obvious.

Healthy boundaries for high productivity: While controlling rogues is a noble goal, we really want a governance model that is *less* about constraint and *more* about "freedom within boundaries". The objective of the governance model is simply to provide healthy boundaries so the developers know where their limits are, but more importantly how to drive their hard-earned functionalities into an architectural core. If we continue to allow our developers to produce tactical functionalities rather than core capabilities, we are not engaging the true spirit of governance. Nor are we honoring the hard work of some of our hardest working people. Nor are we focusing the work of our business users, who may spend most of their days doing deep technical work *that they were not hired to do*.

Developers and technologists like to think that they've built something lasting and useful. If we fail to provide an infrastructure to harness and deploy their work, how can we make it available for redeployment? It becomes one-time-effort for a one-time-fix. If we hold to the rule of one-time-fixes, we will eventually see this as a theme of the architecture, a very disheartening realization.

Governance is about boundaries in structures, conventions, processes, controls, measurements and so many other things. We can't afford to get lost in trying to whip our developers into shape (that sounds kind of violent doesn't it?). We must set the expectations in the governance model so our developers know what we expect *from* the effort, and therefore understand what is expected *of* them. The real key in its activation is to provide the framework within which they work, not just accept their promise to behave themselves. Most developers want to please their end users. Most of what they do is often very thankless, and hearing in the hallway, over email or otherwise that what they've done is making things easier for someone else, is akin to saying "well done".

This is not to suggest that all of our developers are working for the bottom line of the business and not toward their own bottom line (career, experience, etc). But this is a common human-resources problem in every profession. Don't imagine that it's exclusive to technologists. Sometimes it is a problem best solved in human-resource terms, not strictly technical ones. Barring that, a participation framework that keeps them in compliance (and productive) by design is far more effective than something written on paper alone.

Rule #5 Data management - If data management practices are missing, we'll know it. The primary symptoms of a lack of data management include (but are not limited to):

- Manual workarounds for core data processing functions.
- Junk data, contamination, null, duplication, etc in the core data content
- Poorly formed or poorly executed data model
- Systems and siloed (stovepipe) applications that do not easily share information
- Data transport based on replication alone
- No challenge of data from external sources
- No reconciliation of regular external sources
- Information too difficult for average user to navigate

Primer: *Information theory and chaos*. One of the primary rules of the game that we must, above all else, master in the realm of data management, is the simple maxim of information theory concerning entropy. Entropy is the propensity of information to lose integrity. A fax-of-a-fax is a good example. If we continuously fax-a-fax back and forth, it will eventually reduce to nothing more than meaningless dots and lines on a page.

Each time that data transitions from one place to the next, the danger of entropy is ever-present. Not only this, but any decay of the information that was already present, will remain. It will not go away without deliberate effort. This is why our data transportation mechanism should be more formal than simple replication.

Data management means both harnessing *and* stewarding the data.

Harnessing – Deliberately taking the data by the throat and bringing it into submission. It will feel like breaking a horse at first (if you've never broken a horse, watch someone do it to get a feel). But once under control, the horsepower is there for our regular consumption. If we've grown our environment "organically", that is, piecing it together one part at a time, take heart. We have a (mostly) working, functional model that we can use as a baseline to test a new one. Don't fear moving to the new one. It's work, but it's not particularly painful, and the benefits are enormous.

Getting control of our data is more than just installing and loading a data model. We'll dive a little deeper in context for each of these areas: inbound information consists of two primary kinds: transactional and reference. Both are potential sources of woe.

If our transactional data is interacting directly with users, much of the control rests with our developers in how they harness the user's workflow to prevent breakage. It is often an art form in and of itself. We must do ourselves a favor, and put APIs (web services or the like) between the user application and the information systems. This provides us with far more intake control than direct interaction with the database. Views and stored procedures - transactional systems should standardize on them. Service-oriented-architecture is the key, so if we want to formalize on this, great. Just keep in mind that the SOA must not directly access the database, either. Views and stored procedures for all, including and especially the SOA.

Case Study Short: An equities trading firm's data suppliers would send transactional information at the close-of-business each trading day. If a given supplier failed to transmit their file, the firm had no way of knowing this. Periodically a supplier would call up and ask where his data was. The firm's tiger –team would have to chase down the information, or lack thereof, to determine the problem. More than once, the tiger team would make the determination that the data had not been sent, which they would later learn was an incorrect conclusion.

We can avoid these messy, highly manual problems with data exchange protocols. Most vendors are happy to comply, even if they never use your messages. At least, if they are missing data and they have a message that we both received and processed it, we have a place to start looking.

Reference scrubbing - For our reference data, pull it into the environment through a deliberate intake protocol. Don't let it arrive on user desktops or disparate locations. For industry data such as stock ticker symbols, we'll need to provide a means to version the information at the row level. I use stock tickers because the symbols can get recycled within a given exchange, such that over time in our own systems, the presence of a given symbol could mean two different things. Also, since external systems track their own form of the symbol, we could have widely disparate meanings of the same symbol across multiple I/O points. Our brokers might see the symbol as including the exchange or other notation, while another service provider may not care for this extra information. We have to keep all of our publishers and subscribers happy.

So manage the reference data as though it is a source of information not only for ourselves, but for our many constituencies inside and outside the enterprise. We need an intake protocol, a reconciliation protocol, and means to present the final "gold" version to the internal systems so they never see any contamination, and never have to worry about it.

Stewarding – Many people see stewardship as an internal data quality team or governance protocol. While it can (and should) have this form, the protocol is only words on paper without some kind of activating principle. This practice goes beyond simple column-level data scrubbing, or attaching metadata meaning to a data point, and has a simple, universal maxim. It goes like this:

Every time we touch the data, we should make it better for the next downstream consumer.

Rule #6 – A strong architectural approach. A classic maxim is simply this: The surest sign of a good architecture is: good things automatically fall out of it. The surest sign of a marginal architecture is: the environment is constrained from providing much more than it already does.

Sounds almost like we need a crystal ball, or a power-team of heavy-hitters down the hall that are the "go-to" people for architectural excellence. Perhaps we rent-an-architect to get us moving, but without some of his/her brains spilling into buckets for posterity, what is the real lifetime value of what we are doing? Those who come after us will not have taken ownership of the principles, will not appreciate the original sacrifices, etc. Woe is us.

Take a deep breath.

Architecture is *not* rocket science. Don't treat it like some kind of elusive pie-in-the sky goal. Go for *perfection*, but set your heart on *excellence*. Trust me, excellence is easier to achieve and you're not all that far from it. Perfection is a goal. Excellence is a journey. The road to your goal is far more important than the goal itself. No philosophy, that's just the way it is.

The point being, don't go all catatonic trying to get a perfect architecture. Get your core requirements in order and quickly set up a framework architecture, sometimes called a reference architecture or centerpiece-architecture. We'll want this as the springboard for our first iteration and then mature it to its functional and capability edges as we move along.

Notification Framework – We need a consistent means to notify an operator, administrator or interested party when a given event occurs, or what needs to be escalated, and to whom. This goes far beyond operational information. The basic need is to capture an event and send a message. The events could be practically anything we would want to key on, but we don't need to cover everything, of course. The actions could be practically anything we want to do – not just notifying an operator or troubleshooter, but also upstream and downstream systems that are interacting with us.

Data Transportation – How will we get data into the machine? Don't say replication without having some kind of plan. For bulk processing, plain straight replication invokes information entropy and is a regressive model.

Load Control – We need a way to systematically and deterministically load information into our environment with a minimum of overhead and a maximum of visibility and recoverability.

Business Rules – Firstly, we will always want to transform the data into something more consumable. This kind of business rule is proactive in shaping the data according to the desires of the consumers.

Secondly, we will always find anomalies in the data that threaten to affect the user's experience and/or the accuracy of the data. We're talking about *scale* here, so we need rules, not eyeballs, to resolve the anomalies.

If the anomaly is serious enough, we address it with the upstream system as a bug. Otherwise we'll have to scrub or cleanse the anomaly on-the-fly. How does a business rule work? We get together with the users of the data and we deal with them at the highest level (patterns) before we deal with the minutiae. Usually a *rule* is applied in sweeping motions to either cleanse and validate data, or just transform it to a more consumable state.

Exception handling – Whenever one of the above levels should report a failure, we need a means to capture the failure, then fix it with a business rule or drop it into an administrative zone for human eyeballs to review. Tens or perhaps hundreds for each eyeball, not thousands or more. If we have exceptions of this volume, we need to refactor our business rules.

Security Framework – Generally speaking, a framework that provides entry points to the Netezza consumers. This is largely under the control of the Linux host. Don't imagine that Linux will just provide this for free. Security is never for free.

One customer provides a means to log on to a Netezza schema for each of the external user groups who approach the system. This allows for each reporting user, reporting tool, downstream system and ad-hoc user to have their own individually configurable schema.

Outtake Control – Especially if we have a situation where Netezza is an ELT player, producing data for downstream processing systems, we need a means to systematically publish data, validate that it has been consumed by all subscribers, and a means to notify someone when an expected subscriber has not shown up to take the information.

On the higher side – Here are some additional aspects we need to consider:

- **Stability**- the first of three pillars of our environment. If we fail to achieve stability, or if our environment is already unstable, we can stop here. The more and disparate our storage mechanisms, the more the propensity for instability. We must stabilize in order to move forward. Netezza, as a self-contained appliance, offers a means to stabilize rapidly.
- **Adaptability**- the second of three pillars of our environment. While it stands that if an environment is not stable, neither is it adaptable. But without adaptability, we are doomed to endless cycles of rewrite and redeployment, sometimes for the tiniest incremental functionality. Netezza offers adaptability in the flexibility of its framework and the elimination of adaptation constraints. Not the least of which is the absence of index structures. The constant attention to index optimization in a traditional RDBMS is a thorn in the side to administrators and operators, and only offers the constant appearance of instability. In addition, if we adapt once and are no longer adaptable thereafter, we are on a slippery slope toward instability.
- **Scalability**- the third of three pillars of our environment. This aspect is also dependent on the other two pillars. Without stability and adaptability, the whole notion of scalability is never within reach. Likewise if we can scale *only* once, we're not as adaptable as we thought. If we scale multiple times and lose our adaptability along the way, we have only scaled *into* instability. All three pillars must be kept in balance. Netezza allows us to scale in power simply by adding frames, and scale in storage with simple invoice events to unlock ever-present terabytes for our utilization. From there, the scalability is part of the appliance offering and requires far less customer-side direct engineering to achieve our scalability goals.
- **Interface-driven**- Within any enterprise architecture, the harnessing of interfaces provides us with structural and behavioral adaptation. In fact, the majority of adaptation is driven at the interface level, because this is the level that drives the identifying signature of a component. The more unique the interface, the less adaptable the component. So if we right-size our structural interfaces (e.g. views, tables, etc) and we right-size our behavioral activities (rule-driven applications) we effectively provide one more (and significant) level of adaptation. Externally-driven interactions must go through the interface, giving us flexibility under the covers to optimize things without breaking our dependent consumers. Netezza provides the normal entry-points of ODBC/JDBC and views, but we might need

to take additional steps in leveraging these.

- **Capacity-planning metrics**- Our operators and administrators absolutely require these metrics whether they ask for them or not. Netezza provides this kind of information with simple appliance-level statistics. Other environments often require our deliberate application of row counting, disk evaluation and growth pattern tracking. Many of these are custom quantities. Netezza can give us these raw data points but we must package them in context of our own environment and its administrative/operational requirements.

- **Decoupled**- While this is yet another 90's buzzword, it arose for a reason. Decoupling our systems, through both content and interfacing, provide the maximum stability and adaptability. A simple example of decoupling is to define our information storage models and schemas to face their audience and purpose, not to face their sources. By making a clean break from the source structures, we must provide a transformation scenario to restructure the data. Otherwise we are tempted to use bulk replication, inviting the real danger of maintaining more dirt than data. If we clean and restructure the data upon first arrival, we'll have to do less (to none) later in the cycle.

- **Isolated from breakage**- Another aspect of decoupling, but also dives into the data content as well. Strategic use of surrogate keys, for example, both accelerates processing power and decouples us from upstream dependency. Suffice to say that if we can coalesce a five-part key into a unique integer equivalent, we have effectively performed a 10-to-100-fold boost in performance (integer keys are always faster) *and* we've isolated our warehouse from upstream dependency. If any of the natural keys change, we have the freedom to make a call to connect them back together via a surrogate without changing the natural key itself (slowly changing dimension).

- **Performance-centric capabilities**- Performance is not about user-facing functionality. It's about *physics*. User-facing functionality invariably involves software to carefully shape the user experience. Bulk data processing requires hardcore physics. This is founded upon capability, not functionality. If we can successfully separate architectural capability from user-facing functionality, we get an interesting benefit: The user functionality becomes a consumer of our architecture, and can itself change and adapt in high-speed, iterative mode. Capabilities then, change less often and only when the existing capabilities do not meet functional needs. This stabilizes the architectural capabilities and accelerates functional delivery at the same time. Netezza provides a high-capacity, high-capability appliance model that gets us to a stable capability scenario very quickly. We are then a very short distance from providing our users with a robust, agile and responsive experience (both in consuming the functionality, and rapid turnaround on deploying enhanced functionality.

- **User-centric functionalities**- As noted in the prior bullet, we must standardize on driving functionality toward the user while maintaining architectural capabilities in the core. The best way to get this done, is to provide functionalities that are a composite of architectural capabilities. The best technologies to get this done are not necessarily Netezza, since Netezza focuses on core, system-facing capabilities. It is interesting, however that Netezza provides a stable platform core to environments like Business Objects. We then have the ability to rapidly iterate Business Objects deployments against a stable, slowly moving core. The best of all worlds.

- **Administrative error control**- We have two primary options in dealing with errors in a flow-based model. We can deal with them by letting the flow break, and then trying to recover the flow. Or we can deal with them administratively and deliberately, while the flow continues. Once the flow is done, or even while the flow is underway, an administrative person can deal with the erroneous records in a "holding tank". What we must avoid, at all costs, is allowing the holding tank to get too large to handle manually. In one of the examples above, I noted that one architect thought that ten percent was acceptable, even though it represented 100,000 records. When errors occur, it's important to make sure they don't occur again, if there is any remote possibility of automating their recovery, we must do so. Otherwise our scalability factor lies in how many people we need to hire to perform the manual recovery in the absence of an automated one. Don't laugh – I know of enterprises that dogpile people into an error-recovery "war-room", while the development staff is unaware of the problem.
- **Operational visibility**- In an RDBMS environment, we often have stored procedures running the show. These little nuggets are miniature black-boxes to the operational staff. They don't have any visibility to what the procedure is doing, when it will quit, or how far along it is – or if it's ever coming back. It's at least as bad for the testing and troubleshooting staff. Keep the operational flow out of the stored procedures. In Netezza, we have lots of options, including the ability to create checkpointed flows. We can always check the status of any given query, but a checkpointed, restartable and highly visible flow is the only way to truly support operators and testers.
- **Auditable behavior**- Auditable behavior is akin to testable behavior, with the additional ability to gain metrics from the work, and repeat the original work exactly as it was executed Auditability is a high form of testability and traceability. It also means we have a harness on potential corruption of workflow. Let's say we have a multi-stage workload targeting three different downstream data stores. Let's say our workflow dies in the middle of its stream. Two of the stores are loaded, one is partially loaded. Or is it? How can we know where to restart? Or do we back out all the work and restart? What constitutes "all the work"? Can we identify the corrupted parts, remove them and start from a check-pointed location? Can we alert an operator as to what actions to take? What if all the flows continue without breakage, but we find corruption later? How do we track down the source, especially among billions of records?
- **Metadata used throughout**- The industry loosely defines metadata as "information about information". But this definition falls short, because it does not expand on the definition of information, and what about it is *necessary*. Many different forms of metadata are available for free. Others we have to ask for and still others we have produce through built-in metadata factories in our applications.
    - o *Structural*-this defines the structure of the data points, the table/columns and what they mean, their sizes, domains, etc. Usually when someone thinks of metadata,

they think about structure and no further.

o *Behavioral-* this is metadata describing what happens to the data as it moves through the enterprise pipelines. If the data resides over there, and now it is resident here, what happened to get it from there to here, and was it repackaged along the way? Business users think of this as "business metadata" or "functional metadata" expressed in business rule terms. The *behavioral* umbrella includes all the business metadata plus the architectural behaviors it rides on.

o *Statistical-* this is derived information from the data. A fact-table is statistical metadata. It is restructured information to show amounts and counts of data-related activity, and directly involves the data content to derive these numbers. These might include accounting summaries, important synchronizations and other statistical rules.

o *Administrative-* this are often found in the form of logs and the like, and comprise an administrative history of the environment's activity. The administrators only care how much up-time the machine has had, how its resources are distributed and leveraged, whether the machine is behaving in a healthy manner, etc. In Netezza, much of this is already provided for us through the Linux host. Still more is available if we choose to track it. This information is also aligned with machine utilization, availability, peak and low activity levels, etc.

o *Operational-* this provides visibility to the information's operational health. How many files arrived for processing? How many were processed and how many were corrupt? Where are our exceptions tracked? How many transactions were processed and how many failed? What is the longest duration for the workload? What was the longest duration for a given section of workload? What is our most efficient process? Least efficient? When is the peak workload? Many times, this information directly feeds capacity planning, a core responsibility of operations personnel. Environments are often top-loaded with a need for this kind of information, so plan ahead to provide it.

o *Contextual-* A somewhat more nebulous and subjective area, this umbrella can include things like - When system A has a **customer ID**, and system B has a **cust_ id**, and system C has a **c_id**, which one is the master, what does it mean, and how do they relate? In addition, did we have meetings on determining this, what were the outcomes and reasons for the decisions, and who are the stakeholders? One of our colleagues laments that when he entered a new environment and wanted to make some changes to re-align some of these decisions, he put together a case for it and made an impassioned presentation as to why things needed to follow a new and shining path. Unbeknownst to him, three of the people on the architectural board had vested interests in keeping things like they were. Challenging them was tantamount to career suicide.

ABOUT THE AUTHOR

DAVID BIRMINGHAM is an enterprise solution architect who jaunts about in the Overground and the Underground, as it were. He's spoken at Netezza user conferences and generally keeps abreast of the technology in a massively parallel way. If you're reading this, you may have already met him. If not, you might meet him soon, but it's all good.

Mr. Birmingham graduated in 1985 with a degree in Computer Science from Stephen F. Austin State University in Nacogdoches, Texas, still the best computer science school on the planet,

Since that time, Mr. Birmingham's 23 years of derring-do are comprised of adventures in military software engineering, high-speed optical processing, neural networks, artificial intelligence and expert systems, financial services, health care, pharmaceuticals, retail and various adventures with disparate enterprise technologies, spanning a wide range of problem domains, all of them large-scale and high-stakes.

But *yours* is a large-scale and high-stakes problem domain, too, isn't it? You won't hear anything else here but *Welcome to the Club!* Pull up a chair and let's talk war stories. Anyone in this domain is more than welcome and will always find a smile, a coffee, a danish (or two) and we don't turn anyone away!

THE REMEDIATOR is a small cadre of consultants who love to talk-tech and problem-solving, and run about the countryside solving enterprise problems before bedtime. Some of them, like Mr. Birmingham, are a bit more visible than others, but nonetheless, Remediator is more of a *persona* than a person, but none of them work for Netezza or any product vendors mentioned in this book, nor do they work for the same consulting firm, nor ever have - and aren't here to sell the reader anything. Hopefully the reader has received some value for the time spent turning these pages, and that's what it's all about.

But if we must think of The Remediator in personal terms, as you will likely meet one of them along the path of data warehouse derring-do, think of "him" as just a big harmless fuzzball, a teddy-bear type who, apart from days when he's not running breathlessly between client meetings, will probably offer you a coffee and pick *your* brain. While you may not find him shuffling about the underground catacombs with the denizens of data warehousing, you might find him slaying a dragon or two, or just sweeping out the castle keep. Either way, the moniker is *purely* tongue-in-cheek and one should never worry that when the Remediator darkens our door, something is afoot.

However (and you have to watch how people use "however", don't you?) this doesn't mean that something isn't wrong, or that something *could* be wrong. After all, the best preventative medicine to "remediation" is to get it right – or *close* – the first time.

But it probably means we're about to take something that seems daunting and not only fix it, but have a *little* fun doing it. And who doesn't need a *little* more of that? The Remediator has had the odd experience of fork-lifting – usually painlessly so – environments that were stuck in miry clay. They're all big fans of the "wow" effect. The razz-matazz that not only makes the machines talk, but makes them *sing*.

So as we take this journey, just be aware that "Remediator" is just a character on television, not in real life. Okay, that's a lie, we've never been on television. Nevertheless, we may speak wistfully of Remediator's characteristics as though he's a third person in the room, because he speaks for all those who really want to get it right the first time. The real value *is* in getting in right the first time, and then when Remediator shows up, it's to help get the best foot forward and the train on the right track. Once it's out of the station, so to speak, and racing down the track at ninety miles per hour, it really needs to be on the right track - it's very difficult to bring the train back to the station.

You can find Remediator hanging out at the watercooler at ITToolbox.com, although it's an election year, and ITToolbox does not necessarily approve of this message. Remediator has been known to add an essay, a rant, or something in-between, to the Ab Initio Underground blog.

Mr. Birmingham thought it best to deliver the Netezza message to you in person, however. It just seemed like the right thing to do.

In keeping with the spirit of the Underground, none of us have to go by our real names. What happens in the Underground, *stays* in the Underground. Likewise if you discover any errata in the book, forward it on. We like to be accurate more than we like to be first.

With that, one may well ask why this work is self-published and not through a major house. Alas, we're told that the Netezza community is still too rarefied to justify a publisher's cash outlay. While this is changing rapidly, we'd rather not wait for critical mass. It's necessary now, it's time has come, so we invested personal time and cash to make it happen.

If you are reading, this, you have helped recoup the expense so we can all live in the Underground together. Don't imagine that sales will somehow line our pockets. Publishing is expensive, ROI is difficult to non-existent. Still, it's the right thing to do.

Onward and upward.

Index

Cover and other acknowledgements: The following corporations and groups reserve all copyrights and other rights to their registered trademarks and marketing. All descriptions of their respective technologies are likewise registered.

Netezza is a registered trademark of Netezza Corporation.

"It's what's for dinner" is a registered trademark of the Cattlemen's Beef Board and National Cattlemen's Beef Association.

The **Underground** symbol and photo of London's Angel Station (by Chris McKenna) are part of Wikipedia Commons.

Disney and all its wonders are registered trademarks of Walt Disney Corporation.
Microsoft, .NET and SQLServer are registered trademarks of Microsoft Corporation.
Teradata is a registered trademark of NCR and Teradata Corporations.
Sybase and **IQ** are registered trademarks of Sybase Corporation.
Ab Initio is a registered trademark of Ab Initio Software Corporation.
Oracle is a registered trademark of Oracle Corporation.
Jurassic Park is copyrighted by Michael Crichton.

Architecture-centric modeling noted in Configuration Stuff, are copyrighted by VMII, the author and Apress / Expert's Voice.

Boot Camp picture is of Sergeant Paul Nixon, drill instructor, 3rd Recruit Training Battalion, Marine Corps Recruit Depot, Parris Island, S.C., *Semper Fi!*

This book claims no rights or ownership to any registered trademark or copyright, whether used or implied in this work, that at the time of this publication is not already owned or registered by any entity other than Virtual Machine Intelligence Inc.

The views and opinions of Mr. Birmingham and The Remediator are their own. They do not necessarily reflect the opinions of any of the aforementioned entities, current or past employers, clients, vendor partners or any other acknowledged or mentioned entity in this work.

The "Case Studies" and "Case Study Shorts", as well as mention of "RDBMS" have either been generalized ot scrubbed to appropriately hide the identity of the actors and institutions, such that any claims to specificity are inappropriate and unwarranted. For those who would complain otherwise, our standard answer is, "it's not about you."

2321449

Made in the USA